D1994934

SV

Theodor W. Adorno
Nachgelassene Schriften

Herausgegeben vom
Theodor W. Adorno Archiv

Abteilung I:
Fragment gebliebene Schriften
Band 2

Theodor W. Adorno
Zu einer Theorie der musikalischen Reproduktion

Aufzeichnungen, ein Entwurf und zwei Schemata
Herausgegeben von Henri Lonitz

Suhrkamp

© Suhrkamp Verlag Frankfurt am Main 2001
Alle Rechte vorbehalten,
insbesondere das der Übersetzung, des öffentlichen Vortrags
sowie der Übertragung durch Rundfunk und Fernsehen,
auch einzelner Teile.
Kein Teil des Werkes darf in irgendeiner Form
(durch Fotografie, Mikrofilm oder andere Verfahren)
ohne schriftliche Genehmigung des Verlages
reproduziert oder unter Verwendung elektronischer Systeme
verarbeitet, vervielfältigt oder verbreitet werden.
Satz und Druck:
MZ-Verlagsdruckerei GmbH, Memmingen
Printed in Germany
Erste Auflage 2001

Die Deutsche Bibliothek – CIP-Einheitsaufnahme
Ein Titeldatensatz für diese Publikation
ist bei Der Deutschen Bibliothek erhältlich.

1 2 3 4 5 6 – 06 05 04 03 02 01

Inhalt

Aufzeichnungen

Aufzeichnungen I

Aufzeichnungen zu einer Theorie der musikalischen Reproduktion. 1

(NB hierin liegt Auflösung des natürlichen, »organischen« Aspekts der Musik, der ein bloßer gesellschaftlicher Schein ist)

Die wahre Reproduktion ist die Röntgenphotographie des Werkes. Ihre Aufgabe ist es, alle Relationen, Momente des Zusammenhanges, Kontrasts, der Konstruktion, die unter der Oberfläche des sinnlichen Klanges verborgen liegen, sichtbar zu machen – und zwar vermöge der Artikulation eben der sinnlichen Erscheinung. Das Verbergen solcher Beziehungen, wie es selber zuweilen vom Sinn der Werke mag gefordert sein, ist selber nur ein Teil jener Artikulation. Diese Forderung bezieht sich insbesondere auch auf kleinste Einheiten – Themen und Motive. Während die meisten Interpreten die Artikulation der großen Form im Groben zustandebringen, ist ihnen die der Teilganzheiten versagt. Etwa: die Gliederung von Themen in großen – nicht Lied- – Formen nach Vordersatz und Nachsatz. Oder: daß ein Thema, als Nachsatz zu einem anderen wieder erscheinend, einen ganz anderen Sinn hat, und darum anders interpretiert werden muß als beim ersten Auftreten. Von der Genauigkeit und Schärfe, mit der diese mikrologische Arbeit geleistet wird (ihr einfachstes Beispiel ist das Auseinanderhalten von Haupt- und Nebenstimmen in Kammermusik), hängt der *Sinn* der Formen – ihre Übersetzung in Inhalt ab (Beispiel 2. Thema aus cis-moll-Scherzo von Chopin, oder das As-Dur-Thema der f-moll-Phantasie). Und das stets wieder erscheinende Problem der Interpretation ist die Herstellung einer Dialektik von Ganzem und Teil, die weder das Ganze ans Detail verliert noch das Detail durchs Ganze annulliert. In der Tradition der großen abendländischen Musik steht dafür die Einheit des Haupttempos ein. Wann immer durch Tempomodifikationen, selbst differentiale, die Einheit des Satzes gefährdet ist, muß die Artikulation durch andere Mittel: Phrasierung, Agogik, Dynamik, Klangfarbe geleistet werden.

*

Verschiedene Dimensionen des Musizierens substituierbar.
Bei höher organisiertem Musizieren wird unzählige Male ein
Diminuendo, manchmal aber auch ein Crescendo für ein Ri-
tardando einstehen. Tempomodifikationen sind stets das be-
2 quemste, mechanische Mittel – fast ausnahmslos durch Un-
treue gegen den Text bezahlt.

*

Gegen die Phrase, man solle dem Geist, nicht dem Buchstaben treu sein. (NB Toscanini ist dem Buchstaben untreu. Entfalten[1]) NB Goeze und Lessing.[2]

*

Mimetisches Moment in der Reproduktion: die Interpolation der Details der des Schauspielers am ehesten zu vergleichen: interpretieren heißt eine Sekunde lang den Heros, den Berserker, die Hoffnung *spielen* und an dieser Stelle liegt die Kommunikation von Werk und Interpret.[3] Nur wer es nachzuahmen vermag versteht den Sinn des Werkes und nur wer diesen versteht vermag nachzuahmen. Alle Sprachen wenden den Begriff des Spiels auf Musik an.

*

Genaue Analyse als selbstverständliche Voraussetzung der Interpretation. Ihr Kanon ist der fortgeschrittenste Stand der kompositionstechnischen Einsicht.

*

Das Ideal *stummen* Musizierens, schließlich des Lesens musikalischer Texte, im Zusammenhang mit dem Verstummen entwickeln (NB die völlige Zerstörung des sinnlichen Phänomens der Musik durch die Massenreproduktion). Auswendig spielen – das »sich die Musik Denken« – als Vorstufe dazu.

*

Ausgehen von der Frage: was ist ein musikalischer Text. Keine Anweisung zur Aufführung, keine Fixierung der Vorstellung, sondern die notwendig fragmentarische, lückenhafte, der Interpretation bis zur endlichen Konvergenz *bedürftige* Notation eines Objektiven.

*

Wie verhält sich die Notenschrift zur Schrift? Eine der zentralsten Fragen, unlösbar von der: wie verhält Musik sich zur Sprache?

*

Es sind *zwei* prinzipiell falsche Auffassungen vom Wesen der musikalischen Interpretation zu widerlegen: 1) die vom musikalischen Text als Spielanweisung 2) die vom musikalischen 3
Text als Fixierung der Vorstellung. In einem tieferen Sinn ist nicht das Werk die Funktion der Vorstellung sondern umgekehrt (aus der Subjekt-Objekt-Dialektik des Werkes ableiten. NB auch das erkenntnistheoretische Argument der *Unbekanntheit* der Vorstellung – »Ding an sich«. NB Schönbergs Stellung zum Text *gegen* die eigene Auffassung. Es muß aber gesagt werden daß in das Ideal des Werkes als Grenzwerte Vorstellung und Spielanweisung eingehen).

*

Der Begriff des musikalischen *Sinnes* – als des Darzustellenden – ist zu entfalten. Während der Sinn nicht im Phänomen aufgeht, besteht die Möglichkeit seiner Darstellung – wie seines sich Darstellens – allein in den Phänomenen. Das heißt aber: in deren Zusammenhang. Den Sinn von Musik realisieren heißt nichts anderes als alle Momente des Zusammenhangs sichtbar machen. Das ist darzutun an »sinnlosem« Musizieren als dem Unterschied von Lebendem und Totem. Tot ist immer was nicht in seiner Funktion im musikalischen Zusammenhang evident wird. Der Begriff des Ausdrucks ist selber so zu verstehen (aber nicht ganz: d.h. als Ideal; und beim letzten Beethoven ist es desavouiert.). Diese Theorie ist sowohl mit der der Musik als eines intentionslosen Textes wie der von der Röntgenphotographie in Beziehung zu setzen. Die Bestimmung dieser Beziehung ist das eigentliche Anliegen der Arbeit.

*

Es wird eine Analyse des Darstellungsstils von Toscanini zu geben sein. »Interpretation im Zeitalter der Uninterpretierbarkeit«.[4]

Motive:

Auseinandertreten von Text (bloß scheinbare Treue) und Ausdruck (Wirkungszusammenhang).

»Streamlining«: Fetischismus des Funktionierens ohne musikalischen Sinn und Konstruktion. *[Dazu am linken Rand die Notiz:]* Das Funktionieren tritt anstelle der Funktion.

Verhält sich zu den Kompositionen wie eine Dichterbiographie von Zweig zu einer Dichtung.

4 Galvanisierung des Uninterpretierbaren als »Effekt«: Musik wird zugleich zum Konsum und Bildungsgut.

Funktion der Naivetät: Einbruch der Barbarei in die Musik. Sibelius.[5]

In diesem Zusammenhang sind die Motive des Dirigentenaufsatzes aus dem Anbruch[6] zu behandeln.

*

Die Würde des musikalischen Textes ist seine Intentionslosigkeit. Er bedeutet das Ideal des Klanges, nicht dessen Bedeutung. Gegenüber dem optischen Phänomen, das »ist«, und dem Worttext, der »bedeutet«, stellt der Notentext ein Drittes dar. – Abzuleiten als Erinnerungszeichen des vergänglichen Klanges, nicht als Fixierung der bleibenden Bedeutung. – Der »Ausdruck« von Musik ist keine Intention sondern mimisch-nachahmend. Eine »pathetische« Stelle bedeutet nicht Pathos usw. sondern verhält sich pathetisch. Mimetische Wurzel aller Musik. Sie wird festgehalten von der musikalischen Interpretation. Musik interpretieren heißt nicht umsonst Musik *machen* – nachahmende Leistungen vollbringen. Wäre danach die Interpretation die *Nachahmung* des Textes – sein »Bild«? Vielleicht ist das der philosophische Sinn der »Röntgenphotographie« – alles nachahmen was verborgen ist. Schauspieler und Musiker.

*

Den Grenzbegriff des bloßen *Lesens* von Musik einführen. Vielleicht ist – als Rest unsublimierter Mimesis – das »Machen« von Musik schon ebenso infantil wie lautes Lesen (tritt am Chor hervor). Das stumme Lesen als Erbe und Ende der Interpretation. Es ist diese Möglichkeit – das Auswendigspielen komplexer Kammermusik, wie Kolisch[7] es inaugurierte und wie es den absoluten Primat des Textes über dessen Nachahmung statuiert – der gegenüber prinzipiell bereits *alles* »Musizieren« antiquiert klingt. – In der Komposition stehen die Werke Anton Weberns dieser Möglichkeit überaus nahe. / Vgl. Schumann[8]

*

Zwei Aussprüche von Kolisch: »Selbst die virtuose Dirigierkunst Bruno Walters vermochte nicht das NBC-Orchester zur Unpräzision zu veranlassen.« – »An dem Cellisten A.[9] war das beste sein häßlicher Ton.« – Die Kritik des »kulinarischen« Elements der musikalischen Interpretation ist dialektisch zu leisten. Es ist nicht *einfach* zu negieren, aber nur als negiertes festgehalten. Die Negation des »schönen Klanges« ist die eigentliche Leistung aller musikalischen Mimesis – das heißt »charakteristisch«.

*

Das musikalische Werk verändert sich ähnlich durchs Gehört-, Berühmt-, Abgebrauchtwerden wie das Bild unter den Blicken der Unzähligen die darüber gegangen. Das Werk »an sich« ist eine Abstraktion. Wahrscheinlich fällt das *reine* Werk an sich mit dem Uninterpretierbaren zusammen. An Schreker[10] zu zeigen: ist heute schon U-Musik.

*

Die mimetischen Charaktere in den Werken sind historische Chiffern und sie *entweichen* daraus. Was Nägeli[11] an Mozart (analysieren), Hoffmann[12] an Beethoven wahrgenommen ist nicht mehr darin. Zu Nägelis Zeit war Mozart *objektiv* »stilunrein«, nämlich nach dem Stand des musikalischen *Materials*. Heut ist er es nicht mehr. Die historische Veränderung der Werke als solcher erfolgt stets in Relation zum Stand des Materials – eine der wichtigsten Kategorien. Das läßt sich auch so ausdrücken: daß jedes spätere kommensurable Werk jedes frühere objektiv verändert. Die Reproduktion registriert diese Veränderung und bewirkt sie zugleich. Zwischen ihr und dem Werk herrscht ein dialektisches Verhältnis.

*

Nicht nur entweichen Charaktere aus den Werken, es bilden sich auch neue. Das empire-klassizistische Element an Beethoven, das der Romantik entschwand, die ihn zu den Ihren zählte, hat sich heute in eben das konstruktive, ökonomische, integrale umgesetzt, dem die wahre Interpretation gilt. Dies sich Entfalten in der Zeit gilt mehr als für jeden anderen für Bach.

*

Schallplatten so berühmter und wohl auch authentischer Interpreten wie Joachim[13], Sarasate[14], selbst Paderewski[15] haben 6
durchaus den Charakter der Insuffizienz angenommen. Das Joachimquartett, das den Stil der Beethoveninterpretation etablierte, würde heute wohl wie ein deutsches Provinzensemble wirken, Liszt wie die Parodie eines Virtuosen. Das grauenhafte streamline Musizieren der Toscanini, Wallenstein[16], Monteux[17], Horowitz[18], Heifetz[19] – durchaus die Verfallsform der Interpretation – erweist sich als *notwendige* Verfallsform[,] indem, was anders ist, schon schlampig, zurückgeblieben, unbeholfen, eben provinziell wirkt (und auch nicht – beides! Mit größter Vorsicht formulieren)

*

Schrift und Instrument, die Pole der Interpretation.

*

Gesang. Der Gedanke, daß es keinem Steinwayflügel einfällt, ein Konzert zu geben, weil er einen so schönen Ton hat – wohl aber dem Sänger. Die Aufhebung des sinnlichen Wohlgefallens am Klang ist die Idiosynkrasie, in der das Absterben der Interpretation sich durchsetzt. – Dabei der Vergleich von Flügel und Sängern nicht *ganz* wahr – jedoch wahr *geworden* durch den Stimmfetischismus. Auseinandertreten des sinnlichen und geistigen Moments an Musik.

*

Worin ist der Musiker ein »Spieler« und worin nicht. Es gibt keine musikalische Interpretation ohne das Moment des »Danebengreifens« – ohne Risiko. Die interpretative Freiheit vom Risiko untrennbar.

*

Rubato, »Zeit *stehlen«* – was heißt das eigentlich? Mit Recht alle Interpretationsprobleme darum zentriert.

*

Soweit Musik »interpretiert« wird, ist es *stets* »Rubato«.

*

Eine geschichtsphilosophische Interpretation des Überge-
7 wichts der Interpretation über die Sache geben. Erscheinung
gegen Wesen; Mittel gegen Zweck; Person gegen Sache als
ideologischer Reflex der Verdinglichung.

*

Die Fetischisierung der Interpretation ist ein Ausbruchsversuch aus der Verdinglichung – Schein der Unmittelbarkeit – der in die Verdinglichung nur tiefer verstrickt.

*

Die Objektivität der Reproduktion setzt die Tiefe der subjektiven Anschauung voraus, sonst ist sie nur der erstarrte Abdruck der Oberfläche. Dies ist eine der Hauptthesen

*

Ad Dorian[20]

Interpretation als historisches Problem 23 »*The relationship between the performing and the creative artist, however, has changed profoundly in the history of music and continues to do so.*«

Zone der Unbestimmtheit in der Notation (Fermate[21] und Sinn) 27 »*Logically, the objective interpreter of the Fifth will perform the opening measures according to metronomic and other objective determinations, as indicated by the score and not by his personal feelings. If we turn from the particular case of the Fifth Symphony to any classical score, in fact to a score of any period, the inevitable question arises as to whether the score should be interpreted literally or whether the performer should have carte blanche in general interpretation, on the ground that, besides the script of the score, its background must also be freely taken into consideration. [. . .] In spite of this, it would still be conceivable to insure what we call authenticity of interpretation, namely, the* o b j e c t i v e *realization of the author's wishes, if the score as such were explicit enough to protect the composer's intentions against any misrepresentation on the performer's part.*«

Ungenügen der Schrift (28) »*Of course, great composers have superbly transformed their ideas into scores, making the best possible use of musical notation. But it is this very notation that is imperfect and may remain so forever, notwithstanding remarkable contributions to its improvement. There are certain intangibles that cannot be expressed by our method of writing music – vital musical elements incapable of being fixed by the marks and symbols of notation. Consequently, score scripts are incomplete in representing the composers' intentions. No score, as written in manuscript and published in print, can offer complete information for its interpreter.*«

Objektivität = Interpretation des Sinnes aus der Schrift (und umgekehrt: Wechselwirkung, wobei Schrift das »Gegebene«, das kategoriell zur Aufhebung gelangt 28) »*The farther we go back in the different periods of history, the more difficult it becomes to read and know the score, to understand its graphic marks and symbols, and to supplement its meager directions, if any – all of which is necessary for the faithfull performance of the work. Instructions of a type considered indispensable today, such as those for the main tempo of a composition, were frequently omitted in early scores. This means that, from the very start, the interpreter has to supplement the material of the score with his own good judgement. Consequently, even the interpreter of truly objective spirit is bound to find himself occasionally on subjective terrain, irrespective of his loyal inclinations.«*

Mangel an Bezeichnung = noch nicht verdinglicht (hier auf Arbeitsteilung zentriert 29) *»Sketchy as the old score may seem to the modern performer, it fulfilled its function by offering the necessary information in its own day, when the composer and the interpreter were so often one and the same person. Palestrina conducted is own Masses, Handel his own oratorios, Mozart his own operas, and Bach himself sat on the organ bench of the St. Thomas Church in Leipzig, playing his fugues and chorales. Even as late as the beginning of the nineteenth century, it was rather the exception when the composer was not his own interpreter. Chopin dreamed his nocturnes at the piano; and Paganini displayed his demoniacal virtuosity in the rendition of his music on a priceless violin.«*

Tendenzielle Eindeutigkeit moderner Notation 29 *»Today, the interpreter of contemporary works frequently has little or no personal choice, as he is forced to follow the very strict directions of the composer.«*

Strawinskys »Sergeant« 30. *»Stravinsky does not hesitate to compare a good conductor with a sergeant whose duty it is to see that every order is obeyed by his player-soldiers.«*

Meine These gegen background (Stil), für Sinn anschließen an 30f. *»As things are, performers can roughly be divided into two* *groups. They are, according to their attitude toward the score, either objective or subjective executants. And any intepretation, at its very beginning, has to be one or the other. Suppose an interpreter – as many of the best of our day have already done – decides in favour of objective interpretation. If his task is the rendition of a new score of the elaborated type he may secure sufficient clues for his goal of work-fidelity. If he interprets an old work with few or no instructions, then a most difficult task confronts him. He must, because of the elasticity of the old score, reconstruct the work in terms of its musical background. As every score is an integral part of the age in which it is created, every detail of its performance depends upon knowledge of the manners and customs of a particular period.«*

Schwierigkeit der »Vorstellung des Komponisten« 31 »*Nothing is more difficult than his task of rethinking the old works, on the basis of the original elastic score script, in terms of the great masters who wrote them. There are three paths that will lead the interpreter out of this labyrinth. First, he must learn how to read the script and to understand its language. Second, his fantasy must discover the musical essence, the inner language behind the written symbols. Finally, the interpreter should be fully acquainted with the background and the tradition of a work – with all the customs surrounding the score at the time of its creation.«*

Starre Teilung in subjektiv und objektiv. Dagegen: die objektive Interpretation des Sinnes *bedarf* der subjektiven Erfahrung des Zusammenhanges. Gegen naiven Realismus der Musik. Objektivität (31. cf. Hegel Phänomenologie[22])

NB auf der *subjektiven* Seite der Interpretation ist zu unterscheiden zwischen Vorstellung und Realisierung. Jener kommt *heute,* d.h. ohne verbindliche Tradition, der Primat zu. Doch hat die Realisierung eine eigene Dimension: die des Verhältnisses des *Textes* zum Instrument, bezw. [zu] der Stimme.

8 Erleichterung (Rationalisierung) der Notation und Verdummung der Interpreten 42. »*Things are made far more comfortable for the performer today. Unquestionably, there has been a downward trend as regards what the average musician must know. The general present-day level of his training is, in many respects, far lower than that set for his earlier colleague's ambition in his craft.*« (NB dies ist eine *gesamthistorische Tendenz*. Vgl. Fetischarbeit[23])

Das asketische Moment im Beginn der modernen Musik und »Interpretation«: »Tonsprache«: 44 »*Caccini's interpretation attacked whatever seemed opposed to genuine emotional expression. Now, with the humanistic attitude of respect toward the word, the new interpretative goal was to express clearly the true effect of the ›tone language‹, as music was significantly called. This permitted a performance of the new monodic compositions on the basis of a broad subjective treatment of the text as the performer's guide. Emphasis was exclusively on the dramatic meaning of the poem and not on beautiful tone rows.*«

Voce finta, esclamazione 45 f. »*Caccini recognized only two registers: voce plena e naturale (full and natural voice) and voce finta (artificial voice). In his interpretation he wished to restrict male singers to the use of natural voice, rejecting their falsetto as ugly; but sopranos and altos, boys as well as women, were permitted to use both registers. The use of the female falsetto was even considered enjoyable for esclamazione, a singing device of the Renaissance that retained its importance for centuries. Originally the term designated the reinforcing of the voice at the moment when it was about to diminish – a crescendo at the end of the tone. Metaphorically, not only the final crescendo but the whole figure is called esclamazione. Its importance may be judged from the fact that a representative British account of the new style, written as early as 1655, quotes from the Le nuove musiche as follows: [. . .] ›Because Exclamation is the principal means to move the Affections; and Exclamation properly is no other thing, but in slacking of the Voice to reinforce it somewhat.‹*«

Musik als *Sprache* am Anfang der Neuzeit und zentrales Interpretationsproblem. 46 »*The fact that all these references appear at the beginning of Caccini's Le nuove musiche shows how much importance was attached to these devices as a principal means of expression. First and foremost, Caccini expressed his main idea of interpretation in the watchword, una certa nobile sprezzatura di canto – ›a certain noble subordination of the song‹. The singer's task was to speak musically, as it were.*«

Subjektivismus und Identifikation 49 »*STILO RAPPRESENTATIVO. The difference between the old and the new style of madrigal is demonstrated by Sachs: ›The sixteenth-century composer dealt with love through the medium of a madrigal in several parts. No one found any fault in the basses playing the role of a young girl or the sopranos that of a wooer. The music did not try to achieve illusion. In the seventeenth century the singer was merged with the imaginary character to whom the poet's verses were ascribed. The singer had to identify himself with him whose joys and sorrows were depicted in the words. [. . .] After the polyphonic style of the past, les jeunes, around 1600, aspired to a stilo recitativo or rappresentativo, imitating natural diction and expressing even the most delicate and secret emotions of the soul.*‹«

Vorschrift der Freiheit schon 1614 Frescobaldi. 54-55 »*Girolamo Frescobaldi, in the preface to his Toccate published in Rome in 1614, gives a most comprehensive description of organ interpretation. A digest of his rules follows. ›1. First, this kind of performance must not be subject to strict time – as in modern madrigals, which are sung, now languid, now lively, in accordance with the affections of the music or the meaning of the words.‹ We learn, thus, that Italian madrigals were sung with liberty of tempo [. . .]. Obviously, the vocal style influenced the instrumental music. A singing bel canto performance on the instrument was the ideal.*«

Zur Urgeschichte der Massenkultur und ihres Zusammenhangs mit Interpretationsproblemen 55 »›*2. In the Toccate, I have attempted not only to offer a variety of divisions and expressive ornaments, but also to plan the various sections so that they can be played independently of one another. The performer can stop wherever he wishes, and thus does not have to play them all.‹ This almost dangerous admission on the part of Frescobaldi would seem to open up new vistas for subjective interpretation. [. . .] ›5. The cadences, though written as rapid, must be performed quite sustained; as the performer approaches the end of the passage of cadence, he must retard the tempo gradually.‹ [. . .] We see that rubato and phrasing, in interpretation, were not invented with the employment of signs designating these features [. . .].«*

Hauptbeleg der Subjektivierung der Interpretation als Funktion der Verdinglichung 56f. *»From these rules emerge main principles of interpretation for the seventeenth century that also were to prove basic for centuries to follow: (a) subjectivity of reading, as good taste and fine judgment become rulers of performance; (b) the special differentiation of types, such as the dances, according to their characteristics; (c) a general necessity of individual decision, changing almost with every passage; (d) the impossibility of generalizations applicable in more than the broad aspects indicated in rules 1 to 9.«*

Notenschrift und Druck 61 *»The most sweeping change occurred in the sixteenth century, when it became possible to print scores.«*

Renaissance, Funktionsteilung, Quantifizierung, Funktionseinheit, Jazz 62f. *»From the system then adopted to the complicated scores now in use, the way is long and the process is one of logical development. Today it is taken for granted that the orchestra is a group of performers of which each one plays an individually prescribed part. In fact, the young musician who joins an orchestral group can hardly conceive that it could ever have been otherwise. In the early days of the orchestra, however, the employment and grouping of instruments followed no definite order whatsoever. Apparently the only principle was not to have a principle. In those bygone days, whoever happened to be present at a performance played any available instrument. The method was one of extem-*

pore and improvisation. [. . .] The conductor in the early days acted simultaneously as his own arranger. His responsibility was not limited to rehearsing and directing performances. First of all, he had to adjust the res facta, that is, the composer's written score and its tone rows, to the vocal and instrumental forces at hand. How such a metamorphosis of an original score into a variety of versions was brought about, is demonstrated in Syntagma musicum, a treatise published in 1619 at Wolfenbüttel, Germany, and containing invaluable information in many respects. [. . .] We observe here the method called variatio per choros, variations designed for two contrasting choirs.«

Emanzipation der Geige vom Gesang 66 »*Monteverdi also fully realized the potentialities of the violin as the leading melodic instrument of the orchestra. Augmenting its compass from the third to the fifth position, he progressed from the point where the vocal mind of Gabrieli stopped. In other words, he liberated the violin from its function as a substitute for the soprano, and made it an independant orchestral instrument with individual expression.*«

absolutistischer Darstellungsstil: Stampfen 69 »*Here, in front of his musicians and visible to all, stood Maître Jean Baptiste [Lully], pounding the beat with a heavy, decorated stick – a musical commander with military manners, insisting upon instrumental discipline and utmost rhythmical precision. [. . .] Generations later, Jean Jacques Rousseau protested against the noisy beating of conductors in the theater. Rationalist that this philosopher-musician was, he finally became resigned to the idea that without the noise the measure of the music could not be distinctly felt by the singers and orchestra players.*«

Verdinglichung des Komponierens (NB Beethovens Kurzschrift[24]) 70 »*The nineteenth-century opera composer Halévy pictured Lully sitting in his studio inventing only melodies and basso continuo, while two favorite apprentices, Lalousette and Colasse, took one sheet after another from the hand of their master to finish the orchestration – the first assembly-line system in musical history.*«

Konvention regelt Divergenz von Notation + Ausführung 72f. »*In the following illustration Muffat clarifies the considerable contrast that existed between notation and performance.*

We see how the rhythm ist altered in the performance; script and execution are strinkingly inconsistent. Such discrepancies cannot be comprehended from the modern point of view, with its striving for utmost clarity in notation. Yet alteration of rhythm was a common trend in the old practice of music. Therefore, the present-day interpreter, eager to perform these old masterpieces correctly, must reorientate himself in the intricate notation of this music. If the composer wrote those rhythmic patterns as he did – differently from the way they were to sound – he depended on the performer's knowledge of tradition.«

Keine Bachtradition 76f. »*There is clearly a void of one hundred years in which Bach's scores were rarely played, and consequently no tradition of Bach performance could be handed down from the eighteenth to the nineteenth century.*«

Ad Bach: Problem der Ausnutzung *späterer* Resourcen für frühere Musik 81 »*At the same time, to obtain a completely authentic picture of the problems in performing Bach, we must not overlook the facts, first, that today's performances take place in large concert halls and not in the St. Thomas Church, and that therefore the acoustics are different; second, that the master himself might have welcomed an opportunity of increased equipment. The question remains, however, how far he might have gone had he had the facilities of today's conductors. Could he, in his wildest dreams, have imagined the vast orchestral forces that perform today?«*

NB doppelte Front gegen Willkür und Historismus (aus der inneren Geschichte der Werke ableiten)

Das »funktionelle Ornament« (guter Einfall von Dorian, hat viel weitere Konsequenz. Funktion *alles* Akzidentiellen. Akzidentiell ist schließlich die Aufführung selbst, gleichsam die Ornamentierung des Textes die ganz in diesem aufgeht. Das Lesen des Ornaments ist das Schema der Dechiffrierung *aller* Musik. Ad 89) »*To put it paradoxically: ornaments are functional. In other words, they are neither mere embellishments nor musical tapestry.*«

Zum Schlüsselcharakter der Manieren: ad Generalbaß. 91 f. 9
»*Bach's greatest son, with his Versuch [über die wahre Art das Clavier zu spielen], contributed to the musical world something of far more than academic and musicological importance. This volume, coming as it does directly from the workshop of the practical musician [...] offers us in fact a veritable encyclopedia of the interpretative problems of its period. [...] They contain a realization not only of the style and interpretation of the two great baroque masters, Handel and Johann Sebastian Bach, but also of all preceding and contemporary instrumental styles as expressed in English, French, and Italian scores. Thus, the eclectic quality of the treatise becomes obvious and proves to be one of the great advantages of the Versuch. For all these historical and practical reasons, it is convenient to use this treatise as a ground plan for our presentation of ornaments. In the following pages, the different types of graces will be taken up in accordance with Philipp Emanuel's nine chapters on Manieren.*«

Standardisierung des Tanzes 107 »*In dance music, likewise, ambiguity surrounds the meaning of different type names, and to a surpris-*

ingly intensified degree – surprising because, naturally, the dance music accompanied specific step patterns that were inevitably standardized, as in the case of minuet.«

Pulsschlag und Tempo 115 *»Not only in the ever changing minuet, but in all the other fluctuating dance forms, the first and principal question to be settled is: What is the correct tempo? [...] It was the methodical mind of Quantz that solved this problem half a century before the advent of Maelzel's invention. In his Versuch einer Anweisung die Flöte traversière zu spielen, Quantz presents a method based on the human pulse. He assumed that there are eighty beats to the minute. This figure, in turn, is analogous to eighty time units on the metronome. Taking full advantage of Quantz's scheme, we easily translate his pulsations into the standard units of Maelzel's metronome. By mutual adjustment, any tempo can be stated precisely, eliminating ambiguity.«*

Zeugnis des Schnellerwerdens im Rokoko (116f., ad neue Tempi) *»A cross section of rather confusing courante designations can be gleaned from the following: ›swift corantos‹ (Shakespeare); ›largo‹ (Bassani); ›rather quickly‹ (Kuhnau); ›pompously‹ (Quantz). The reason for the variety of modes is the fact that the old dance has practically nothing in common with the later types called by the same name. As the Rococo lightened everything up, so the stately court courante gradually developed a moderate and eventually a fast tempo.«*

Affektenlehre, das mimetische Element der Interpretation und der Wirkungszusammenhang 139 *»Modern renditions of eighteenth-century music, aspiring to recall the spirit of that old time, cannot ignore substantially the ramifications of the Affektenlehre. Today it must be remembered that it laws controlled the old interpretation and that every eighteenth-century performer was expected to obey its rules. Reviewing first the general statements of various authorities, we learn that the musical expression of human emotions emerges as the final goal of interpretation.«*

Erkenntnis des Affekts und Nachahmung 140 *»Unequivocally, Quantz demands that the performer recognize the affections expressed in a piece, always keeping his rendition in conformity with them. Thus, only interpretations based on an appropriate scrutiny of the affections, and their suitable musical application, are sanctioned.«*

Interpretation als Nachahmung 144 *»As Lohlein in his Supervision in Violin Playing, Sulzer in his General Theory, and others have concluded, it is only when the performer fully experiences the composer's feeling, that he is capable of arousing the corresponding emotion in those who listen to his performance.«*

crescendo: Einheit von Komposition und Interpretation 149 *»However, beginnning with Jommelli, the choice of modulation to piano or forte, crescendo or decrescendo, no longer resided in the will of the performer, but had to be sought in the instructions of the composer himself.«*

crescendo als Spezialität (Arbeitsteilung) 151 *»The difference between the earlier interpretations and those of Mannheim, as Rosamond Harding, G. Schünemann, and others show, is that an already recognized type of dynamic performance achieved a new tone-poetic effect and finally became a speciality, celebrated through the splendor of the Mannheim orchestral renditions.«*

Ende des Generalbasses und Ende der interpretativen Freiheit 157 *»The comparison of the classical score with its predecessor reveals a further departure: the basso continuo has vanished from the script. In the orchestral and vocal scores of preclassical times, we see the figured bass part as an inevitable characteristic of concerted rendition. Thus, the keyboard part was executed ad libitum, interpreted in an improvisatory way. But improvisation, as the art of making music extemporaneously, ceases to be a factor in classical interpretation.«*

Dorians undialektische Auffassung von Subjekt und Objekt

[157] »*If interpretation as a subjective art could not become fully entrenched in music prior to the Renaissance and the awakening of individualized expression, then objective interpretation found its logical inception in the classical score. It is only since the latter part of the eighteenth century that sufficient clues had been made available, by the new classical script, to provide all the information necessary for a performance of work-fidelity.*«

Phrasierung 159 (NB Phrasierung eines der Kernprobleme des »Sinnes«). »*Phrasing is a feature common to both speech and music: it serves the same purpose in the language of words as in the language of tones. What may be called articulation in music is equivalent to diction in speech. Thus it is clear that phrasing occurs everywhere: in the tune of the torch singer and in the aria of Caruso; in the speech of the idiot and in that of Shakespeare. While phrasing is universal and ageless, in the sense that it has been exercised since Adam an Eve and the archbeginnings of musical utterance, the applied discipline of phrasing in the performance of music is young.*«

Sulzers Warnung vorm guten Taktteil 162 (zum Alter der Modernität) »*In Sulzer's encyclopedia,* General Theory of the Fine Arts, *the following explanations is provided: ›After the first note of each measure, the other strong beats should be less marked. The first note of a bar within a phrase must not be overaccentuated. Failure to heed this may spoil the whole performance. The caesuras are the commas of the song, which, as in speech, must be made manifest by a moment of relaxation.*‹«

Zusammenhang von Dynamik und Phrasierung: Einheit der Elemente (NB diese Einheit *ist* der musikalische Sinn. Dies ist eine der zentralen Thesen). 162f. »*In 1834, Pierre Baillot (with Beethoven's friend Kreutzer, a leading exponent of the French violin school) states in* L'art du violon: *›Slight separations, such as rests of short duration, are not always indicated by the composer. The player must therefore provide them, when he sees that it is necessary, by letting the last note of the phrase die away. Indeed, in* *certain cases he must even let it end shortly before the completion of its normal duration.‹«*

Gute Stelle gegen falsche Objektivität 163. *»Today there are many interpreters who, in a conscientious attempt to be objective, believe that the omission of bowings in the manuscript forces them to make the same omission in their playing.«*

Begriff des musikalischen Sinnes und Phrasierung (zentral: 164) *»It suffices to quote Rousseau's Dictionnaire de musique (1775), which contributes the following on the topic »phrase«: ›A singer who feels his phrases and their accent is a man of good taste. But one who renders only notes, keys, scales, and intervals, without comprehending the meaning of the phrases – even if he be precise otherwise – is nothing but a »note-gobbler«‹ (n'est qu'un Croque-sol).«*

Stärke und Dissonanz (ad Wagnerarbeit[25]. 168) *»Further clues to dynamic distinction are provided by the harmony as such. Philipp Emanuel Bach points out that every tone foreign to the key can very well stand a forte, regardless of whether it occurs in dissonance or consonance. This is very convincing: the dissonance had been the enlivening element of all music since the era of medieval counterpoint.«*

»Thema« und Dynamik: Zusammenhang von Form und Dynamik 168 *»He [scil. Quantz] also explains that the theme of the composition calls for dynamic emphasis.«*

Haydn und Fortschritt 177 *»However ›Papa‹ certainly has no place as a clue to Haydn interpretation today, in an attempt to produce an old-fashioned gemütlich atmosphere of music-making, whereas in reality Haydn's scores represent the spirit of progress, depth, and artistic courage.«*

Dorians Regel des Tempos (das musikologische Tempo) 180

»The life-work of Mozart and Haydn falls into a time before the invention of the metronome, and so the difficult task of determining the right tempo in classical and earlier scores can be based only on the musical material in the script, in conjunction with musicological facts.«

historische Relativität der Schrift 181 (ad neue Tempi) *»In other words, notes that look long to the modern eye meant something quite different in their day: the brevis 𝅜, the semibrevis 𝅝, and the minim 𝅗𝅥 are laden with connotations of slowness only in the minds of certain modern interpreters.«*

Schnellerwerden durch Wiederholung (ad Historizität des Tempos 185 f.) *»Hence Quantz's precept: ›When a composition (especially a fast one) is repeated (for instance, an allegro of a concerto or a symphony), it must be somewhat quicker the second time, in order not to put the listener to sleep. [. . .]‹ On the contrary, it is almost a criterion of acceptable classical performance that the tempo primo be resumed at every recapitulation.«*

NB die *Abstraktheit* des Begriffs espressivo ist zu retten. Er bezieht sich nicht auf den Ausdruck eines Bestimmten sondern auf den Sprachgestus der Musik.

Mozarts Rubato 189 (kritisieren) *[Dorian (S. 188) zitiert aus einem Brief Mozarts vom 24. Oktober 1777:] »›No one seems to understand the tempo rubato in an adagio, where the left hand does not know anything about it.‹ First, it now becomes clear that Mozart himself played rubato – a discovery of great importance, since the majority of acclaimed performers strictly avoid the rubato as absurd in Mozart, which in turn is in keeping with the point of view of the dictionary on this very problem. Second, an insight is gained into the specific rubato technique of Mozart, according to his own description. The master himself discloses the secret – ›the left hand does not know anything about it‹. This, as will become apparent later, is the foundation of any rubato playing. Moreover, if one substitutes melody for the right hand and accompaniment for the left hand, it becomes a general prescription for performing music rubato.«*

Rubato als Ausdruck 190 »*The purpose of his [scil. Pier Francesco Tosi] technique of ›robbed‹ time was expression. Rubato was thus used where a particular phrase required special expressive emphasis.«*

NB Das Problem der Interpretation liegt in der Dialektik von Ausdruck und Konstruktion

Beethovens Ambivalenz zum Metronom 198 »*On the manuscript of his song Nord oder Süd, Beethoven wrote the notation, ›100 according to Maelzel. But this must be applicable only to the first measures, for feeling also has its tempo and this cannot be entirely expressed in this figure‹«*. (NB Doppelgesicht der Verdinglichung. Protest des »Lebens«. Cf. später Debussy-Bergson 300).

espressivo als ritardando 207 »*We can find nowhere in Beethoven a specifically prescribed rubato. As we shall see in a later section, the literal instruction, tempo rubato, was introduced by Chopin. Yet there are evidently passages where the aggregate of Beethoven's markings amounts to what the rubato instruction represents in later periods: a variation of time with gradual modification. For example, in the opening movement of Opus 111, the original instruction, allegro con brio ed appassionato, dissolves completely upon the very first appearance of the second theme. Here, meno allegro appears in the second half of the measure, followed by two measures marked ritardando.«*

Phantasieelement und Treue 220 »*In striking contrast to the attitude of wilfulness toward the score, there also prevails, during the nineteenth century, the contrasting thought of allegiance to the score.«*

Das Originalmanuskript 224 »*One of the most characteristic features in modern interpretation is the increasing tendency to turn to the original manuscripts of great composers as the dependable basis for proper rendition. Studying the composer's manuscript, rather than the printed edition, is the ideal way of approaching a master's score.«* Schumanns Kritik 224f. »*Nevertheless, while Schumann stresses the objective approach by insisting upon reference to the manuscript, he at the same time warns the interpreter against blind acceptance of every detail of the manuscript and against an exaggeration of the conception of objectivity.«*

Charakter durch musikalischen Inhalt 227 zentral (NB Stelle bei Schumann[26] suchen) »*In the composer's own view, then, the Schumann interpreter must, first of all, grasp the character of his scores from the musical content – from the very structure of the score. [. . .] If we trace Schumann's ideology further, we see how he stamps himself as an aesthete of the* A f f e k t e n l e h r e, *with the following viewpoint on tempo: ›You know how I dislike quarreling about tempo, and how for me only the inner measure of the movement is conclusive. Thus, an allegro of one who is cold by nature always sounds lazier than a slow tempo by one of sanguine temperament. With the orchestra, however, the proportions are decisive. Stronger and denser masses are capable of bringing out the detail as well as the whole with more emphasis and importance; whereas, with smaller and finer units, one must compensate for the lack of resonance by pushing forward in the tempo.‹«*

Wagners schmiegsame Tempi (ad Vitalismus)

funktionelles Rubato 239 »*Another observer of Chopin's time variation is Ignaz Moscheles, who explains Chopin's rubato as a specified means of gliding over harsh modulations in a fairy-like way with delicate fingers. Thus, rubato was applied in a purely functional way, so unlike the abuse of it by many modern executants with whom it degenerates from slight variation into a disregard of time – a vulgarized license of meter and confusion of rhythm smuggled into the Chopin performance in the guise of so-called tradition.«*

»objektive« Interpretation gerade subjektivistischer Musik 246f. *»In spite of the obvious emphasis on the composer's subjective experience, there is, in his expressed views, an insistence on objectivity in interpretation. It is strictly demanded that the interpreter regard himself as nothing more than the loyal medium of the composer.«*

Tempo als Kernproblem 280 *»Taking literally Beethoven's word ›tempo is the body of performance‹, Wagner demonstrates how the technique of correct interpretation centers around the setting of the right tempo [...].«*

extremes Adagio + Allegro. »Tempovariation« bei Wagner 281f. *»The true adagio can hardly be played too slowly; the naïve allegro is usually a quick* alla breve. *[...] After considering the problem of* tempo primo, *Wagner approaches that of tempo modification, bitterly complaining that the technique of time variation was utterly unknown to performers. But his mind this very factor was the vital principle of all music-making.»*

Meistersingervorspiel 282 *»For the modern interpreter, the composer's own illustration of the proper rendering of his* Meistersinger *prelude, in a flexible four-four time, is most important. Here modifications serve the purpose of exposing discriminately the diverse themes as interwoven in the polyphonic web.«*

Wagner für Tempomodifikationen 283 *»Wagner demands tempo changes in the course of the opening movement; yet this was generally treated by conductors as a single unit.«*

Das subjektive Element objektiver Interpretation (gegen Dorian 284) *»Summing up, we realize that Wagner's interpretative ideology is that of his age. All the traits of Romanticism are embodied in this one great mind: extreme subjectivity seeks the strange company of a passionate striving for extreme loyality.«*

Dorians undialektische Auffassung 285f. *»The fact is, Verdi* *went even farther in emphasizing radical objectivity of rendition than did Wagner. Not torn like the latter between antagonistic ideologies (of work-fidelity on the one hand, and the claim to the interpreter's right to re-create on the other), Verdi was most tyrannical in demanding unconditional obedience to his scores.«*

Gegen die Antithese »theatralisch-historisch« 293 *»Bülow believed, however, in a third power also, namely, in himself. And so he sails in completely subjective waters, recklessly changing eternal words, such as Bach's Chromatic Fantasy, and showing, in his editing of Scarlatti or Beethoven, his own theatrical showmanship rather than a true historical approach.«*

Virtuos und Zirkus (Naturbeherrschung) 299 *»The attraction of the virtuoso for the public is very much like that of the circus for the crowd. There is always hope that something dangerous may happen. M. Ysaye may play the violin with conductor Colonne on his shoulders, or M. Pugno may conclude his piece by lifting the piano with his teeth.« [Claude Debussy, La Revue blanche, 1. Mai 1901]*

Debussys Antimechanismus 300 *»In La revue blanche [vom 15. Mai 1913], we read his [scil. Debussys] comment: ›At a time like ours, in which mechanical skill has attained unsuspected perfection, the most famous works may be heard as easily as one may drink a glass of beer, and it only costs ten centimes, like the automatic weighing machines. Should we not fear this domestication of sound, this magic that anyone can bring from a disk at his will? Will it not bring to waste the mysterious force of an art which one might have thought indestructible?‹«*

Satie, Dada, Jazz 304 f. *»If one reads the list of instruments intended to be used for background noises in the performance of Satie's ballet Parade – sirens, typewriters, airplanes, dynamos – it becomes clear that our machine age has fully entered the realm of performance.«*

historische Korrektheit: Durchschneiden der dialektischen Beziehung 311 »*The principle of historical correctness, one of the most significant trends in modern interpretation, had its beginning long before the dawn of the twentieth century: we have only to recall the work-fidelity of the romantic era to realize that the objective approach is not an achievement of our age. [. . .] Supported by great scores, important ideologies, undreamed-of technical accomplishments, the trend to correctness in musical rendition is now an established principle.*«

NB Objektivität ist nicht historische Korrektheit. Diese gerade ist heut meist kunstgewerblich, candle light – schlecht subjektiv d. h. in Widerspruch zu den Bedingungen des objektiven Geistes.

Keine prästabilierte Harmonie zwischen Komposition und den historisch verfügbaren Mitteln der Interpretation (gegen Historismus 312) »*With such a general turning to the past world of music, emphasis on a legitimate old style of performance is but the logical consequence. If baroque scores are to be played with historical correctness, then the historical instruments actually used in readings by their composers, and not our modern ones, must be employed.*«

Schönbergs Bach[27] 312f. »*Not only the need for the return to the old sound ideal, but simultaneously the absurdity of certain modern arrangements is indicated: it is historically incorrect to substitute the modern orchestra palette for the old one [. . .].*«

Problem 318 diskutieren »*Probably the best-known example [scil. für Beethovens Verwendung des Horns] is found in the opening movement of the Fifth Symphony. In the fifty-ninth measure, the theme is given to the horns; the analogous passage of the recapitulation, however, is given only to the bassoons. Why Beethoven resorted in the second version to bassoons is obvious: since he could not use the stepped notes of the E flat horn for the expressive power of this phrase in C major, the only alternative available was to substitute bassoons for horn. With the advanced technique of the instrument today, conductors do what Beethoven could not have done in 1805, and use the horn in both cases, relieving the bassoons from a task for which they are not well suited.«*

Strawinskys Positivismus[28] 329 *»For the schooling of the young interpreter, Stravinsky's suggestion is noteworthy that it would be wiser to start the education of the young musician by first giving him a knowledge of what is, and only then tracing backward, step by step, to what has been.«*

Schönbergs Erkenntnisideal 333 *»The romantic method necessarily consists of a heightening of the surface luster, rather than what Schönberg demands – balance and symmetry of presentation, where true insight into the construction governs the outline as well as all the details of the interpretation.«*

11 Eliminierung des Interpreten als »middleman« (342) *»We have only to think of the possibility of an apparatus that will permit the composer to transmit his music directly into a recording medium without the help of the middleman interpreter.«*

Standardisierung der Aufführung durch Schallplatte 342f. *»One of the direct consequences of recordings is the means they provide for improving the average interpretative standards. With the renditions of the great musicians available on disks, the mediocre performer has a priceless opportunity to orientate himself by model performances. [. . .] But there is another side of the picture: such a second-hand interpretation, accomplished through imitation, is bound to lack the conviction of a personalized conception. The student, before the convenient availability of the gramophone, was forced to acquire his knowledge of a masterwork by direct study of the score, playing it on the piano, or just reading it. This approach sharpened his ear and imagination.«*

Zum *Ende* der musikalischen Interpretation 343-44
1) das Uninterpretierbarwerden der Werke[29]

2) das »Schreiben« des Klanges
3) die Standardisierung der Interpretation
4) keine Wechselwirkung von Ausführendem + Hörer *»Such interaction of artist and audience does not exist in the case of the electric rendition. Neither is the interpreter before the microphone stimulated by an audience, nor can the listener to a record or a broadcast performance be influenced beyond the aural sensation.«*

*

Zu Richard Wagners »Über das Dirigieren« (G. S. 8, p. 261 ff[30])

264: *»Da auf diese Lieblingsopern auch von den großen Theaterintendanten, nach dem rühmlichen Geschmacke ihrer Höfe, am allermeisten gehalten wird, so ist es auch nicht zu verwundern, daß Anforderungen, welche sich auf diesen Herren durchaus unbeliebte Werke begründen, bei ihnen nur dann durchzusetzen sein würden, wenn der Kapellmeister eben ein Mann von Gewicht und ernstem Ansehen wäre, und wenn er namentlich selbst recht ordentlich wüßte, was für ein heutiges Orchester nöthig ist.«*
Nachdruck auf der *Autorität* des Dirigenten. (NB mit dem Anwachsen des Sinnes der Reproduktion wächst auch ihr repressiver Charakter an: ad Philosophie der neuen Musik. Mit anderen Worten: die Fetischisierung der Reproduktion, das sinnlose Toscanini-Ideal, wird durch die radikale Verfolgung des musikalischen Sinnes selber erzeugt. Die »Monopolisierung« der Musik entsteht in deren eigenem Schoß).

268 f.: *»Meine besten Anleitungen im Betreff des Tempo's und des Vortrages Beethoven'scher Musik entnahm ich einst dem seelenvoll sicher accentuirten Gesange der großen Schröder-Devrient; es war mir seither z. B. unmöglich, die ergreifende Kadenz der Hoboe im ersten Satze der c-moll-Symphonie*

[Takt 268] so verlegen herunterblasen zu lassen, wie ich dieß sonst noch nie anders gehört habe; ja, ich empfand nun, von dem mir aufgegangenen Vortrage dieser Kadenz aus zurückgehend, auch, welche Bedeutung und welcher Ausdruck bereits an der entsprechenden Stelle dem als Fermate ausgehaltenen [g] der ersten Violine [Takt 21] zu geben sei, und aus dem rührend ergreifenden Eindrucke, den ich von diesen zwei so unscheinbar dünkenden Punkten her gewann, ging mir ein den ganzen Satz belebendes neues Verständniß auf.« rückschließende Interpretation (von der Oboenkadenz der V. aus). D. h. Totalität als Rück- und Vorblick. Die sinnvolle Interpretation transzendiert die bloße Gegenwart. Es ist das Zeichen der schlechten, daß sie in der Darstellung des je Gegenwärtigen aufgeht: das positivistische Verkümmern der Erinnerung. Definition des Effekts als bloßer Gegenwart. Dazu Wagners »Wirkung ohne Ursache«[31] (NB Wagner *widerspricht* dem S. 285 *[»Keiner unserer Dirigenten getraut sich dem Adagio diese seine Eigenschaft im richtigen Maaße zuzuerkennen; sie spähen vom Anfange herein nach irgend welcher darin vorkommenden Figuration aus, um sogleich nach der muthmaßlichen Bewegung derselben ihr Tempo einzurichten.«]*)

269: *»Von dem Orchestervortrag unserer klassischen Instrumentalmusik ist mir aus meiner frühesten Jugend ein auffallender Eindruck der Unbefriedigung verblieben, welchen ich, sobald ich noch in neuester Zeit einem solchen Vortrage beiwohnte, stets wiederum erhielt. Was mir am Klaviere, oder bei der Lesung der Partitur, im Ausdrucke so seelenvoll belebt erschienen, erkannte ich dann kaum wieder, wie es meistens ganz unbeachtet flüchtig an den Zuhörern vorüber ging.«* »seelenvoll belebt«: der musikalische Sinn ist bei Wagner *zunächst* durch den Ausdruck definiert.

271: *»Das Orchester hatte eben gelernt, in jedem Takte die Beethoven'sche M e l o d i e zu erkennen, welche offenbar unseren*

braven Leipziger Musikern damals gänzlich entgangen war; und diese Melodie sang das Orchester.«
die Forderung, die »Melodie zu erkennen«. Dazu: 1) Interpretation als Erkenntnis. 2) Melodie heißt hier soviel wie »roter Faden«, d.h. Zusammenhang. (Beweis 286 *[»Die bedeutendsten Allegro-Sätze Beethoven's werden meistens durch eine Grundmelodie beherrscht, welche in einem tieferen Sinne dem Charakter des Adagio's angehört, und hierdurch erhalten sie die* s e n t i m e n t a l e *Bedeutung, welche diese Allegro's so ausdrücklich gegen die frühere,* n a i v e *Gattung derselben abstechen läßt.«]*)

273: *»Auf welchem Wege ward es jenen Pariser Musikern möglich, so unfehlbar zu der Lösung dieser schwierigen Aufgabe zu gelangen? Ersichtlich zunächst nur durch den gewissenhaftesten Fleiß, wie er bloß solchen Musikern zu eigen ist, welche sich nicht damit begnügen, sich gegenseitig Komplimente zu machen, sich nicht einbilden, daß sie Alles von selbst verstünden, sondern dem zunächst Unverstandenen gegenüber sich scheu und besorgt fühlen, und dem Schwierigen von der Seite beizukommen suchen, auf welcher sie zu Hause sind, nämlich von der Seite der Technik.«*
zur Wechselwirkung der wahren Interpretation: »Dem Schwierigen von der Seite der Technik beikommen.« Durchs Umsetzen der Darstellungsprobleme in technische macht sich *notwendig* zugleich das subjektive Element der Interpretation geltend. (Verdinglichung – Subjektivität). Aber darin zugleich wieder das für den Progressiven Wagner so charakteristische positivistische Element (Auseinandertreten von Sinn und Technik; daher Gesamtkunstwerk usw.)

274: *»*N u r d i e r i c h t i g e E r f a s s u n g d e s M e l o s ' g i e b t a b e r a u c h d a s r i c h t i g e Z e i t m a a ß a n: *beide sind unzertrennlich; eines bedingt das andere. [. . .] Will man Alles zusammenfassen, worauf es für die richtige Aufführung eines*

Tonstückes von Seiten des Dirigenten ankommt, so ist dieß darin enthalten, daß er immer das richtige Tempo angebe; denn die Wahl und Bestimmung desselben läßt uns sofort erkennen, ob der Dirigent das Tonstück verstanden hat oder nicht. Das richtige Tempo giebt guten Musikern bei genauerem Bekanntwerden mit dem Tonstück es fast von selbst auch an die Hand, den richtigen Vortrag dafür zu finden, denn jenes schließt bereits die Erkenntniß dieses letzteren von Seiten des Dirigenten in sich ein. Wie wenig leicht es aber ist, das richtige Tempo zu bestimmen, erhellt eben hieraus, daß nur aus der Erkenntniß des richtigen Vortrages in jeder Beziehung auch das richtige Zeitmaaß gefunden werden kann.« Tempo als Funktion des »Melos« (Zusammenhangs) *und*
12 Kriterium des Verstehens. Die einander widersprechenden Sätze Wagners (Widerspruch aufdecken) unten auf der Seite, sind der genaueste Ausdruck eines dialektischen Sachverhalts, den der Antihegelianer Wagner am letzten würde zugegeben haben.

275: *»Hierin fühlten die alten Musiker so richtig, daß sie, wie Haydn und Mozart, für die Tempobezeichnung meist sehr allgemeinhin verfuhren: ›Andante‹ zwischen ›Allegro‹ und ›Adagio‹, erschöpft mit der einfachsten Steigerung der Grade fast Alles ihnen hierfür nöthig dünkende. Bei S. Bach finden wir endlich das Tempo allermeistens geradesweges gar nicht bezeichnet, was im ächt musikalischen Sinne das Allerrichtigste ist. Dieser nämlich sagte sich etwa: wer mein Thema, meine Figuration nicht versteht, deren Charakter und Ausdruck nicht herausfühlt, was soll dem noch solch' eine italienische Tempobezeichnung sagen? – Um aus meiner allereigensten Erfahrung zu sprechen, führe ich an, daß ich meine auf den Theatern gegebenen früheren Opern mit recht beredter Tempo-Angabe ausstattete, und diese noch durch den Metronomen (wie ich vermeinte) unfehlbar genau fixierte. Woher ich nun von einem albernen Tempo in einer Aufführung, z. B. meines ›Tannhäuser‹, hörte, vertheidigte man sich ge-*

gen meine Rekriminationen jedesmal damit, auf das Gewissenhafteste meiner Metronom-Angabe gefolgt zu sein. Ich ersah hieraus, wie unsicher es mit der Mathematik in der Musik stehen müsse, und ließ fortan nicht nur den Metronomen aus, sondern begnügte mich auch für Angebung der Hauptzeitmaaße mit sehr allgemeinen Bezeichnungen, meine Sorgfalt einzig den Modifikationen dieser Zeitmaaße zuwendend, da von diesen unsere Dirigenten so gut wie gar nichts wissen.«
die romantische These vom Primat des Sinnes über die Notation. Wagners Kernstück, die Lehre von der »Tempomodifikation«, hängt unmittelbar davon ab.

282: *»Hier liegt eben der entscheidend wichtige Punkt, auf dessen sehr deutliches Erfassen es abgesehen sein müßte, wenn es über den oft so sehr vernachlässigten und durch üble Gewöhnungen verdorbenen Vortrag unserer klassischen Musikwerke zu einer ersprießlichen Verständigung kommen sollte. Die üble Gewöhnung hat nämlich ein scheinbares Recht, auf ihren Annahmen über das Tempo zu bestehen, weil sich eine gewisse Übereinstimmung des Vortrages mit diesem gebildet hat, welche einerseits den Befangenen das wahre Übel verdeckt, andererseits aber zunächst eine offenbare Verschlimmerung dadurch gewahren läßt, daß der im Übrigen gewöhnte Vortrag bei nur einseitiger Veränderung des Zeitmaaßes sich meistens ganz unerträglich ausnimmt.«*
Wagners Zugeständnis des relativen – historischen – Rechts der falschen Interpretation (als zweiter Natur. Hat sehr weitreichende Konsequenzen).
»Um dieß an einem allereinfachsten Beispiele klar zu machen, wähle ich den Anfang der C moll-Symphonie [von Beethoven]: Über die Fermate des zweiten Taktes gehen unsere Dirigenten nach einem kleinen Verweilen hinweg und benutzen dieses Verweilen fast nur, um die Aufmerksamkeit der Musiker auf ein präzises Erfassen der Figur des dritten Taktes zu konzentriren. Die Note Es wird gewöhnlich nicht

länger ausgehalten, als bei einem achtlosen Bogenstriche der Saiteninstrumente ein Forte andauert. Nun setzen wir den Fall, die Stimme Beethoven's habe aus dem Grabe einem Dirigenten zugerufen: ›Halte du meine Fermate lange und furchtbar! Ich schrieb keine Fermaten zum Spaß oder aus Verlegenheit, etwa um mich auf das Weitere zu besinnen; sondern, was in meinem Adagio der ganz und voll aufzusaugende Ton für den Ausdruck der schwelgenden Empfindung ist, dasselbe werfe ich, wenn ich es brauche, in das heftig und schnell figurirte Allegro als wonnig oder schrecklich anhaltenden Krampf.‹«
[Am linken Rand, quer zur folgenden Aufzeichnung:] NB Rheingold-Vorspiel
Die grandiose Stelle über den *Ton*. (NB der absolute Ton ist der reine Ausdruck, der ins Ausdruckslose umschlägt. Er bezeichnet den Gegenpol zum Sinn, d.h. der absoluten Konstruktion, die in den Ausdruck umschlägt), nämlich:

283: *»›Und nun beachte du, welche ganz bestimmte thematische Absicht ich mit diesem ausgehaltenen Es nach drei stürmisch kurzen Noten hatte, und was ich mit allen den im Folgenden gleich auszuhaltenden Noten gesagt haben will.‹«*
der expressive Sinn als *»thematische Absicht«* (!)
»Doch ist dieser gleichmäßig stark ausgehaltene Ton die Basis aller Dynamik, wie im Gesang, so im Orchester: erst von ihm aus ist zu allen den Modifikationen zu gelangen, deren Mannigfaltigkeit zunächst den Charakter des Vortrages überhaupt bestimmt.«
der gleichmäßig starke Ton.
»Ohne diese Grundlage [scil. des gleichmäßig ausgehaltenen Tons] giebt ein Orchester viel Geräusch, aber keine Kraft; und hierin liegt ein erstes Merkmal der Schwäche unserer meisten Orchesterleistungen.«
Wagner gegen »Schwäche« (begrenzt: Ideal der Monumentalität)

285: *»Hier steht nun das Adagio dem Allegro gegenüber, wie der gehaltene Ton der figurirten Bewegung. Dem tempo adagio giebt der gehaltene Ton das Gesetz; hier zerfließt der Rhythmus in das sich selbst angehörende, sich allein genügende reine Tonleben.«*
die berühmte Stelle übers Adagio und der reine Ton.

286: B. Walters Theorie[32] vom Adagiocharakter der kantablen Themen. *»Selbst im Allegro dominirt, bei genauer Beachtung seiner bestimmendsten Motive, immer der dem Adagio entlehnte Gesang.«*
Mißverständnis des Eroikathemas (ausführen). *[Adorno notierte am Rand des Notenbeispiels des 1. Themas des ersten Satzes der »Eroica« in Wagners Schrift:* dies ist keine »Adagio-Melodie« – überhaupt nicht »Melodie«].

287: *»Hier [scil. im Finale von Mozarts Es-Dur-Symphonie und dem der A-Dur-Symphonie Beethovens] feiert die rein rhythmische Bewegung gewissermaßen ihre Orgien, und daher können auch diese Allegro-Sätze nicht bestimmt und schnell genug genommen werden. Was aber zwischen diesen äußersten Punkten liegt, ist dem Gesetz der gegenseitigen Beziehungen zu einander unterworfen, und diese Gesetze können nicht zartsinnig und mannigfaltig genug erfaßt werden. denn sie sind in einem tiefen Grunde dieselben, welche den gehaltenen Ton selbst in allen erdenklichen Nüancen modifizirten [. . .].«*
das »Gesetz der gegenseitigen Beziehungen zueinander«.

(288: *»Die vollendetsten dieser Art [scil. der ›Mozart'schen schnellen Alla-breve-Sätze‹] sind die Allegro's seiner Opern-Ouverturen, vor allem der zu ›Figaro‹ und ›Don Juan‹. Von diesen ist bekannt, daß sie Mozart nicht schnell genug gespielt werden konnten [. . .].«*
Extreme. Mozarts ¢)

290: *»Mir konnte zunächst nur darum zu thun sein, das Dilemma selbst aufzudecken, und dem Gefühle eines Jeden es klar zu machen, daß seit Beethoven hinsichtlich der Behandlung und des Vortrages der Musik eine ganz wesentliche Veränderung gegen früher eingetreten ist. Was früher in einzelnen abgeschlossenen Formen zu einem Fürsichleben auseinandergehalten war, wird hier, wenigstens seinem innersten Hauptmotive nach, in den entgegengesetztesten Formen, von diesen selbst umschlossen, zu einander gehalten und gegenseitig aus sich entwickelt. Natürlich soll dem nun auch im Vortrage entsprochen werden, und hierzu gehört vor allen Dingen, daß das Zeitmaaß von nicht minderer Zartlebigkeit sei, als das thematische Gewebe, welches durch jenes sich seiner Bewegung nach kundgeben soll, selbst es ist.«* Hauptbeleg bei Wagner für den historischen Charakter der Interpretation (»seit Beethoven hinsichtlich der Behandlung und des Vortrages der Musik eine ganz wesentliche Veränderung gegen früher eingetreten«)

292-93: *»Die eigentliche Schwäche der Variationenform als Satzbildung wird aber dann aufgedeckt, wenn ohne jede Verbindung oder Vermittlung stark kontrastirende Theile nebeneinander gestellt werden. [. . .] Die unangenehmste Wirkung von dieser achtlosen Nebeneinanderstellung erfahren wir, wenn sogleich nach dem ruhig getragenen Thema eine unbegreiflich lustig bewegte erste Variation eintritt. Die erste Variation des so über Alles wundervollen Thema's des zweiten Satzes der großen A-Dur-Sonate für Klavier und Violine von Beethoven [op. 47] hat mich, da ich sie noch von keinem Virtuosen anders behandeln hörte, als es eben eine zur gymnastischen Produktion dienende ›erste Variation‹ überhaupt verdient, stets zur Empörung gegen alles fernere Musikanhören gebracht. [. . .] Somit liegt es doch nun für den Vortragenden, der in solchem Falle, wie in dem mit der sogenannten Kreutzer-Sonate, die Ehre beansprucht, für den Musiker voll und ganz einzutreten, recht nahe, daß er wenigstens den*

Eintritt dieser ersten Variation mit der Stimmung des soeben beendeten Thema's etwa dadurch in eine milde Beziehung zu bringen sucht, daß er im Betreff des Zeitmaaßes eine gewisse Rücksicht durch anfänglich milde Deutung des neuen Charakters, in welchem – nach der unabänderlichen Ansicht der Klavier- und Violinspieler – diese Variation auftritt, ausübt: geschehe dieß mit rechtem künstlerischem Sinne, so würde etwa der erste Theil dieser Variation selbst den allmählich immer belebteren Übergang zu der neueren, bewegteren Haltung bieten, somit, ganz abgesehen von dem sonstigen Interesse dieses Theiles, auch noch diesen Reiz eines freundlich sich einschmeichelnden, im Grunde aber nicht unbedeutenden Wechsels des im Thema niedergelegten Hauptcharakters gewinnen.«
Wagners Manie des Übergangs. Er ist außerstande, den Kontrast als Mittel des Zusammenhangs zu begreifen. Gerade dieser common sense der Vermittlung als des Graduellen führt zur *Verzerrung* der Interpretation (cis-moll-Quartett [op. 131 von Beethoven]). NB alles bei Wagner »überbestimmt«, das Musikdrama ist die Totalität als Tautologie[33].

294: *»Dieser Allegrosatz [scil. der 2. – Allegro molto vivace überschriebene – von op. 131, der nur durch eine Fermate vom 1. Satz getrennt ist] folgt demnach unmittelbar einem Adagio von so träumerischer Schwermuth, wie kaum ein anderes des Meisters sich findet [. . .]. Hier handelt es sich nun offenbar darum, in welcher Weise dieses [scil. das Thema des 2. Satzes] an die schwermüthige Erstarrung des unmittelbar vorangehenden Adagio-Schlusses herantreten, gleichsam aus ihr auftauchen soll, um nicht durch die Schroffheit seines Eintrittes unsere Empfindung eher zu verletzen als anzuziehen. – Ganz angemessen tritt dieses neue Thema auch zunächst im ungebrochenen pp, eben wie ein zartes, kaum erkennbares Traumbild auf, und verliert sich alsbald in ein zerfließendes Ritardando, worauf es sich zur Kundgebung seiner Wirk-*

lichkeit gleichsam erst belebt, und durch das Crescendo in die ihm eigene bewegte Sphäre tritt. – Offenbar ist es hier eine zarte Pflicht des Vortragenden, dem genügend angezeigten Charakter dieses Allegro's angemessen, seinen ersten Eintritt auch durch das T e m p o *zu modifiziren [...].« – [Adorno notierte dazu am Rande des Notenbeispiels:]* NB da der Zusammenhang doch schon motivisch hergestellt ist, wäre es pleonastisch, auch das Tempo stetig [?] zu halten. Es wäre unleidlich.
das Beispiel des cis-moll-Quartetts kritisieren.

298: *»Nachdem ich so dem einleitenden Adagio [der Freischütz-Ouvertüre] seine schauerlich geheimnißvolle Würde zurückgegeben hatte, ließ ich der wilden Bewegung des Allegro's vollen leidenschaftlichen Lauf, wobei ich durch die Rücksicht auf den zarteren Vortrag des sanften zweiten Hauptthema's in keiner Weise gebunden war, weil ich mir sehr wohl zutraute, zur rechten Zeit* d a s T e m p o w i e d e r s o w e i t z u e r m ä ß i g e n, *daß es unmerklich zu dem richtigen Zeitmaaße für dieses Thema gelangte.«*
Furtwängler als Erbe Wagners.

299: *»Um mich für jetzt in meiner Erzählung von jener Aufführung der Freischütz-Ouvertüre mit dem Wiener Orchester nicht länger zu unterbrechen, berichte ich nun des Weiteren, daß ich, nach äußerster Erregung des Zeitmaaßes, den ganz dem Adagio entlehnten, lang gedehnten Gesang der Klarinette:*

dazu verwendete, von hier an, wo alle figurative Bewegung im gehaltenen (oder zitternden) Tone aufgeht, das Tempo durchaus unmerklich so weit zurückzuhalten, daß es, trotz der wiederum bewegteren Zwischenfigur:

mit der hierdurch so schön vorbereiteten Kantilene in Es-dur in der gelindesten Nüance des immerhin festgehaltenen Hauptzeitmaaßes angekommen war.«
das Moment der *Vernunft* in Wagners Modifikationen.

299 ff.: *[Die Stelle schließt an die in der vorangehenden Anm. zitierte unmittelbar an:] »Wenn ich nun für dieses Thema*

darauf hielt, daß es gleichmäßig piano, also ohne die übliche gemeine Accentuation beim Aufsteigen der Figur, sowie mit gleichmäßiger Bindung im Vortrage, also nicht

gespielt werde, so war dieß zwar mit den sonst so trefflichen Musikern Alles erst zu besprechen, der Erfolg dieses Vortrages war aber sogleich so auffällig, daß ich für die wiederum unmerkliche Neubelebung des Tempo's mit dem pulsirenden

nur die leiseste Andeutung der Bewegung zu geben hatte, um auch für den Wiedereintritt der energischesten Nüance des Haupttempo's mit dem folgenden Fortissimo das ganze Orchester im verständnißvollsten Eifer zu finden.«
die großartige Analyse der Interpretation der Frei- 13
schützouverture (bes. 299 unten). Hier ist aber die Mo-

difikation legitimiert durch die konstruktiven *Mängel* der Komposition. D.h. der Raum der interpretativen Freiheit ist stets die Brüchigkeit des Zusammenhangs im Werk. Eine meiner Hauptthesen. Die Interpretation ist die Rettung des Werkes.

308 f.: »*Wie ich dieß mit dem Vorangehenden bereits öfter berührte, sind Versuche zur Modifikation des Tempo's zu Gunsten des Vortrages klassischer, namentlich Beethoven'scher Tonstücke von dem Dirigenten-Gremium unserer Zeit immer mit Widerwillen aufgenommen worden. Ich wies ausführlicher nach, daß einseitige Modifikation des Zeitmaaßes, ohne entsprechende Modifikation des Vortrages im Betreff der Tongebung selbst, ein anscheinendes Recht zu Einsprüchen gäbe, wogegen ich den hier tiefer zu Grunde liegenden Fehler ebenfalls aufdeckte, somit diesen Einsprüchen keinen anderen Grund als den der Unfähigkeit und Unberufenheit unserer Dirigenten im Allgemeinen übrig ließ. Ein wirklich giltiger Grund zur Abmahnung von dem mir unerläßlich dünkenden Verfahren in jenen bezeichneten Fällen ist allerdings wiederum der, daß in jenen Tonstücken nichts schädlicher werden müßte, als willkürlich in ihren Vortrag gelegte Nüancen auch des Tempo's, wie sie sofort dem phantastischen Belieben jedes, etwa auf Effekt losarbeitenden oder von sich eingenommenen eitlen Taktschlägers Thür und Thor öffnen, und unsere klassische Musiklitteratur mit der Zeit zu gänzlicher Unkenntlichkeit entstellen würden. Hiergegen läßt sich natürlich nichts Anderes einwenden, als daß es eben traurig um unsere Musik steht, da solche Befürchtungen aufkommen können, weil damit zugleich ausgesprochen ist, daß man an eine Macht des wahren Kunstbewußtseins, an welcher jene Willkürlichkeiten sich sogleich brechen würden, in unseren gemeinsamen Kunstzuständen nicht glaubt.*«
Diskussion der *Einwände* gegen Wagners Subjektivismus (NB Wagners Theorie in Zusammenhang mit dem Nominalismus seines ganzen œuvres bringen)

310: *»[Man] muß sich jetzt deutlich machen, welches der Zustand des Vortrages nur sein kann, in welchem diese Werke uns unter dem Gesetze jener Unfähigkeit und Trägheit eifrigst konservirt werden, wenn man andererseits rücksichtslos erwägt, in welchem Sinne selbst ein Meister wie Mendelssohn sich mit der Leitung dieser Werke befaßte! [...] Und deßwegen unterwerfe ich hier diese pietistische Abwehr desjenigen Geistes, den ich als den richtigen für den Vortrag unserer großen Musik bezeichnet habe, einer schärfer eingehenden Betrachtung, um den sonderbaren renitenten Geist, welcher jene Abwehr eingiebt, in seiner wirklichen Armseligkeit aufzudecken, und vor Allem ihm den Heiligenschein zu benehmen, mit welchem er sich als keuscher deutscher Kunstgeist zu schmücken herausnimmt. Denn dieser Geist ist es, welcher jeden freien Aufschwung unseres Musikwesens hemmt, jeden frischen Luftzug von seiner Atmosphäre ferne hält, und mit der Zeit wirklich die glorreiche deutsche Musik zu einem farblosen, ja lächerlichen Gespenst verwischen kann.«*
gegen Historismus: Wagners Einsicht, daß gerade die Konservierung zerstört.

312 ff: *»Bei uns blieb der Musiker immer nur ein eigenthümliches, halb wildes, halb kindisches Wesen, und als solches ward er von seinen Lohngebern gehalten.«*
Wagners soziologische Theorie des Musikers.
Der »neue«, »elegante« Interpret als Zirkulationsagent (antisemitische Theorie), als parasitär am Werk. »Gebildetheit« *»Wie nun aber z. B. den Juden unser Gewerkwesen fremd geblieben ist, so wuchsen auch unsere neueren Musikdirigenten nicht aus dem musikalischen Handwerkerstande auf, der ihnen, schon der strengen wirklichen Arbeit wegen, widerwärtig war. Dagegen pflanzte sich dieser neue Dirigent sogleich auf der Spitze des musikalischen Innungswesens, etwa wie der Banquier auf unserer gewerkthätigen Sozietät, auf. Hierfür mußte er sofort Eines mitbringen, was*

dem von unten auf gedienten Musiker eben abging, oder von ihm doch nur äußerst schwer, und selten genügend zu gewinnen war: wie der Banquier das Kapital, so brachte dieser die Gebildetheit mit.« (sehr genau abwägen).

314: *»Im Allgemeinen ist es ein Hauptcharakterzug dieser Gebildetheit, bei nichts stark zu verweilen, sich in nichts tief zu versenken, oder auch, wie man sich ausdrückt, von nichts viel Wesens zu machen. [. . .] Bei dem Ungeheuren, Göttlichen und Dämonischen, ist daher nicht zu verweilen, schon weil an ihm etwas Nachzuahmendes eben durchaus nicht aufzufinden glückt, weßhalb es dieser Gebildetheit geläufig ist, z.B. von Auswüchsen, Übertreibungen u. dergl. zu reden, woraus dann wieder eine neue Ästhetik hervorgegangen, welche vor Allem sich an Goethe zu lehnen vorgiebt, weil dieser ja auch allen Ungeheuerlichkeiten abhold gewesen wäre, und dafür so eine schöne, ruhige Klarheit erfunden habe. Da wird denn die ›Harmlosigkeit‹ der Kunst gepriesen, der hier und da zu heftige Schiller aber einigermaaßen verächtlich behandelt, und so, in kluger Übereinstimmung mit dem Philister unserer Zeit, ein ganz neuer Begriff von Klassizität gebildet, zu welchem in weiteren Kunstgebieten endlich auch die Griechen herbeigezogen werden, bei den ja klare, durchsichtige Heiterkeit so recht zu Hause war.«*
Gebildetheit als Konformismus, »Harmlosigkeit«.

315: *»Hier ist nur noch zu erklären, was es mit diesem, von Mendelssohn so dringend empfohlenen ›Darüberhinweggehen‹ für einen heiteren griechischen Sinn hatte. [. . .] Bei Mendelssohn hieß es: die unvermeidlichen Schwächen der Ausführung, unter Umständen vielleicht auch des Auszuführenden, verbergen; bei Jenen [scil. seinen Anhängern und Nachfolgern] kommt nun aber noch das ganz besondere Motiv ihrer Gebildetheit hinzu, nämlich: überhaupt zu verdekken, kein Aufsehen zu machen.«*
Konformistische Aufführung als »Verdecken« (Gegen-

teil der Röntgenphotographie) NB: ideologischer Charakter gerade des Positivismus.

316: *»Ein großer Theil ihrer Bildung bestand seither eben darin, auf ihr Gebahren mit der Sorgfalt Acht zu haben, wie der mit dem Naturfehler des Stammelns oder Lispelns Behaftete, welcher in seiner Kundgebung alle Leidenschaftlichkeit vermeiden muß, um nicht etwa in das ungebührlichste Stottern oder Sprudeln zu verfallen. [. . .] Der Deutsche ist eckig und ungelenk, wenn er sich manierlich geben will: aber er ist erhaben und Allen überlegen, wenn er in das Feuer geräth. Das sollen wir nun Jenen zu Liebe zurückhalten?«*
Wagners Einsicht in den klassizistischen Darstellungsstil als verdrängte Mimesis.

317: *»Zunächst, und für unsere Untersuchung am wichtigsten, äußerte sich der Erfolg dieser negativen Maxime eben im Vortrage unserer klassischen Musik. Dieser ward einzig durch die Furcht davor geleitet, etwa in das Drastische zu fallen.«*
»Furcht . . . etwa in das Drastische zu verfallen« (großartig)
»Von dem großen Franz Liszt wurde mir denn auch erst meine Sehnsucht, Bach zu hören, erfüllt. Gerade Bach wurde zwar mit Vorliebe auch dort kultivirt; denn hier, wo vom modernen Effekt, oder auch von Beethoven'scher Drastik gar nicht die Rede sein konnte, war die seligmachende glatte, durchaus gewürzlose Vortragsart scheinbar so recht eindringlich beizubringen. Von einem der namhaftesten älteren Musiker und Genossen Mendelssohn's [. . .] erbat ich mir einmal den Vortrag des achten Präludiums mit Fuge aus dem ersten Theile des wohltemperirten Klaviers (Es moll), weil dieses Stück mich stets so besonders magisch angezogen hatte; ich muß gestehen, daß ich selten einen ähnlichen Schreck empfunden habe, als ihn mir die freundlichste Ge-

währung dieser meiner Bitte brachte. Da war denn allerdings von düsterer deutscher Gothik und all' den Alfanzereien nicht mehr die Rede; dagegen floß das Stück unter den Händen meines Freundes mit einer ›griechischen Heiterkeit‹ über das Klavier hin, daß ich vor Harmlosigkeit nicht wußte wohin, und unwillkürlich in eine neu-hellenische Synagoge mich versetzt sah, aus deren musikalischem Kultus alles alttestamentarische Accentuiren auf das Manierlichste ausgemerzt war.«
die »neu-hellenische Synagoge«.

319: *»Diese Scheu [scil. die Maxime: ›nur keinen Effekt‹], wie sie ursprünglich nämlich nur eigene Impotenz verdeckte, wird jetzt zur Anklage der Potenz, und diese Anklage gewinnt aktive Kraft aus der Verdächtigung und Verleumdung. Der nährende Boden, auf welchen dieß Alles für sein Gedeihen sorgt, ist eben der arme Geist des deutschen Philisterthums, des im kleinlichsten Wesen verwahrlosten Sinnes, unter welchem wir auch unser Musikerwesen mit inbegriffen gesehen haben.«*
Objektivismus als Ressentiment (Nietzsche-ähnliche Theorie. Triebschen?) cf. Newman IV, 337[34]

321: *»Vor einiger Zeit warf ein süddeutscher Zeitungsredakteur meinen Kunsttheorien ›muckerische‹ Tendenzen vor: der Mann wußte offenbar nicht, was er damit sagte; es war ihm einfach um ein böses Wort zu thun. Was ich dagegen von dem Wesen der Muckerei in Erfahrung gebracht habe, bezeichnet die sonderbare Tendenz dieser widerlichen Sekte damit, daß hier dem Anreizenden und Verführerischen auf das Angelegentlichste nachgetrachtet wird, um an der schließlichen Abwehr desselben seine Widerstandskraft gegen den Reiz und die Verführung zu üben.«*
»Mucker« (Wagner selbst!)

327: *»[Das Tempo wird] nirgends aber mit der sinnvollen Modifikation zu Gunsten eines verständlichen Vortrages behandelt,*

auf welche ich mit nicht minderer Bestimmtheit, wie auf das Richtigspielen der Noten selbst rechnen muß.«
Modifikation im Dienst von Verständlichkeit.
»Das Hauptzeitmaaß dieses Stückes [scil. des Meistersingervorspiels] ward von mir mit ›sehr mäßig bewegt‹ vorgezeichnet; dieß bedeutet also nach dem älteren Schema etwa: Allegro maestoso. Kein Tempo ist mehr als dieses, bei längerer Andauer, und namentlich bei stark episodischer Behandlung des thematischen Inhaltes, der Modifikation bedürftig, und es wird zur Ausführung ›mannigfaltiger Kombinationen [Marginalie Adornos: »d. h. doch wohl: sukzessiv«*] verschiedenartiger Motive gern gewählt, weil seine breite Gliederung im regelmäßigen* $\frac{4}{4}$ *Takte diese Ausführung durch die Nahelegung jener Modifikation mit großer Leichtigkeit unterstützt.« [Die Analyse des Meistersingervorspiels erstreckt sich bis auf die Seite 330.]*
Die nicht ganz luzide Analyse des Meistersingervorspiels (ich habe sie interpretiert[35]).

334: *»Wir sind im tiefsten Grunde versucht, daran zu zweifeln, daß diese Herren [scil. ›aus dem Generalstabe unserer Taktschläger-Armee‹] wirkliche Musiker seien: denn offenbar zeigen sie gar kein musikalisches Gefühl; aber sie hören wirklich sehr genau (nämlich mathematisch genau, wenn auch nicht idealisch: die Fatalität mit den falschen Orchesterstimmen begegnet immerhin nicht Jedem!); sie haben einen scharfen Überblick, lesen und spielen vom Blatte (wenigstens sehr Viele unter ihnen); kurz, sie erweisen sich als wahre Leute von Fach; auch ist ihre Bildung – trotz Allem – von der Beschaffenheit, wie man sie eben doch nur einem Musiker hingehen lassen kann, so daß, wollte man diesen an ihnen leugnen, nichts übrig bliebe, am wenigsten etwa ein geistvoller Mensch.«*
mathematisches und idealisches Hören.

*

Ad Stil.: die bösartige Wucherung.
Intimitäten[36]

14 Zum historischen Charakter der Interpretation ist auf die jüngste Erfahrung zu rekurrieren. Im Deutschland von Furtwängler und dem Buschquartett[37] haben wir ein im gewissen Sinn »positivistisches« Musizierideal polemisch vertreten müssen (freilich *stets* im äußersten Gegensatz zum »neusachlichen«); im Amerika Toscaninis ein »expressives«; und dies nicht nur theoretisch, sondern bis in Nuancen der tatsächlichen Wiedergabe hinein. Daraus vielleicht: die wahre Interpretation ist stets polemisch (sehr deutlich bei Wagner).

*

Titel der Arbeit: Die wahre Aufführung (??)

*

Unter den Argumenten gegen den musikalischen Historismus ist nicht das geringste, daß in älterer – »vorklassischer« – Musik die Farbe überhaupt kein konstitutives Element ist.[38] Das »Kolorit« der Bachischen Orgel und des Bachischen Orchesters ist der Komposition unvergleichlich viel *äußerlicher* als bei Wagner oder Schönberg und darum hat »Authentizität« hier einen viel unsachlicheren Sinn – sie ist Sache des Stils und nicht des musikalischen Sinnes. Man braucht das Gebundensein auch jener Musik an ihr Klangmaterial, zumal in der zarten Sphäre des Clavichords, nicht zu verkennen, um doch das Opfer in den Kauf zu nehmen. (Alle Interpretation involviert ein Opfer. Wagner hat darum wohl gewußt. Er hat auch für Musik, die Natur-Blechbläser voraussetzt, die Ventilinstrumente gefordert und in diesem Sinne Beethoven retouchiert[39], während er im Vorwort zur Tristanpartitur den Verlust des echten Horncharakters durch die chromatische Mechanik zugesteht[40]). Zudem sind die entscheidenden vorklassischen Instrumente, die den Continuo ausführen, ihrem Wesen nach so mechanisch (nämlich Orgel und Cembalo), daß eine strukturelle, mehr als stilistische Beziehung zum musikalischen Inhalt ausgeschlossen ist, ja daß sie zu dessen weit entwickelter Differenziertheit in Widerspruch treten. Die authentische Wiedergabe der Bachschen Konstruktion fordert also die Auflösung des authentischen Bachischen Klanges.[41] Etwas von diesen Fragen betrifft – wie Wagner nachwies – auch Beethoven und *alle* Musik vor der Emanzipation des Orchesters.

*

Die Kritik des Historismus ist in engster Fühlung mit Wagners Abhandlung über den Vortrag der IX. Symphonie (G. S., 9, p 231 ff.)[42] zu führen, die durch ihre Materialnähe von Wagners theoretischen Schriften die bedeutendste sein dürfte. Dazu:

231: *»Mir sind bei einer neuerlich von mir geleiteten Aufführung dieses wunderbaren Tonwerkes verschiedene Bedenken aufgestoßen, welche, weil sie die mich unerläßlich dünkende Deutlichkeit des Vortrages betreffen, mich so stark einnahmen, daß ich nachträglich auf Abhilfe der von mir empfundenen Übelstände sann. Das Ergebniß davon lege ich hiermit ernstlich gesinnten Musikern, wenn nicht als Aufforderung zur Nachahmung meines Verfahrens, so doch als Anregung zu sinnvollem Nachdenken hierüber, vor.«*

der Grund der Retouchen ist die *Deutlichkeit*, d. h. die Realisierung des musikalischen Zusammenhangs. Formulierung wie die musikalische Konzeption über die Leistungsfähigkeit des Orchesters hinausgeht, d. h. die Konstruktion über das Klangmaterial.

»Im Allgemeinen mache ich darauf aufmerksam, in welche eigenthümliche Lage Beethoven bezüglich der Instrumentation seiner Orchesterwerke gerieth. Er instrumentirte ganz nach denselben Annahmen von der Leistungsfähigkeit des

Orchesters, wie seine Vorgänger Haydn und Mozart, während er im Charakter seiner musikalischen Konzeptionen undenklich weit über diese hinausging. Das, was wir im Betreff der Auseinanderhaltung und Gruppirung der verschiedenen Instrumentalkomplexe eines Orchesters sehr wohl als Plastik bezeichnen können, hatte sich bei Mozart und Haydn zu einer festen Übereinstimmung des Charakters ihrer Konzeptionen mit der bis dahin ausgebildeten und gepflegten Zusammenstellung und Vortragsart des Orchesters gestaltet.«

Begriff der *Plastik* im Auseinanderhalten der instrumentalen Komplexe.

232: *»In diesem Bezug bleibt seine ›Sinfonia eroica‹ nicht nur ein Wunder der Konzeption, sondern nicht minder auch ein Wunder der Orchestration. Nur muthete er bereits hier dem Orchester eine Vortragsweise zu, welche es sich bis auf den heutigen Tag noch nicht aneignen konnte: der Vortrag mußte nämlich von Seiten des Orchesters ebenso genial sein, wie die orchestrale Konzeption des Meisters selbst es war. Von hier, von der ersten Aufführung der ›Eroica‹ an, beginnen daher die Schwierigkeiten des Urtheils über diese Symphonien, ja selbst die Behinderungen des Gefallens an ihnen, welches den Musikern der älteren Epoche nie wirklich hat ankommen wollen. Es fehlte diesen Werken an der Deutlichkeit der Ausführung, weil die Hervorbringung dieser Deutlichkeit nicht mehr, wie bei Haydn und Mozart, in dem verwendeten Organismus des Orchesters gewährleistet war, sondern einzig durch die, bis in das Virtuosenhafte gehende, musikalisch geniale Leistung der einzelnen Instrumentisten und ihres Dirigenten ermöglicht werden konnte.«*

Einwand der *Undeutlichkeit* der instrumentalen Realisierung bei Beethoven seit der Eroica.

233: *»Daher z. B. die Beethoven so eigenthümlich gewordene Forderung eines Crescendo, welches auf dem äußersten*

Punkte sich nicht in das Forte entlädt, sondern plötzlich in das Piano umschlägt: diese eine, so häufig vorkommende Nüance ist unseren Orchesterspielern meistens noch so fremd, daß vorsichtige Dirigenten, welche sich wenigstens des rechtzeitigen Eintrittes des Piano versichern wollten, ihren Musikern eine kluge Umkehr des Crescendo und Einlenkung in ein behutsames Diminuendo zur Pflicht machten. Der wahre Sinn dieser so schwierigen Nüance liegt gewiß darin, daß hier dieselben Instrumente etwas ausführen sollen, was erst dann ganz deutlich wird, wenn es verschiedenen, mit einander abwechselnden Instrumenten übergeben ist. Dieß wissen neuere Komponisten, welchen das bereicherte heutige Orchester und seine üblich gewordene Verwendung zur Verfügung steht. Diesen würde es möglich gewesen sein, gewisse von Beethoven beabsichtigte Wirkungen ohne alle exzentrische Anforderung an die virtuose Leistung des Orchesters, bloß durch die ihnen erleichterte Vertheilung an unterschiedene Instrumentalkomplexe, mit großer Deutlichkeit sicher zu stellen.«

Hauptbeleg für instrumentales Konstruieren: das Beethovensche < p nur zu realisieren durch instrumentale Melodieteilung (dies ist im Grunde schon das Prinzip der Schönbergschule, vermittelt wohl durch Mahler dessen gesamte Instrumentationspraxis wohl die Probe auf Wagners Arbeit über die IX. ist[43]).

233 f.: *»Hier [scil. in Beethovens späten Streichquartetten] hat der einzelne Spieler, in einem gewissen technischen Sinne, oft für eine Mehrzahl von Spielern einzutreten, so daß ein ganz vorzüglich aufgeführtes Quartett dieser späteren Periode den Zuhörer häufig zu der Täuschung verführen kann, als vernehme er dicht neben einander mehr Musiker, als wirklich spielen.«*

die Stelle über das illusionäre Moment an den letzten Quartetten.

»Diese Deutlichkeit beruht nun, meines Erachtens, auf

nichts Anderem, als auf dem drastischem Heraustreten der Melodie.*«*
Deutlichkeit = »drastisches Heraustreten der Melodie«.

235f.: »*Zwar glückt es schon Beethoven zuweilen, durch Betheiligung der Blechinstrumente den Holzblasinstrumenten die entsprechende Prägnanz zu geben: allein hierin war er durch die zu seiner Zeit einzig erst gekannte Beschaffenheit der Natur-Hörner und -Trompeten so kläglich beschränkt, daß gerade aus seiner Verwendung dieser Instrumente zur Verstärkung der Holzbläser diejenigen Verwirrungen hervorgingen, welche wir jetzt eben als unzubeseitigend dünkende Verhinderung des deutlichen Hervortretens der Melodie empfinden. Dem heutigen Musiker habe ich nicht nöthig, die hier berührten Übelstände der Beethoven'schen Orchester-Instrumentation erst aufzudecken, denn sie werden von ihm, bei der uns jetzt allgemein geläufig gewordenen Verwendung der chromatischen Blechinstrumente, mit Leichtigkeit vermieden; zu bestätigen ist nur, daß Beethoven sich genöthigt sah, in entfernten Tonarten die Blechinstrumente plötzlich abbrechen, oder auch in grellen einzelnen Tönen, wie sie gerade die Natur der Instrumente einzig darbot, völlig störend, und von der Melodie wie von der Harmonie ableitend, mitwirken zu lassen.«*
Kritik des Naturblechs und strukturelle Notwendigkeit der Retouche.

237: »*Im Betreff der höchst störenden Mitwirkung der Trompeten im ersten* Forte *des zweiten Satzes der A-Dur-Symphonie entschloß ich mich jedoch mit der Zeit zu einer energischeren Abhilfe. Ich ließ hier die beiden Trompeten, die nun doch einmal nach dem von Beethoven sehr richtig gefühlten Bedürfnisse mitspielen sollten, leider aber durch ihre damalige einfache Beschaffenheit dieß in der nöthigen Weise zu thun verhindert waren, das ganze Thema im Einklange mit den Klarinetten blasen. Die Wirkung hiervon war so vortrefflich,*

daß keiner der Zuhörer einen Verlust, sondern nun einen Gewinn empfand, welcher andererseits als Neuerung oder Veränderung Niemandem auffiel.«
die – apologetische – Stelle über Gewinn und Verlust der Retouche.

238: *[Wagner diskutiert das 2. Thema des »Scherzo« aus Beethovens IX. Symphonie, Takt 93ff., das den Holzbläsern überlassen ist.] »Die Unterstützung, welche ihnen hierbei von den Blechinstrumenten [scil. Hörner in D und B] zu Theil wird, fällt in der zuvor bezeichneten Art so aus, daß sie die Deutlichkeit des Thema's durch lückenhaft eingeführte Naturtöne weit eher stört als fördert. Ich rufe einen Musiker auf, mit gutem Gewissen zu behaupten, daß er diese Melodie jemals in Orchesteraufführungen deutlich gehört habe, ja, ob er sie nur kennen würde, wenn er sie nicht aus der Lektüre der Partitur oder aus dem Spiele des Klavierauszuges sich entnommen hätte? In unseren üblichen Orchesteraufführungen scheint man noch nicht einmal zu dem nächstliegenden Auskunftsmittel, das ff der Streichinstrumente beträchtlich zu dämpfen, gegriffen zu haben, denn so oft ich noch für diese Symphonie mit Musikern zusammenkam, fuhr hier Alles mit der wüthendsten Stärke hinein.«*
»Störung der Deutlichkeit des Themas durch lückenhaft eingeführte Naturtöne«.

239: *»Die Erfahrung bestätigte aber meine Annahme nie, oder nur höchst ungenügend, weil immer den Holzblasinstrumenten eine schneidige Energie des Tones zugemuthet blieb, die ihrem Charakter, wenigstens im Sinne der hier angetroffenen Zusammenstellung [scil. im 2. Thema des Scherzos der IX.], stets zuwider bleiben wird. Ich wüßte, sobald ich jetzt diese Symphonie wieder einmal aufzuführen hätte, gegen das unläugbare Übel des in Undeutlichkeit, wenn nicht in Unhörbarkeit Verschwindens dieses ungemein energischen Tanzmotives, keine anderes Abhilfsmittel zu versuchen, als die*

Zutheilung einer ganz bestimmten thematischen Mitwirkung wenigstens an die vier Hörner.«
wie Wagners Theorie immer weitertreibt: der absolute Mangel der Holzbläser an »schneidiger Energie« als
16 konstitutiver Widerspruch der klassischen Instrumentation zum musikalischen Inhalt.

240: *»Es wäre nun zu versuchen, ob die hier angedeutete Verstärkung der Noten des Thema's [vgl. das Zitat der vorangehenden Anm.] genügte, um das Quintett der Streichinstrumente in dem vom Meister vorgezeichneten ff die begleitende Figur ausführen zu lassen, worauf es andererseits vorzüglich ankommt; denn der Gedanke Beethoven's ist hier ganz unverkennbar derselbe übermüthig ausgelassene, welcher bei der Rückkehr des Hauptthema's des Satzes in D moll zu dem unvergleichlich wilden Exzesse führt, wie er je nur durch die originellsten Erfindungen dieses Einzigen, Wunderbaren zum Ausdruck kommen konnte. Bereits dünkte es mich daher eine sehr üble Abhilfe, vermöge welcher das Hervortreten der Blasinstrumente durch ein Zurückhalten der Streichinstrumente befördert werden sollte, weil sie den wilden Charakter der Stelle bis zum Verkennen aufheben mußte. Mein letzter Rath geht demnach dahin, das Thema der Blasinstrumente so lange, und sei es durch die Trompeten, zu verstärken, bis es, selbst bei dem energischesten Fortissimo der Streichinstrumente, im rechten, durchdringenden Sinne deutlich hervortritt und herrscht.«*
für Beethovens »wilde Exzesse«. (ad Berlioz[44])
Retouche für *Wildheit* (Technifizierung und Archaik). (NB die Dialektik der Aufklärung ist viel verwickelter als wir sie bis jetzt gefaßt haben.)

241: *»Bei der Entscheidung solcher Fragen handelt es sich nur darum, ob man bei der Anhörung eines ähnlichen Musikwerkes eine Zeitlang von den Intentionen des Tondichters nichts Deutliches wahrzunehmen, oder dagegen das zweckmäßigste Auskunftsmittel, ihnen gerecht zu werden, vorzieht.«*

Wagners Gesetz der Retouche, freilich im Sinne der Vorstellungstheorie (Intentionen des Tondichters), aber doch nach »Deutlichkeit« formuliert.

245: *»So entsinne ich mich nie den Anfang der achten Symphonie (in F) gehört zu haben, ohne im sechsten, siebenten und achten Takte durch das unthematische Hinzutreten der Hoboe und der Flöte über dem melodischen Gesang der Klarinette im Erfassen des Thema's gestört worden zu sein; wogegen die vorangehende Mitwirkung der Flöten in den vier ersten Takten, trotzdem sie ebenfalls nicht genau thematisch ist, das Verständniß der Melodie nicht verhinderte, weil diese von den stark besetzten Violinen hier im Forte zur eindringlichen Deutlichkeit gebracht worden ist.«*
der sehr gute Einwand gegen die Instrumentation des Anfangs der VIII. Symphonie. (NB es wäre z.B. eine Instrumentationskritik des Anfangs der Durchführung der IX. möglich, der in der Tat das neudeutsche Orchester verlangt, das dann diese Stelle, ebenso wie die Coda, stets imitierte.[45])

246: *»Es dürfte nun zu gewagt und dem Charakter der Beethoven'schen Instrumentation, in welcher wir sehr wohl berechtigte Eigenthümlichkeiten zu beachten haben, nicht richtig entsprechend erscheinen, wolle man die Flöte hier [scil. IX. Symphonie, 1. Satz, Takt 138ff.] gänzlich auslassen, oder sie nur als unisone Verdoppelung der Hoboe zur Verstärkung herbeiziehen.«*
das Moment der *Vorsicht* der Retouche, sehr gute Stelle. NB die Stelle mit den übergebundenen Sechzehnteln klingt immer noch unverständlich.

251: »Wenn wir gehörig erwägen, von welcher einzigen Wichtigkeit es bei jeder musikalischen Mittheilung ist, daß die Melodie, werde sie uns durch die Kunst des Tondichters auch oft nur in ihren kleinsten Bruchtheilen vorgeführt, unablässig uns gefes-

selt halte, und daß die Korrektheit dieser melodischen Sprache in gar keiner Hinsicht der logischen Korrektheit des in der Wortsprache sich gebenden begrifflichen Gedankens nachstehen darf, ohne uns durch Undeutlichkeit ebenso zu verwirren, wie ein unverständlicher Sprachsatz dieß thut, so müssen wir erkennen, daß nichts der sorgfältigsten Mühe so werth ist, als die versuchte Aufhebung der Unklarheit einer Stelle, eines Taktes, ja einer Note in der musikalischen Mittheilung eines Genius', wie des Beethoven's, an uns [. . .].«
Hauptstelle zum Zusammenhang der Kategorien »musikalische Sprache« – Ausdruck – Deutlichkeit. Umschlag des subjektiv-mimetischen Desiderats in das objektiv-konstruktive.

252: Interpretation und *Erkenntnis:* man soll »über keinen Takt einer Tondichtung, wie der Beethovens, ohne deutliches Bewußtsein davon hinweggleiten«.

253: *»Selbst mit der sorgfältigsten Beachtung der hiermit gegebenen Vorschrift würde aber in den, im letzten Theile desselben ersten Satzes wieder vorkommenden Stellen, der übelsten Folge der verfehlten Intention des Meisters nicht abzuhelfen sein, weil hier das dynamische Misverhältniß der abwechselnden Instrumentalkomplexe die Abhilfe durch zarte Behandlung der vorgeschriebenen Nüancen bis zur Unmöglichkeit erschwert. Dieß gilt zunächst den zwei ersten Takten der ähnlichen Stelle auf S. 47 der Partitur [= Takt 359f. des 1. Satzes der IX. Symphonie], wo die erste Violine mit sämmtlichen Streichinstrumenten sofort bereits in einem crescendo zu spielen hat, welches die darauf mit dem entsprechenden Gange folgende Klarinette mit geeigneter Stärke und Steigerung fortzuführen außer Stande ist: hier mußte ich mich zu einer vollständigen Aufgebung des crescendo für die beiden ersten Takte entschließen [. . .].«*
Dynamisches Proportionsproblem und instrumentale Farbe (ad Einheit der musikalischen Elemente).

255 ff.: *»Aus eben dem angeführten Grunde für alle meine Bemühungen in dem Sinne einer wahrhaftigen Verdeutlichung der Intentionen des Meisters, habe ich dagegen schließlich noch eine äußerst schwierige Stelle des Solo-Quartetts der Sänger zu besprechen, in welcher ich erst nach langer Erfahrung den Übelstand aufgefunden habe, der sie, die an und für sich so wundervoll entworfen ist, bei jeder Ausführung einer wahrhaft erfreulichen Wirkung beraubt. Es ist dieß die letzte Sologesangs-Stelle am Schlusse der Symphonie, das berühmte H-dur: ›wo dein sanfter Flügel weilt‹ [Takt 836-841]. [. . .] Dagegen liegt die nur durch radikale Abhilfe zu beseitigende Verhinderung einer reinen und schönen Wirkung dieses Satzes in der Tenorstimme, welche durch eine unzeitig eintretende figurirte Bewegung einerseits die Deutlichkeit des Gesammtvortrages beeinträchtigt, andererseits aber eine unter allen Umständen ermüdende Aufgabe sich zugetheilt sieht, welcher sie nach jedem Gesetze einer zweckmäßigen Respiration nicht entsprechen kann, ohne in ein beängstigendes Abmühen zu gerathen. Betrachten wir die Stelle näher, so löst sich vom Eintritte des Quartsextaccordes mit der Vorzeichnung H-dur [. . .] der fesselnde melodische Gehalt derselben in einen figurirten Gang des Sopranes auf, welchen, nach der Tiefe zu abwechselnd, Alt, Tenor und endlich Baß, mit freier Imitation fortsetzen. Denken wir uns die diesen melodischen Gang nur begleitenden Stimmen hinweg, so vernehmen wir die Intention des Meisters deutlich folgendermaaßen sich ausdrücken:*

Nun sekundirt aber bereits im zweiten Eintritte der Tenor dem figurirten Gange des Altes vollständig in Sexten und Terzen [= Takt 837], wodurch sein darauf im dritten Takte [= Takt 838] mit der Fortsetzung der Melodie erfolgender Eintritt nicht nur seine Bedeutung, sondern auch seine Wirkung auf das von ihm zuvor bereits zur Aufmerksamkeit auf ihn gelenkte Gehör verliert, welches jetzt des Anreizes verlustig geht, den hier die im Tenor wiedererscheinende melismische Figur des Sopranes gewähren soll. Nicht nur aber, daß die melodische Intention des Meisters hierdurch undeutlich wird, sondern daß der Tenorist die zwei figurirten Takte hinter einander nicht mit der Sicherheit bewältigen kann, wie ihm dieß mit der Figur des zweiten Taktes allein durchaus unschwer fallen würde, schadet der Wirkung dieser herrlichen Stelle. Ich habe mich daher, nach reiflicher Überlegung, entschlossen, dem Tenor künftighin die seinem Haupteintritte vorangehende, in der Sekundirung der Altstimme bestehende, schwierige Figuration zu ersparen, indem ich ihm nur die wesentlichen harmonischen Noten derselben zutheile; demgemäß er dann so singen würde:

Ich bin überzeugt, daß jeder Tenorist, der sich bisher mit dieser Stelle erfolglos abquälte, wenn er statt dessen

singen mußte, mir sehr dankbar sein, und nun desto schöner den ihm wirklich gehörenden melodischen Gang vortragen wird, welchem er nach meinem Rathe folgende dynamische Nüance

angedeihen läßt, um ihren richtigen Ausdruck ganz in seine Gewalt zu bekommen.«
die Dialektik der Retouche. Die Änderung der H-dur-Soloquartettstelle aus dem Finale der IX. Symphonie. Die Forderung der Verdeutlichung der Komposition führt hier zu deren entscheidender Antastung. Ist die wahre Interpretation die Rettung des Werkes, so ist sie zugleich dessen Auflösung. Die Realisierung von Wagners Forderung der rein sinngemäßen Aufführung zerstört das Werk – und zwar unbedingt jedes – weil die Erkenntnis, die das Ideal der Interpretation abgibt, zu- 17
gleich notwendig den Nachweis der Brüchigkeit des Sinnes liefert (NB beim letzten Beethoven ist die Brüchigkeit des Sinnes selber ein Element dieses Sinnes. Der »verwirrende« Takt des Tenors ehe er imitatorisch den roten Faden übernimmt, höchst charakteristisch für den letzten Beethoven, wäre zu *retten!*). Es ist dabei entscheidend, daß es hier keine Grenze zwischen dem legitimen Eingriff und dem Mißbrauch gibt. Deren Etablierung ist nichts als die mittlere Linie des Konformismus. Mit unabdingbarer Konsequenz vielmehr treibt die am Ideal des Werkes gemessene Vernunft Wagners zur Veränderung des Werkes und dieser ist kein Einhalt zu gebieten. Das Werk verändert sich und zerfällt am Ideal seiner eigenen Wahrheit – das ist das Geheimnis seiner inneren Historizität.

*

Die Interpretation gilt der Darstellung des dialektischen Bildes der Komposition. Die Überlegung zum Freischütz.[46] 1820 wurde genau so wenig, ja vermutlich weniger an Geister »geglaubt« als heute. Trotzdem war damals die illusionäre Wiedergabe der Wolfsschlucht möglich, die heute ein Kinderspott wäre. Und nicht nur wegen des Absterbens der Phantasie, die damals die Geisterwelt ohne empirische Realität konzipieren konnte, während sie ihr heute nur als »Faktum« erträglich wäre. Sondern: in Schicksalsdrama und der Romantik der »finsteren Mächte« spricht sich in Wahrheit die Innervation der Entzauberung der Welt aus. Die Romantik lebt vom Schauer der Aufklärung und daß dieser Schauer – Hugos nouveau frisson über Baudelaire und Poe[47] bezeichnet die Schwelle – verfiel, ist der Grund der »Lächerlichkeit« der Zauberoper. Der Gegenstand der Interpretation ist die Erweckung des dem Werke je innewohnenden Schauers. Ist er entwichen, so ist das Werk uninterpretierbar – während es zugleich der Interpretation *bedarf*. Dieser Schauer aber ist die Aura der aus dem Werke objektiv sich entfaltenden, geschichtlichen Bilder.

18 Der Nachweis fürs Uninterpretierbarwerden von Werken ist an Problemen der in dieser Hinsicht besonders sensibeln *Opernregie* zu führen. Wolfsschlucht des Freischütz und Schwan des Lohengrin.[48] Die wilde Jagd und der Schwan, sinnlich vorgeführt, sind unmöglich – ihre Apologie verwandelt die Werke in Bilderbogen. Gibt man sie auf und verwandelt sie etwa in Natursymbole oder solche Zeichen wie den Schwan als Lichtkegel, so werden die Werke auf jenes Allgemein-Menschliche nivelliert das das Ende jeglicher Kunst bedeutet. Selbst Wagners Opernallegorik einer extrem geschichtsfremden Philosophie hat an der drastischen Theaterillusion zäh festgehalten und der König Ludwig, der am Lohengrin nichts als den Schwan wahrnahm, hat mehr verstanden als die spirituellste Auslegung. Denn der Gehalt – der keineswegs mit dem philosophisch Vermeinten zusammenfällt – ist das geschichtliche Bild: dessen Vergänglichkeit allein ist die

»Ewigkeit« des Werkes, der Geschichte innewohnt. An den Requisiten gehen die dialektischen Bilder auf. Das gilt aber auch für die Musik, deren gestische Charaktere – wie der Virtuos sie nachahmt – das Äquivalent der Requisiten sind. Die Chiffern der Leidenschaft der Appassionata – der mitbrummende d'Albert.[49] Diese Gesten sind heut einzig noch beschwörbare – Furtwängler – und treten in Widerspruch zur Konstruktion. Bleibt aber diese allein, rein, unmimetisch zurück – wird das Werk gewissermaßen »an sich« interpretiert, so ist sein Gehalt entsunken, der eben in dem Gestus für andere, dem geschichtlichen Aspekt besteht. Das an sich interpretierbare Werk ist zugleich – indem es dem Subjekte sich verschließt – das objektiv uninterpretierbare

L. A. 16. Juni 1946.

*

Zur Kritik des Historismus: Daß das Prä-Subjektive, das onto-
logische Ansich der Musik, auf welches das historisch objek-
tive Ideal abzielt, im *äußersten* Falle gerade als Reiz genossen
wird, so wie Strawinsky aus der archaischen Reiz-Sphäre bei 19
Debussy und Ravel hervorgetreten ist. Also, die Reaktions-
form auf den Historismus dementiert dessen eigenen Inhalt –
die Objektivität ist bloße Maske der Subjektivität, während
die wahre Objektivität gerade durch die Subjektivität hin-
durchgeht. – Meist freilich ist der gegenwärtige Objektivis-
mus bloßes Regressionsphänomen, der musikalische Reflex
einer Anthropologie, die das Subjekt liquidiert, weil – und in-
dem – es *keine* Gesellschaft gibt. Daher, geschichtsphiloso-
phisch, das Moment des Ressentiments im Objektivismus. Es
reflektiert die Unwahrheit des Kollektivs. Das Schema der Ju-
gendbewegung.[50]

In der Musik ist das Ausdruckslose Ausdruck.[51]

*

Die an Wagners Arbeit über die IX. Symphonie zu entfaltende Dialektik der Retouche wird kompliziert [dadurch,] daß sie, in der von der Interpretation herzustellenden (und das Werk auflösenden) Stimmigkeit den Begriff des integralen Werkes voraussetzt. Der ist aber zunächst nur der deutschen Tradition eigen und auch dieser nicht unbedingt; Schubert, Bruckner spotten dieses Begriffs (und nicht *nur* aus Insuffizienz sondern auf Grund des Gehalts. Schlecht ist an Beiden nicht das Dissoziationsmoment als solches, sondern ihre Pseudomorphose an die integrale Musik – der »falsche« Beethoven); große Komponisten wie Mussorgskij oder Janáček stehen ganz exterritorial dazu. Ich muß also:

entweder die Zerfallskategorie auf die integralen Werke, die Tradition des musikalischen »Systems« einschränken (was mir willkürlich und äußerlich erscheint)

oder einen *tieferen* Begriff der Idealität und Konsistenz des Werkes einführen als den der Einheit in der Mannigfaltigkeit der motivisch-thematischen Konstruktion. Das letztere schwebt mir längst vor, aber es entfernt sich von der »Gegebenheit« der materialen Beschaffenheit der Musik so weit daß es in eigentlich musikalischen Kategorien kaum mehr sich fassen läßt. *[Am linken Rand, quer zum Text:]* NB also Beethoven wäre nur als extremes *Modell* der Dialektik des Integralen zu behandeln

Vielleicht liegt die Lösung darin, daß der Verfall der Werke, der ja diesen immanent ist, ein Stück ihrer *Intention* ausmacht, daß also die Einheit bei Schubert gerade im Zerfall der Einheit besteht (NB hier die entscheidende Bedeutung des bei Wagner übersehenen *Kontrasts* – das *Unvermittelte* bei Schubert. Die klassische Totalität ist, wie Hegels Philosophie, die universelle *Vermittlung),* sodaß die wahre Interpretation Schuberts die Darstellung des Zerfalls als eines aus der Totalität *entspringenden* wäre – die epische Totalität ist die, die *an sich* »müde wird«[52], einschläft, sich dissoziiert. Dies alles setzt freilich die Theorie Beethovens, und zwar besonders des epischen Charakters und des Spätstils *voraus.*

*

Reproduktion ist eine Form (an den Eingang stellen)
D.h. das Werk bedarf ihrer ohne daß sie aus dem Werk folgt.

Zu den älteren Materialien

Drei Dirigenten Anbruch 8,7: p. 315 ff.[53]
Rettung als Beschwörung (*nur* Furtwängleraufsatz)
Ad Nachtmusik.[54]
Nachleben der Werke im Zerfall. Leichte Musik[55]
(NB das Problem der 2 Sphären Musik gehört in die Reproduktionstheorie)
S. 2 Formel über Freiheit, Erkenntnis, Objektivität.[56]
Die These vom Zerfall der Werke *an sich,* ihrer objektiven historischen Dynamik[57], ist nicht herzubeten sondern zu begründen.

*

Zur Mechanisierung ist beides zu sagen: die immanente Notwendigkeit, und die objektive – »technische« – *Nichtauthentizität.*

*

Aussagen über den Ursprung der Notenschrift sind, solange die Unkenntnis der griechischen Musik währt, unverbindliche Mutmaßungen. Doch rechtfertigt sich die Kritik der scheinbar natürlichen, vernunftgemäßen Auffassung philosophisch, die Notenschrift sei als Gedächtnisstütze entstanden: um die lebendige Musik, Lied und Tanz, vorm Vergessenwer-

den zu bewahren. (Belege) Die These ist rationalistisch, eine Projektion später Bedürfnisse in die Archaik. Gedächtnisstützen werden notwendig wenn das Gedächtnis – angesichts der
21 universalen *Vermittlung* des Erfahrens, welche die ursprüngliche Beziehung von Subjekt und Objekt durchschneidet, die im Gedächtnis die kräftige Spur hinterläßt – problematisch wird: in der Belastung mit zahllosen fernen, nicht »erfahrenen« Daten, schließlich in der Schwächung des Gedächtnisses, des Organs fürs Gewesene, durch totale Anpassung an das was je ist. Kinder brauchen keine Gedächtnisstütze; schwer fällt ihnen nicht die sprachliche Erinnerung sondern gerade deren »stützende« Vergegenständlichung, nämlich eben die Schrift. Mit den Primitiven kann es nicht anders gewesen sein. Wann immer traditionell, ohne Bindung an die fixierte Schrift musiziert wird, erweist sich das Gedächtnis als *stark:* die rhythmischen Modelle, die von primitiven Völkern behalten werden, sind so komplex, daß kein Zivilisierter es sei denn der geschulteste Musiker die gleiche Leistung aufbrächte (noch im Jazz etwas davon). Und die Modifikationen im primitiven und traditionalen Musizieren (dieses das Rudiment von jenem) sind eine Funktion des Gedächtnisses, nicht von dessen Versagen: so gegenwärtig ist das Vergangene, daß es nicht als Entfremdetes sich absetzt sondern weiterlebt: seine Veränderung verbürgt daß es da ist – identisch festgehalten, verdinglicht wird es gerade als *Vergessenes,* sodaß man leicht genug die Notation als Feind der Erinnerung, des Gedächtnisses selber, und dessen Wiederherstellung durch Vernichtung bezeichnen könnte. Es kann also die musikalische Notation nicht als einfache Erinnerungsstütze, als harmloses Bewahren eines Flüchtigen entstanden sein. Sondern sie verweist gerade auf die *Störung* jener naturwüchsigen Verhältnisse, in denen das Gedächtnis beheimatet, die Trennung von jetzt und früher nicht starr vollzogen ist. Nämlich: auf die Herrschaft. Die musikalische Notation ist ein Stück Disziplin. Sie enteignet das Gedächtnis, indem sie es stützt. Die kultischen Tänze und Lieder werden der Einheit von Erinnerung und Veränderung entzogen. Sie sollen ver-

gessen werden um sich zu fixieren, sie sollen in die identische Wiederholung übergehen, welche die Musik der barbarischen Kulturen bezeichnet. Der Stamm soll sich der Spontaneität des Ausdrucks entäußern; er soll gehorchen, nicht verstehen, nicht antasten. Der musikalische Text ist im Ursprung, als was er sich in der späten Reife der Kunstmusik wieder darstellt: Tabu. Die ersten musikalischen Schriftzeichen sind die starr regelmäßigen Trommelschläge der Barbaren und vielleicht ist die musikalische Schrift überhaupt ursprünglich Nachah- 22
mung jener rhythmisch-disziplinären Systeme, die selber bereits die musikalischen Zeitverhältnisse durch die »zeitfremde« Regelmäßigkeit der Abstände *verräumlichen.* Jedes Notenzeichen ist das Bild eines Schlages: die Objektivierung der Musik, das Umsetzen des Zeitverlaufs in einen räumlichen, ist nicht nur formal Verräumlichung, sondern ihrem ursprünglichen *Inhalt* nach, die Verräumlichung nämlich von Erfahrung zum Zwecke ihrer Beherrschbarkeit. »Alle Verdinglichung ist ein Vergessen«[58] – das Verfügbarmachen des Gewesenen macht es zugleich unwiederbringlich. Darin liegt die verzweifelte Utopie aller musikalischen Reproduktion: durch Verfügung das Unwiederbringliche wiederzubringen. Alles Musizieren ist eine Recherche du temps perdu. (NB es gehört also Notation zum geometrisch-musikalischen Typus, ist im *Ursprung* bereits antimimetisch, anti-expressiv und entfaltet sich später in diesem Wesen). Das schließt aber nicht weniger ein als die Dialektik der gesamten Musik bis zu deren Liquidation. Die Entfaltung der Musik ist durch ihre graphische Vermittlung, Verdinglichung, Verfügbarkeit möglich erst geworden – die musikalische Schrift ist das Organon der musikalischen Naturbeherrschung, und in ihr ist gerade die musikalische *Subjektivität* entstanden als Trennung von der bewußtlosen Gemeinschaft. Die Verdinglichung, Verselbständigung des musikalischen Textes ist die Voraussetzung der ästhetischen Freiheit. Zugleich aber liegt in der musikalischen Schrift ein dem Musikalischen – ihrem eigenen Inhalt – Entgegengesetztes. Die Rationalisierung, Bedingung aller autonomen Kunst,

ist deren Feind zugleich. Die Notation reguliert, hemmt, unterdrückt immer zugleich, was sie notiert und entwickelt – und daran laboriert alle musikalische Reproduktion. Genauer gesprochen: im Aufschreiben von Musik ist *konstitutiv* bereits die Differenz von dieser mitgesetzt. Die Verräumlichung des Zeitlichen ist notwendig, nicht bloß empirisch inadäquat. Autonomie und Fetischismus sind zwei Seiten des *gleichen* Sachverhalts. Die Treue zum Werk ist der Gehorsam der schließlich das Werk zerstört. Einzig der gesellschaftliche Gehorsam jener Treue hat die Musik befähigt der existierenden Gesellschaft zu widersprechen. Er reißt sie am Ende in den gesellschaftlichen Betrieb hinein (NB alles viel spezifischer auf Schrift – Interpretation beziehen)

20. Juni 1946

*

23 Das *Auswendigspielen* des genauen Textes als Rekonstruktion des der Musik immanenten Moments des Gedächtnisses. Schon von Schumann advoziert[59] (suchen!). Von Kolisch in die Kammermusik eingeführt. Strenges Auswendigspielen ist die wahre Freiheit.

*

Auseinandersetzung mit dem *Relativismus* der musikalischen Interpretation, wohl nach »Veränderung der Werke«. Der Relativismus ist stets der der Sache *transzendenten* Behandlungsweise eigen und zergeht sobald in deren immanente Gesetzlichkeit eingedrungen wird. Das ist aber nicht im Sinne des dogmatischen Absolutismus (dem Komplement des Relativismus) sondern der Arbeit des Begriffs zu verstehen. Konkret entfalten. Jede musikalische Arbeit setzt die Möglichkeit der Unterscheidung von Richtig oder Falsch voraus, beim Komponisten wie beim Interpreten: die Apperzeption jeden musikalischen Sinnes besteht geradezu in dieser Unterscheidung, und es gilt mit Bezug auf sie für die musikalische *Erfahrung* gar kein Unterschied zwischen der »elementaren« Unterscheidung richtiger und falscher Töne (die ja bereits keine physikalische ist sondern bereits die ganze kategoriale Apparatur der Musik in sich trägt) und dem Urteil über die richtige oder falsche Wiedergabe der Interpretation eines ganzen, komplexen Stückes. Gegenüber der sich bestimmenden Notwendigkeit der musikalischen Erfahrung ist der Relativismus ganz äußerlich und abstrakt. Es *könnte* formallogisch anders sein, es kann es *nicht* in der Erfahrung, weil jeder Schritt tiefer in die Sache zugleich einer in die Notwendigkeit ihrer Darstellung ist. Das Wesen des Werkes kommt mit dieser Notwendigkeit geradeswegs überein. Philosophisch gesprochen, der Relativismus setzt in der *Zufälligkeit* der Interpretation die dinghafte Trennung des Objekts vom Subjekt, das jene verschieden »auffassen« kann, voraus, die als *produzierte* zu begreifen ist und in deren *Dialektik* die Reproduktion gerade besteht. Wer vom Werk eine Auffassung hat, ist diesem entfremdet; wer es spontan versteht, erkennt es.

*

Soviel ist am Relativismus wahr: der *Zugang* in die Objektivität bleibt zufällig. Die Erfahrung beim Arbeiten mit Musikern, daß es am wichtigsten ist, *überhaupt* etwas zu sagen. Die monadologische Organisation des Kunstwerks erlaubt es, daß *jede* 24
Tür ins Zentrum führt, jedes Moment ins Gesetz. Selbst die unbestimmte oder falsche Ausstellung bei der Arbeit, wenn sie in die Disziplin des Werkes eingeht, ist ein Moment der wahren Interpretation. Dazu Kolischs »irgend etwas ist immer falsch«[60].

*

Würde man dem Leiter eines Streichquartetts bei der Arbeit die Relativität seiner Forderungen entgegenhalten, er würde nicht verstehen und sich auf die technische Kasuistik berufen, und diese Borniertheit ist gerade philosophisch der höhere Stand der Erkenntnis.

*

Ein Taktierer stellt ein Werk in sinnwidriger, mechanischer Symmetrie dar. Das Bewußtsein erkennt den Widerspruch zur Sache und drängt auf die Darstellung des Sinnes. Diese gerät in Widerspruch zum Text und zur Einheit. Also: relativiert. Aber in *bestimmter* Negation. Furtwängler vertritt gegen Wendel[61] die Wahrheit. Indem jener dabei in die Unwahrheit übergeht, wird dieser nicht wahrer. Die Kritik ist die objektive Entfaltung der im Werk verschlossenen Dialektik. Musikalische Interpretation ist wesentlich stets Kritik. Die Relativität ist nicht Gleichberechtigung der »Auffassungen« sondern das Organ von deren Abschaffung. Die wahre Interpretation ist eine streng vorgezeichnete, aber um der tragenden Antinomie der Kunstmusik willen prinzipiell nicht zu verwirklichende Idee.

*

Auswendigspielen Schumann I, S. 147-148. Sehr wichtig.

*

Es gibt in der äußersten Strenge der Interpretation ein Moment der Freiheit, nicht das der *Insuffizienz* der Schrift, also des Hohlraums, der in »objektiver« Musik dem Interpreten gelassen wird, sondern ein *prinzipiell* der Notation enthobenes *gestisches* Element – das Moment des Idiomatischen. Kreisler[62], Kolisch sprechen ihre Sprache nicht trotz sondern in der Strenge und hier ist der legitime Ort der Subjektivität des Interpreten. Kategorien wie Geigenton, Anschlag usw., überhaupt ein die Sprache des Instruments Sprechen. Auch Caruso[63]. Ohne dies Moment keine große Interpretation. Es bezeichnet das Moment der Wahrheit an der Virtuosität. Ist nicht dies über die Wiedergabe hinausgehende, selbständige Moment der vokalen oder instrumentalen Sprache beim Interpreten vorhanden, so ist gerade die *Objektivität* des Werkes nicht zu realisieren, die aufs Subjekt als auf ein in ihr nicht Aufgehendes verwiesen bleibt. Dies ist einer der tiefsten Ansatzpunkte der Dialektik der Interpretation. Es ist genau *dies* Moment, das bei den positivistischen Interpreten abstirbt und dies gerade wird als Treue mißverstanden. – Jenes idiomatische Moment allein ist die Bedingung der Konkretion. Gerade das Nichtaufgehen begründen. 25

*

Zur Begründung des Nichtaufgehens davon ist auf das Problem Werk – Material zu rekurrieren. Im Idiom vertritt der Interpret gegen das Werk dessen Material – gewissermaßen die Musik gegen die Komposition. Das Idiom, das absolut Besondere, ist gerade gegenüber dem Werk das Allgemeine. – Vielleicht läßt sich vom *Charakter* des interpretierenden Subjektes reden.

*

Warum ist die Veränderung der Werke *objektiv?*

1) das naiv-realistische Werk an sich ist unerkennbar
2) es existiert nicht sondern stets nur als Verhältnis zum Material
3) das Werk je als ein Verhältnis zum Material
4) das Werk als ein gesellschaftliches Verhältnis
5) das Werk ist nicht »rekonstruierbar«; gerade die Rekonstruktion hat das Moment der Willkür.
6) die Erkenntnis des Werkes als Gegensatz zu seinem naiven an sich sein, löst dies gerade auf.
7) der Wechsel der Interpretation nicht frei, sondern untersteht Richtig und Falsch.
8) die Veränderung gesetzmäßig.

vgl. Benjamin S. X[64]

Darin das subjektive Moment mitenthalten, aber nicht als ein von der Sache Ablösbares, Kontingentes, sondern dieser verschränkt. Die Interpretation ist keine Sache des Geschmacks. Wo die Frage des Geschmacks noch entscheidet, ist das Problem der Interpretation im Ernst noch nicht gestellt.

*

Ad antike Notenschrift. Riemann I,1. 238ff[65]:

238 »mutmaßlich«. *»Wir kommen zum Schluß unserer Darstellung der Musik des Altertums, wenn wir nun wenigstens in kurzen Zügen die Beschaffenheit der griechischen Notenschrift erörtern und uns über deren mutmaßliche Entwicklung ein Bild zu machen suchen.«*

Ton*abstände »Durch die paarweise Zusammenstellung sämtlicher Zeichen der Singnotenschrift mit den gleichbedeutenden der Instrumentenschrift noch dazu in Skalentabellen, welche über die Tonabstände keinerlei Zweifel lassen, ist die Aufgabe der Übertragung der antiken Notierungen in unsere Notenschrift so bequem gemacht, wie man nur wünschen kann.«*

Instrumentalnoten älter als Singnoten *»Das übereinstimmende Ergebnis der Forschungen der gleichzeitig an die Öffentlichkeit getretenen Hauptwerke auf diesem Gebiete (Fr. Bellermann, ›Die Tonleitern und Musiknoten der Griechen‹ 1847 und K. Fortlage, ›Das musikalische System der Griechen in seiner Urgestalt‹ 1847) ist, daß die Singnotenschrift offenbar auf die Verhältnisse des enharmonischen Tongeschlechts von Hause aus berechnet ist, während die Instrumentalnotenschrift vielmehr demselben nachträglich angepaßt zu sein und vielmehr auf diatonischer Grundlage zu beruhen scheint. Daraus muß man natürlich schließen, daß die Instrumentalnoten, oder wenigstens Elemente derselben, älter sind als die Singnoten.«*

219 »Ausnutzung des Notenbildes zu verstärkten ästhetischen Wirkungen«. *»Ein Irrtum ist es auch, wenn Westphal behauptet (a. a. O. S. 80), daß bis zur Zeit Bachs schnellere Tonstücke mit kleineren, langsamere mit größeren Notenwerten geschrieben worden seien; vielmehr hat schon die Stilwandlung um 1600 mit der Einführung der Tempobezeichnungen Allegro, Adagio usw. die Ausnutzung des Notenbildes zu verstärkten ästhetischen Wirkungen (eilende Ganze und Halbe, gehemmte Achtel, Sechzehntel usf.) gebracht und nicht erst die Zeit nach Bach.«* 26

cf. die ganze Stelle.

die rhythmische Notation nach »Füßen« *»Das [scil. daß ›Aristoxenos die normale Zählzeit doch bereits ebenso wie uns heute als eigentliche Grundlage des Rhythmus vorschwebt‹] ergibt sich bestimmt aus der Unterscheidung monopodischer, dipodischer und tripodischer, tetrapodischer und pentapodischer Versbildungen, bei denen 2,3,4,5, Einzelfüße zu höheren Einheiten zusammengeschlossen werden und der Einzelfuß zum Zählwert wird.«*

4 Zusammenhang des Ursprungs der Musik mit Sport usw. *»Nicht nur Dichtung, Musik und Mimik oder Tanz galten den Griechen als zu enger Einheit verbunden, sondern auch die Körperkraft und Körpergewandtheit erschienen ihnen im Lichte künstlerischer Vollkommenheit.«*

5 »andreia« *»So erwarben sie in der Musik wie in der Körperbildung mannhaften Ernst (ἀνδρεία), und auch für die Bewegungen in Waffen übten sie sich nach dem Rhythmus des Gesanges (μετὰ τῆς ᾠδῆς).«*

der beste Tänzer sei der beste Krieger (dem Sokrates zugeschrieben) *»Das daselbst [scil. in den ›Deipnosophisten‹ des Athenäus, geschrieben zu Anfang des 3. Jahrhunderts n. Chr.] zitierte Wort des Sokrates, daß der beste Tänzer auch der beste Krieger sei, wird durch diese Ausführung wohl verständlich.«*

NB das griechische musische Verhältnis zur Gewalt spiegelt den Ursprung des Musischen in dieser zurück.

8 Es gibt bereits eine griechische Wissenschaft vom Vortrag[66]:
Ἐξαγγελτικόν[67]
Mimik als ὑποκριτική, also Verstellung, neben Gesang und Instrumentalvortrag.

9 Riemann leugnet Mimik als musikalisches Element. *»Im Sinne unserer heutigen strengeren Scheidung der Künste gehört ja freilich die Mimik (als Gebärdenspiel und Tanz) ebensowenig wie die Dichtung, ja noch weniger, zur Musik im engeren Sinne. Denn wenn der Sprache zweifellos noch spezifisch musikalische Elemente im musikalischen Klange innewohnen, kann das gleiche von der lediglich zum Auge sprechenden Mimik nicht ausgesagt werden.«*

31 Möglichkeit der Entstehung der Neumen aus Cheironomie, d. h. den Handbewegungen des Dirigenten. *»Es ist sogar nicht unmöglich, daß die Neumenschrift selbst griechischen Ursprungs ist und sich aus der Cheironomie, den Handbewegungen des die Melodiebewegung und die ihr entsprechenden Bewegungen des Chors leitenden Chordirigenten des Altertums entwickelt hat.«*
Cf. II, 84.[68] *»Schon sechs Jahre vor Erscheinen des ersten Bandes der ›Neumenstudien‹ [von Oskar Fleischer], nämlich 1889, überschrieb Dom Mocquereau das dritte Kapitel der einleitenden Studie zu der Faksimile-Ausgabe des Cod. 390 von St. Gallen ›Notation oratoire ou chironomique‹ und wies auf die enge Verwandtschaft von Gesten und Erhebungen und Senkungen der Stimme hin, [. . .] bezeichnet die Akzente als eine Art Nachmalen der Tonbewegung (pictographie), betont auch sehr bestimmt, daß im Mittelalter sowohl in der griechischen als in der römischen Kirche Handbewegungen des Dirigenten dazu dienten, die Hebungen und Senkungen der Melodie und zu-*

gleich den Rhythmus und das Tempo anzudeuten und somit den Chor bestimmt zu leiten.«

II. Teil[69]

83: Coussemakers[70] Theorie des Ursprungs der Neumen aus Akzentzeichen (Prosodie). Auch O. Fleischer[71] »*Ed. de Coussemaker hat als erster in seiner Histoire de l'harmonie au moyen âge (1852, S. 158) die Vermutung ausgesprochen, daß die Neumen sich aus den griechischen Akzentzeichen (Prosodien) der alexandrinischen Grammatiker entwickelt haben, und dieser Gedanke ist seither nicht wieder fallen gelassen worden. Mit besonderer Ausführlichkeit hat ihn Oskar Fleischer in seinen Neumenstudien (Teil 1-2, 1895-97) aufgenommen, aber dabei durch Anhäufungen von allerlei fernliegendem historischen Detail (er zieht sogar die Chinesen und Inder mit heran) den Mangel einer eigentlichen strikten Beweisführung verdeckt.«*

84: Nachmachen von Handbewegungen[72]

85: Hauptstelle. »*[. . .] bis endlich zu Anfang des 8. Jahrhunderts der Angelsachse (Neumenstudien II. 8) oder Ire (das. S. 68) Ceolfried den ersten Versuch machte, aus den Schlagzeichen der Cheironomie eine den Texten überschriebene Tonbezeichnung zu entwickeln und damit der Erfinder der Neumenschrift wurde.«*
– Unten: Akzentuationssysteme »*Weiter entwickelt sodann Fleischer auf Grund eines im 16.(!) Jahrhundert geschriebenen irischen Traktats und eines (nicht näher bestimmten) ›alten Druidenwerk‹ französisch-gallischer Provenienz, daß die Iren ein eigenes altes Akzentuationssystem besessen haben, das sich von dem von Fleischer für die Griechen und den Orient angenommenen mit Sekundschwankungen um den Mittelton dadurch unterschied, daß die gewöhnlichen Stimmbeugungen Terzen statt Sekunden betrugen.«*

NB wenn die Notenschrift die Musik nachahmt, muß Aufführung die Schrift nachahmen.
Die Aufklärung der Notenschrift ist verwandelte Mimesis.
Sie ist intentionslos.
Sie ist rhythmisch und melodisch zugleich (ad Einheit der Elemente).
Sie ist autoritär: Gestus des *Dirigenten*.
Heute noch zeichnet die Hand des Dirigenten die Linie.

89 Riemann hält Frage nach dem Ursprung der Neumen für von sekundärer Bedeutung (kritisieren) *»Deshalb ist auch die Frage nach den letzten Wurzeln der Neumenschrift für uns von sekundärer Bedeutung. Nicht die Beschaffenheit und Bedeutung der Notenschriftzeichen, sondern vielmehr die Beschaffenheit der Gesänge, welche sie fixieren sollen, ist das uns in erster Linie Interessierende und wir haben schwerwiegende Gründe gefunden für die Annahme, daß die Gesänge schon in den ersten Jahrhunderten des Christentums einen Reichtum der melodischen Gestaltung hatten, welchem primitive Stadien der Entwicklung der Notenschrift wie die von Coussemaker oder Fleischer angenommenen in keiner Weise voll gerecht werden könnten.«*
Meine Hypothese: es ist in der Notenschrift zum chironomischen (mimetischen) Element ein zweites, signifikatives, die Buchstabentonschrift *hinzugetreten* das erst die Eindeutigkeit geschaffen hat. Siehe:

92 *»Eine eigentliche Notenschrift ist darum die Neumenschrift vor ihrer Verbindung mit der Buchstabentonschrift (durch das Liniensystem) überhaupt nicht gewesen.«*
(NB dieselbe doppelte Wurzel der *griechischen* Schrift??)

95 direkte Anschaulichkeit unserer Notenschrift. *»Wir erkennen dann mit Staunen und Bewunderung, daß das unsere heutige Notenschrift so himmelhoch über alle anderen Notierungsweisen erhebende Moment der d i r e k t e n A n s c h a u-*

lichkeit ein Erbteil der Neumenschrift ist, daß unsere Notenschrift nur eine im Laufe der Jahrhunderte konsequent ausgebaute Neumierung ist. Also erste Vorbedingung für eine gerechte Beurteilung des Wertes der Neumen ohne Linien ist die Annahme einer beschränkten Anzahl durch direkte Überlieferung mittels Vorsingens und Nachsingens weitergegebener Melodien; nicht die Festlegung dieser Melodien in einer jeden Einzelton bestimmenden Notierung ist ihr Zweck, sondern vielmehr die besondere Art ihrer Anpassung auf den jedesmaligen Text. [. . .] Haben die Chorleiter wirklich, wie gut verbürgt ist, mit Handbewegungen die Melodieführung angedeutet, so werden doch zweifellos sie sich dabei graphisch fixierter Vorlagen bedient haben. Daß nicht auch jedem Chorsänger ein Buch mit solchen Notierungen zur Verfügung stand, ist dagegen selbstverständlich, schon wegen der Kostbarkeit der Singbücher. Der Chor lernte in der Singschule die Melodien, und auch die vielen Texte mußte er auswendig wissen; beim jedesmaligen Vortrage aber sorgte der cheironomierende Chorleiter dafür, daß die Textunterlegung in der für den Fall gebotenen Weise durchgeführt wurde. Dafür war aber mit einer beschränkten Zahl von Zeichen wohl auszukommen.«
(äußerst wichtige Seite)
Neumen setzen unmittelbare Überlieferung voraus. 27
Zweck der Neumierung: nicht Festlegung der Melodien sondern Anpassung auf Text (kultische Disziplin). Hauptstelle.
Gestische Darstellung der Melodie. (NB also nicht bloß Rhythmus sondern *Melos* gestisch: d. h. aber intentionslos).

96 das Notenzeichen als Akzentzeichen *»Tatsächlich ist denn auch die Zahl der eigentlichen Elemente der Neumenschrift nur eine kleine; da sind zunächst die zweifellos mit Recht auf die Akzente der alexandrinischen Grammatiker zurückgeführten, jedenfalls in der Idee mit denselben übereinstimmenden für Einzeltöne.«*[73]

106 f. Hinzukommen der lateinischen Buchstabennotierung. *»Zweifellos steht fest, daß im 10. Jahrhundert eine* I n s t r u m e n t a l n o t i e r u n g *(für Orgel, Rotta usw.) mit den ersten Buchstaben des Alphabets im allgemeinen Gebrauch war und zwar zuerst nördlich der Alpen. Die urpsrüngliche Bedeutung der Tonbuchstaben war ABCDEFGA=cdefgahc' [...].«*
(NB meine Auffassung: die Neumisierung ist keine eindeutige signifikative Bezeichnung sondern ein Regulativ der Tradition. Die Schwierigkeiten der Dechiffrierung, weil man rationalistisch nach etwas Falschem – der Eindeutigkeit sucht.)
(NB alle Probleme der Neumisierung sind in der modernen Notation *enthalten)*

169 Guidos Reform als Synthese von Neumen und Buchstabenschrift. *»Guido selbst sah also im Grunde die von ihm geschaffene neue Tonschrift einerseits als eine bequemere Verwendung der Buchstabentonschrift, andererseits aber auch als eine Fortbildung der Neumenschrift an.«*

188 Mensuralnotation als Ausdruck der *Dauer* der Noten = Loslösung der Musik vom Textrhythmus. *»Die Verkoppelung verschiedener Texte tritt vielmehr erst gleichzeitig mit der gänzlichen Emanzipation der Melodie vom Rhythmus des Textes auf, welche noch ganz andere Dinge gestattet als die Verbindung verschiedener Texte, z. B. den Vortrag desselben Textes in beliebiger zeitlicher Verschiebung oder die Gegenüberstellung von Texten ganz anderer Gliederung. Diese Emanzipation wurde möglich durch eine neue Reform der Notenschrift, welche die Dauer der einzelnen Töne durch die Gestalt der Noten ausdrückte, also durch Aufnahme eines derselben bis dahin so gut wie gänzlich fremden Elements in die Notenschrift. Was eigentlich auf diese vollständige Revolution der Kompositionstechnik geführt hat, liegt vollkommen im Dunkel.«*

199 Einfluß der Mensuralnotation auf das *Komponieren.* *»Man kann nicht ohne weiteres sagen, daß die Emanzipation des musikalischen Rhythmus von der immanenten Rhythmik des Textes durch Einführung von Notenwertzeichen sogleich durchaus einen Fortschritt der Kunst bedeutete. Daß sie aber einen solchen anbahnte, steht natürlich außer Zweifel; ja man wird annehmen müssen, daß die Männer, welche diese Reform vollzogen, das deutliche Bewußtsein hatten, der Kunst ganz neue Wege zu öffnen. Den Anstoß zu der Reform mögen die Bedürfnisse der Instrumentalmusik gegeben haben, die ja mangels eines führenden Textrhythmus darauf angewiesen war, Mittel der Fixierung der Rhythmen zu finden, wenn sie von der freien Improvisation oder der Festhaltung einiger konventionellen rhythmischen Typen, wie sie die Tänze erforderten, zu freieren Gestaltungen gelangen wollte.«*

*

Die wahre Interpretation ist die vollkommene Nachahmung der musikalischen Schrift.

*

Ritters Theorie usw. Ursprung des deutschen Trauerspiels 212 ff.[74]

*

Zwei Elemente der Notenschrift Riemann I, 1, 61. *»Daß die Instrumentalnotenzeichen auf zwei Elemente hinweisen, die bereits eine frühere Zeit verschmolzen haben wird, habe ich bereits in meinen Studien zur Geschichte der Notenschrift (1878) angemerkt. Die Zeichen der tieferen Oktave weisen offenbar auf eine diatonische Skala mit dem ersten Buchstaben des Alphabetes hin A B Γ Δ E Z H Θ = g f e d c H A G*[75]*, die der Mittellage dagegen auf eine*

Bezeichnung der Töne mit dem Anfangsbuchstaben der Namen der Saiten der Kithara: Nete, Paranete, Trite usw. Es liegt nahe, die erstere als die erste Notenschrift der Auleten, die letzere als die der Kitharöden anzusehen.«

*

NB das mimische Wesen der Musik ist zerfällt in den Ausdruck (der Pseudomorphose mit Sprache Intention Gegenständlichkeit eingeht) und Konstruktion die das gestische Moment rein festhält aber als solches, ohne Ausdruck, gleichsam ohne Subjektivität festhält und objektiviert. Musik als Kunst ist Versuch der Versöhnung dieser Elemente und dieser Versöhnung dient die Reproduktion die Ausdruck in Konstruktion verwandelt und Konstruktion in Ausdruck.

*

28 Zur Intentionalität in Musik und Sprache

Jedes Schriftzeichen eines Wortes ist wie ein Gitterwerk, durch welches der Sinn hindurchleuchtet indem er von seiner sinnlichen Spur, dem Echo im Laut, sich befreit. Jede Note ist der bewußtlose Abdruck eines Lautes und Anteil gewinnt sie an Bedeutung einzig durch Konfiguration.

*

Veränderung deduzieren

(a) die Starrheit des Zeichens verfehlt den Gestus der Musik

(b) das »Notenbild« verfehlt die Konstruktion (Vorsicht gegen ?[76] Schluß des vorigen Kapitels.)

Die Noten haben ein Eigenleben das sich bewegt: dies ist die subjektive Seite, die die Musik, weil nicht an sich eindeutig, sondern nur durch Gewalt des Bedeutens verdinglicht, bewegt sich weiter gegen die Verdinglichung.

Die Willkür der Beziehung von Notation u. Musik macht beide gegen einander Schwanken.

Der immanente Gestus der Musik ist immer Gegenwart, gerade *nicht* ewig, d. h. auch die alten Zeichen der Musik gelten dem *Jetzt,* das damit in sie hereinfällt.

Das Bild reicht an die Konstruktion nicht unmittelbar heran, diese entfaltet sich vielmehr erst aus ihm.

Man muß die Zeichen in Nachahmung verwandeln und das Bild in die Erkenntnis. Beides nicht an sich in der Schrift gegeben sondern erfragt. Daher trägt diese ihre Dynamik in sich.

Das Eigenleben der Noten: daß ihr *Gestalt*zusammenhang wechselt.

Die Konfigurationen sind verschieden. Die reine Note, an sich, ist ein physikalischer Grenzbegriff.

Was Zeichen was Bild ist wechselt. Beleg: Notenkopf und Ligatur. Es werden immer mehr Bilder zu Zeichen und diese treten zu immer neuen Bildern zusammen.

In den immanenten Sinn der Werke schlägt die Zeit herein. (Beleg, die Schubertstellen).

*

Eine Theorie des musikalischen *Hörens* muß eingeschlossen 29
werden. In der Produktion von Musik ist Hören *nicht* das Primäre. Der Laut ist ein Reflex. Ihn zu hören ist die erste Stufe der Verinnerlichung, Vergeistigung – im »Zuhören« des Lautes ist, als dessen Festhalten, Identifizieren schon Hören als *Vorstellung* gesetzt. Hören als ungegenständliche Objektivation. Die Aufklärung der Musik ist ihre Verlegung in den inneren Sinn. Hören als das Gegenteil des Mimetischen, die eigentliche *Vermittlungs*kategorie von Geste und Sinn, sinnliche Vergeistigung. Das Komplement von Schrift: je mehr Schrift, desto mehr bedarf es des Hörens. Grenzbegriff der reinen Vorstellung. – Alles musikalische Hören ist ein *Nach*hören wie beim Echo und in jeder musikalischen Erfahrung ist mit dem Hören das Nichtgehörte, die Gebärde. Dies Nachhören

in der Interpretation, die von der Vorstellung ausgeht, diese in die Geste retrovertiert und diese wiederum an der Vorstellung mißt. Selbst Komponieren nicht absolute Sache des Hörens, nicht einmal im Sinne der inneren unsinnlichen Hörfunktion. Haydn, Strawinsky die am Klavier schreiben, Bergs mangelhaftes Gehör. Komponieren als Abhören. Das Hören ist in der Interpretation das Rationale, die Kontrollinstanz.

*

Es gibt eine *echte* Mehrdeutigkeit der Texte, d. h. mehrere objektiv in ihnen angelegte Interpretationen, aber noch diese Mehrdeutigkeit ist eine *bestimmte,* und sie ist historisch im Schwinden.

*

Es muß, als eines der philosophischen Grundmotive der Arbeit, hervortreten, daß die Objektivität von Erkenntnis – und Darstellung – nicht ein *Weniger* an Subjektivität, ein Weglassen erheischt sondern ein *Mehr* an Subjektivität. Nachmachen heißt daß dem Subjekt um so mehr vom Objekt sich erschließt wie es hineingibt. Das ist das zentrale Argument gegen den Positivismus. Aber dies Hineingeben spielt im Text, nicht als ein von ihm Abgespaltenes – und das ist die Schwelle gegen die Romantik. Das subjektive Moment der Objektivität ist die Interpretation.

August 1949

*

Benjamins Sprachtheorie[77] behandeln.

*

Abhängigkeit einzelner Darstellungscharaktere von der Formtotalität. Es ist z. B. ein entscheidender Unterschied, ob die gleiche melodische Gestalt als Thema gespielt, gesetzt wird, ob sie in den Fluß einer Entwicklung hineingezogen erscheint, oder ob sie schließlich als Resultat einer Entwicklung wieder eintritt. Dies heißt weitgehend: interpretieren.

*

Interpretation deckt Konsequenzen auf. Z. B. Sforzati sind oft durch minimale Akzente bezw. Akzentverschiebungen vorzubereiten.

*

Dissonanzen spielen. Darin spielt Geschichte. Unter der Vorherrschaft der Tonalität treten sie zurück. Teleologisch haben sie, die Akzidentien, als das treibende Wesen sich enthüllt, während die vorgegebene, abgegriffene Tonalität der Bestätigung nicht mehr bedarf. Die Interpretation muß die Dissonanz ins Licht rücken. – Sehr Verwandtes gilt für die schlechten Taktteile.

*

Desiderate 31

1) es muß zwischen der Theorie der Notenschrift und der Reproduktionstheorie der eindeutigste Zusammenhang hergestellt werden und zwar so, daß die Prinzipien von dieser aus jener abgeleitet werden
2) es muß, zu dem signifikativen und bildlichen Moment, das tonsprachliche in dem in dem Brief an Ingolf Dahl[78] entwickelten Sinn als drittes, gleichberechtigtes hinzutreten. (Dies hat *nichts* mit der im Text kritisierten Auffassung von Musik als Sprache zu tun.)

Dies Moment ist das eigentliche Medium der Geschichte im Werk.

3) es muß eine weitgehend ausgeführte positive Lehre von der Reproduktion gegeben werden wie sie heute fällig ist. Die Notizen auf der vorigen Seite sind rhapsodische Beispiele einer solchen Lehre.

*

Die Terminologie möchte ich wie folgt festlegen: der musikalische Text enthält 3 Elemente

1) das mensurale (das bisher als signifikativ bezeichnete, der Inbegriff alles durch Zeichen eindeutig Gegebenen)
2) das neumische (bisher: mimisch, mimetisch oder gestisch genannt, das aus den Zeichen zu interpolierende strukturelle)
3) das idiomatische (bisher: musiksprachliche, d. h. die aus der je vorgegebenen und das Werk *einschließenden* Musiksprache zu erschließende. Dies muß noch genau entfaltet werden. Vielleicht auf *Wien* exemplifizieren. Bergs Vorschrift »wienerisch«).

Thema der Arbeit ist eigentlich die Dialektik dieser Elemente. Es fehlt noch der Übergang von der Notationstheorie zur Reproduktionstheorie, und die Verfeinerung der Notationslehre durch die moderne Forschung.

*

32 Aufgabe der musikalischen Interpretation ist es, das idiomatische Element durchs Mittel des mensuralen ins neumische umzusetzen. »Ursprung ist das Ziel«.[79] These meines Buches.

*

Das idiomatische Element ist der Inbegriff aller Konventionen, innerhalb deren ein Text erscheint. Es ist aber nicht dem neumischen bloß äußerlich, sondern enthält das neumische in unreiner Gestalt in sich, während umgekehrt unproblematisch – d. h. ohne Beziehung auf den Untergang des Werkes – das neumische nur soweit existiert wie das idiomatische gilt. Mahlers Satz »Tradition ist Schlamperei«[80] bezeichnet genau die je sich wiederholende Situation, in der das neumische und idiomatische Element auseinandertreten.

*

Es muß der Anschein eines *Fetischismus* des musikalischen Textes vermieden werden. Aufgabe der Interpretation ist natürlich nicht die Treue zum Text *an sich,* sondern die Darstellung »des Werkes« d. h. der Musik für die der Text einsteht. Die Reflexion auf Text, Notation, Elemente des Textes usw. ist notwendig bloß, weil diese »Musik« weder als solche selbstevident, noch unmittelbar gegeben, noch eindeutig ist. Dies ist der Hebel der Methode und das muß hervortreten.

*

Idiomatisches und neumisches Element. »Neumen setzen unmittelbare Überlieferung voraus.« Vgl. S. 27 dieser Aufzeichnungen. NB gilt das nicht gerade fürs Idiomatische?

*

Es gibt in der Interpretation ein Analogon zum Verhältnis von Ontogenese und Phylogenese. Wie die objektive Geschichte des Werkes nämlich so führt die Erfahrung des individuellen Interpreten stets vom idiomatischen Element durchs mensurale zum neumischen, und schlecht ist sowohl die welche beim idiomatischen wie beim mensuralen stehenbleibt.

*

33 Als ein Nebenprodukt der Arbeit muß sich die Bestimmung des Begriffs »musikalisch« ergeben (gegen Busoni[81]). Er ist der Oberbegriff alles dessen was jenseits des Mensuralen von der wahren Interpretation gefordert wird. Primär ist es das subjektiv gegenwärtige idiomatische Element (musikalische und unmusikalische schlechte Komponisten: die Musik von Rachmaninoff oder Gershwin bewegt sich im idiomatischen Medium; die von Sibelius nicht), in einem höheren Sinn das (vermittelte) Bewußtsein des neumischen. Man kann sagen daß die Aufgabe der wahren Interpretation die Aufhebung und Wiederherstellung des »Musikalischen« sei. Dazu vielleicht eine Diskussion des Falles Schnabel.[82]

*

Das idiomatische Element variiert zwischen verschiedenen Komponisten und »Schulen«. Es ist sehr stark bei Schubert, in einem ganz anderen Sinn bei Wagner, bei Mahler, und die sogenannten nationalen Schulen machen das idiomatische Element zum Prinzip (auch z. B. der Jazz) – daher vieles von ihrer Schwäche. Umgekehrt tritt es bei Bach, Beethoven, Schönberg ganz zurück und ist bei Haydn und Mozart weitgehend sublimiert. Der klassizistische Impuls der großen Musik ist weitgehend der der – transzendental-subjektiven – *Bewältigung* des idiomatischen Elements. – Musikantentum ist der Primat des idiomatischen Elements in der Interpretation.

Lake Tahoe, 8. September 1949

*

Der Begriff des Idiomatischen verweist auf den der Sprache. Aber es ist die These des Buches, daß Musik keine Sprache sei. Danach stehen beide Kategorien nicht im einfachen Gegensatz sondern haben ein Moment gemeinsam das in beiden verschieden sich entfaltet, und von dessen Explikation scheint das Gelingen der Arbeit abzuhängen. Ihm kommt wohl der *Dia-*

lekt am nächsten. Musik keine Sprache, aber kennt Dialekte und deren Inbegriff wird vom Begriff des Idiomatischen getroffen. Was aber ist Dialekt ohne Sprache? Oder vielmehr: ist Dialekt nicht das sprachlose Element der Sprache?

*

Wahre Reproduktion ist nicht einfach die Realisierung des 34
analytischen Befundes (der übrigens prinzipiell nicht als abgeschlossener vorzustellen ist). Sondern sie enthält das idiomatische Element als aufgehobenes in sich. Und damit schließt sie *notwendig* die Subjektivität des Interpreten ein, die jedem Werk gegenüber das idiomatische Element repräsentiert (Schlüssel zur Subjekt-Objekt-Theorie). Sie ist also weder die irrationale (idiomatische) noch die chemisch-reine, analytische, sondern die Wiederherstellung des mimischen Elements durchs analytische hindurch. Das Neumische als ihre Idee (? Oder ist es nicht selber nur *eines* der Elemente das mit den anderen in dialektische Konfiguration tritt? Zentral)

*

Notenlesen und musikalisches Bezugssystem. Das schnelle Vorauslesen beim Abspielen, Erraten von Fortsetzungen usw. setzt das tonale System voraus (und allgemein das idiomatische Element; vgl. Schumanns Definition wer musikalisch sei[83]). Sonst unendlich viel schwieriger, obwohl auch in nichttonaler Musik nicht unmöglich, weil deren objektive Tendenz gewisse Antezipationen stiftet. – Die Arbeit muß eine Theorie des Abspielens liefern. – Ich kann im Allgemeinen, beim Überblicken und Erfassen des Notenbildes, eine Musik beurteilen, noch *ehe* ich sie mir exakt vorstelle. Ein wesentliches Moment des Neumischen.

*

»Tempo giusto« – das ist der Ausdruck des Vertrauens der Notation aufs idiomatische Element.

*

Interpretation ist dem *Wesen* nach ein dialektischer Prozeß.

*

35 Der in der Philosophie der neuen Musik ausgesprochene Gedanke, daß die traditionelle große Musik, Beethoven zumal, das Allgemeine und das Besondere zum paradoxen Einstand bringe[84], ist auf die Reproduktionstheorie anzuwenden. Es herrscht eine enge Beziehung zwischen Idiomatischem und Allgemeinem einerseits, Besonderem und Neumischem andererseits, und in gewissem Sinn ist die Interpretation die Nachahmung jenes in der Komposition selbst spielenden Prozesses – daher dialektisch.

*

1953

Die Arbeit muß in »Regeln« terminieren wie der: Die Klangfarbe, der Ton ist ein Mittel zur Charakteristik musikalischer Gestalten, zur Artikulation, nie »Selbstzweck« sondern Funktion der Darstellung des musikalischen Sinnes, vor allem auch der *Unterscheidung.* Hat z. B. ein Geiger einen schönen, süßschluchzenden und zugleich aggressiven Ton, und spielt das Mendelssohnkonzert, so hat er den langsamen Satz nicht mit diesem Ton zu spielen, sondern den Charakter des Verträumten, nicht ganz Präsenten durch die Modifikation des Tons zu realisieren. Grundsätzlich sind *alle* Differenzen von Charakteren, noch die subtilsten, in klangliche zu übersetzen. Gilt insbesondere für die Singstimme.
Oder: die harmonische Determiniertheit des Melos in der späteren tonalen Musik seit etwa Mozart ist von der Reproduktion dadurch herauszubringen, daß der Klang der melo-

dischen Hauptstimme die Harmonie nachfühlt, sie gewissermaßen spiegelt (z. B. Farbwechsel beim Wechsel der harmonischen Funktion eines Tons).
Die Analyse der richtigen Darstellung von Werken muß auf ein Corpus von dergleichen Regeln führen.

*

Zur Theorie der *Phrasierung:* Die Phrasierung muß nicht nur 36
gliedern und artikulieren, sondern die *Proportion* der Formteile darstellen; also in der Trennung nach dem *Gewicht* des zu Trennenden unterscheiden (es wird, infolge der idiomatischen Eingeschliffenheit, durchweg *zu wenig* phrasiert). Im Grunde reicht die Phrasierung bis zu jedem Ton, jedenfalls zur kleinsten sinngebenden Gruppe. (Beispiel Chopin E-Dur-Etüde [op 10,3].) – Man kann durch Phrasierung den Schwung einer ganzen Form herausarbeiten; etwa indem man die Cäsuren immer kleiner werden läßt weil sie schon etabliert sind (Revellers[85]), oder indem man dort, wo die Form zusammenschießt, nach zuvor sehr deutlicher Phrasierung lange Bogen bildet (Chopin, z. B. As-Dur Etüde).

*

Man findet in der Romantik, zumal bei Schumann und Chopin, »spleen«, fixe Ideen, Obsessionen. Dazu muß man den »Geist« solcher Musik verstehen. Aber wie man das *darstellt,* läßt sich präzis musikalisch sagen: etwa durch Akzentuierung des ersten Tones einer solchen Gruppe, als eines unabweislich sich Anmeldenden, z. B. in der Moscheles-Etüde[86] von Chopin:

usw.

[Am linken Rand der Aufzeichnung:] d.h. das neumische Element *und* das idiomatische

*

Bei Beethoven sind Sechzehntelfiguren kaum je Passagen oder Läufe: man muß den *Widerstand* mitspielen.

*

37 Es gibt Musik, zu deren Sinn es gehört, die Struktur *nicht* durchsichtig zu machen – aber das ist dann selbst ein Teil der Struktur, auf den die Analyse führen muß. – Analytisches Resultat: Verschleierung der Analyse. – Bei der Analyse muß man alles Idiomatische vergessen, bei der Darstellung wieder die Analyse. – Musikalisch sein ist die Kraft, der Analyse trotz des idiomatischen Elements mächtig zu sein und des Neumischen trotz der Analyse. Überhaupt, die Kraft, die musikalischen Momente in ihrer Antithesis festzuhalten (dies ist die eigentliche Definition[)]. – Das Idiomatische ist die *Voraussetzung* jeder Interpretation, welche von dieser aufgezehrt wird. Das Mensurale ist das *Medium,* in dem das Idiomatische ins Neumische übergeht; Notation als *Mittel* der Analyse. – NB die Beziehung zu dem Fragment über Sprache und Musik[87] muß hergestellt werden.

*

Nicht nur müssen Begleitsysteme zurücktreten, sondern dürfen nicht als Melodien gespielt werden. Da sie es nicht sind, erheben sie einen falschen Anspruch und klingen albern (NB das musikalisch Dumme). Z.B. Klavierbegleitung im langsamen Satz des Es-Dur-Konzerts von Beethoven nicht »ausspielen«.

*

Rosé sagte mir einmal von einem Quartett: die können ja kein
Thema spielen.[88] Etwas sehr Richtiges. Die Interpretation
muß Setzungscharaktere (und den Unterschied von diesen)
zum Ausdruck bringen. Dazu etwa Beethovens Bezeichnung 38
»mit Nachdruck« beim Rondothema des Es-Dur-Konzerts. –
Alle derartigen Charaktere in Darstellung übersetzen. Aber
wie: das ist das Problem.

*

Wenn am Riemannschen Begriff des toten Intervalls[89] etwas daran ist, so implizierte das eine tötliche[90] Kritik an den Werken, oder an der Interpretation, oder am Hörer. Einer wahren Interpretation dürfte es wohl keine toten Intervalle geben. Das führt aber auf einen in meinem Entwurf[91] bis jetzt ganz vernachlässigten Aspekt: die Interpretation als *Korrektur* der Werke, Versuch, Sinnloses sinnvoll zu machen. Wer je im Ernst Werke interpretiert hat, weiß, daß alle Analyse Kritik ist (– denn es gibt kein *Verstehen* von Kunstwerken, das nicht ihre Kritik implizierte), auf Schwaches oder Falsches stößt, und daß die eigentlichen Probleme der Interpretation untrennbar sind vom Versuch, das Falsche doch durch die Darstellung zu rechtfertigen. Interpretation ist apologetisch, darin dem Kommentar verwandt; diese Erfahrung habe ich besonders an Eduard [Steuermann][92] gemacht. Aber auch dies hat seine Dialektik, denn je strenger die Interpretation der Logik des Werkes sich anmißt, je schärfer sie es belichtet, um so tiefer läßt sie die Schatten seiner Fehlbarkeit zugleich hervortreten. – Zwischen diesem Problem und dem der Herstellung des musikalischen Sinnes herrscht der tiefste Zusammenhang, denn wo ein solcher am wenigsten sich kristallisiert hat, ist der Text am vieldeutigsten, die Interpretation am schwierigsten.

*

Noch in neuerer Zeit stehen Werke, die einer festen Tradition angehören, in denen das idiomatische Element überwiegt,
39 ganz anders zur Notation als eigentlich autonome. Beim Barbier von Sevilla wirkt der Notentext kaum als solcher, sondern fast wie eine unverbindliche Erinnerungsstütze. Wer nicht weiß, wie das musiziert wird, kann es kaum aus den Noten entnehmen, trotz der gar nicht schablonenhaften Kompositionsweise.

*

Insuffizienz der Notenschrift: man weiß z. B. sehr oft, bei kleineren modifizierenden crescendi, nicht, wie weit sie führen, von sf wie stark es ist; bei crescendo ebenso wie accelerando nicht ob stetig oder in geometrischer Proportion. All dies kann nur aus dem Zusammenhang erschlossen werden. Aber meist zwingend (z. B. Relativität des sf auf die Dynamik der betreffenden Gestalt – obwohl dies nicht ausnahmslos gilt z. B. bei Beethoven).

*

Die Theorie der Phrasierung wird sehr zu differenzieren sein. Phrasierung relativ auf Kompositionskategorien wie Übergang und Kontrast. Phrasierungen, die Kontraste darstellen, naturgemäß stärker als solche, die kontinuierliche Flächen artikulieren. Wahrscheinlich verschiedene *Typen* von Phrasierung wie die funktionelle, darstellende; die interpunktierende; die *unmittelbare,* mimische. Wie denn überhaupt keine mechanische Identität der Interpretationsmittel des Ganzen und des Einzelnen gilt, sondern – da diese Kategorien qualitativ variieren – qualitativ verschiedene und *zugleich* identische; Identität in der Nichtidentität. Äußerst wichtig.

*

Dies hat viel weitere, prinzipielle Geltung für *alle* von Zeichen indizierten Elemente der Darstellung. Denn sie *alle* haben außer ihrer »mensuralen« ihre »neumische« Bedeutung d. h. sie sind zu differenzieren nach ihrer *Funktion*. So kann ein cre- 40
scendo formdynamische Bedeutung haben oder agogische in einer Phrase. So kann der Klang einer Stelle deren Charakter gelten und deren Beziehung zum Ganzen (er muß immer *beides*). Zugleich aber haben alle musikalischen Zeichen immer auch eine Bedeutung *an sich,* und zu den Postulaten der wahren Interpretation gehört, diese mit der funktionellen auszugleichen.

*

Die Interpretationslehre darf sich nicht bei der arbeitsteiligen Scheidung musikalischer Elemente und deren Spiegelung im Zeichensystem (Noten + akzidentielle Bestimmungen) bescheiden, sondern muß, indem sie die Unterschiede festhält, zugleich die Relationen bestimmen. Ein crescendo kann anstelle einer Tempomodifikation (z. B. eines falschen ritardando) treten, oder ein Akzent auf einem dissonierenden Ton kann den harmonischen Sinn realisieren. All dies steckt natürlich in der Komposition, und diese ist das Maß dafür. Grundsätzlich kann in der Musik jedes Element für alles stehen. *[Längs des linken Randes:]* Gesetz: »Dissonanzen spielen«.

*

Vom Standpunkt des *Subkutanen* aus (s. den großen Schönbergaufsatz 1952-53[93]) ergeben sich eine Reihe Regeln wie: die Auftakte fallen lassen, nie automatisch gute Taktteile, in Figuren die erste Note betonen; latente thematische Beziehungen spielen, das durchs Schema Selbstverständliche zurücktreten lassen usw. (diese Regeln sind in weitem Maß die Phänomenologie der falschen Interpretation, die beim idiomatischen stehen bleibt: die Kritik des Musikanten[94]). Aber

auch dies ist nicht mechanisch zu verstehen, denn das Subku-
41 tane ist nicht *an sich,* sondern nur als Negation des Anderen, und darzustellen ist diese Dialektik, die Relation. Also *nicht:* den schlechten Taktteil spielen und den guten fallen lassen, sondern den Prozeß zwischen beiden deutlich machen.

*

Grundregel heute ist selbstverständlich: das Erkannte, die Vorstellung realisieren, sich nicht vom Idiom, vom Klang, von der Stimme oder vom Instrument treiben lassen. Aber selbst dies ist zu differenzieren. Denn es herrscht im musikalischen *Sinn,* dem neumischen Element, vielfach ein Verhältnis zur instrumentalen Spielweise. Beethoven schon ist vielfach objektiv in Klaviergriffen gedacht; es verstieße vielfach gegen den Sinn, wenn man gegen die Hand spielen wollte (z. B. in den letzten Sonaten, bes. op. 111).

*

Zur Darstellung *neuer* Musik: es ist wohl, nächst der Verdeutlichung des »roten Fadens«, das wichtigste, daß *Identisches* als solches kenntlich ist. Ich hörte z. B. eine Aufführung von Bergs op. 3 (jetzt, April 1953 in L. A.), in der in der Durchführung des 1. Satzes kurz vor dem Höhepunkt, infolge der Drängung, Takt 91 f das $\frac{1}{32}$ nach dem punktierten Achtel nicht zu erkennen war. Dadurch ging aber verloren, daß das Thema identisch ist mit der Gestalt des Cellos Takt 51-52 – und damit der Sinn der Durchführung und eigentlich des ganzen Satzes. Von *einer* Note, die unter den Tisch fällt, kann eine Formtotalität abhängen, und die übliche Darstellung neuer Musik besteht *nur* aus solchen Versäumnissen. Daher ist sie dann *mit Recht* unverständlich. – In Weberns op. 5 waren vielfach die Temporelationen so verzerrt daß die der Form verschwanden; z. B. im I. Satz Takt 14-16 schon viel zu rasch. Ebenso das a tempo Takt 51 außer aller Proportion schnell – Am Anfang von III. [ging] das col legno Sechzehntel verloren und damit *alles* Spätere. In V war nicht zu verstehen, daß der Pizzicato Akkord Takt 9 *identisch* ist mit dem vorausgehenden arco. 42

*

Der erste Satz der V. von Beethoven sehr rasch – jeder Versuch der Monumentalisierung schlägt in Gemütlichkeit um. Die Wirkung der ersten Takte keinesfalls durch Breite, sondern im vollen Tempo, aber am Frosch und mit schwerem Gegenakzent auf der ersten – auf den schlechten Taktteil fallenden – Note:

wenn man das nicht lieber nur liest.

*

Zum B-Dur-Trio von Beethoven[95], Aufführung Heifetz-Feuermann-Arthur Rubinstein. – »Zu schön«. D. h. hier: der sinnliche Wohllaut des Klangs schiebt sich vor die Realisierung der Konstruktion. Es wird alles geglättet. Z. B. das Überleitungsmodell des 1. Satzes gegen Schluß, unmittelbar vorm Seitensatz, verliert den Charakter der *Ferne,* des nicht ganz Da, der Aura, die für den ganzen Satz (wie für die Ferne Geliebte[96]) charakteristisch ist. Das 2. Thema setzt sich zu wenig als Charakter ab. Im Trio des Scherzos (das schon zu schön, gemildert einsetzt) geht der *Ausbruch* – damit der Kontrast zu dessen Nachsatz – dadurch der *Formsinn* verloren. Unmöglich der Strich der Wiederholung des Trios und der abermaligen des Scherzos, d[ie] hier wie in der VII. Symphonie eine architektonische Funktion hat. – Im langsamen Satz ist das Thema

43 mit Recht *fließend,* nicht geweiht genommen. Aber das bedeutet eine Verpflichtung – man kann dann nicht, um die Sechzehntel gemütlich zu spielen, in einer Variation viel langsamer werden (Eduard [Steuermann] sagt in solchen Fällen: man kann nicht hier und da den Rebbach haben). Solche »Verpflichtungen« – analog den von der Komposition selber eingegangenen – sind eines der *zentralen* Interpretationsprobleme. Der letzte Satz zu rasch, zu flüssig, ohne das Moment des Störrischen, des Widerstands, das »Flämische« (Rubinstein verfehlt einige der Akzente auf schlechtem Taktteil im Thema). Das ist aber keine Sache des »Geschmacks«. Sondern: die große Coda hat ihren Sinn gerade in der *Auflösung* des Widerstandsmoments in Bewegung. Fehlt jener, so findet diese nicht statt: es herrscht also Wechselwirkung zwischen Charakter und musikalischem Zusammenhang. – Man kann an dergleichen Dingen, wie den »absenten« Überleitungstakten oder dem verfehlten Themencharakter, erkennen, daß interpretative Phantasie die Bedingung der Realisierung der *objektiven* Gestalt ist. Diese das Gegenteil des »Residuums«.

*

Es ist nicht zu schwer, die richtigen Charaktere, und ebensowenig, die richtigen Tempi zu finden. Aber beides zugleich – das ist fast unmöglich, und das verweist auf einen notwendigen Widerspruch in der Sache.

*

In der guten Interpretation eines hochorganisierten Stückes
44 werden kaum je zwei Viertel chronometrisch einander gleichen. Aber es wird auch nicht zwei geben, die man nicht als auf eine *latente,* identische Zählzeit bezogen fühlte.

*

Über den richtigen Vortrag eines *Themas:*

1) es ist unbedingt notwendig, daß die charakteristischen Elemente eines Themas hervortreten. Ich hörte den Seitensatz der Melusinen-Ouvertüre[97] so, daß es anstatt

usw.

klang. Dadurch das *Ganze* unverständlich.

2) Der Seitensatz im 1. Satz der Pastorale hat einen ganz unscheinbaren Baß, der dann aber im doppelten Kontrapunkt erscheint, enggeführt wird usw. – es ist die Pointe der ganzen Stelle, daß ein an sich homophones Gebilde polyphon ausgelegt und dadurch, trotz seiner Unscheinbarkeit, dynamisiert wird. Dem muß aber die Darstellung Rechnung tragen, indem der Baß sogleich thematisch »gesetzt« wird, *ohne* aber durch den Vortrag überfordert zu werden, nämlich:

usw.

Und den Flöteneinsatz danach muß man *hören*.

*

Die Vortragsbezeichnung espressivo sagt: mit Ausdruck, aber nicht, was ausgedrückt wird, und das ist richtig. Aber nicht, weil ein allgemeiner, abstrakter Ausdruck wie ein Rahmen 45 den bestimmten, spezifischen einschlösse, sondern weil der musikalische Ausdruck nicht Ausdruck eines fixierten intentionalen Objekts ist. Er flammt gleichsam auf, um zu erlöschen. Was aber von der Darstellung durch espressivo verlangt wird, ist, daß sie diesen in der Musik gelegenen Gestus mitmacht. Espressivo spielen heißt: den immanenten Vollzug der Musik *nachmachen;* nicht an sich sein lassen, sondern durchs Subjekt sich zueignen, und darum stets in gewissem Sinn: die Musik übertreiben – etwa so, wie man übertreibt, wenn man ein Gesicht oder eine Stimme nachmacht. Die Augenblicke des espressivo sind die in denen das Neumische zum Konflikt mit dem Mensuralen kommt, wo dieser Konflikt zugunsten des Neumischen entschieden wird – und wo dieser Sieg als Vortragsbezeichnung in die Notierung der Komposition selbst aufgenommen ist. Daher hat das espressivo *immer* etwas vom Rubato, und Beethoven hatte den genau richtigen Instinkt, wenn er im Prestissimo von op. 109 nach espressivo »a tempo« schrieb. Dagegen sind Anstrengungen wie die Schnabels, den jeweiligen Inhalt des Ausdrucks festzulegen, bloße Spielerei.

*

Es ist erstaunlich, wie arm die *Skala* der meisten Interpreten ist. So kennen sie im Großen oft nur 2 Charaktere: den brillanten (Allegro) und den lyrisch Gesanglichen (Adagio); und darauf reduzieren sie eigentlich alles und fassen, was sich nicht so reduzieren läßt, als bloßen »Übergang« auf; z.B. Herr Bruno Walter, der so etwas auch theoretisch vertritt[98]. Der
46 Unsinn läßt sich an seinen Mahler-Platten im einzelnen dartun. – Oder: Instrumentalisten kennen nur: Melodie, Akzente (Ecknoten), »Läufe«, die laufen aber fallen gelassen werden; wissen nicht, daß man auch rasche Sechzehntel melodisch spielen kann (technisch gesprochen: nicht zugunsten der Akzentnoten vernachlässigen, durchwegs Skepsis gegen die guten Taktteile).

*

Zur Dialektik der Interpretation: wenn man, um des lyrischen Ausdrucks willen, Gesangsthemen z. B. bei Chopin zu *langsam* spielt, so fallen sie so auseinander, daß sie den Ausdruck verlieren, der stets einer überschaubaren Gestalt bedarf.

*

Man kann Musik auch *zu sehr* »darstellen«, »zelebrieren«, »zu ernst nehmen«, außer Verhältnis zu ihrer Substanz sie mit dem Gestus »seht einmal« vor Augen stellen. Oft bei Schnabel, z. B. den langsamen Satz des B-Dur-Konzerts von Beethoven. Die Intensität und Versenkung muß in Proportion zum Gehalt von Musik stehen; sonst wird diese überbelichtet und dadurch zerstört. – Sonst *sehr* hohes Niveau Schnabels, z. B. in der großen A-Dur-Sonate von Schubert. Nur manchmal das Abschmeckende, sich selbst Genießende. Aber wie schwer, das in technischen Kategorien zu fassen.

*

Im langsamen Satz der V. Symphonie (ist er übrigens wirklich
so gut?) nimmt Karajan den Forte-Einsatz der Celli und Bässe
in 32teln (kleine Partitur 60f.) nicht nur ff anstatt f, sondern
non legato, während ein Bindebogen steht. Da die Gestalt
sonst *überall* gebunden ist, kann es sich kaum um eine Kor- 47
rektur handeln. Sondern durch die Instrumentation ist die Hauptstimme sonst kaum zu hören; die Begleitung hat in der Tat das Übergewicht. Aber: durch Karajans Trick wird der *Charakter* entstellt und ein Kontrast durch den Klang gesetzt, den die Komposition nicht einlöst. Eine Änderung der Instrumentation, wie die Celli durch Bratschen und Fagotte zu verdoppeln wäre *weniger* treulos als die Darstellung, die den Wortlaut festhält (natürlich müßte dann das ganze Begleitsystem umgesetzt werden, was aber möglich wäre wohl ohne eine Note zu opfern). – Übrigens keine rechte Freude an der ganzen, sehr virtuosen Aufführung. Die Blechmelodien vielleicht

zu melodisch und ausgeglichen, im Widerspruch zur Idee von Beethovens Orchester; die monumentalen oder »charakteristischen« Gestalten im 3. u. 4. Satz auf Kosten des Tempos; alles zu sehr da, zu wenig aufblitzend und untergehend – dieser großartige Dirigent hat den *Hegel* an Beethoven nicht verstanden; man könnte sagen: die Darstellung des Geistes von Beethovens Musik tut ihrem geistigen Element Unrecht. Aber wie soll man das begreiflich machen, und wem?

*

Es muß *stets* Proportion zwischen Darstellung und Musik herrschen z. B. auch in dem Sinn, daß es läppisch ist, sehr einfache Musik, die keine Widerstände setzt, wie die beiden Sonatinen von Beethoven, zu *rasch* zu nehmen. (NB: auch das *Umgekehrte:* das Unbelastete darf nicht »ausgetitscht« werden!)

*

Wenn man den Satz streng nimmt, daß die Musik der Interpretation bedarf, so liegt der Gedanke nahe, daß diese jener
48 zuhilfe kommen muß. In der Tat weiß man etwa vom Operntheater, wie der Dirigent bei Stellen nachlassender Spannung das Tempo forciert und Ähnliches. Diese Tendenz wird sich überall da verstärken, wo der Gedanke an die Wirkung wesentlich ist. Aber gerade das weckt Zweifel am Prinzip. Die Interpretation, die »hilft« ist immer zugleich *verdeckend* und wird dadurch immer zugleich zum *Unrecht* an dem Gegenstand. Je höher Musik geartet ist, um so tiefer sind ihre Unvollkommenheiten und Fehler mit ihrem Besten verschränkt – wie oft ist das Beste gerade der gestaltete *und* die Gestalt sprengende Widerspruch. Schnabel »hilft« dem im herkömmlichen Sinn im Mittelteil sicher mißlungenen langsamen Satz der nachgelassenen A-Dur-Sonate von Schubert[99]. Er nimmt ihn improvisando und eilt über die wolkigen und brüchigen Stellen hinweg. Dadurch aber mutet er dem Satz eine Idee geschlossener

dynamischer Totalität zu, die er nicht einlöst, und macht die Sache nur schlimmer. Ist nicht das Fragmentarische, Diskontinuierliche, auch das skizzenhaft Unausgeführte *gegen* Beethoven gerade die *Idee* dieser Musik. Ist es nicht dem sehr bedeutenden Satz *wesentlich,* in die Brüche zu gehen[?] Ich erinnere mich aus meiner Jugend, eh ich nach Wien ging, meiner Neigung, bei Schubertsonaten wie der großen in a-moll mich *ganz* den Gestalten, auf Kosten der Tempi, zu überlassen, und ich glaube, das war richtiger als Schnabels Intention. Interpretation rettet die Musik indem sie sie in ihrer Fehlbarkeit – und deren Sinn – aufdeckt und ihr *vergibt.* Musik bedarf der Interpretation: als *Kritik,* die ihr die Ehre der absoluten Wahrheit antut.

*

Ich hörte den alten Mascagni, auf Platten, die Cavalleria dirigieren. Es war alles viel zu langsam, bis zum Grotesken, und 49
daher völlig unwirksam. Es gefiel ihm so gut; er war so stolz; er konnte sich von keinem Takt trennen. Und damit hat er sein chef d'œuvre zerstört. Zur wahren Interpretation gehört ein Stück *Wut* auf die Musik, die ihrer Idee in all ihren Erscheinungen geopfert wird. »I just hate music.«[100]

*

Die falsche Darstellung, die auf das sinnlich Einzelne, den Wohllaut, die schöne Melodie aus ist, bescheidet sich nicht beim Atomistischen. Sie hat, als notwendiges Komplement dazu, ein falsches Bewußtsein von Totalität. Das ist Brio, Schwung – regelmäßig damit assoziiert (Toscanini, Walter). Anstatt daß der Fluß aus der Sache, den Impulsen des Einzelnen gewonnen wird, sind diese stillgestellt, werden aber in einen ihnen äußerlichen, vorgegebenen Fluß – den des »Temperaments« der Darstellung – gewissermaßen eingetunkt. Dies ist eines der Hauptphänomene des üblichen Musizierens und es wird eine der Hauptaufgaben sein, es konkret zu bezeichnen. Es besteht meist in einem abstrakten Vorrang des Tempos über die Charaktere, der ebenso verkehrt ist, wie wenn die Charaktere sich undialektisch verselbständigen –

*

Die Regel, gegen das Schema zu musizieren, das Subkutane herauszubringen, schlechte Taktteile, Dissonanzen zu spielen usw. darf nicht mechanisch-undialektisch aufgefaßt werden. Denn das Schema war der traditionellen Musik nicht *nur* äußerlich, und je größer sie war, um so weniger äußerlich war es. Vielmehr war es konstitutiv und hat die Gegenkräfte selbst mitgezeitigt. Das heißt aber: sie war ein Spannungsfeld (daß es
50 keine radikal nominalistische Musik gibt, daß auch die radikale neue Musik, wie sehr immer verborgen, Rudimente traditioneller Formen enthält, ist eine andere Seite des gleichen Sachverhalts). Die Interpretation muß dies Kraftfeld aktualisieren. Also nicht *nur* die Dissonanzen spielen und die Konsonanzen fallen lassen, sondern die *Spannung* zwischen beidem nach Maß des kompositorischen Sinnes realisieren. Man muß die Konsonanzen, die guten Taktteile, die Grundzählzeiten durchfühlen – nur in Relation zu ihnen lebt das andere. Was wären die $\frac{3}{2}$-Takte, die im letzten Satz des Klavierkonzerts von Schumann im Seitensatz sich ergeben, wenn man sie nicht als eine Art Paradoxie gegenüber dem tragenden $\frac{3}{4}$-Takt empfände? Das heißt aber: auch dieser muß, als Hintergrund, verwirklicht sein. Solche Besinnungen gelten *vor allem* für die Beethovensche Synkope, und für die Konstruktion bei Brahms.

*

(nach einer älteren Notiz[101]) Vielleicht (!) läßt sich etwas allgemeiner sagen: die wahre Reproduktion ist *nicht* einfach die Realisierung des Befundes der Analyse. Das ergäbe einen un-

erträglichen Rationalismus und setzte tendenziell die Musik-
wissenschaft als Instanz der musikalischen Darstellung ein.
Sondern sie muß das idiomatische Element als aufgehobenes
in sich enthalten. Insofern die Notenschrift nicht nur Zei-
chensystem sondern Modell einer Nachahmung ist, muß die
Analyse das Nachzuahmende herausstellen das im Text sich
verschließt, aber es nachzuahmen bleibt nach wie vor die Auf-
gabe der Reproduktion und in ihr ist das Moment der Sponta- 51
neität gefordert. Ich muß wissen was ich nachahmen will, aber
um es nachahmen zu können, bedarf es der Musikalität. Bei
Schnabel z. B. war das Wissen ums Nachzuahmende außeror-
dentlich, hatte aber zugleich das nachahmende Vermögen *ge-
stört*. Ein Schulfall war ein Pianist wie Heinz Hirschland[102]; die
Gefahr meiner Reproduktionstheorie ist nicht unähnlich der
welche von der Psychoanalyse droht. Wahre Interpretation ist
weder die irrational-idiomatische (Kritik des Musikanten)
noch die analytisch reine, sondern die Wiederherstellung des
mimetischen Elements durch die Analysis hindurch. Das
Neumische ist eigentlich die Anweisung darauf. – Exempla-
risch in meinem Sinn ist Kolisch.

*

Notenlesen und musikalisches Bezugssystem. Das schnelle Vorauslesen beim Abspielen, das Erraten der Fortsetzungen, das Schumann geradezu als ein Kriterium des Musikalischen betrachtet[103], setzt die Tonalität voraus (übrigens ist es vielleicht eines der merkwürdigsten Charakteristika Bruckners, daß er diesem Kriterium *nicht* genügt, ohne doch zu »überraschen«. Das meine ich mit dem Gegen den Strich Komponieren. Enorm das Auflösungsfeld des Hauptthemas der VII.[104], wo, nach einem Augenblick der unerhörtesten Epiphanie, der in der Reprise *nicht* wiederholt wird, ein Flüstern anstatt der »Konsequenz« folgt. *Warum* – das muß die wahre Reproduktion zeigen). In einem gewissen Sinn setzt die neue Musik den traditionellen – idiomatischen – Begriff des Musikalischen außer Kraft; das sehen, wie sehr vieles, ihre Feinde richtiger als die Freunde; dem hat die wahre Reproduktion Rechnung zu tragen und von da aus die traditionelle Musik zu verfremden. Und durch diesen Prozeß muß die Reproduktion einem höheren Begriff des Musikalischen zur Geburt verhelfen. Übrigens erlaubt auch in nicht-tonaler Musik die Erfahrung der Tendenz, des »Triebleben der Klänge«[105], gewisse Antizipationen.

*

Lärmempfindlichkeit ist die Musikalität der Unmusikalischen.
52 Folgerung daraus: keine Scheu vor den dynamischen Extremen, auch dem dreifachen Fortissimo. Die Zonen, in denen Musik unhörbar oder unerträglich wird sind die, in denen sie das Einverständnis aufsagt. Nichts schädlicher als das Maß des mf.

*

In den Orchesterwerken des Wiener Klassizismus sind das Hauptproblem die Blechbläser, die im Forte wie Melodieträger hervortreten, es meist aber nicht sind, sondern bloße harmonische Verstärkung. Der Eindruck des Sinnlosen, der dadurch entsteht. Ich weiß nicht, was tun. Einmal, meine ich, soll die Interpretation nicht »helfen«; zum anderen kann man kaum Entstellungen der Struktur dulden. Immerhin, glaube ich, lassen Instrumentationsretuschen sich vertreten. Denn hier schmückt ja nicht die Retusche einen Mangel der Komposition (vgl. S. 48), sondern macht sie deutlich. Aber wo ist die Grenze? Wie weit gehört nicht gerade das »sinnlos« verstärkende Blech bei Beethoven zu dessen *Sinn?* Und wenn man mit den Retuschen anfängt, hört man dann nicht mit Hollywood-Adaptionen und Herrn Korngold[106] auf? Man stößt hier auf die Kontroverse über den Historismus.

*

Agathe[107] pflegte von gewissen verlogenen Stimmen zu sagen: die singt wie eine Sängerin. Von Toscanini, Sommernachtstraumouvertüre: die Geißen des Apennin haben den deutschen Wald abgefressen. – Von einem ihr verhaßten Brucknersatz: Ganghofers Leichenbegängnis mit ausgestopften Hirschen.

*

Bowl 14. Juli 53[108]

Auch die Phrasierung ist aus dem musikalischen Sinn zu entwickeln. Wenn z. B. im langsamen Satz der Pastorale – einem bei Beethoven völlig exterritorialen Stück – ein Takt dreimal hintereinander wiederholt wird, so bedeutet dies eine Stauung, gleichsam ein nicht Loskommen, in äußerster Absicht (Form als Mittel des Ausdrucks). Also darf auch die Interpretation nicht »fließen«. Mit anderen Worten, die wörtlich wiederholten Phrasen müssen, wie erneute Ansätze, durch seis noch so minimale Luftpausen von einander getrennt sein. 53
Bruno Walter sucht sie sinnwidrig im »Fluß« zu halten und läßt das Fagott ohne jede Phrasierung spielen, wie er überhaupt die Neigung hat, Phrasen zu verschleifen. Sein Musizieren ist durch die *Angst* determiniert, der Hörer könnte »ausgelassen« werden, nicht durch die Sache. Entweder er verliert sich, pikfein abschmeckend, an Details (was Karl Kraus für die Liebe sagt, gilt genau für die Musik – Trennung vom »Tisch«[109]), oder er treibt, wo er Langeweile fürchtet. Er spielt bewundernswert auf dem Orchester Klavier, aber das Orchester *ist* kein Klavier d. h. es muß eine Proportion herrschen zwischen der Art des Modifizierens und dem Material – ein Orchester kann nicht auf die gleiche Weise frei spielen wie ein Quartett oder ein Klavier, weil sonst das Improvisatorische scheinhaft wird; die Abweichungen müssen im Orchester viel *feiner* sein. Walter weiß das nicht – etwas Ordinäres in seiner Empfindungsweise, Differenziertheit, die mit Keulen dreinschlägt. Lyrischer Theaterkapellmeister; ohne Sinn fürs Anti-

thetische, Durchbrechende. Bei Beethoven zum Beispiel, im letzten Satz der Pastorale, der Einsatz des Fortsetzungscharakters

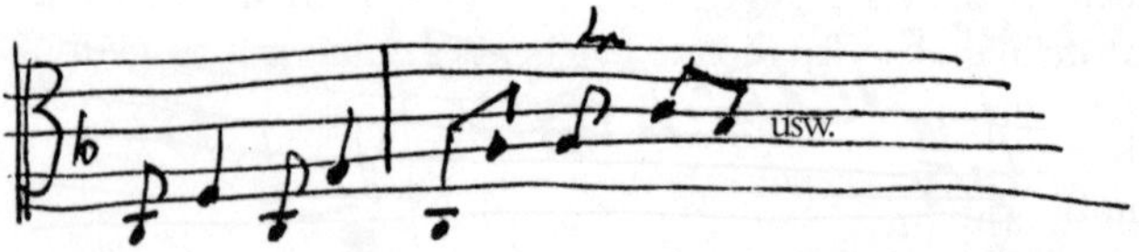

so wenig marcato, daß das Moment des Weitertreibens durch den subjektiven Eingriff, so zentral bei Beethoven, völlig verloren geht. In der Egmont-Ouvertüre vertuscht er die Dissonanzen; bei der Modulation im Seitensatz, wo er um der Perspektive willen ausspielen lassen müßte, hastet er aus Angst vorm rhythmischen Stillstand weiter. – Bewundernswert nur seine Abwehr des Mechanischen (alles bei Walter ist Abwehr). Wie er z. B. den Vogelimitationen in der Pastorale durch ein minimales, Mahlersches Unregelmäßiges der Einsätze, das Lächerliche nahm, das macht ihm so bald niemand nach. Einzelne vorzügliche Tempi mit dem Moment des Gebremsten, auch Gelassenen (1. und 3.Satz); nur hält ers nicht lang aus, es muß etwas geschehen.

*

54 Es ist *richtig,* wie Walter das Siegfriedidyll chorisch, nicht solistisch aufzuführen, denn: 1) das Perspektivische, »Auratische« fordert das *Unendliche* des chorischen Streichertons, nicht das Endliche, Abgesetzte des solistischen. 2) der al fresco-Charakter der Komposition erlaubt nicht die Distinktheit, das Thematischwerden des Einzelnen, wie es im Sinn einer zu nahen, zu »deutlichen« solistischen, kammermusikalischen Aufführung läge. Gegenteil einer Kammersymphonie. Also: Besetzungsfragen, Klang im Verhältnis zum musikalischen Sinn.

*

Wesentliche Forderung, daß sukzessive Melodienoten stets als auf einander bezogen faßlich werden. Z. B. im langsamen Satz der Pastorale (S. 37):

Dies ist besonders schwierig wegen des Registerwechsels der Klarinette und wegen des fp auf dem f. Man kann es erreichen: 1) indem man auf das g *crescendiert,* sodaß der Akzent auf dem f nicht die Linie zerreißt; 2) indem man das kritische Intervall, die None g-f, *legato* spielt, um keinen Preis zwischen beiden die geringste Atempause (wie bei Bruno Walter). – Analoge Probleme auf erweiterter Stufenleiter in kontrapunktischer Musik, wo die Hauptstimme von einem zum anderen Part springt. Es muß nicht nur immer H‾ hervortreten, sondern vor allem auch der Anschluß jeder Hauptstimme an die andere klar werden, entweder phrasiert oder *lückenlos, nie* aber dem Zufall überlassen. Die sogenannte Unverständlichkeit neuer Musik beruht in weitem Maß auf Verstößen gegen diese Regel. Die sukzessiven, nicht nur die simultanen Verhältnisse der Stimmen zueinander müssen realisiert *werden.*

*

»Tradition ist Schlamperei« – der Satz Mahlers ist der genaue 55
Ausdruck fürs Absterben des idiomatischen Elements, das dem mensuralen und neumischen das Feld räumt.

*

Die Forderung nach *Deutlichkeit* des musikalischen Zusammenhanges geht doch jeder anderen vor (obwohl sie von der

des Sinnvollen nicht getrennt werden kann, ja endlich mit dieser konvergiert). Z. B. in der Aufnahme der VII. von Beethoven, Furtwängler und Wiener Philharmoniker, in der Einleitung, kleine Partitur S. 3 [Takt 15 f.] ist einmal, unglücklich gesetzt, der cantus firmus in den 2. Geigen unter einem ff-Akkord der gesamten Bläser und über dem ff-Sechzehntelmotiv in den Bässen. Bei Furtwängler waren die 2. Geigen nicht zu hören und dadurch entstand ein thematisches Loch, durch das die ganze Einleitung, wüßte man sie nicht auswendig, sinnlos geworden wäre. Man müßte natürlich den Bläserakkord (und die Bratschen) mit einem schweren sff einsetzen lassen, dann aber sofort ihn diminuieren, damit die Hauptsache durchkommt. Furtwängler hält sich ans Geschriebene (kein diminuendo steht da), zerstört den Zusammenhang. Die ganze Einleitung ist fast prohibitiv schwierig, und zwar um, nachdem man sie erst in Halben hört, in die Sechzehntelbewegung hereinzukommen, die man natürlich auf Viertel bezieht (Beethoven hat *nicht* Alla breve geschrieben). Im Takt 2 der 2. Seite [Takt 9], bei der Ausweichung, wird man fast immer konfus. Ich glaube, am besten *ritardiert* man diesen Takt (was mit dem diminuendo sich ganz von selbst macht), so weit, daß man gut quasi a tempo in die $\frac{1}{16}$ auf der Dominante kommt. Ganz sicher bin ich nicht (ähnliche Probleme in dem großen Präludium in Es aus dem 1. Bd. des Wohltemperierten Klaviers). Übrigens hat man bei Furtwängler bereits den (halb-thematischen) Flöteneinsatz im 6. Takt nicht gehört. – Nach dem crescendo im 4. Takt [Takt 66] des Hauptsatzes, unmittelbar vorm p-Einsatz des Hauptthemas, kann man leider *keine* minimale Luftpause machen wegen des Sechzehntelauftakts der Streicher. Es muß also die Dynamik, das p subito, *anstelle* der Phrasierung treten, deren Funktion übernehmen. – In der Schlußgruppe S. 31
56 [Takt 52-55] der Hauptrhythmus in den Bässen nicht zu entnehmen, wieder unverständlich. – Gegen *unmotivierte* Modifikationen, z. B. die Neigung, Homophones rascher zu nehmen als Polyphones. Furtwängler nimmt die etwas verwickelte Durchführungsepisode S. 42 f [Takt 220-235] vorsichtig, un-

merklich langsamer. Das mag man gern konzedieren. Aber dann bekommt er Angst (Grundgefahr *aller* Interpretation) und wird ab S. 44 [Takt 236] viel zu plötzlich viel zu rasch ohne den leisesten Grund in der Komposition (viel eher verlangt die harmonische Spannung im Steigerungsteil eine *Stauung* des Tempos). – Das Allegretto wie alle anderen *viel* zu langsam aber doch schön; Furtwängler wäre der größte lebende Dirigent, wenn er zufällig dirigieren könnte. Nur das Trio nicht genug ausgespielt, Klarinetten Einsatz S. 88 [Takt 117] zu schwach, S. 89 [Takt 128] nicht genug hergegeben. Unvergleich[lich] schön brachte Furtwängler im letzten Satz die Dissonanz S. 173 [Takt 66] u. 199 [Takt 277]. Überhaupt keine sinnlose Note; aber völliges Überwiegen des Neumischen übers Mensurale.

*

Die Frage des Uninterpretierbarwerdens müßte sich an technischen Tatbeständen konkretisieren lassen. Z. B. Beethoven VII. Symphonie, Finale, die im letzten Takt auf S. 169 [Takt 36] beginnenden imitatorischen Streichereinsätze. S. 170 [Takt 37 f. u. 41 f.] sind durch die Setzweise und die unglückliche Lage 2. Geigen und Bratschen wohl nicht durchzuhören. Würde man retouschieren, etwa durch Klarinetten und Fagotte verdoppeln, die sogar frei sind, so käme ein Beethoven ganz fremder Klang herein; das Zufahrende der Streicher würde gemildert und vor allem das Ungemischte, »Reine« von Beethovens Farbe (seine *refus,* das heroisch-Asketische, sind ein integrales Element der Komposition). Läßt man die Stelle wie sie ist, so wird sie im strengsten Sinn unverständlich. Sie ist also wirklich uninterpretierbar. War sie es schon immer? Eigentlich glaube ich es nicht – wahrscheinlich weil man *alles* leiser, weniger monumental spielte und weniger »deckte«; aber auch das wäre heute unmöglich und klänge, wie wenn man Beethoven eine Perücke aufsetzte. – Einen Ausweg wüßte ich: wenn man an dieser Stelle, und *nur* ihr und analogen, die Streicher durch zusätzliche *Streicher* verstärkte. Dann

bliebe das Kolorit gewahrt, und die Einsätze kämen durch.
57 Aber kein Kapellmeister ließe darauf sich ein, und es muß zugegeben werden, daß die außer in ein paar Takten herumlungernden Geigen und Bratschen etwas Lächerliches und Dilettantisches hätten (schon das Piccolo in Schönbergs op. 26 ist etwas komisch). Solche optischen Dinge sind vom Sinn der Musik schwer zu trennen, so äußerlich sie scheinen.

*

1954 Frankfurt

Der Text muß zentral eine Theorie der *Improvisation* enthalten, denn was Interpretation im prägnanten Sinn ausmacht, ihr »Problem«, ist immer dem Improvisatorischen verwandt. Es ist beides: archaistisch, »musikantisch«, falsches Zurück hinter die Objektivität des Textes durch das *Als-ob* der Unmittelbarkeit d. h. daß das Notierte aussieht als wäre es das Produkt der Spontaneität des Spielers (»kommt a Walzer heraus«) – und die *Aufhebung* der Verdinglichung durch den musikalischen Sinn der den Text suspendiert, die Brechung des Mythos der Musik als da ist: die Philologie, das mensurale Element. Zwischen diesen Polen spielt die *Dialektik* der Improvisation und sie wird zu entfalten sein. Alle Wahrheit und die meiste Unwahrheit der Interpretation ist improvisatorisch: es führt eine gleitende Skala von *jeder* sinnvollen Wiedergabe zu[r] vollen Interpretation. – Meine alte Beobachtung daß »colla parte«, »frei« usw. Bestandteile des *Textes* wurden. Das improvisatorische Element wird eingebaut als Schutz gegen die Schrumpfung und eben das ist unmöglich und befördert nur die Herrschaft der Vergegenständlichung des Textes, der Entfremdung. Am Problem der Improvisation läßt etwas von der Unmöglichkeit von Musik selber sich ablesen. – Improvisation auf der Schwelle zur *Komik,* enger Zusammenhang mit dem musikalisch Dummen. – Wie Beethoven improvisierte, läßt an der Solophantasie für Klavier sich entnehmen, offenbar einer für einen Freund aufgeschriebenen Lieblingsimprovisa-

tion: die Form des abschnittweisen Komponierens in »Intonationen«[110] (wie auch in den Phantasien von Mozart): *ohne Wiederholungen.* – Oberste Regel der Interpretation des Im- 58
provisatorischen: nichts Improvisatorisches darf wiederholt werden. – Das irreversible *Absterben* der Kunst des Improvisierens ist ein *Hauptargument* für meine These vom Absterben der Interpretation überhaupt.

28. März 1954

*

Zu meiner in dem großen Bachaufsatz[111] niedergelegten Anschauung von dessen Interpretation lassen noch einige sehr zentrale Argumente sich beibringen. Vor allem: wenn man schon den *vokalen* Ursprung der Bachischen Polyphonie hervorhebt, das *Gesungene* der Stimmen, dann ist es unsinnig, für die Darstellung gerade das Moment zur Ausschließlichkeit zu erheben, das dem Gesang, als dem von Subjekten, schlechterdings versagt ist. Polyphonie des Chors heißt: Objektivität durch die Vereinigung der Subjekte, nicht durch deren Eliminierung (NB enger Zusammenhang mit meiner Kritik an der Residualtheorie der Wahrheit[112]). – Dann: Bach hat, außer für Orgel und Cembalo, ja nicht nur fürs Clavichord sondern für *Streicher* geschrieben, also ein *an sich* den mechanischen Instrumenten entgegengesetztes Medium. Wie könnte man also jene zum Kanon der Interpretation erheben?

*

Meine These, daß die Differenzierung der begrifflichen Mittel zur Erkenntnis von Musik weit hinter dieser zurückgeblieben ist, gilt auch für die Interpretation. Es gibt eine Menge kritischer Kategorien, die etwas Wahres treffen, ohne ins Material selbst sich hereinzubegeben und sie wären von einer zureichenden Theorie zu »übersetzen«. Ich nehme einige der am bedenklich klingendsten, journalistischen, wie das »Fluidie-

59 rende« oder die aus dem Witz über Nikisch berühmte »Faszination«[113]. Das *gibt* es. Aber weder ist es ein musikalisch Unerklärliches, etwa bloß Psychologisches (das Psychologische, die Suggestion oder Übertragungskraft, ist bloßes Vehikel; übrigens: was bedeutet sie? Hat sicher viel mit dem neumisch-mimetischen Element zu tun), noch lassen sich, wie Rudi [Kolisch] einmal dachte, *einfache* technische Korrelate dafür angeben (wie es z. B. bei einer Kategorie wie *Schwung* wahrscheinlich noch möglich ist als der durch bestimmte Verbindungsmittel wie Phrasierung und Dynamik herzustellenden Einheit relativ getrennter Gestalten in der Darstellung: das Hinwegtragen über äußerliche und tiefere Cäsuren); aber einer zum Selbstbewußtsein erhobenen Interpretationslehre, der in sich selbst reflektierten Technik, müssen sie zufallen. Fluidum ist wohl der musikalische Sinn, soweit er durch die Interpretation als unmittelbar, als musiksprachlich erscheint; darin das Positive *und* Negative dieser Kategorie. Weiter verfolgen. Unter keinen Umständen darf die Theorie *je* mit Kategorien wie Persönlichkeit usw. sich abspeisen lassen.

*

Lieder werden fast ausnahmslos viel zu langsam dargestellt, weil Sänger die Stimme zeigen und Ausdruck oft auf Kosten der Musik geben wollen (meine Erfahrung mit Karl Erb[114] in Reutenen). Paradoxie: die Stimme, als Träger des Menschen, also des Zwecks, zugleich Mittel, Instrument, und dies wird ihr sehr schwer um ihres Leibhaften, Lebendigen willen. Sie muß zum Instrument gemacht *und* darin bewahrt werden. Wird sie *nur* Instrument, ganz sich entfremdet, dann tritt das von Agathe bezeichnete Phänomen »wie eine Sängerin singen« ein. – Lieder werden oft schon vom Komponisten zu langsam bezeichnet, z. B. die Mainacht von Brahms die natürlich in Halben, nicht in Vierteln geht. – Eine für Sänger sehr
60 charakteristische Verzerrung der Anfang von Brahms' »Auf dem Kirchhof«. Sie singen:

 anstatt 

wodurch die Musik sich in Unsinn verwandelt. Über die Darstellung dieses Liedes ließe sich eine ganze Abhandlung schreiben. – Was ich von Bruno Walter sagte, gilt vor allem auch für *Pianisten:* sie verfügen nur über 2 Charaktere, den »schöner Anschlag« und den »brillant«. Dadurch wurde z. B. die Berceuse von Chopin bei Karolyi[115] ganz entstellt. Von den $\frac{1}{32}$eln an Fiorituren, nicht – schnelle – Melodie; dadurch der Zusammenhang des Ganzen, die quasi Variationsform, unverständlich, keine *Vermittlung.* Überhaupt: Charakter der Vermittlung.

*

Berg, Kammerkonzert, vor meinem Vortrag in Stuttgart »Das Altern der neuen Musik«[116]. Ungeheuer *vorsichtige* Aufführung, kein Mensch wagt eine Melodie auszuspielen, nicht einmal der Pianist die 1. Variation, und vor lauter Vorsicht, ohne Wagen, wird es unartikuliert, konfus, genau so wie Dilettanten die moderne Musik sich vorstellen. Demut, Zurückhaltung sind in der Musik zweifelhafte, gefährliche Tugenden, so wie wenn man im Leben vor extremen Entschlüssen zurückschreckt und nichts riskiert, man alles verlieren kann. In diesem merkwürdigen Sinn ist Musizieren wirklich Spielen. – Mein Vortrag hatte viel mehr Erfolg als die Musik meines Alban. Ich hätte mich vor Scham verkriechen können. Auch dies, daß die Leute lieber über Musik reden hören als diese selbst, gehört in eine Geschichtsphilosophie der Interpretation.

*

Gegen primitive, unlautere Mittel der Darstellung, z. B. wenn man bei Chopin ein klingendes Piano dadurch darstellt, daß

61 man nur die Begleitung p oder pp, die Melodie aber mindestens mf spielt. Real spielen. Sehr wichtiges modernes Kriterium.

*

Bei vielen in der Tempogestaltung schwierigen Sätzen findet sich ein Takt oder eine Stelle, von der aus das ganze Tempo sich erhellt. Im ersten Satz der (überhaupt, wegen Rudimenten von Unreife, sehr schwer darzustellenden) c-moll-Sonate op. 10, No. 1 von Beethoven schwankte ich, ob er in Vierteln oder ganzen Takten zu nehmen sei. Mit der Modulationsgruppe aber (nach der Generalpause) wird deutlich, daß der Satz nur in ganzen Takten gedacht werden kann, trotz der sehr großen Schwierigkeiten, die sich dadurch für eine der Hauptgestalten ergeben. – Übrigens, bei Interpretationsschwierigkeiten dieser Art stimmt meist etwas in der Komposition nicht.

*

sehr wichtig

Meine Theorie, daß alle musikalische »Form« sedimentierter Inhalt ist[117], muß für die Reproduktionstheorie fruchtbar gemacht werden. Aber das nächstliegende: die Reproduktion müsse den sedimentierten Inhalt »erwecken«, wäre viel zu grob. Einmal ist der Gehalt der Musik nicht jener Inhalt, sondern viel eher der Prozeß seiner Sedimentierung; und dann wäre sie jenes Inhalts auch gar nicht mächtig. Vielmehr also müßte die Reproduktion, als ein Vollzug, der immanenten Historizität der Komposition – die selber ein kodifizierter Vollzug ist – habhaft werden; ja hier liegt eines der Zentralprobleme von Interpretation überhaupt. Dazu der Gedanke von den aufblitzenden und sogleich *negierten* Intentionen – ist das nicht überhaupt das Gesetz der Interpretation als der Spannung von Ausdruck und »Ganzem«? – Überhaupt ist das Fragment über Musik und Sprache in die Reproduktionstheorie zu verarbeiten.

*

An *schlechten* Orchesteraufführungen (mein alter Palmengarten!) läßt sich lernen: wie jedes Orchesterwerk analytisch ist d. h. das Ganze farblich in seine Formelemente *zerlegt*. Die
Aufgabe der Reproduktion ist es, das von der Komposition 62
zerlegte wieder zu vereinen, und gerade das mißlingt: die Elemente bleiben unverbunden. Was aber hier so handgreiflich-stofflich sich zeigt, ist in einem höheren, geistigen Sinn das Problem *aller* Interpretation. Sie ist notwendig Auseinandernehmen und Zusammenfügen.

*

Natürlich gibt es mehrere Schichten der falschen Interpretation, eine ist die stoffliche des Nicht-Zusammenbringens (von falschen Noten usw. angefangen, rohem Klang usw.), die andere die der *unwahren* Interpretation, d. h. des Verfehlens des Komponierten. Aber beides hängt viel mehr von einander ab als der Laie weiß, der starre »Niveaus« unterscheidet. Der rohe Klang eines Militärorchesters kommt zum Teil von falschen Akzenten; und die geistige Insuffizienz von Toscanini führt zu stofflich falschen Tempi. Alles Geistige in der Musik hat seinen klangmateriellen Repräsentanten; man muß beides nur unterscheiden, um die Unterscheidung aufzuheben.

*

Aufzeichnungen nach der Darmstädter Vorlesung
gemeinsam mit Kolisch, August 1954[118]

Der Gedanke, daß kein grundsätzlicher Unterschied von alter und neuer Musik, ist in Beziehung zu setzen zum Begriff des Subkutanen, meinem Schönbergaufsatz und dem Radiovortrag zu dessen 80. Geburtstag[119]. D.h. die Idee der Aufdekkung des Subkutanen der traditionellen Musik durch die Interpretation entspricht dem Vorgang des das Innere nach außen stülpen, den die neue Musik selbst vollzogen hat. Dabei ist aber zu betonen, daß es sich nicht um die Darstellung des Skeletts handelt sondern des *Prozesses* des von innen nach außen Tretens. Mit anderen Worten, des Prozesses zwischen Tonalität (im umfassendsten Sinn) und Komposition.

*

Negativ ist die Theorie damit zu begründen, daß die *gesamte*
63 offizielle Interpretation der traditionellen Musik, die auf die Fassade abzielt, nicht nur das Innere verfehlt sondern ein Stück Kulturindustrie ist und daher selbst mensural *falsch* (Toscanini). Die alte Musik aus der neuen interpretieren. Was kann man an Schönberg über Beethoven lernen? – Die Kritik der Klangfassade entspricht der funktionalistischen am Ornament.[120]

*

Jede Interpretation steht prinzipiell vor *unlösbaren* Problemen. Es gibt eine absolut richtige Interpretation oder wenigstens eine zählbare Mannigfaltigkeit von solchen, aber sie ist eine *Idee:* nicht einmal rein zu erkennen, geschweige zu realisieren. Die Interpretation mißt sich an der Höhe ihres Mißlingens. – Daher: Zufälligkeit des Einsatzes bei der Arbeit des Interpreten, weil etwas *immer* falsch ist. Es gibt ins Kunstwerk unendlich viele Zugänge, aber nur ein Zentrum. Wenn ich ein Beethovenquartett wie op. 59, 2 analysiere, so ist es gleichgültig, ob ich von dem Rhythmus 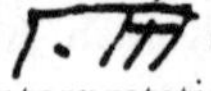 oder von dem Intervall der Quint[121] ausgehe – die Interpretationen müssen konvergieren.

*

Wenn auch die wahre Interpretation unbekannt und unrealisierbar ist – die falsche läßt sich stets, konkret agnoszieren.

*

Das gilt vor allem für den Begriff des musikalischen *Sinnes* als einen der bestimmten Negation par excellence. Er entzieht sich der Definition, ist nur höchst vermittelt zu bestimmen (dazu vgl. die Arbeit Über das gegenwärtige Verhältnis von Philosophie und Musik[122]). Aber was *sinnlos* ist: das läßt an jedem Augenblick von Komposition wie Interpretation bündig sich angeben. – Idee der Interpretation wäre: die integrale Darstellung des musikalischen Sinnes, des Komponierten. – Oder vom einzelnen her: eine Darstellung, in der es keine tote Note, kein totes Intervall, keine tote Pause gibt. Riemanns Begriff des toten Intervalls kritisieren. Er gehört dem abstrak- 64
ten Schema, grundsätzlich nicht der konkreten Komposition.

*

Die Theorie von der geschichtlichen Veränderung der Werke und der wahren – d. h. nicht historistischen – Interpretation ist vermittelt dadurch, daß der Prozeß, als den die Interpretation die Komposition darzustellen hat, eben der geschichtliche ist: daher die ältere von der fortgeschrittensten her. Das Kraftfeld, als welches die Interpretation die Musik je zu bestimmen hat, ist immer zugleich das Geschichtliche – die Dialektik von Besonderem und Allgemeinem. Dies halte ich für den *entscheidenden* Gedanken.

*

Zur Problematik des »Willens des Autors«, als einer Hilfskonstruktion, ist zu verweisen auf den »Willen des Gesetzgebers«. Dagegen

1) meist ist er unbekannt und nicht zu ermitteln.

2) die Musik – vermittelt durch den Text – hat gegen den Autor ein Eigenrecht. Dem hat Schönberg sich gebeugt.[123] Wie wenig an einem Werk, als der Einheit von Material und objektivem Sinnzusammenhang, gehört schon dem Autor. Meist nicht mehr als der spontane Akt der Synthesis. Der ist zwar entscheidend – aber durch den *Text* zu erschließen, nicht außerhalb von ihm
3) die Werke verändern sich: das heißt auch: gegen den Willen des Autors.

*

Zum Begriff des *mensuralen* Elements:
1) es allein gibt keine Musik. Der Inbegriff der Realisierung des Mensuralen allein wäre sinnlos. Gegen den
65 Begriff einer chemisch reinen Sprache der Musik. Sie wäre genau die, welche das innere Moment der Historizität eskamotiert, vergleichbar dem Logikkalkül im Verhältnis zur Sprache. Dazu auch: es gibt ein Idiom des *Interpreten,* Kreislers, d'Alberts, Kolischs und dies hat ein Recht, innerhalb der mensuralen Schwellen in die Darstellung einzugehen, ja es hat viel mit jenem Subjektiven zu tun, durch das hindurch die Objektivität des Sinnes sich konstituiert. Vielfach gewahrt der Interpret den Sinn des Mensuralen durchs Medium seines Idioms, das dann freilich hinter der Darstellung des Sinnes zurückbleibt, gleichsam abfällt.
2) das Mensurale ist *ungenau,* d. h. reicht nicht an die Musik heran. Die musikalische Schrift ist Gedächtnisstütze. Sie trägt nicht das Ganze, ist unvergleichlich viel zu undifferenziert, und dies ist ein Grundsätzliches, das auch bleibt, womöglich sich verstärkt, je feiner man notieren lernt (Beispiel der späte Webern!). Diese Ungenauigkeit ist aber genau das Maß der Differenz von Notation und Sinn.

3) die Notation ist nicht rein mensural, sondern zugleich weniger und mehr. Weniger: siehe (1) und (2). Mehr: sie hat neumische Rudimente. Daher Heranziehung nicht nur von Urtexten sondern von Autographen in denen meist das neumische Element dem mensuralen sich einprägt.

*

Beim Begriff des Mensuralen prinzipiell auf den Unterschied von Signum und Mimesis aus der Dialektik der Aufklärung[124] rekurrieren.

*

Zum Begriff des *Neumischen*. Er, als das eigentliche Element
der Unmittelbarkeit, ist durch den Sieg des Mensuralen zu 66
dem Vermittelten geworden und dies macht den genauen Sinn von Interpretation als einem Erschließen aus dem Text aus. Aber dies darf deshalb nicht zu primitiv verstanden werden, weil nicht nur die Schrift immer noch neumische Elemente (wie z. B. die Balken zusammengehörender Notengruppen) enthält sondern *Ersatzfunktionen* für die entschwundenen neumischen ausgebildet hat. Sehr gutes Beispiel die *Phrasierungsbogen*. Denn sie sind *nicht* mensurale Bogen – sonst bezeichneten sie legato, was sie nicht tun – sondern Einheiten der Struktur, des Sinnes. Die Interpolation des Sinnes im Text hat stets zum Hilfsmittel dessen neumische Elemente.

*

Der Begriff »Schlüssel« (in allen Sprachen) ist sehr interessant weil er genau den Übergang des Neumischen ins Mensurale festhält. Er bedeutet: dies musikalische Bild soll *exakt* dies und jenes bedeuten. Und es ließe sich sagen, daß der Weg der Interpretation der umgekehrte der Verschlüsselung sei. Der

Schlüssel sagt: das Bild ist ein Zeichen für dies; die Interpretation: das Zeichen ein Bild von jenem.

*

Die moderne Orgelbewegung und aller Objektivismus der Interpretation ist nicht bloß, wie ich bislang verfuhr[125], zu kritisieren, sondern abzuleiten. Es liegt ihm zugrunde die Erfahrung vom Absterben des idiomatischen Elements. Diese setzt sich um in eine Empfindlichkeit gegen musiksprachliche Elemente überhaupt. Vor allem gegen den *Ausdruck,* der als ar-
67 chaisch wahrgenommen [wird,] etwa wie der Kaftan von alten Juden. Aber in dieser Erfahrung verschränkt ein Legitimes sich mit einem Falschen. Das Legitime: nicht länger von dem Musikstrom, der eingeschliffenen und verfallenen Sprache sich tragen lassen. Das Falsche: Idiosynkrasie gegen den Sinn überhaupt, der an das Verdrängte mahnt, das eigentlich Mimetische. Anstelle von dessen Rekonstruktion, Vermittlung tritt die Beschränkung aufs Mensurale, als wäre es die Musik. Es wird die Emanzipation vom Idiom mit der Liquidation des Neumischen verwechselt. Aber das Verdrängte kehrt in falscher Gestalt wieder. So etwa in den oft grellen und skurrilen Registrierkünsten, von denen man wähnt, sie wären gegen das mensurale neutral. Oder allgemeiner, »sozialpsychologisch«: in der sektiererhaften, paranoiden Besetzung der objektivistischen Sphäre, mit sacred cows und Hexenjagd und Reinheit. Die Verdrängung des Affekts zieht allen Affekt auf sich. Dies gilt, in gewissem Maß, auch für Strawinsky. – Es bedarf aller subjektiven Innervation, um im Objekt zu erlöschen. Gegen Residualtheorie der Wahrheit. Der rein mensural gespielte Bach ist sensu strictissimo *sinnlos* d. h. falsch, unmusikalisch.

*

Das Verhältnis auch zum idiomatischen Element ist nicht einfach negativ, sondern dialektisch. Man muß es haben, um es

aufzuheben. Die wahre Interpretation muß gegen den Strich
musizieren d. h. gegen das musiksprachliche Gefälle die Kom-
position durchsetzen. Aber dazu muß immer zugleich das
musiksprachliche Gefälle mitvollzogen sein. Der Fehler der
Walchas[126] ist, daß sie es einfach ignorieren. Hier wird auf
Schnabel einzugehen [sein]. Er hat – wahrscheinlich als Reak-
tionsbildung auf ein sehr stark idiomatisches Element der
eigenen Musikalität, auf sehr viel »Dialekt« – besonders heftig
sich dagegen gesträubt, ist aber bei der abstrakten Negation 68
stehen geblieben d. h. hat es nicht als Vermittlung des Neumi-
schen in seine Darstellung mit aufgenommen. Daher das Ge-
walttätige; z. B. der Glaube, daß es schon geleistet sei, wenn
man eine Nebenstimme, einen Akzent hörbar macht, der
sonst unter den Tisch fällt, und darüber die Hauptstimme als
solche zu spielen versäumt.

*

Der Begriff der Rekonstruktion des Neumischen aus dem Mensuralen, die eigentliche Interpretation qua Dechiffrierung, hat als wichtigste Vermittlungskategorie die der *Analyse* als einer notwendigen Bedingung der Interpretation. Aber ihr Begriff ist vor dem rationalistischen Mißverständnis zu schützen. Zunächst heißt Analyse beinahe – nicht ganz – das Gegenteil dessen was gemeinhin darunter verstanden wird. Also nicht die Reduktion auf die traditionellen Formteile sondern auf die *spezifischen,* dem je einzelnen Werk eigenen Elemente, Triebkräfte, und vor allem ihren Zusammenhang zum Ganzen: wobei freilich die Dialektik dieser Elemente und der »offiziellen« der Form einen wesentlichen Gegenstand ausmacht, vor allem bei Beethoven, der mit der Komposition die Tonalität »konstruiert«, das Allgemeine nochmals aus dem Besonderen erzeugt[127] (die allgemeine Form und die Tonalität, das sind korrelative Begriffe). – Dann: die Interpretation ist nicht einfach die Darstellung des analytischen Befundes, oder nur die eines sehr radikal verstandenen, der wie die Elemente die Ge-

stalten und Zusammenhänge einbegreift. Was z. B. vom thematisch-motivischen Inhalt als solcher hervortreten soll, hängt immer von den ebenfalls von der Analyse herauszuarbeitenden *Funktionen* der Elemente ab, obwohl man wohl erwarten
69 darf, daß gegenüber dem sprachlichen Gefälle die Realisierung des spezifisch thematischen Inhalts meist schon sehr viel bedeutet. – Aber es liegt zwischen der Analyse und der Darstellung noch ein sehr wesentlicher Vorgang, der theoretisch noch zu entwickeln bleibt. Die Rede, daß man zur wahren Interpretation erst zu analysieren und dann die Analyse zu vergessen habe, kommt vermutlich dem Tatbestand recht nahe. Und genau die Phase ist das Erlöschen des Subjekts, der Intention, in der Sache (auch dem entspricht ein Moment der Komposition, s. das Fragment über Musik und Sprache).

*

Es gibt immer die Möglichkeit der *negativen* Darstellung. Man kann z. B. einem Thema die strukturell geforderte Emphase verleihen nicht nur durch Hervorheben, sondern auch durch extremes Pianissimo, und auch dies ist strukturell vorgezeichnet. Die Möglichkeit der negativen Darstellung bezieht sich auf *sämtliche* musikalischen Dimensionen.

*

Der Begriff der Phantasie, als des analytisch-rekonstruktiven Moments, bleibt *objektiv* zu bestimmen als genau jene Spontaneität, deren es zur Aufdeckung des Subkutanen bedarf. Sie erfindet nichts sondern durchbricht die Oberfläche; die Imagination eines verborgenen musikalischen Sinnes. Etwa Eduard [Steuermanns] Deutung zweier Takte aus den Variationen von Webern[128]. Benjamins Definition der Phantasie[129] heranziehen. – Rudi [Kolisch] und ich hatten im Kurs die Trennung von Gefühl und Verstand in der Musik angegriffen. Michael Mann[130] definierte sehr hübsch Phantasie als die Zone der Indifferenz von beidem. Gehört zur Theorie der »Analyse«.

*

Gegen die Trennung von Gefühl und Verstand in der Darstellung von der Sache her argumentieren. Hochorganisierte Mu- 70
sik heißt immer Gegenwart des Nichtgegenwärtigen, also Erinnerung und Vorblick, und dies ist vom Interpreten her stets eine geistige, kategoriale Funktion. Nur wer Musik nicht bloß fühlt sondern denkt, fühlt sie richtig. – Dies ist zugleich von der Sache her – abgesehen von der Kritik der Massenkultur – die Argumentation gegen das kulinarische Hören und Spielen, easy listening, die Passivität der Auffassung. Wer sich rein überläßt, verfehlt die Sache, der er sich überläßt.

*

Aufgabe der Analyse ist die Rekonstruktion des Neumischen aus dem Text. Die herkömmliche Interpretation, die um der Not des Mensuralen willen dieser Aufgabe sich nicht ganz entziehen kann, löst sie falsch, indem sie anstelle der immanenten Dechiffrierung den *Stil* von außen heranzieht und in ihm die Bürgschaft des Sinnes zu besitzen wähnt. Aber die Rekonstruktion läßt sich nur am konkreten Werk, nicht an dessen allgemeinem Begriff leisten; der Stil ist dem Sinn äußerlich, dessen bloßes Surrogat. Die wahre Interpretation *liquidiert* den Stil. Das läßt sich besonders an Mozart zeigen. Vgl. dazu Schönberg, Style and Idea.[131] Auch meine Definition von dem Stil als dem *Sprachähnlichen*[132].

*

Der Gedanke vom Absterben der Interpretation ist abzuleiten aus der Idee der wahren Interpretation und der *grundsätzlichen* Unmöglichkeit ihrer Realisierung.

*

Gegen das tonale Gefälle musizieren: das heißt zunächst einmal die musikalische Vorstellung realisieren. Und die steht im Gegensatz nicht nur zu den allgemeinbegrifflichen Momenten der Komposition, sondern ebensosehr auch gegen die von den instrumentalen (scil. und vokalen) *Spielweisen* herrührenden.
71 den. Kolisch insistiert darauf, daß die wahre Interpretation sich nichts soll von Stimme oder Instrument vorgeben lassen. Aber das bedarf einiger Einschränkung. Bis zu Beethoven hat man kaum eine Vorstellung unabhängig von der Spielweise in der Komposition realisiert; sein Wort von der erbärmlichen Geige[133] bezeichnet wohl eine Schwelle. Andererseits ist auch bei ihm noch kaum gegen die Klaviergriffe zu musizieren, die eher eine implizite Darstellungsregel litten. Erst der Klaviersatz von Schönberg ist ganz aus der Vorstellung des Klavierklangs aber nicht der pianistischen Realisierung geschöpft, vor allem seit op. 23. Und die instrumentalen Spielweisen sind seit der Wagnerischen Emanzipation der Farbe selbst zu einer kompositorischen Produktivkraft geworden, bei den Franzosen, bei Strawinsky, vor allem bei Hindemith, wo sie den Primat einnehmen (»Kritik des Musikanten«[134]). Es würde also nicht genügen, einfach *gegen* die Spielweisen oder unter deren Vernachlässigung die Musik darzustellen, sondern die Analyse muß auf den Stellenwert der Spielweise im musikalischen Zusammenhang führen, und danach hat dann die Wiedergabe zu verfahren.

*

Gegenüber jeglicher Konvention hat die rekonstruierende Reproduktion zunächst einmal das zu vollbringen, was Brecht *Verfremdung* nennt; ohne dies Moment ist die Aufgabe der Interpretation noch nicht einmal erkannt. Aber die Verfremdung ebenso wie die Grundthese, daß die traditionelle nur von der neuen Musik her dargestellt werden kann, ist polemisch zu setzen gegen den Begriff des Modernistischen. Es kann sich nicht darum handeln, die traditionelle Musik wie streamline-

Möbel neu aufzuputzen sondern die Verfremdung muß sich nach dem Kanon des musikalischen Zusammenhangs gegen die klangliche Oberfläche vollziehen. – Der Unsinn dessen, was mir ein Student in Darmstadt vorbrachte. Ein junger Münchner Komponist habe erklärt – offenbar unter Beziehung auf mich – die Dissonanzen bei Beethoven seien mittlerweile so abgebraucht, daß sie die ihnen zugemutete Funktion nicht mehr erfüllten. Um Beethoven zu aktualisieren, müsse 72
man ihm andere, gepfeffertere Harmonien unterlegen. Ob das nicht auch meine Meinung sei. Aber das verfehlt sich nicht nur gegen das mensurale Element und verletzt die Grundforderung der objektiven Realisierung, sondern isoliert auch naiv eine an sich richtige geschichtsphilosophische Erfahrung vom Zusammenhang. Denn Beethovens Dissonanzen sind nicht bloß für sich sondern im Verhältnis zu den Konsonanzen und haben nur gegen diese ihren Stellenwert. Ja ihre innere Struktur ist immer und ausnahmslos an der Tonalität gebildet; sobald diese Beziehung entfällt, wird das Ganze sinnlos. Von der neuen Musik her interpretieren heißt nicht Piscator, oder Hamlet im Frack.

*

Zur Frage der temperierten Stimmung. Schulfall des Musizierens traditioneller Musik von der neuen her, gegen die Spielweise. Daß neue Musik Galimathias wird, wenn man nicht enharmonische Töne identisch spielt, weil dann die Akkorde nicht mehr zu erkennen sind, liegt ja auf der Hand. Aber das gilt auch für die traditionelle, sobald man den Zusammenhang realisiert. Beispiel Beethoven op. 59, 2 erster Satz, Takt 72 f. Die einzelnen Akkorde blieben ja vielleicht noch verständlich, wenn man das es tiefer spielt als das darauf folgende dis. Aber der Sinn der Stelle ist die Identität in der Nichtidentität, d. h. die harmonische Differenz der beiden Akkordfolgen wird gefühlt nur gegen den verbindenden Ton als ihr *Gleiches*. Und das Schwanken zwischen entfernter Ober- und Unterdomi-

nantregion vom Ende der Schlußgruppe der Exposition ab
entscheidet zugleich über den *Formsinn* des Ganzen; nur wenn
die Extreme es-moll und h-moll deutlich sind, wird das Takt
82 erreichte As-Dur als vorläufiger Ausgleich gefühlt und da-
mit der ganze weitere funktionell harmonische Verlauf des
Satzes. Mit anderen Worten, folgt man der Spielweise, die
nicht enharmonische Identität anstrebt, so wird der gesamte
musikalische Zusammenhang sinnlos. – Es folgt übrigens dar-
73 aus, daß die kritischen Differenztöne f d bezw. e cis besonders
deutlich gespielt werden müssen.

*

Zum Problem des Kulinarischen, des schönen Tons. Es handelt sich nicht um ein Gegenbild des Klanges, sondern einfach darum, daß der Klang ein Mittel der Darstellung des Sinnes, des Modellierens ist und zwar ein um so wichtigeres, je mehr Oberflächenmittel der Artikulation wie Tempomodifikationen usw. entfallen. Modell der Behandlung des Klanges ist die Kunst des Ausinstrumentierens in der Komposition. Eigentlich muß jedes musikalische Element, je nach seinem Sinn und dem Sinnzusammenhang, *anders* klingen. Bestritten wird also jeder verselbständigte, von der Komposition abgelöste Klang und Ton (und damit implizit der meiste Musik-, zumal Gesangsunterricht). Er entspricht in der Interpretation notwendig einem atomistischen Musizieren. – Dann: wenn irgendwo, gilt beim schönen Ton wie allem sinnlich Wohlgefälligen der Einwand des Relativismus, der *hier* gerade vergessen wird. Der Ton des Zigeunergeigers, der das kleine Mädchen entzückt, ist mir widerwärtig. Es gibt überhaupt keinen Ton an sich – gerade das »Unmittelbare« ist vermittelt; der Ton des Zigeunergeigers klingt nach Nepp, der ganze Amüsierbetrieb ist in ihm sedimentiert (und noch in den crack-Geigern[135]). Und insofern freilich ist das Urteil über die sinnliche Qualität doch nicht willkürlich und zufällig sondern bestimmte Negation. Der Ton »an sich«, die »schöne Stimme« ist der Musik feind.

Dies steht hinter Rudi [Kolischs] Ausspruch.[136] – Natürlich ist nicht, wie jemand in Darmstadt meinte, der schlechte Instrumentalist vorzuziehen. Aber der gute muß über alle Möglichkeiten des Klanges in Freiheit, nach dem Maß der Komposition verfügen.

*

Zum Begriff der *Deutlichkeit*. Er hat zwei Bedeutungen. Einmal die klangmaterielle, daß man alles hört, was geschrieben ist, daß die Stimmen sich plastisch von einander abheben, daß kein Klangnebel entsteht, außer wo er in der kompositorischen Intention liegt. Hier wiederum der Begriff des deutlichen *Instrumentierens* der Kanon: so spielen, wie es deutlich, bei Mahler etwa, instrumentiert wäre. Dies ist als musikalische Forderung selbstverständlich, wird aber meist vor allem zugunsten des mittleren, ausgeglichenen Klangideals vernachlässigt. – Es gibt aber auch eine höhere, konstruktive Deutlichkeit, die in der Analyse fundiert ist. Sie ließe etwa so sich formulieren: daß der musikalische *Sinn* einer jeden Phrase im Ganzen deutlich werden muß – was keineswegs stets mit der klangmateriellen Deutlichkeit identisch ist. Es darf nichts von ungefähr gespielt werden, weil es so dasteht, ohne daß die Funktion genau erkannt und realisiert wäre (dies Versäumnis ist einer der Hauptgründe für die Unverständlichkeit vieler Aufführungen neuer Musik). Illustrieren mit op. 59, 2, erster Satz, Takt 82, die Dehnung (die Phrase ist $2\frac{1}{2}$ Takte lang anstatt der regulären 2). Grund: 1) es ist hier der erste (vorläufige) Ausgleich zwischen den divergenten tonalen Regionen, und damit ein Ruhepunkt erreicht. 2) Es beginnt hier der eigentliche erste Durchführungsteil, der wie oft bei Beethoven im Gegensatz zum zweiten entspannten, phantasierenden Charakter hat. Dies muß die Interpretation leisten durch große Deutlichkeit des Halts, also 74

1) quasi fermate, »frei«, sehr deutlich ausgehalten (aber dies bezieht sich mehr auf den Charakter, kaum aufs

Mensurale: es muß durch eine *Nuance,* nicht wie eine *wirkliche* Fermate bewirkt werden).

2) Akzent auf dem c als Ziel, aber dann sofort weg.

75 3) transparenter, irrealer ppp Klang, der sich deutlich von dem »thematischen«, realen Klang vorher unterscheidet. Vgl. dazu die Quint as-es der 2. Geige in [Takt] 83. Der Grund dafür ist die Baßnote zu besetzen und das Cello für das Hauptmotiv freizubekommen, aber wie in jeder guten Musik erzeugt hier die Komposition durch den Satz den richtigen Klang.

Es ist zu beachten, und zu realisieren, daß die Stelle ihre *Konsequenz* hat in der Coda, wo ihr [Takt] 215 f entspricht, bezeichnet f und diminuendo. Dies ist in [Takt] 82 so vorzubereiten, daß die Identität wahrgenommen wird.

*

Dem kulinarischen Einzelklang entspricht im Ganzen die Tendenz zu *glätten,* auszugleichen, Extreme zu vermeiden, zu vermitteln. Dies geschieht stets auf Kosten der Charaktere – der Deutlichkeit im höheren Sinn.

*

Thematisch musizieren heißt keineswegs stets die Themen hervorheben, »mit Nachdruck« spielen, wie Beethoven einmal verlangt, sondern *charakteristisch* spielen, also so, daß das Thema qua Thema sich unterscheidet, z. B. in op. 59, 2 durch das rasch Gleitende.

*

Der Behandlung der Darstellung der einzelnen musikalischen *Elemente* ist weit nachdrücklicher voranzustellen, daß ihre Trennung eine Verdinglichung ist, die aus der Schule kommt und nicht aus der Komposition. Nicht nur lassen sie sich für einander substituieren (z. B. Dynamik anstelle von Tempo-Modifikationen), sondern sie hängen überhaupt funktionell von einander ab, z. B. Klang von Phrasierung (als deren Mittel); Dynamik von Thematik, Tempo von Form. Dies wird zumindest zu belegen, vielleicht aber bis ins Einzelne zu entfalten sein aus der Idee des musikalischen Sinnzusammenhangs. – Der falschen Trennung der Elemente entspricht aber ihre Kontamination, z. B. die von Akzentuierung und Rhythmik. Man muß auch hier unterscheiden, um zu vereinen. 76

*

Grundregel fürs *Tempo:* durchwegs vertritt das Tempo die Totale, selbst den Oberbegriff, gegen das Einzelne, das Detail, so wie dieses von Klang und Charakterisierung gegen das Ganze in der Dialektik der Interpretation vertreten wird. Das Tempo ist als Einheit des Satzes so weit durchzuhalten wie es ohne Verletzung des musikalischen Sinnes möglich ist (Schnabels Tempomodifikationen in der Beethovenausgabe[137] ein zu *plumpes* Mittel der Artikulation. Dazu aber wichtige Einschränkung von Rudi [Kolisch]: das durchzuhaltende Hauptzeitmaß ist eine *Idee,* d. h. es braucht im ganzen Satz nicht eine einzige Zeiteinheit der metronomischen zu entsprechen und diese kann doch, als Resultante, herauskommen. – Meine eigene These geht sehr weit: es werden in thematischer Musik bei sinnvoller Darstellung niemals auch nur 2 Schläge einander chronometrisch gleich sein. – Die Identität des Tempos hat ihre Grenze am musikalischen Sinn, d. h. der Bedeutung des Einzelnen. Es ist leicht das Tempo in abstracto durchzuhalten, fast prohibitiv schwer im durchgehaltenen zumal *raschen* Tempo zu differenzieren. – Die Forderung der *raschen* Tempi hängt wesentlich mit der Einheit zusammen. Je rascher das Tempo, um so eher läßt ein Satz als Ganzer, als Einheit sich auffassen. Aber eben darin bereits wieder die Gefahr des Mechanischen, zumal diese Forderung vom positivistischen Musizieren falsch übernommen wurde. Grundsätzlich, etwa ge-

gen Wagner, vertreten, aber genau so »zart« wie dieser das langsame Extrem vertrat[138]. – Zur Theorie des Tempos des Ganzen die symphonische Idee des Einstandes der Zeit.[139] Das Tempo ist das beste, das dieser Idee am besten dient. Das kann
77 aber unter Umständen das chronometrisch *langsamere* sein, nämlich wenn dann die Gestalten deutlicher werden, deren Proportion den »Augenblick« zeitigt.

*

Wir diskutierten Rudi [Kolischs] Theorie der Tempi Beethovens[140]. Ihr zufolge gibt es eine zählbare Mannigfaltigkeit von Grundtypen, Grundcharakteren, den[en] jeweils ein identisches Tempo zugeordnet ist. Ich will das nicht bestreiten; es ist das eines der »mechanischen«, veranstalteten Elemente Beethovens, für welche die Abkürzungen seiner Schrift sprechen und etwa der Ausspruch über Naturgenie und verminderten Septimakkord[141]. Aber abgesehen von der – im Buch zu behandelnden – Frage, ob und wie weit die wahre Interpretation dem Werk in seiner Bedürftigkeit zu Hilfe zu kommen hat (und jeder wirkliche Interpret versucht das, das Finden der richtigen Lösung ist gar nicht zu trennen von der Suche nach dem kleinsten Übel, dem, was der Komposition relativ am besten bekommt), müßte doch im Rahmen der von Rudi entdeckten Identität weitgehend differenziert werden. Ich nannte den langsamen Satz von op. 59, 2 und den lydischen aus op. 132; Rudi fügte noch den der IX. Symphonie hinzu. Fraglos gehören alle drei zum Typus des langsamen Alla breve, mit sehr langsamen *Halben* als Einheit; die Viertel würde Rudi durchwegs = 60 ansetzen. Aber die Halben im E-Dur-Adagio und dem der Neunten sind Melodie-Halbe, die in op. 132 Choralhalbe, die als Melodie viel schwieriger aufzufassen sind. Ich würde also, um das Thema überhaupt erkennbar zu machen, diesen Satz am *raschesten* von den dreien spielen und damit im schärfsten Gegensatz zur Tradition. Nur so ist zu verhindern, daß der Satz nichts verbreitet als eine feierliche Stim-

mung, die in seiner Unverständlichkeit, einem Falschen,
gründet. Dazu kommen Erwägungen der Form und Propor-
tion. Wenn man die Halben in op. 132 nicht fließend nimmt,
ist das Tempo des $\frac{3}{8}$-Teils zu weit weg, eine Einheit überhaupt
nicht mehr wahrzunehmen. Nur der Satz der IX. hat den gro-
ßen Abgesang, dessen Sechzehntelsextolen den Halben des
Themas eine obere Grenze vorschreiben. Es ist auch für die 78
Proportionen zu berücksichtigen, daß hier der Mittelsatz $\frac{3}{4}$ ist,
also seine Einheit doch wohl *langsamer* als im lydischen Satz,
dessen Mittelsatz ich mir aus harmonischen Gründen in gan-
zen Takten denke. Vor allem aber, die *geistigen* Charaktere der
drei Sätze, des subjektiv-lyrischen aus op. 59, der Choralvaria-
tionen und des symphonischen Adagiotypus, sind so grund-
verschieden, daß es mir positivistisch dünkt, alle wegen der
relativ *abstrakten* Kategorie »Adagio-Halbe« im Tempo über
einen Kamm zu scheren.

*

Die grundsätzliche Unlösbarkeit des Tempos – daß es eigentlich für kein Stück ein richtiges gibt – ist Ausdruck des kompositorischen Antagonismus, der Unversöhnlichkeit von Ganzem und Teil in thematischer Musik.

*

Die Vorstellung des Tempos ist immer gebunden an die des *Gesamtcharakters* eines Satzes, der sich dann nach den Einzelcharakteren modifiziert – [aber] beim Tempo *minimal.*

*

Tempogestaltung als Funktion des musikalischen *Inhalts.* Beispiel Bergsonate.[142] Alles ineinander gearbeitet, vermittelt, auch die gegensätzlichen Charaktere. Gefahr des Dickichts. Daher hat hier die Tempogestaltung das Gegenteil des sonst

Notwendigen zu besorgen; die Differenzierung bei Innehaltung der Übergänge, schon bei der als rascher bezeichneten neuen Gestalt im Hauptthema. Aber all dies *innerhalb* der Spanne des einheitlich, aber als »Spielraum« vorgestellten Haupttempos. Ein scheinbar Äußerliches wie die *klein geschriebenen* Tempomodifikationen hat daran seinen genauen Sinn.

*

Erste Forderung der Tempogestaltung: Ermittlung der Einheit und ihres Maßes. Z. B. Beethoven, c-moll-Konzert, falls nicht schon notiert. Allegro con brio bezieht sich *nicht* auf die Alla breve-Halben, sondern das 𝄵 sagt nochmals dasselbe. Also *nicht:* 𝅗𝅥 = 138, sondern so rasche ♩, daß man 𝅗𝅥 denkt, also etwa 𝅗𝅥 = 80.

*

79 Daß das Tempo vom musikalischen Inhalt abhängt, heißt, daß es bei thematischer Musik innerhalb der mensuralen Grenzen grundsätzlich *flexibler* sein soll als bei einthematischer[143]

*

Musik muß verweilen können, – aber nicht sich selbst zuhören.

*

Das Tempo muß »neumisch« die Musik nachzeichnen (das wissen die Dirigenten, nur wird bei ihnen die Angst vor der langen Weile als eine vorm Hörer daraus). Also etwa in der Eroica kleine Partitur S. 12, nach der Generalpause[144] *nicht schleppen,* »vorwärts« (die Frage ist kaum zu schlichten, ob man damit den Sinn der Komposition realisiert oder ihr hilft – beides konvergiert). – Vom Sinn aus einen Satz »im Fluß halten«; zuweilen fordert der Sinn den *Eingriff* des Themas, z. B. op. 59, 2, 1. Satz, Takt 55-56, wo mit dem Quartsextakkord eigentlich schon die Kadenz erreicht ist. Die Musik aber interpoliert und diese Interpolation wird dadurch als *Kraft* der Form fühlbar, daß man nicht innehält, sondern die Musik weiterzieht. Dagegen ist es ganz *falsch,* die darauf folgende homophone Synkopengestalt zu accelerieren, weil man hier die Stauung nur soweit fühlt wie man der guten Taktteile bewußt ist, und da man keine Binnenbetonungen machen darf, so muß man die Zählzeiten streng innehalten. Das letzte Achtel in Takt 64 (aber ohne ritardando) schwer betonen, sodaß 2 Akzente auf einander folgen – Wiederherstellung des Gefälles, die komponiert ist, muß ausgespielt werden. Bei den Synkopen genau unterscheiden zwischen  in Takt 68 und den darauf folgenden ! Alles andere *nur* durch die Dynamik, das crescendo substituiert ein stringendo, das più crescendo ein ritardando. – Zum »die Musik weiterziehen« vgl. auch Eroica, kleine Partitur S. 16[145].

*

Je rascher und einheitlicher das Tempo wird, um so mehr nimmt die konstruktive Funktion anderer Darstellungsmittel besonders auch Akzente zu, insbesondere die von Klangdifferenzierung und Dynamik.

*

Grundaufgabe der Tempogestaltung: die Ermittlung der Haupteinheit bezw. des Temporaumes. Sie ist prinzipiell paradox. – Je rascher das Tempo desto wichtiger die Phrasierung – aber auch beim langsamen Extrem. 80

*

Zur *Dynamik:* gegen das mf als Norm (Rudi [Kolisch] sagt, Beethoven kenne kein mezzoforte). Wenn es eine Normalstärke gibt, wäre es die ohne alle Forcierung, also das p. Das Grund mf kommt von der falschen kulinarischen Vorstellung vom vollen satten Klang. Aber wahrscheinlich ist die Idee einer Normalstärke an sich schon falsch. – Von der neuen Musik her, die sich aus Extremen komponiert, dynamische Gestaltung nach den Extremen, wider range. Dies als Mittel der Artikulation und Freisetzung des Subkutanen besonders wichtig. Nicht einen mittleren Klang abwandeln, sondern die Stärke aus den Charakteren und ihrer Proportion entwikkeln. – Forderung weit größerer dynamischer Differenzierung: sie muß so weit gehen wie die Differenzierung der Komposition. Läßt sich vielfach aus den Charakteren ableiten, wo sie nicht notiert ist.

*

Dynamik ist nicht nur ein quantitativer sondern auch ein qualitativer Begriff d. h. *wesentlich* mit den Klangcharakteren verbunden. Es gibt z. B. ein p das da ist, ein reales p, und ein nichtpräsentes – dies ist vielleicht mit misterioso gemeint. NB die Arbeit sollte vielleicht eine Phänomenologie *aller* solcher Bezeichnungen enthalten, die sie in Kategorien des musikalischen Sinnes übersetzt und genau ausführt, was sie präzis musikalisch heißen. Oder wenigstens die *Idee* einer solchen Phänomenologie, und einige ausgeführte Modelle. *[Längs des linken Rands:]* sehr wichtig

*

Die Forderung nach dynamischer Charakteristik schließt die nach dynamischer *Ökonomie* ein. Um die Charakteristik zu ermöglichen, darf man die Stärkegrade nicht *verbrauchen.* Vor al-
81 lem größte Vorsicht mit Forte-Flächen. Oft genügt für das, wozu die übliche Darstellung den festgehaltenen Stärkegrad

einer ganzen Phrase braucht, ein Akzent; bei sf sofort weg anstatt den Akzent zu »halten« (dies in die Orchesterpraxis eingeführt zu haben[).] – Dies Desiderat berührt sich mit einem der wichtigsten der Darstellung von Polyphonie: für die Stimmen Luft schaffen. Dynamische Plastik heißt nicht nur Stimmen hervorheben, sondern mehr noch, die anderen zurücktreten lassen, vor allem *unbedingt* alles, was keinen melodischen Sinn hat. Akkordisch gedachte Stellen wie z. B. im ersten Satz der C-Dur-Symphonie von Schubert muß man akkordisch spielen (sehr vieler musikalischer Unsinn folgt daraus, daß man melodisch spielt, was nicht melodisch ist!). Also: nicht verbinden sondern (minimal) trennen; die Oberstimmen nicht stärker als die anderen; deutlich nur jeweils die harmonisch kritischen Töne.

*

Die Schönbergsche Unterscheidung von H¬, N¬ und unbezeichneter (d. h. absolut zurücktretender) Stimme ist prinzipiell auf die gesamte traditionelle Musik anzuwenden, jedenfalls die thematische; bei im strengsten Sinn polyphoner liegen die Verhältnisse, wie Schönberg richtig gesehen hat[146], etwas anders. – Die übliche Darstellung zumal von Kammermusik ist in dieser Hinsicht viel zu primitiv; sie begnügt sich in der Regel mit dem »roten Faden«. Ich gab ein Beispiel aus Beethovens e-moll-Quartett, die im Verhältnis des dreifachen Kontrapunkts stehenden Takte 13 und 21. Beidemale ist die Oberstimme Hauptstimme; beidemale muß der liegende Baß unbedingt zurücktreten. Das Problem sind die Mittelstimmen. Aber man kann die Oberstimme von [Takt] 21 f als Hauptstimme nur verstehen, wenn man ihre Identität mit der Bratschenstimme [Takt] 13 f erkennt. Also ist diese N¬ und muß deutlich sein, während die 2. Geige ganz zurücktritt (gewöhnlich ist es umgekehrt). Man kann also die dynamischen Verhältnisse von durchbrochenem Satz streng aus dem musikalischen Sinn entwickeln. Übrigens erfordert der für den

ganzen Satz konstitutive Rhythmus  besondere dynami-
82 sche Sorgfalt. Z. B. [Takt] 21 ist das vorschlagende Sechzehntel der 2. Geige zu betonen d. h. nicht fallen zu lassen und so durchwegs (die Betonung der Sechzehntel des Auflösungsfeldes in Vierergruppen folgt daraus[)]. Entsprechend [Takt] 156f keine Lücken; die Differenzierung darf *nur* durch die Farbe erfolgen.

*

Crescendi und decrescendi viel differenzierter aus dem musikalischen Sinn. Beispiel Takt 48-49 im ersten Satz von op. 59, 2. Takt 49 fährt als neue Gestalt »subito« dazwischen ähnlich wie die Gestalt mit den Sechzehnteln im 1. Satz der Eroica[147]. Also darf das crescendo von [Takt] 48 nicht *stetig* in [Takt] 49 führen. Andererseits aber auch keine Luftpause, weil sonst das subito verloren ginge (man wäre auf die Überraschung vorbereitet wie durch Gedankenstriche in schlechter Prosa). Also ist die einzige Lösung, einen dynamischen Grad gewissermaßen zu *überspringen*. Dies der *genaue* Sinn des sf. Modell dafür, wie Dynamik aus dem musikalischen Sinn zu entwickeln sei. (NB Exkurs über die Beethovenschen crescendi, die in ein p führen.[148] Sie haben *stets* einen Formsinn. Hier ist die »negative« Darstellung schon komponiert.

*

Dynamik und Verhältnis der Elemente zu einander. op. 59, 2, Takt 34. *Kein* ritardando Bratsche *und* Cello diminuendo, aber Cello nicht kontinuierlich ins p führen und vorm p-Eintritt des Seitensatzmodells phrasieren (minimale Luftpause). Dagegen die Stetigkeit wahren durch *kontinuierliches* diminuendo in der Bratsche, welche die beiden kritischen Takte legato, ohne jede Phrasierung miteinander verbindet. NB im Cello Takt 35 das g unter keinen Umständen fallen lassen, damit die Identität des Motivs mit der Fortsetzungsgestalt [Takt] 39 ganz deutlich wird. Dafür diese nicht kulinarische ausmelodisieren, sondern im strengen Fluß halten; keinerlei Verzögerung. Dies ein Modell für die entscheidende Kategorie des thematischen Musizierens.

*

Charakteristische N⁻ bei Beethoven im Adagio von op. 59, 1, 83
der Kontrapunkt der 1. Geige Takt 9 f. (S. 34)[149]

*

Beispiel wie Dynamik fürs *Tempo* eintreten kann Eroica kleine Partitur S. 7.[150]

*

Bei der Kritik der Normalstärke, des Normalklangs ist darauf zu rekurrieren, daß Musik überhaupt kein *Normalzustand* ist und darum unter keinen Umständen als ein solcher dargestellt werden darf. Musik als Normalzustand: so wird sie als Kontrebande in die positivistische Welt eingeschmuggelt, etwa Hindemith, Musikant (vgl. die These von der Entkunstung der Kunst in »zeitlose Mode«[151]). Genau diesem Schein muß die wahre Interpretation entgegenarbeiten. Man muß nur richtig interpretieren und es wird schon verfremdet. Der Sinn der Musik ist nicht die Einpassung in den Betrieb (durchs Funktionieren) und nicht dessen Verschleierung (durch Glätte, Harmonisierung, Kulinarisches), sondern der bestimmte Widerstand durch ihre immanente Konsequenz. Das ist der eigentliche Zusammenhang der Reproduktionstheorie mit meiner Philosophie.

*

Thematisch musizieren: das heißt die *Geschichte* eines Themas darstellen[152] und nicht etwa einfach: die Themen verdeutlichen. Diese Verdeutlichung kann (z. B. im Verlauf Bachischer Fugen) gerade *falsch* sein. Es gibt eine Deutlichkeit *höheren* Grades, etwa wie die höhere Kritik in der Geschichtswissenschaft, nämlich die der thematischen Geschichte, und sie hat vor der positivistischen Deutlichkeit des je einzelnen thematischen Tatbestandes die Priorität. – Man kann den 1. Satz von op. 59, 2 begreifen als einen Verlauf, in dem ein Exterritoriales – das Quintintervall e-h des ersten Taktes – hereingezogen, immanent, thematisch *wird*. Daran ist die ungemein schwierige Interpretation des Hauptthemen-Komplexes zu messen. Z. B. im ersten Takt muß die Oberstimme
84 deutlich genug sein, um als Substrat der Geschichte aufgefaßt zu werden, aber nicht schon so deutlich, um das Resultat, das Thematischwerden, vorwegzunehmen, und die Schwierigkeit besteht darin, diese materiale Logik der Musik ins Mensurale zu übersetzen. Oder in Takt 3 muß der Zusammenhang

und

fühlbar sein, aber nicht unterstrichen (also wohl: die 1 unbetont, die 4 mit einem Akzent, der auch auskomponiert ist (die Verdopplung durch die 2. Geige und die Dehnung). – Man muß aber auch den Sextenschritt verstehen, weil von ihm das Verständnis von Takt 18 abhängt, von diesem Takt 48 und damit das Verständnis des ganzen Satzes (NB. der Rhythmus von [Takt] 48 ist wieder das Band zu dem Auffang-Motiv Takt 55 Bratsche). Dabei darf aber all dies nicht unterstrichen – es muß gewußt und dann gleichsam wieder vergessen werden. Und das führt ins Herz der Reproduktionstheorie, an die Stelle, wo sie sich selbst aufzuheben beginnt. Denn man könnte sehr ernst fragen: daß diese Zusammenhänge subkutan sind, gehört selbst zu ihrem Sinn: sie enthüllen, würde ihn verletzen d. h. schlüge in Pedanterie um. Aber das wäre undialektisch gedacht, und die Logik der Musik ist die dialektische. Der ganze, unendlich feine, aber entscheidende Unterschied ist: ob durch die »Haut« (die bei Beethoven auch zum Komponierten gehört) das Subkutane *durchscheint* oder ob sie, als Phänomen, anstelle des Wesens *hypostasiert* wird. Die ganze Aufgabe besteht darin, diesen Gedanken in die Sprache der Musik zu übersetzen. Zur Haut »zurückkehren«. Die als Erscheinung gewußte Erscheinung ist *objektiv* verschieden von der unreflektierten; dasselbe und nicht dasselbe, und in diesem Sinn ist die Darstellung von Musik dialektisch. Interpretieren heißt in der Erscheinung die Identität des Nichtidentischen, die Nichtidentität des Identischen verwirklichen. *[Längs des linken Rands:]* dies ist das Zentralproblem der gesamten Theorie

*

Ad *Phrasierung*. Die meisten Probleme von Sinn und Sinnlo- 85
sigkeit im *Einzelnen* sind solche der Phrasierung, zumal bei neuer Musik. Das Phänomen des unverständlichen *Satzes*. Sie setzen sich vor allem aus zwei Aspekten zusammen, dem des Absetzens, der »Interpunktion« (submensurale Pausen, die meist auch mensural sich schreiben ließen), und der *Akzentuierung* (die streng genommen in die Dynamik fällt[)]. – Die *Einheit* der Phrase ist die der musikalischen Gestalt in ihrer Selbständigkeit und Unselbständigkeit. In ihr spielen gute Taktteile, überhaupt Taktstriche meist eine Rolle, ihr Verhältnis ist aber nicht prinzipiell mit der Phrasierung identisch. Vielmehr haben die Phrasen melodische Schwerpunkte, die oft mit harmonischen koinzidieren aber nicht stets. Phrasierungskategorien sind: ansetzen, fortsetzen, absinken, wieder aufnehmen, Abgesang. Genaue Phrasierungsanalysen geben bei Schönberg, dem Hauptthema aus op. 23, 1, und der Klari-

nettenmelodie des Liedes op. 22, 1, evt. auch das Hauptthema von op. 16, 1. – Bei emanzipierter Melodik die Bedeutung der Höhen- und Tiefenpunkte. – Sinnvoller Vortrag von Themen vielleicht am Hauptthema des Violinkonzerts von Schönberg, einer falschen Darstellung d. h. der *unartikulierten* gegenüberstellen. Das Sinnlose ist das Unartikulierte; daher hat der Ausdruck immer zugleich auch konstruktiven Sinn. – Die richtige Phrasierung muß genau das leisten, was in schlechter Interpretation das Rubato leistet. – Phrasieren heißt nie allein die Gestalt artikulieren, sondern immer zugleich das Verhältnis der Gestalten zueinander. Man muß vorfühlen, auf etwas hin Phrasieren, über etwas hinweg Phrasieren; die Phrasierung ist nie statisch, sie lebt von den musikalischen Kräfteverhältnissen. Man muß genau so fühlen: jetzt kommt etwas, wie: dies löst es ein. In der Phrasierung ist das Moment der Sprachähnlichkeit von Musik positiv aufgehoben; durch die Phrasierung allein *spricht* Musik. – Es gibt auch rückbezogene Phrasierung. – Jede Phrase muß wissen was sie will, bestimmt sein, und wo sie mehreres will (Überkreuzung!) muß auch dies mehrere deutlich werden. Es gibt keine vage Phrasierung außer wo die Verschleifung von Phrasen ihrerseits einer Absicht der Konstruktion dient, wenn z. B. gegen Ende einer Komposition symphonischen Wesens die Musik die – als solche fühlbaren – Dämme überflutet. Über-
86 haupt läßt sich an der Phrasierung besonders die zeitliche Dynamik der Musik entnehmen: der Verlauf tendiert dazu, die Phrasenenden zu überwinden. Interpunktion viel deutlicher als gemeinhin: es läßt eine ähnliche Entwicklung sich beobachten wie in der Sprache der Verfall der großen Perioden. Insbesondere Doppelpunkt und Semikolon musizieren. – Phrasierung von *Parenthesen* (sehr wichtig!) – Einwürfen, Ausweichungen. – Problem der Phrasierung bei Absenz äußerlicher Formgliederung (Schönberg, op. 23, 4). – Die Totalität der Phrasierung fällt zusammen mit der musikalischen *Form*. Daher ist jede Einzelphrasierung an der Formtotalität zu messen. – Grundregel der Betonung »kritischer« Töne. Grund-

sätzlich keine Binnenbetonungen übergebundener Noten. Differenzierung der Akzente siehe Schönbergs Bezeichnungen.

*

Nachtrag zu op. 59, 2. Takt 67 2. Geige nur sf, dann sofort weg (Beispiel für »Luft schaffen«). – Takt 78-79 Mittelstimme thematisch spielen. – Takt 107, bei der Wendung der Durchführung, muß der phantasierende Charakter aufhören, sehr streng. Bratsche + Cello hier erstmals voll thematisch. – Im 2. Satz in der 2. Strophe des Themas ab Auftakt zu [Takt] 9 ist die 1. Geige und gerade *nicht* der Choral Hauptstimme.

Locarno, 1. September 1954

*

Hübscher Ausspruch von Rudi [Kolisch] in Kranichstein: es ist mit den kleinen Noten wie im Monopolkapitalismus. Nicht nur sind sie *an sich* klein – die Großen machen sie noch kleiner, entziehen ihnen Zeit und Kraft. Das Fallenlassen kürzerer Noten ist wohl das Hauptübel der falschen Darstellung.

*

Man muß sich über die *Strategie* der Arbeit klar werden. Sie richtet sich gegen 2 Fronten. Auf der einen Seite das offizielle
Musikleben, das längst, und gerade auch in seinen gefeierten 87
Vertretern, ein Stück der Kulturindustrie ist, *zugleich* galvanisiert, temperamentvoll und kulinarisch. Kultiviertes und barbarisches Musizieren konvergieren. Auf der anderen die abstrakte Negation, die Flucht ins Mensurale. Dort der falsche Subjektivismus, hier die Residualtheorie der Wahrheit, die Ausrottung des Subjekts (*alle* Formen des Objektivismus, von Stockhausen bis Walcha, meinen eigentlich dasselbe. Die sogenannte Jugend protestierte gegen das »überspitzte espressi-

vo« in Eduard [Steuermanns] Schönbergdarstellung[153]). – Schüler aus der Ostzone, von Bloch, kamen begeistert zu mir: so etwas hätten sie überhaupt noch nicht gehört.

*

In Kranichstein gab es einige Fragen, welche die Theorie zu beantworten hat. So wollte ein Student wissen, ob aus unserer Kritik des konventionellen Musizierideals nicht folge, daß schlechte Instrumentalisten usw. den guten vorzuziehen seien. Das ist natürlich Unsinn. Die Wahl von Klängen[,] Spielweisen usw. nach den Erfordernissen des Komponierten muß aus *Freiheit* kommen, der Verfügung über die Möglichkeiten, nicht aus der Not der angeblich musikalischen Sängerinnen, die Schönberg singen, weil sie für die Butterfly keine Stimme haben. Ob diese Verfügung relativ selbständig oder nur an den Kompositionen gewonnen werden kann, ist eine pädagogische Frage. Zur Erwerbung der Freiheit ist die Verselbständigung der Technik wohl unvermeidlich, sonst gibts Halbdilettanten à la Bobi[154]; sobald die Verselbständigung der Mittel aber erfolgt ist, gravitieren die Künstler bereits von sich aus zur Kulturindustrie, efficiency, »service«. Man stößt also auch hier auf eine Antinomie. Immerhin wäre jenem Studenten zu konzedieren, daß *soziologisch* junge, noch nicht arrivierte Künstler besser zur richtigen Interpretation taugen als berühmte, die durchwegs unansprechbar sind. – Ein anderer meinte, ob aus unserer Theorie ein Verbot gegen jede persönliche Charakte-
88 ristik, jedes Idiom des Interpreten abzuleiten wäre. Rudi [Kolisch] und ich haben das unisono verneint: gegen »chemisch reinen« Ton. Auch dies wäre eine musikalische Residualtheorie der Wahrheit. In der wahren Interpretation ist dies Moment *bewahrt:* genau dies heißt »Vortrag« und dessen Kategorie bleibt zu entfalten. Auch hier ist radikal nicht ratzekahl.

*

Harmonische Verhältnisse müssen durch die *Form* dargestellt werden. Rückungen etwa, im Gegensatz zu Modulationen, durch Plötzlichkeit, Unvermitteltsein, also *minimale* Luftpausen. Durchführung der Pastorale.

*

Die Darstellung des musikalischen Sinnes: das ist doch wesentlich die Artikulation. Dazu formosus als schön: formenreich, gegliedert. Ist aber nicht die Artikulation an jedem Kunstwerk – an allem Schönen – dessen Sprachähnlichkeit? Wäre das nicht das Verhältnis der wahren Interpretation zur Sprache?

*

Aus einem Gespräch mit Rudi [Kolisch] vom 2. Oktober 1954: dieser meinte, die Vermittlung zwischen neuer Musik und der Darstellung von traditioneller sei zunächst ganz handgreiflich, daß man an jener eine Differenzierung der Sache und daher der Darstellung gelernt habe, die dieser – der traditionellen – zugute komme aber zugleich von dieser selbst gefordert sei. – Man müsse den Begriff des Subkutanen von der Vorstellung einer musikalischen Hinterwelt scheiden. Auch das Subkutane gehöre zum Phänomen, zu dem was real erklingt, nur falle es eben bei der herkömmlichen Interpretation unter den Tisch. Dies ein wichtiger Einwand gegen das Mißverständnis des Intellektualismus. 89

*

Die Theorie ist zu behüten gegen das progressive education-Mißverständnis, die wahre Interpretation wäre rein, unmittelbar aus dem Werk zu entwickeln, ohne daß der Interpret geistig und technisch schon etwas mitbringt. (Vgl. dazu Aufzeichnung auf S. 87) Die Verselbständigung des Instrumentalen, als ein Moment von Arbeitsteilung, Rationalisierung, ist nicht einfach zugunsten eines unmittelbaren Verhältnisses zur Sache selbst zurückzunehmen. Um so weniger, als das Steigen der Komplexität der Werke selbst verlangt, daß die Interpreten immer mehr von sich aus können. An dieser Stelle hat die Theorie sich scharf von der musikpädagogischen Jugendbewegung zu trennen. Diese reduziert die Werke, um den Sprung der verdinglichten Technik und der Sache zu überwinden, und bewirkt Regression hier wie dort. Aber es kommt darauf an, die Trennung durch die eigene Konsequenz, durch ihr Extrem aufzuheben. Wie die Komposition, je mehr sie sich von der Interpretation scheidet, durch ihre Anforderungen diese um so mehr steigert, so wird der Interpret, je vollkommener und differenzierter er wird, je besser er sein Naturmaterial beherrscht, desto fähiger, der Komposition gerecht zu werden. Das Entscheidende ist nur die bewußte Wendung alles dessen auf die Sache, die Selbstreflexion der Interpretation als eines *für sich* Bestehenden – »Kritik des Musikanten«. – Einfacher wohl nur beim Gesang, wo der Stimmenfetischismus bewirkt, daß das Meiste, was ein Sänger »kann«, der Sache nur im Wege steht. Aber selbst hier gilt es zu differenzieren: schlecht ist nur alle »Stimmbildung«; ganz anders steht es mit Singen als einer instrumentalen Technik, der Koloratur.

*

Vielleicht muß man noch weiter gehen. Es gibt einstweilen in
90 der Interpretation immer noch legitime und notwendige Elemente, die sich nicht rein in die Sache auflösen lassen, und die vom Interpreten herkommen. So gehört zu aller wirklichen Darstellung ein gewisses den Klang aus dem Klavier herausmeißeln, körperhaft gleichsam im Klavier spielen. Das definiert den Pianisten, es ist genau das, was mir abgeht. Aber wer nicht so Klavier spielt, kann auch keine Beethoven-Sonate richtig darstellen, obwohl dies plastische Klangideal nur sehr vermittelt, wenn überhaupt, in ihm enthalten ist. Nur wenn es losgelassen, Selbstzweck wird, wird es schlecht. – Und schließlich:

wie steht es mit der Stimme Carusos? Schlägt da nicht der Fetisch Stimme in die Sache selbst um? Solche Extreme müssen bedacht und hereingenommen werden, wenn die Theorie nicht stur fachmännisch geraten soll.

*

Es müssen *höhere* Interpretationsfragen zumindest *angezeigt* werden. Ich notiere die sehr schwierige Stelle, wo die c-moll-Etüde von Chopin vor dem Mittelteil nach B-Dur moduliert[155]. Problem ist, daß die Höhepunkte in beiden Händen nicht zusammenfallen; die Melodie der Rechten, in größeren Werten, erreicht ihr F *vor* dem G der Sechzehntel in der Linken. Dies über den Zielton hinausgreifende g ist in gewissem Sinne eine *Überschreitung* des vorhergehenden f; zugleich aber *absolut* darunter. Spielt man darauf das Ganze hin, wird die ohnehin sehr schwer zusammenzufassende Linie der Rechten lahm und sinnlos; fallen lassen darf man es erst recht nicht. Einzige Auskunft: volle Unabhängigkeit des Vortrags beider Hände; auf 2 Ebenen spielen. (Genau bezeichnen)

*

Zur Theorie des *Dirigenten*. Der Dirigent hat zwei ganz ver- 91
schiedene, zunächst unverbundene Aufgaben zu bewältigen. Zunächst die der Koordinierung der Spieler (und Sänger), die oberhalb einer gewissen Zahlengrenze von den Einzelnen nicht mehr geleistet wird; also die Kontrollfunktion, vom primitiven Zusammenhalten zu höheren technischen Aufgaben wie dem Nicht-schleifen-lassen, den Stimmen ihr Recht schaffen und Ähnlichem. Dann aber die Aufgabe des Musizierens: das Werk, durch die Imagination des einzelnen Subjekts hindurch, in der Vielfalt des Orchesters als Einheit zu realisieren. Der zweiten Aufgabe stehen nun außerordentliche Schwierigkeiten entgegen. Eine solche Imagination haben überhaupt nur wenige Musiker; die meisten ersetzen sie durch

eine unmittelbare, mimische Beziehung zum Instrument. Das ist beim Orchester nicht möglich; man kann nicht auf dem Orchester Klavier spielen, das gegenüber der mimetischen Unmittelbarkeit eine Schicht der Vermittlung setzt, und wer es doch tut, macht es schlecht, schauspielerhaft, indem er jene Schicht der Vermittlung verleugnet (Bruno Walter). Darüber hinaus setzt das von dem Imaginierenden physisch Getrennte, verselbständigte, entfremdete Medium der Verwirklichung der Imagination Widerstände wie eine zähe Masse entgegen, am meisten wohl beim Chor, weil das Singen selber eine Art Unmittelbarkeit ist, die dem Vermittlungsprozeß grundsätzlich sich entzieht (daher der besondere Typus des Chordirigenten, der dieser besonderen Bedingung in einer Art von Resignation sich anpaßt. Übrigens besteht das, was man so Dirigierbegabung nennt in der Fähigkeit jene Widerstände durch einen psychologischen Mechanismus von Übertragung und Identifikation zu brechen, ja ihre Energie in den Dienst der Aufführung zu stellen – an diese Stelle gehört die längst
92 projektierte Sozialpsychologie des Orchestermusikers[156]). Die Konsequenz dieser Schwierigkeit ist, daß die Lösung der ersten Aufgabe durchwegs für die zweite unterschoben wird; daß die Kontrollfunktion und was zu ihr gehört, wie Präzision des Schlags, Nicht locker lassen, Einteilung der Dynamik (des Orchesters, nicht der Komposition) so erscheint, als wäre sie bereits die zweite; und der Schwindel besteht darin, daß subjektiv der Dirigent den Anschein zu erwecken versteht, als wäre die Fähigkeit zu solchen Leistungen bereits die des Gestaltens, während objektiv durch die eingeschliffene Tradition, solange nicht verfremdet wird, die Unterscheidung von beidem außerordentlich erschwert ist, und anstelle der eigentlich musikalischen Wirkung, die ganz fehlt, beim Publikum eine Fortsetzung der psychologischen tritt, die mit den Widerständen des Orchesters fertig wird.

Frankfurt, 22. März 1955

*

Wie in manchen Kompositionen die Reproduktion vorgedacht ist. Es gibt Stücke oder Stellen bei Chopin, wie die Presto-Etüde in f-moll oder der Zweiunddreißigstel-Teil des Fis-Dur-Impromptus, die, in einem sehr sublimen und vergeistigten Sinne verstanden, durch den Klaviersatz bereits damit rechnen, daß die Kraft der Finger kaum je ganz gleichmäßig ist, sodaß unwillkürlich und *zufällig* einzelne Töne auffallen, etwa wie in der Sonne Reflexe auf dem Wasser aufleuchten. Das kompositorische Moment der Kontingenz, das tief zum Wesen der Romantik gehört, realisiert sich vermöge der unabdingbaren Fehlbarkeit der Wiedergabe.

*

Nichts in der musikalischen Reproduktion ist läppischer, als
wenn ein Rubato mit dem Charakter der Willkür, des Beab- 93
sichtigten, Gemachten auftritt – so wie meine Mutter[157] mit überwältigender Komik zu imitieren wußte, wie eine pseudoitalienische Sängerin eine Stelle aus einer Sopranarie der Forza del destino (Pace, pace) vortrug mit einem accelerando

[Rechts neben dem Notenbeispiel:] NB. zur Theorie des musikalisch *Dummen* als einer kritischen der Interpretation.
Da aber das Problem *aller* Reproduktion im Verhältnis von Freiheit und Notentext liegt – sollte hier nicht ein Kanon des Reproduzierens *selber* zu finden sein?

*

Zur Theorie des Dirigenten: Die Forderung des Zusammenhaltens läuft bei schwierigeren Werken meist darauf hinaus, daß die Aufmerksamkeit der Präzision in der Vertikale gilt, der ja auch der Schlag entspricht. Aber für die Darstellung des musikalischen Zusammenhanges ist die Horizontale viel wichtiger. *Alles* kommt auf den »roten Faden« an, zunächst die von Hauptstimme zu Hauptstimme springende Melodie, dann auf die syntaktische Artikulation der einzelnen Linien in sich. Daß das, zugunsten eines ganz äußerlichen Präzisionsideals, vernachlässigt wird, ist der Hauptgrund der Unverständlichkeit neuer Musik. – Große Dirigenten sind selten die »präzisesten«.

*

Konstruktion (im Werk) und Deutlichkeit (in der Reproduktion) sind Äquivalente. Das ist das Mahlerische Element an Schönberg. Ja beide Kategorien sind vertauschbar; man muß deutlich komponieren und durch die Reproduktion konstruieren. Diese Schicht ist die der Indifferenz von Werk und Wiedergabe: in ihr entscheidet sich ihr Verhältnis.

*

Januar 1956.

94 Ausdrücke wie virtuos, con bravura (bei Chopin) und ähnliche deuten auf ein wesentliches Moment der musikalischen Reproduktion: das eines Rituals von *Natur*beherrschung. Der Interpret ist immer zugleich, und zwar aus objektiver Notwendigkeit, vermöge der Spannung zwischen dem Werk und der Wiedergabe, etwas wie ein Bändiger, ein Dompteur, am meisten als Dirigent und Pianist, aber auch als Koloratursängerin. Dies ist der *in der Sache* gelegene Grund für die Affinität der Reproduktion zum Zirkus- und Zigeunerwesen und zugleich für die soziologische Sonderstellung des Reproduzierenden: Privileg des als Institution zugelassenen Verfemten;

und hier liegen zugleich wesentliche Kräfte und entscheidende Schwierigkeiten der wahren Reproduktion (auf Eislerbuch rekurrieren und die beiden Momente entfalten[158]). Es wird aber dabei vorausgesetzt, daß die darzustellende Musik »Natur« sei – freilich auch das Rohmaterial der Reproduktion, wie Klavier, Orchester, Stimme – vermutlich dieses mehr. Daß die Reproduktion ein *doppeltes* Material: nämlich die Klangmaterie, aus der gestaltet, und das Werk, das gestaltet wird, hat, ist wohl der objektive Grund für die Verselbständigung der Reproduktion. – In gewissem Sinn ist das Werk immer wieder, *wird* immer wieder gegenüber der Interpretation Natur; das ist ihr Recht und ihre Notwendigkeit. Zugleich aber ist diese Natur selber vermittelt und insofern unwahr; das verleiht der Interpretation ihren Scheincharakter, gefährdet sie mit Lächerlichkeit, arbeitet an ihrer Abschaffung. Das hier bezeichnete Element ist das fragilste und hinfälligste der Reproduktion, aber eines ihrer eigentümlichsten. *Sehr wichtig;* weiterverfolgen.

*

Gutes Beispiel für das Verhältnis des zu wählenden Tempos 95
und der Komposition: das erste Prélude von Chopin, in C, Agitato überschrieben. Die Idee des genialen Stückes ist das Verhältnis der nachschlagenden Bewegung zum guten Taktteil, auf den die Bewegung übergreift, als ob sie sich nicht halten könnte. Diese Idee ist zugleich die des Ausdrucksgehalts, des Augenblicks von überströmendem, passioniertem Enthusiasmus. Nach diesem erreichten Augenblick spielen dann die beiden Elemente, das nachschlagende und das auf die eins eintretende, miteinander, so wie die gelungene Erfüllung, und sie allein, es erlaubt, mit der Versagung zu spielen. Es kommt aber alles darauf an, daß diese Idee und ihre äußerst differenzierte Entfaltung *deutlich* werden. Das fast unlösbare Problem der Darstellung – jede echte Darstellung führt auf Aporien und Antinomien, keine Musik ist rein darstellbar – ist daher, den

leidenschaftlichen Schwung des Gesamtcharakters mit jener Deutlichkeit zu verbinden. Das heißt aber, unverführt von den Sechzehnteln und von jenem Schwung, das Tempo so weit zu *mäßigen,* daß die Pausen auf 1 so klar sind, daß man dann deren Überwindung auch fühlt. Dazu gehört auch vorsichtigste Pedalisierung, vor allem also Pedal weg *vor* der eins und nicht, nach Pianistenart, erst nachklappend. Ich habe das Stück noch *nie* richtig gehört, auch von mir selbst nicht.

*

Die Literatur *systematisch* auf dergleichen Belegstellen durchgehen; auch Schönberg. Dies bleibt noch zu leisten.

*

Daß in der musikalischen Reproduktion die Objektivität der Sache einzig der Anstrengung der subjektiven Phantasie sich verdankt, wird im Einzelnen zu erweisen sein. In dem fis-
96 moll-Nocturne von Chopin op. 48, Nr. 2 folgt in der ersten Strophe des Hauptteils, nach vollständiger Kadenz in Gis-Dur, ein Nachsatz, das Hauptthema, der dies Gis-Dur in die Wechseldominante der Grundtonart umdeutet. Dieser Nachsatz tritt mf ein und wird dann bis zum pp diminuiert. Aber es ist ein *uneigentliches* mezzoforte, d. h. die absolute Tonstärke ist nicht leibhaft gemeint, sondern unwirklich, wie auf einer anderen Ebene liegend, umgefärbt; das reale mf in der Tenorlage drückt etwas Absentes, gleichsam ein piano aus, und gerade die absolute Tonstärke ist das Mittel, dies Imaginäre herbeizuziehen, so wie Gespenster um so gespenstischer wären, je realer sie sind. Natürlich gibt es für das Phänomen technische Korrelate wie hier den *Nachsatzcharakter* der Stelle; es ist alles schon geschehen, »nachher«; das mf hat in dem wiederhergestellten Grund-piano-Charakter keine Funktion mehr und wird darum zum Als-ob; dergleichen Phänomene sind ungemein schwer in Worten zu fassen und bisher, außer gelegentlich

von Kurth[159], kaum je beschrieben worden. Am Pianisten ist es, den Sinn der Stelle zu realisieren, indem er eine Farbe, einen Typus des Anschlags findet, der das mf entwirklicht. Ich zweifle nicht an der Verbindlichkeit der Einsicht, also der *Objektivität* solcher Interpretation; ich kann sie auch bis ins Einzelne formanalytisch begründen, aber all das setzt einen Akt von Spontaneität, Phantasie voraus; ohne Subjekt des Interpreten geht der objektive Sinn der Komposition verloren. Interpretation ist mimetisch auch in dem Sinn, daß sie im Komponierten gleichsam das Komponieren nachmacht, die Objektivation in den flüssigen Aggregatzustand wieder auflöst, und das allein ist der Weg in dem sie objektiviert. Diese Theorie steht Marcel Proust überaus nahe, wie denn dessen Werk – im außermusikalischen Bereich – zum großen Teil aus Erfahrungen besteht wie der hier an Chopin angedeuteten. Die hier erreichte Paradoxie ist das eigentliche Problem der Reproduktion.

». . . so wie das Spiel eines großen Musikers . . . das eines so 97
großen Pianisten ist, daß man nicht mehr weiß, ob man überhaupt einen Pianisten vor sich hat, weil eben dies Spiel . . . so durchsichtig geworden ist, so ganz von seiner Aussage erfüllt, daß man es selbst gar nicht mehr bemerkt oder doch nur wie ein Fenster, das den Durchblick auf ein Meisterwerk eröffnet.«

Marcel Proust, Guermantes, S. 66.[160]

*

Zu S. 90 dieser Notizen. »Höhere Interpretationsfragen« – das ist eigentlich unkünstlerisch. Denn alles im Kunstwerk ist gleich nah zum Zentrum, gleichen Ranges. Und: alle geistigen Fragen der Darstellung sind durch die konkreten technischen vermittelt. Ja noch mehr: die das Ganze, die Anlage der Form betreffenden Fragen sind nicht abstrakt, an sich, unabhängig von den Details zu lösen, sondern nur durch diese hindurch. Aber auch umgekehrt. Dies muß sehr stark hervortreten.

*

Zur Theorie des Dirigenten, S. 91. Es ist sogar fraglich, ob es *wünschbar* wäre, so auf dem Orchester zu musizieren wie auf dem Klavier, oder Kammermusik. Denn alle Orchestermusik, und gar die Oper, ist ihrem eigenen Sinn nach auf eine gewisse *Distanz* angelegt; *will* gar nicht so ganz ausgehört werden wie die andere. Von der Distanz des Phänomens zum Hörenden hängt aber die wahre Interpretation wesentlich ab. Dazu, daß die Orchesterwerke Beethovens, und bei Mozart wenigstens die Opern, in der Faktur wesentlich einfacher, lapidarer sind als die große Kammermusik.[161] Dies ist eine wichtige Vermittlung der Theorie mit der Gesellschaft, die hier in die ästhetische Immanenz selbst hineinreicht.

*

98 Eine sehr wichtige Kategorie ist die der *Signifikanz* bezw. ihres Gegenteils. Unendlich viel schlechtes Musizieren besteht einfach darin, daß Signifikantes insignifikant gespielt wird. Das ist *nicht* stets mit Stärke oder auch nur Hervortreten identisch, ja zuweilen nicht einmal mit Akzenten. Mir fiel in Soltis Figaro[162] auf, daß die Terzen in der ersten Pagenarie

usw.

abfielen, das Ganze schleifte durch mangelnde Signifikanz, eine bestimmte Mattheit hatten. Vielleicht korrigierbar durch einen Akzent auf dem Auftakt; ich bin aber nicht sicher. – Die ganze, sehr schwierige Arie litt daran, daß die Sängerin das Thema nicht als Thema exponierte, d. h. daß der Rhythmus

so verschleift war, daß er als solcher nicht mehr deutlich wurde.

*

Sehr viel über Interpretationsfragen ist aus meinem ungedruckten Einleitungsvortrag zum Kammerkonzert von Berg[163] zu entnehmen und heranzuziehen. Bei mehrfarbiger Musik besteht der rote Faden wesentlich darin, daß bei rasch umschlagenden Farben, selbst bei identischem Stärkegrad, keine »Farblücke« entsteht; bei schwierigen Stücken kann sonst sogleich das Verständnis gefährdet werden. Gilt auch für klassische
Musik, z. B. die erste Fortsetzung des Diskantthemas gleich zu 99
Beginn der Figaro-Ouvertüre. – NB im langsamen Satz Berg die Stelle, die ich wegen Unverständlichkeit der Interpretation als Beispiel wegließ (Engführung mit Vergößerung und Verkleinerung)[164]. Wäre zu analysieren, d. h. zu zeigen, was man hören muß, warum man es nicht hört, mit welchen Folgen. Hier ist der Grund der Unverständlichkeit zu greifen.

*

Geheimnis der wahren Interpretation: in jedem Augenblick seiner selbst mächtig bleiben. Dadurch wird sie fähig, das Werk, das immer nur vermittelt wird durch die Imagination, ganz zu realisieren. Also das genaue Gegenteil von Spielwelt, Spieltrieb, der Fetischisierung des Mechanismus. Zusammenhang mit »Kritik des Musikanten«.

*

Die Kritik des Historismus ist zusammenzudenken mit der am Arrangement. Was über dieses im Fetischcharakter steht (ad Beethoven) widerspricht scheinbar dem in der Bacharbeit gesagten[165]. Aber doch nur scheinbar. Die Schwelle ist die Beziehung der Farbe zur Konstruktion. Aber nicht ganz. Es muß präzis die Frage beantwortet werden: warum ist es legitim, Orgelwerke von Bach zu orchestrieren, scheußlich, Symphonien von Beethoven umzuinstrumentieren. Das Element der *Geschichte* spielt wesentlich herein. Aber ganz klar bin ich mir selbst nicht. Äußerst wichtig.

*

zentral

Was man so musizieren nennt ist im allgemeinen nur Ichschwäche, das bloße sich Überlassen an Instrument und Idiom. Und gerade das stellt sich vor das Werk (NB der Musikant als der nicht voll Individuierte. Slawische, vorbürgerliche Nationen!). Das ist die genaue Vermittlung des Satzes, daß die Objektivität nur durchs Subjekt hindurch sich realisiert.

*

100 Es wird auch von den sozialökonomischen Bedingungen der Interpretation zu handeln sein. Im Kapitalismus, wo die Ware Arbeitszeit getauscht wird, krankt tendenziell *alle* musikalische Interpretation, vorab aber die Oper, an Unterprobieren aus Zeitnot. Die meisten Aufführungen finden statt, wenn das Probieren erst beginnen müßte. Das sich Verständigen, das Funktionieren im Groben ersetzt die eigentliche Darstellung. Maßlose, den Sinn tangierende Vergröberung. Dazu das Problem der Gewerkschaft und seine Dialektik, vor allem in U. S. A. Die Hoffnungslosigkeit, das Bewußtsein daß alles zu wenig sei, sedimentiert sich als Defaitismus. Rottenbergs[166] »Scheußlich, weiter«. – Der deutsche Repertoirebetrieb, das

Nachdirigieren, der Zerfall der Aufführungen. Stagione kein Ausweg. Toscaninis Leistung: das zulängliche Probieren. Bayreuth. All das hereinziehen. Die sozialen Bedingungen sind zum Teil für die falsche Interpretation auch so verantwortlich, daß sie keine andere gestatten – nicht nur so, daß sie sich in ihr ausdrücken. Musikalische Mangelwirtschaft und zugleich die Rücksicht auf Verkäuflichkeit bis ins Klangideal hinein. Wenn diese Zusammenhänge nicht dargestellt werden, wird das Ganze zu ideologisch.

*

Ob eine Phrase sinnvoll musiziert ist, das läßt sich genau in technische Korrelate wie Akzente, Luftpausen usw. umsetzen. Aber um diese Umsetzung zu vollziehen, muß man erst den Sinn der Phrase verstehen. Sehr wichtig, weiter verfolgen. Gegen Intuitionismus *und* Positivismus.

*

Sils Maria, August 1956

Der Unterschied in der Darstellung traditioneller und neuer Musik ist eigentlich nur der, daß jene, dem äußerlichsten Schein nach, etwas von der Last seiner Arbeit abnimmt, indem die fixierten Akkordverbindungen und das Gefälle der Tonalität einen gewissen Oberflächenzusammenhang herstellt, der
in der neuen Musik fehlt. Strukturell, vom Subkutanen her 101
sind die Probleme hier wie dort die gleichen. Immerhin ist die Sinnlosigkeit in der Darstellung neuer Musik fast allgemein und trägt das Ihre zum Widerstand bei. Sie rührt wesentlich von dem Mangel an Probenzeit her. Vor allem bei Dirigenten tritt eine verhängnisvolle Verschiebung der Aufmerksamkeit ein. Es wird auf Zusammenhalt, nicht auf Zusammenhang probiert, während jener die bloße Voraussetzung für diesen ist. Wenn es »klappt«, meint man schon, es wäre richtig, auch wenn der greulichste Galimathias herauskommt. Zilligs Äu-

ßerung[167] über seine Aufführung des Kammerkonzerts von Berg und der Unsinn bei der Engführung im langsamen Satz. Es wird nur *vertikal* musiziert, vom Schlag aus, und das heißt: überhaupt nicht. Faustregeln:

1) der rote Faden, Zusammenhang von Stimme zu Stimme. Besondere Aufmerksamkeit bei Stimmendungen und Fortsetzungen (Anfang d. Bergkonzerts). Rudi [Kolischs] Desiderat: Impulse aufnehmen
2) wirkliches Klarlegen des Verhältnisses von Haupt- und Nebenstimmen. Nicht das Thema, das man eh hört, ist stets die Hauptsache. Exemplifizieren am Berg-Konzert und an Bach, II. D-Dur Fuge.
3) Melodiestruktur (am Hauptthema des Bläserquintetts von Arnold Schönberg). Dazu: der Augenblick wo es zu schwimmen beginnt (Phrasierung) und: die Löcher in Melodien.
4) genaueste Rechenschaft über den Formsinn einer jeden Stelle – ja Note! – geben und danach spielen. Z.B. beim Anfang des Quintetts: Bau des Hauptthemas (Mittelsatz!!!) und Zeugma im Nachsatz; »Einsatz« der Fortsetzung mit den Achteltriolen (wie in einer Mozartsonate); relatives Gewicht der Cäsuren.
5) Wörtlichnehmen der Dynamik im Sinn von Extremwerten der Deutlichkeit, besonders wichtig bei Holzbläsern. p wird *fast immer* zu stark gespielt.

102 6) die Tempogestaltung ist stets, unbedingt der musikalischen Deutlichkeit unterzuordnen.

7) Ritardandi usw. stets aus dem musikalischen Zusammenhang, nie absolut, verselbständigt. Sonst tritt Unsinn ein, die ganze Form, ja die musikalische *Sprache* kann unverständlich werden. Wo die Sprache nicht verstanden ist, werden meist die Ritardandi übertrieben. Beispiel vor dem f-moll-Einsatz in der 1. Kammersymphonie op. 9 [von Schönberg]. Diese, vor allem die Exposition, überhaupt voll solcher Probleme. Vielleicht einige entfalten (die Hornimitation in der Umkehrung,

am Anfang, meist schon unverständlich. Klang und Verständlichkeit).

8) beim Probieren erst *nur* die Folge der Hauptstimmen, dann die N‾ hinzunehmen, dann erst die eigentlichen Begleitungen. Diese Systemweise probieren.

*

Die wenigsten Musiker wissen, daß es auch *rasche* Melodien gibt. Ob etwas Melodie, hat zunächst mit dem Tempo gar nichts zu tun.

*

Oberster Grundsatz Bruno Walters: der Kunde darf nicht ausgelassen werden, nie sich langweilen. Also entweder schwelgen oder mitreißen, mitnehmen. Was dabei aus der Musik wird, ist ihm gleichgültig.

*

Von einer bestimmten Phase der Reflexion an will die Notierung, über das mensurale und neumische Moment hinaus, *von sich aus,* als subjektive Intention etwas sagen, und Aufgabe des Interpreten ist es, das zu lesen. In der Appassionata entscheidet der Unterschied von  und 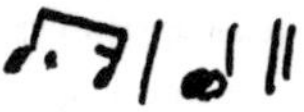 über den Charakter der Komposition.

*

Der Satz von Bülow: crescendo ist piano, diminuendo ist forte[168] gilt viel allgemeiner. Ein Sechzehntel ist nicht nur weniger als ein Achtel sondern vor allem auch mehr als ein Zwei- 103
unddreißigstel. Das wird meist vergessen.

*

Im Sinne des Postulats der Deutlichkeit aller ästhetischen Kategorien wäre wohl prinzipiell zu formulieren, daß jedes musikalische Zeichen – Note, Pause, Vortragsbezeichnung – gegen die nächstangrenzenden auf *beiden* Seiten absolut unterschieden werden muß außer in Fällen kontinuierlicher Übergänge – und dann muß der Charakter des Übergangs *selber* absolut deutlich werden.

*

Es muß etwas für die absolute Durchführung des temperierten Intonierens gesagt werden. Die »natürlichen« Unterschiede sind archaische Rudimente und mit der rationalen chromatischen Skala, dem Gleichgewicht ihrer Stufen, der *prinzipiell stets* möglichen enharmonischen Umdeutung unvereinbar. Für Sevčiks Halbtonmethode.[169] Sehr wichtig.

*

In den Text muß eine genaue Anweisung für die Darstellung verwickelter Polyphonie aufgenommen werden, mit einem Beispiel.
Motive:

1) jede neu eintretende Stimme muß auffallen, vor allem Modelle als solche exponiert werden
2) jede Stimme, die so pointiert war, daß man sie weiter verfolgt, muß in der Fortsetzung zugunsten der nächsten zurücktreten.
3) zu betonen sind Einsätze, nicht Taktteile. Oft genügt ein ganz kurzes Markieren, dann kann die Stelle zurücktreten
4) besondere Aufmerksamkeit für *nicht* zusammenfallende Phrasierungen, Akzente usw. Gleichzeitige Phrasen verschiedener Länge genau auseinanderhalten.
5) Hierarchie des Hervorhebens: thematisch gegen nichtthematisch, profilierte Stimmen gegen bloße Kontra-

punkte, Stimmen die wichtig sind aber leicht verloren gehen gegen solche, die man ohnehin hört. Diese Desi- 104
derate geraten oft in Konflikt. Dann entscheidet der kompositorische Sinn. Fälle wo alle Stimmen gleich wichtig sind, sind äußerst selten – und kurz.

6) Stimmen nicht *nur* durch die Dynamik auseinanderhalten sondern durch Strichart, legato vs. staccato, Klangfarbe, lang gegen kurz usw. (systematisch).
7) So weit als möglich Luft schaffen. Pausen immer aushalten. Cäsuren und Atempausen
8) *Klangraum* herstellen. Wie?

*

Fortsetzung

Vermeidung der mf-Sauce, eines pedalähnlichen Grundklangs, auf dem alles schwimmt. Klangraum herstellen heißt: die Möglichkeit von einander abgehobener Extreme schaffen. – Aber all dies trifft noch nicht ins Zentrum der Darstellung von Polyphonie. Diese muß vielmehr vom Wesen der Sache ausgehen: der Dialektik der Stimmen, davon, daß eine die negative Funktion der anderen ist. *Hauptregel:* weder nur vertikal spielen, harmonisch, noch bloß horizontal im Sinn unabhängiger Melodien, sondern das *Ineinanderpassen* der Stimmen erkennen und realisieren. Dies wäre an einem Einzelbeispiel zu erläutern. Eine Stimme muß gewissermaßen als Negativ, Komplement der anderen gespielt werden. Zu realisieren sind nicht bloß die Stimmen sondern ihr *Verhältnis:* die Polyphonie muß durch die Interpretation als Medium der *Formbildung* sich erweisen.

*

Klangraum: ein Akzent kann unter Umständen ersetzen, daß eine ganze Linie forte gespielt wird.

*

Man muß beim Begriff Klangraum genau unterscheiden: die Herstellung eines – gewissermaßen leeren – Raums, in dem die Ereignisse sich von einander abheben (und das ist hier, in
105 der Reproduktionstheorie gemeint), und der Räumlichkeit der Komposition selber, wie sie früher von der harmonischen Perspektive, heute von der kontrapunktischen Arbeit besorgt wird (wie in meinem Kurs über Schönberg und den Kontrapunkt[170] entwickelt). Beides hängt aber zusammen. In der Reproduktion setzt die Realisierung des zweiten Moments die Herstellung des ersten voraus.

*

Die Hauptregel für die Darstellung von Polyphonie läßt sich vielleicht, sehr cum grano salis, auf die Formel bringen: alle Stimmen müssen zusammen eine Melodie bilden. Es ist vor allem auf das Ineinanderpassen hin zu probieren. Dabei auch Rudi [Kolischs] Kategorie: Impulse aufnehmen. Die Stimmen müssen *eine* sein – aber gerade dadurch, daß sie sinnvoll von einander *unterschieden* werden.

*

Eine der Hauptquellen des schlechten – unartikulierten, sinnwidrigen – Musizierens ist das Bedürfnis nach falscher Verbindung d. h. der an der Klangoberfläche. Je weniger offenbar die Musikanten der strukturellen Einheit gewahr werden, desto mehr fürchten sie das Auseinanderfallen und helfen sich durch das möglichst bruchlose Ineinanderziehen. Hereinspielt die infantile Unfähigkeit, Pausen zu halten (NB das mensurale Moment muß *gestärkt* werden, wenn es dem Andern zugute kommen soll). Der Elementarfall ist der hörbare Lagenwechsel schlechter Streicher; es reicht aber über das Verschleifen von Phrasenende und Anfang bis zur großen Form, wo sie im Grunde Cäsuren verabscheuen (NB Bruno Walter). Der Zusammenhang von Musik besteht aber nicht im Weitergehen sondern im *inneren* Fluß d. h. dem dialektischen Spannungsverhältnis *unterschiedener* Teile. – Die hier bezeichnete, zentrale Unsitte entspricht genau dem bumble-bee-Typus des Komponierens. Die meisten reproduzierenden Musiker stehen auf dem Standpunkt der bumble bee. Die nach außen projizierte Angst vor der *eigenen* Leere.

*

Der sehr verbreitete Fehler des *Fallenlassens* bezieht sich nicht
nur auf kurze Noten und schlechte Taktteile, sondern vor al-
lem auch auf ganze Phrasenenden. Dabei spielt herein daß in 106
tonaler Musik jene vielfach antizipiert werden können, »sich
von selbst verstehen«. In Wahrheit handelt es sich, wie bei den
meisten Fehlinterpretationen, um Mangel an *Kraft:* man hat
sich gewissermaßen in der Setzung des Anfangs verausgabt,
und schleift den Rest bloß flüchtig mit. Dadurch werden die
Zusammenhänge, vor allem die Fortsetzungen so leicht un-
verständlich. Die Forderung des *Ausspielens* bezieht sich vor
allem auf dies Phänomen. – Der Gegensatz zur musikalischen
Kraft ist das mit dem Gefälle des Idioms sich Treiben lassen.

*

Geheimnis der Interpretation: An sich halten und doch nicht gegen sich selbst Musizieren. Der eigene Impuls muß noch in dessen Negation leben. Eben dies ist die Kraft des Interpreten.

*

Munteres Musizieren, von Kindern, Amateuren, Unterhaltungsmusikern und ähnlichem, bietet der Theorie das wichtigste Anschauungsmaterial. Denn einmal erscheint hier die Musik gewissermaßen mit all ihren Brüchen und Löchern, auseinandergenommen, in den Teilen jeglicher Dimension, aus denen sie sich zusammenfügt, und wie an kaputtem Spielzeug läßt an ihr sich studieren wie sie »funktioniert«. Die Risse sind soviel Fenster auf die Probleme der Interpretation, welche der gelungene Vollzug sonst verdeckt, dann aber zeigt sich an den Verfahrungsweisen jener Subjekte all das, was auch das schlechte *offizielle* Musizieren inspiriert, dort aber durch gute Manieren, den »guten Musiker« zugedeckt wird; die übliche musikalische Erziehung ist nichts als die Geschichte solcher Verdeckung. Man muß Toscanini aus dem Frankfurter Palmengartenorchester, aus dem Salontrio des Hotels Waldhaus in Sils-Maria Bruno Walter verstehen und deduzieren.

*

Die Theorie kann und will nicht alle Interpretationsprobleme vollständig entwickeln – sie sind unendlich –; wohl aber Modelle aufrichten, wie zu lösen sei. Die Arbeit und Anstrengung erspart sie nicht. Jedes Kunstwerk ist eine Monade; es gibt kein übergreifendes Schema für die Bewältigung der Probleme. Zur Einleitung.

*

107 Jede Komposition enthält – gegenüber dem reinen Notentext – Elemente ihrer eigenen Interpretation. Zu ihnen gehört, außer den Angaben und Vortragszeichen, vor allem auch seit dem 19. Jahrhundert die Instrumentation, die immer das Werk interpretiert, dafür Sorge trägt, daß es so und nicht anders erscheine. Aus diesen Elementen muß die Darstellung extrapolieren. Wenn im Tagesakkord am Anfang des II. Aktes Tristan Trompeten, Posaunen, Tuba fehlen, so besagt das etwas über den Charakter des Klanges – und damit der ganzen Partie, eine Anweisung für die Darstellung. Damit ist der Satz von Berg zusammenzunehmen, jede Musik lasse mehrere Weisen der Instrumentation zu.[171] Die je gewählte ist der Kanon der authentischen Interpretation.

Frankfurt, Dezember 1956

*

Höhere Darstellungsprobleme: auskomponierte Ritardandi bei Brahms. Sie wirken fast stets – fälschlich – wie Vergrößerungen, also mensural, und nicht wie Ritardandi, also mensural[172]. Z. B. in dem überhaupt sehr schwierigen ersten Satz der zweiten Symphonie: Ende der ersten Hauptgestalt vor der Unisonostelle (kleine Partitur S. 2). Man wird das wohl so bringen müssen, daß der Bläsernachsatz der 2. Strophe, der schon vor der Vergrößerung auf deren Motiv hängen bleibt, dabei so weit ritardiert wird, daß man als *Konsequenz* daraus die 4 Abschlußtakte als Vergrößerung hört. Es ist aber auch möglich, daß das von Brahms bei den 3 kritischen Takten vor der Vergrößerung geschriebene crescendo *ohne* Tempomodifikation die Ritardandowirkung vorbereiten soll (Dynamik kann Tempo substituieren!). Das *stellt* dann aber erst das Problem, d. h. wie ist dann so zu verfahren, daß die intendierte Wirkung *eintritt.* Äußerst schwierig. Übrigens die Idee des auskomponierten ritardando im ganzen Satz, so schon vor A (S. 3). – Das einzigartige des Stückes: daß ein in all seinen Elementen lyrisches Gebilde als Totalität gleichwohl symphonisch ist. Wie das zu realisieren ist – das sind die *eigentlichen* Interpretationsprobleme, zu deren Bewältigung es nur nie kommt.

*

Die in der vorigen Notiz bezeichneten »höheren Darstellungsprobleme« sind, wie bereits vermerkt, nicht eine *Schicht,* die auf den niedrigeren aufzubauen wäre. Sie folgen aber genau so wenig, als ob sie selbstverständlich wären, aus der bloßen sachgerechten Darstellung der Details. Zwischen beiden Momenten herrscht vielmehr in den Kompositionen, und darum auch in der Darstellung, stete Spannung: ihre Identität ist das Problem, die des Nichtidentischen. Zur Dechiffrierung der Details bedarf es ebenso des Wissens vom Gesamtcharakter wie dieser dadurch zusammenschießt, daß den Impulsen der Details nachgegangen wird. Keine prästabilierte Harmonie 108 waltet zwischen beiden sondern die Identität ist immer eine erst herzustellende und es ist vielleicht die innerste Aufgabe der Interpretation – die, um deretwillen das Werk der Interpretation bedarf – jene Identität, welche der Text nur als Potentialität und Problem enthält, zu aktualisieren. Darin liegt, daß die Interpretation, wie Hilfe, so auch *Kritik* der Texte impliziert, nämlich überall dort, wo sie auf die Unmöglichkeit jener Identifikation stößt. Diese ist immer dialektischen Wesens, nie »induktiv« oder »deduktiv«. Übrigens hängt die Interpretation des Verhältnisses von Ganzem und Teil selber auch von dem Werk ab. Wo das Ganze den blinden Vorrang besitzt – bei Händel, bei Strawinsky – muß die Interpretation faute de mieux ihr folgen, und ebenso umgekehrt, wo die Musik nur aus »Einfällen« sich zusammensetzt. Mit anderen Worten: die »höheren« Darstellungsprobleme gibt es eigentlich nur in hoher, in sich dialektischer Musik.

*

Eine von Rudi [Kolisch] bezeichnete Kategorie: das Aufnehmen von Impulsen. Z. B. in der Aufführung des letzten Klavierkonzertes von Mozart ließ Solti eine Staccatostelle mit Vorschlägen sehr spitz, charakteristisch spielen; die Haskil[173], die die Stelle danach hat, spielte sie weich, verschwommen und bewirkte eine Anticlimax dort, wo das Soloinstrument ein Gesetztes einzulösen hätte. Dies ist ein Problem allen Ensemblespiels.

*

Generell läßt sich sagen, daß die Probleme der Interpretation
109 im eigentlichen, geistigen Sinn immer die der Komposition sind. Einmal muß die Interpretation die Idee der Komposition – derart wie ich sie S. 107 bei der II. Symphonie von Brahms bezeichnete – herausbringen, ihr zuhilfe kommen. Dann: sie hat die *Probleme* auszutragen, die in der Komposition

gelegen sind. Die Schwierigkeiten, Antinomien hat sie nicht, wie es fast allerorten geschieht, zuzuschmieren sondern deren eigenen *Sinn* zu begreifen und ihm zu gehorchen. Durch Darstellung dieses Sinnes der Probleme, nicht indem sie überspielt werden, trägt die Interpretation zu ihrer Lösung bei. Sie geht auf die *Extreme* des kompositorischen Gehalts, nicht auf deren mittleren Ausgleich. Die Interpretation ist gewissermaßen eine Berufungsinstanz, vor der die Komposition als Prozeß nochmals ausgetragen wird. Interpretieren heißt: die Komposition so komponieren, wie sie von sich aus komponiert sein möchte. Dem liegt zugrunde die Vorstellung vom Werk als Kraftfeld; dazu die Selbstanzeige des Wagner[174].

*

Die musikalische Interpretation hat mehrere recht drastisch unterschiedene Schichten: die analytische Erkenntnis des Sinnes, also die Wahrheit des Werkes; die adäquate Imagination, an der alles Erscheinende zu messen ist; die Realisierung d. h. der dialektische Prozeß mit dem klingenden Material. Das meiste Unglück geschieht bereits auf dieser gröbsten Schicht, die übrigens in der herrschenden Praxis fast stets die erste und meist die einzige ist, während sie die letzte sein sollte. Fast stets kommt es anders heraus als man es sich denkt, durch Reibungskoeffizienten, die teils am eigenen Spiel- und Singmechanismus liegen, teils an dem Instrument, teils an der Aufspaltung der *einen* imaginierten Musik an mehrere Subjekte (Ensemble: Forderung daraus die unbedingte Autorität des für die Interpretation je verantwortlichen!); teils im »sozialen Hohlraum« etwa zwischen Dirigenten und Orchester, teils in besonderen Widerständen der Materie, wie etwa des Chors und der Bühne. Dabei ist aber auch dies Verhältnis zum Klangmaterial durchaus dialektisch. Während alle der Imagination widerstehen, tragen viele auch zu ihr bei und zwar nach dem Kanon des Verhältnisses der Komposition *selbst* zum Ma- 110
terial. Das Klavier – oder sind es nicht Arm, Handgelenk und

Finger, ist nicht gerade das Klavier *freundlicher?* – will nicht so wie ich gern will, aber zugleich sagt es immer auch: so kann es sein, so soll es sein, d. h. es ist selber wieder ein Moment der Imagination, zuweilen auch deren Korrektur (aber gerade hier ist die höchste Vorsicht gegen das Mißverständnis des Musikanten angezeigt!). Diese verwickelten Verhältnisse sind genau darzustellen.

*

Dabei zeichnet sich nun eine Antinomie ab. Im Gegensatz zu Ideen, wie sie in der Jugend- und Laienbewegung geistern mögen, ist es nämlich, um den Interpretationsaufgaben gewachsen zu sein, unbedingt notwendig, den Spiel- (und auch Sing-)mechanismus *selbständig* auszubilden, für sich zu entwickeln, unabhängig von den konkreten Aufgaben, und zwar in einem sehr hohen Maße. Wie in der Wissenschaft ist die Trennung von Methode und Sache – und zwar um der *Sache* willen – geboten. Während in Wahrheit jegliche Art der Darstellung einzig aus der *spezifischen* Sache zu entwickeln wäre und jede abstrakte Methode, indem sie das Werk unter die Verfahrensweise der Interpretation subsumiert, eigentlich a priori ihrer Aufgabe widerspricht, bedarf es doch wieder einer solchen Methode, um überhaupt ein Niveau der Darstellungsmittel herzustellen, das überhaupt an die Aufgaben heranreicht. Man kann nicht mit jedem Werk von vorn anfangen. Insofern partizipiert die Interpretation an der Dialektik von Arbeitsteilung (dies gilt viel allgemeiner: weil nämlich die Musik *selber* daran partizipiert). Aber dadurch verselbständigt sich der Spielmechanismus derart, daß er sich den Aufgaben der Komposition entfremdet. Wenn die Finger des Dilettanten nicht an die rechte Stelle kommen, so laufen die des professionals von selbst, und dies auch im übertragenen Sinn, geistig-musikalisch. Es ist daher prinzipiell eines der Hauptprobleme der Interpretation, daß die erworbene und notwendige Habitualität des Spielers je wieder von der spezifischen Erkenntnis des Werkes gebrochen, negiert, aufgehoben wird. Dieser Übergang ist der zur wahren Interpretation. Das Unvergängliche an Schnabels Leistung besteht darin, daß er im *Prinzip* als erster ihn vollzog, konkret freilich vielfach bei der abstrakten Negation der habituellen Spielweise stehen blieb. Webern, Steuermann, Kolisch haben es dann wirklich realisiert. – Im Licht dieser Erörterung zeichnet sich ab, daß der *Widerstand* gegen die richtige Interpretation von der Habitualität, der *subjektiven* Spielweise herrührt (das Problem des in jedem Augenblick seiner selbst mächtig Seins der Interpretation), die Hilfe von der *objektiven* Spielweise des Instruments, das gerade als ein dem Interpreten antithetisch gegenüberstehendes sich gegen ihn in gewisser Weise mit dem Werk verbündet. *[Darunter:]* vgl. S. 99 111

*

Rudi [Kolischs] Weigerung, die Differenz traditioneller und neuer Musik überhaupt anzuerkennen, hängt zuinnerst mit der Reproduktionstheorie zusammen. Denn die traditionelle verfremden, heißt ja: sie wie neue anschauen (etwa so, wie Brecht von »Übungen zu dem Trauerspiel Hamlet«[175] spricht). Und die Anstrengung, die subkutane Schicht der traditionellen Musik zu erschließen und zu realisieren, ist sicher nicht geringer als die, in der neuen, wo sie schon nach außen gekehrt ist, darzustellen. D. h. von einem zentralen Standpunkt der Interpretation aus ist alle Musik gleich schwer. Damit aber auch zum Hören. Der Aufsatz »Neue Musik Interpretation Publikum«[176] ist im Text zu verarbeiten.

*

1957

In der traditionellen Musik genügt es *nicht,* unabhängig vom Taktstrich zu musizieren, sondern man muß *zugleich* die absoluten und die Taktbetonungen fühlen, d. h. den Konflikt beider austragen. Besonders bei Schumann, wo dies zuweilen ausdrücklich verlangt wird (er hat sehr richtig gefühlt, daß bei

der vorherrschenden 8-Taktigkeit Mittel solcher Differenzierung notwendig sind). Z. B. im 2. Thema des Finales des Klavierkonzerts darf man nicht *nur* den Scheintakt $\frac{3}{2}$, sondern immer zugleich die $\frac{3}{4}$ durchhören also gewissermaßen die Pause im 2. Takt betonen. Das heißt technisch: die 1 des Modells etwas hervorheben (verlängern, nicht akzentuieren!); die 3 des ersten, die 2 des 2. Taktes usw. *relativ* fallen lassen. – Solche Wirkungen sind der neuen Musik, durch den Fortfall des rhythmischen Schemas, verwehrt, analog den entsprechenden harmonischen. Von hier fällt Licht auf eine wirkliche Funktion des Jazz: nämlich solche Differenzierungen, die sonst verschwinden, zu bewahren. Wie übrigens überhaupt die *Inter-*
112 *pretation* manches vom Jazz zu lernen hat.

*

Im Fledermauswalzer macht Solti vor dem Akzentton im 4. Takt 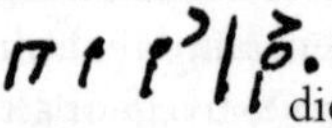 eine kurze (minimale) Luftpause, welche die Elastizität ungemein verstärkt. Aber eine solche quasi-rubato-Wirkung ist nicht wiederholbar, ohne komisch zu werden. Andererseits aber muß sie, um organisch zu sein, Konsequenzen haben. Er löst instinktiv das Problem indem er die Luftpause *auflöst,* d. h. in der 1. Sequenz verkleinert und dann ganz verschwinden läßt. Ganz ähnlich die Revellers in »In a little Spanish town« – Was man von der popular music lernen kann –

*

Zum Sinn der Koloratur – des Balletts der Stimme – gehört ein eigentümliches Mehr können als es können. Es muß das Schwierigste »leicht« klingen, mühelos, nie bloß realisiert. Zum Gefühl der Naturbeherrschung gehört, daß nicht die Fähigkeit bloß der Aufgabe gleiche sondern ihr überlegen sei. Denn sonst ist es wirkliche Naturbeherrschung und nicht deren Rückkunft als *Spiel.* Hier öffnet sich ein Spalt in die Metaphysik – und die Rettung – des virtuosen Elements. Denn es ist nicht einfach Naturbeherrschung als Herrschaft über Material und Spielmechanismus, sondern indem mit jener Beherrschung, vermöge ihrer Vollkommenheit, gespielt wird, verliert sie die Gewalt, den Ernst, wird zu Imagination und dadurch versöhnt: Herrschaft über Natur erscheint »natürlich«, wird ihrer selbst als Natur inne. Rastelli als Schlüsselfigur zur musikalischen Interpretation.

*

Wie wenig die Vorstellung des Komponisten – der ominöse »Wille des Gesetzgebers« – einen Kanon der Interpretation abgibt, zeigt die folgende Überlegung. In seiner Imagination rückt alles zusammen, sie meint das Ganze, ist im Idealfall momentan, gleichzeitig. Außerdem: was man genau an Eigenem kennt, ist einem fad, (Nietzsche![177]), one wants to get over with it! Daher stellen die Komponisten, mit Recht, ihre Sachen vielfach rascher sich vor als sie objektiv, d. h. als Entfaltung des musikalischen Sinnes sind. Metronomisierungen etwa bei Schumann und Schönberg, gelegentlich auch bei Beethoven, dürften zu rasch sein. Die Interpretation aber ist
die angemessene Übersetzung des musikalischen Sinnes in die 113
Erscheinung. Auch sie beruht auf der Imagination aber einer von ganz anderem Typus als die des Komponisten. – Hierher auch das Problem der Uraufführungstempi.

*

Zum geschichtlichen Wesen der Interpretation. In den zwanziger Jahren, in Opposition gegen den deutschen Irrationalismus, mußten Kolisch und ich rasche Tempi, Verzicht auf Pathos, das Anti-Brucknerische vertreten. Im Amerika Toscaninis dann, gegenüber dem herrschenden Positivismus, änderte sich das, und diese Modifikationen sind nicht den Sachen äußerlich, sondern spielen in diesen selber sich ab d. h.

werden durch die Dialektik von Einheit und Mannigfaltigkeit vorgezeichnet. – Vor 30 Jahren klagten Maria und Agathe[178] über den Verfall der italienischen Gesangskunst. Heute klagt Solti schon darüber, daß es keine Wagnersänger mehr gibt – ohne daß dafür das Ältere sich wiederhergestellt hätte.

*

Zur Frage der mitkomponierten Interpretation den Satz von Schönberg zitieren, ein guter Komponist habe die Umblätterstellen mitzukomponieren[179].

*

Zum Problem der Charaktere. Die Motivfragmente am Anfang der IX. Symphonie [Beethovens]. Sie dürfen nicht als Vordergrund, espressivo gespielt werden, weil ja das Hauptthema aus ihnen erst sich bildet. Sie dürfen aber auch nicht einfach fallen gelassen werden, weil sonst die Beziehung nicht mehr verständlich ist. Es muß ein Mittleres gefunden werden; deutlich aber doch nicht unterstrichen. Genau das können die Dirigenten nicht, die immer »zweiwertig« denken. Furtwängler nimmt das Motiv grob espressivo. Überhaupt die Vergröberungstendenz im Zusammenhang mit dem Bestreben der Dirigenten nach Sinnfälligkeit. – Bei Bruckner gibt es einen Charakter der unterdrückten Ekstase, z. B. bei der Einführung des 2. Modells im Hauptthema der IV. (*vor* dem Forte)[180], oder beim Verklingen des Hauptthemas der VII. ins Säuseln[181]. Dieser Charakter wird *nie* getroffen. In genaue Angaben übersetzen warum nicht.

*

Das Verhältnis von Haupt- und Nebensache: entweder es wird
114 roh ignoriert, oder es wird visiert, aber grob im Sinn des Hervor- und Zurücktretens gelöst. Aber das Verständnis des Hauptthemas der IV. Symphonie von Bruckner hängt *wesent-*

lich daran, daß die Führung der Bässe gegen das Horn, die erst die Perspektive schafft, *deutlich* wird: nur *relatives* Zurücktreten. Wie man überhaupt die Hauptstimmen dann *nicht* hervorheben soll, wo sie von selbst da sind. Bei jenem Anfang ist es wichtiger, daß das Horn verschleiert, als daß es »da« ist – *da* müssen aber, auch im pp, die rauschenden Streicher sein.

*

In der Arbeit muß klar gesagt sein, daß heute fast alle musikalische Interpretation sinnwidrig und falsch ist, und die *Gründe* dafür gegeben [werden]. Dazu vgl. das Filmmusikbuch[182].

*

Zum Problem der mechanischen Reproduktion. Die alten, relativ primitiven Grammophone sind den pseudo-perfektionierten modernen Plattenspielern vorzuziehen, weil sie nicht den *Schein* des Originals erwecken sondern als Schatten auftreten. Je näher aber die mechanische Wiedergabe der lebendigen zu kommen trachtet, um so mehr tritt die Unwahrheit – zumal als der »vergößerte«, aufgequollene und daher undeutliche Klang – hervor. Die Schwelle ist wohl die elektrische Aufnahmetechnik. Freilich vermag die Quantität in die Qualität umzuschlagen d. h. die Imitation so sich vervollkommnen daß die Kategorie des Originals ihr Recht verliert.

*

Dem Mangel an Innenspannung in der Interpretation – also der Unfähigkeit, die Elemente sinnvoll dynamisch auf einander zu beziehen – entspricht genau die omnipräsente Angst, äußere Spannung nicht zu verlieren. Daher der ungeheuer verbreitete Fehler, Phrasen nicht wirklich ausspielen zu lassen. Ungeduld als Surrogat von Spannung. Während die meisten Darstellungsmittel in der Interpretation übertrieben werden,

werden die Phrasierungen meist untertrieben. So werden die wichtigsten Cäsuren im Wiener Klassizismus, wie die zwischen den beiden Hauptkomplexen der Exposition, meist zu *kurz*, d.h. einfach nach der Zählzeit genommen. Harmonische Doppelpunkte, oft auch Pausen, erlauben das, ohne daß offen ein Bewußtsein des Mechanischen sich herstellte; aber die subkutane Organisation gerät durch solche falsche Exaktheit unweigerlich in Unordnung. Die Teile sind zwar
115 äußerlich getrennt, aber das *Gewicht* der Trennung geht verloren.

*

Die Darstellung musikalischer Formen darf nie bloß die der Formschemata und Teile sein sondern immer die der musikalischen *Textur*, oder genauer des Verhältnisses zwischen Textur und Gliederung – dies ist eine der wichtigsten, wenn nicht *die* wichtigste Regel. Der Begriff der Textur als ein Zentralbegriff der Interpretation.

*

Kritik der Heteronomie der Interpretation. Alles ist schlecht, was von sedimentierten Schwierigkeiten der Sing- und Spielweisen herrührt, wie das Tremolo des Sängers oder der hörbare Lagenwechsel der Streicher, besonders der Celli. (meist handelt es sich um Archaismen!) Aber auch hier äußerste Differenzierung geboten, denn andererseits sind die Sing- und Spielweisen auch wieder ein positives Moment der Interpretation. Cf. S. 109 und 110 dieser Notizen. Wann gut, wann schlecht? Kriterium ist wohl wieweit zwischen den »Manieren« der Darstellung und der Interpretation ein sinnvoll durchsichtiger Zusammenhang besteht. Hier Zusammenhang mit dem *neumischen* Element.

*

Im Text wird auf die Schriften Hugo Riemanns einzugehen sein. Er hat, bei aller akademischen Enge, das sehr große Verdienst, Reproduktionsfragen aus der *Sache* – d. h. der Komposition – angefaßt zu haben; er ist über das bloße Vertrauen auf das »Musikalische« herausgekommen, das zwar eine notwendige aber nicht zureichende Bedingung der Reproduktion ist und, um sich erhalten zu können, durch die Reflexion hindurch muß. Das gilt vor allem für seine Lehre von der *Phrasierung*[183], die er in einen sinnvollen Zusammenhang mit der Komposition gebracht hat, unter Beziehung auf bedeutende ältere Autoren wie J. A. P. Schulz (NB den Artikel »Vortrag« in Sulzers Theorie der schönen Künste von 1772 beschaffen). Darüber hinaus hat Riemann eine relativ hohe *Differenzierung* erreicht, indem er nicht einfach seine gewiß starren Schemata aufstellte sondern versuchte, mit deren Hilfe das zu erklären, was ihm Abweichung dünkte. Die Schwäche liegt in dem gesamten Ansatz. Er hat die achttaktige Periode, mit *allem*, was sie mit sich führt, hypostasiert, als wenn sie eine Art musikalisches Urphänomen wäre, auf das schließlich alle Strukturmomente sich
zurückführen lassen. Aber die Achttaktigkeit ist selber ein Ent- 116
sprungenes und gilt nur für den an der Sublimierung der Tanzformen bestimmten musikalischen Bereich. Bach weicht nicht von der Achttaktigkeit ab sondern ist in den entscheidenden Schichten seines Werkes exterritorial zu ihr: es gilt wohl der Satz, *daß alle polyphone Musik wesentlich n i c h t achttaktig ist* und zwar deshalb, weil die Polyphonie in der Komposition selbst das leisten will was die Achttaktigkeit ihr von außen aufstülpt (man kann das an Fugen von Mendelssohn und Schumann studieren, in denen die Symmetrie wesentlich der Formidee *widerspricht;* dazu vgl. die Fugenregel – von wem sie stammt – daß ein Fugenthema prinzipiell keine Periode oder Halbperiode sein soll[184]). Die Achttaktigkeit ist ein problematischer und relativ äußerlicher Aspekt des Rationalisierungsprozesses. Daher sind denn auch die späteren Komponisten, die ihr nicht gehorchen, Schubert vor allem und Schönberg, auch Mozart, nicht sowohl als Nuancen, Deviationen zu verstehen, die mit Kunst dann

doch unter das Riemannsche Schema sich bringen lassen, sondern Ausdruck einer Gegentendenz, der zum je Einzelnen, zum »Triebleben der Klänge«[185] als einem archaischen Erbe, einem unausrottbar Mimetischen. Riemann aber denkt musikalisch umfangslogisch, quasi »realistisch«; alles soll aus dem abstrakten Oberbegriff folgen wie in einer deduktiven Wissenschaft. Es ist eine *undialektische* Reproduktionstheorie; sie verfehlt das Werk als ein *Kraftfeld* zwischen dem Allgemeinbegriff und dem Individuellen, nicht Subsumierten; Klassifikation anstatt Begreifen (das gilt für fast die gesamte offizielle systematische Musikwissenschaft). Dadurch wird seine Theorie einerseits zu schematisch, andererseits – wo sie das nicht Subsumierte und diesem inkommensurable Schema bringen will, zu kompliziert, eine Art Epizykelntheorie, welche das *Zählen* zur obersten Kategorie erhebt und am Wesen des Phänomens vorbeizielt (ich habe verwandte Einwände im Harmonikkapitel des Wagner[186] gemacht). In meiner Sprache:
117 Riemann sucht die gesamte Reproduktionstheorie auf mensurale Begriffe zu bringen. Die Wahl von Abstraktionsschnitten und Bezugssystemen ist aber der Sache gegenüber nicht indifferent. Indem Riemann das metrisch-harmonische Kraftfeld verkennt, versagt er als Anweisung zum Reproduzieren überall dort wo der Sinn der Musik die Spannung jener Elemente ist und vollends dort, wo in einem *äußeren* Sinn der abstrakte Oberbegriff depotenziert ist – latent, subkutan gibt es ja diese Spannung in *aller* Musik. Die Fehlanweisung wird konkret zu belegen sein.

*

Allgemein gilt für die Reproduktion die funktionelle Abhängigkeit der musikalischen Dimensionen von einander. Z. B. Form und Agogik. Es kann an bestimmten Stellen ein Desiderat der Form sein, das Tempo im Fluß zu halten, d. h. irgend ein Nachlassen von deren Spannung zu kompensieren durch ein unmerkliches Anziehen des Tempos. In der Reproduktion sehr erfahrene Komponisten bringen das oft durch Bezeichnungen wie »Nicht schleppen« zum Ausdruck.

*

Aus der Kontrapunktarbeit[187] die reproduktionstheoretischen Konsequenzen ziehen, wie: nicht nur *deutlich* durch dynamische Abstufung des Simultanen, Zurücktreten nach Einsätzen, Unterscheidung von Legato und Staccato, sondern auch: die Stimmen in einander passen, also die Ergänzungen und Relationen herausbringen, »beantworten« usw. Das ist der *objektive* Sinn von »Impulse aufnehmen«. Dies letztere Element – die Realisierung von *Ähnlichkeiten* – wird im kontrapunktischen Musizieren fast nie auch nur erreicht.

*

Schumannkonzert, I. Satz, ein Takt nach B[188]. Die tiefsten Töne der Begleitfiguren bilden eine Begleitung. Aber sie dürfen keinesfalls *betont* werden. Also nur: sehr kurz. Durchs Abheben, nicht durch Akzente werden sie zur Linie. Substituierbarkeit: Längenverhältnisse können anstelle dynamischer treten.

*

Allgemeine Regel: wo immer eine musikalische Dimension 118
eine Anforderung an die Interpretation stellt, die zugleich sich verbietet, ist diese Anforderung durch eine andere Dimension zu realisieren. Das entspricht dem kompositorischen Sachverhalt der Substituierbarkeit einer Dimension durch die andere.

*

Ähnlichkeiten müssen als Ähnlichkeiten, Kontraste als Kontraste, Modifikationen, Varianten als solche deutlich werden.

Jedes musikalische Ereignis hat nach solchen Kategorien seinen Formsinn: er ist zu erkennen und das Erkannte darzustellen. Wird aber etwa zwischen Verschiedenem vermittelt, so ist die *Vermittlung* deutlich zu machen. Man kann also, ebenfalls vom kompositorischen Sachverhalt her, von *funktioneller* Interpretation reden. Interpretieren heißt: jedes musikalische Moment so darstellen, daß die Funktion, die es an sich in der Komposition erfüllt, in der Erscheinung erfüllt [wird]. – Wenn die Komposition das Wesen in die Peripherie setzt, dann ist genau dieser Prozeß der, welcher der Interpretation das Formgesetz vorschreibt. – Durch die Interpretation soll die Komposition, als das an sich Seiende, zum an und für sich Seienden werden – nicht zu einem für andere. – Wahre Interpretation: die Komposition hört sich selber zu.

*

Das Impulse aufnehmen als bloße *Ähnlichkeit* ist viel zu arm, und oft falsch. Es kommt immer darauf an, die *Relation* eines Ereignisses zu vorhergehendem, anstatt bloß das Ereignis als solches darzustellen, und diese Relation kann äußerst vielfältig sein; sie erschöpft sich nicht in Ähnlichkeiten und Kontrasten. Sie kann z. B. eine *Antwort* sein, oder ein Einholen, Ausfüllen, Überbrücken eines vorher bloß Gesetzten; oder dessen Auflösung. An diesen konkreten Bestimmungen hat die Interpretation (wie die Komposition) ihr wahres Leben; die formalen Kategorien wie Ähnlichkeit und Kontrast sind eigentlich nur Mittel zu ihrer Realisierung, nie die Träger des musikalischen Sinnes, und der Interpretation, selbst. Die eigentliche Schicht der Interpretation wird durch die Verdeutlichung von Ähnlichkeit und Kontrast erst *erschlossen,* nicht schon durchdrungen. Der hier angedeutete, im Text verschlossene *Prozeß,* zu realisieren durch die Verhältnisse der Einzelmomente zu einander, ist das Leben der Werke wie der Darstellung und er eigentlich ist es, der von der herkömmlichen Interpretation
119 überhaupt nicht erreicht wird. Hier entscheidet die Nuance

über den *ganzen* Sinn. Zu kritisieren die Auffassung, als wäre die Wahrheit der Interpretation so gebaut, daß es im Ganzen stimmen muß und die Details, gewissermaßen als Luxus, *hinzutreten.* In der Kunst entscheidet das *kleinste* über die Totale: vgl. S. 41 – wie übrigens auch in der Philosophie. – Das ist natürlich nicht *unmittelbar* auf die Technik des Probierens zu übertragen. – Der sogenannte gute Musiker ist genau der, welcher das hier angedeutete, *zentralste* Problem sei's nicht kennt seis absichtlich ignoriert. Schlüssel zum »Musikanten«: Hindemith.

*

Beispiel zur vorhergehenden Notiz: daß es nicht auf den bloßen Kontrast ankommt sondern dessen spezifische Funktion: Anfang des A-Dur-Quartetts von Schumann[189]:

(oder so ähnlich)

Die Funktion des Nachsatzes: Ausfüllen des Intervalls, Übersetzung des Rufs ins Menschliche, auch etwas wie Antwort, muß in der Interpretation herauskommen. Also: die kritischen Ecknoten, die ausgefüllt werden, müssen als solche noch fühlbar sein durch minimale Betonungen. Durch die dabei sich ergebenden Gruppen fällt dann ein natürlicher Akzent auf den Höhepunkt des Nachsatzes, e, der dann wieder als »Schritt« gegenüber dem ersten fis, im Vordersatz, gehört wird (Binnenmelodie). Diese Struktur schafft zugleich *metrische* Variation durch die Bildung von *Zweiviertel*gruppen, »Scheintakten«, die aber gerade die *wahren* Takte sind. Sie werden gewissermaßen durch den letzten Takt »verifiziert«. Das abschließende e ist dann sinngemäß ein (fallen zu lassender) *guter* Taktteil, schwache 1, und Auftakt zur Wiederholung des Vordersatzes (*kein* totes Intervall; dieser Begriff von Riemann steht zur Kritik!). Also eine latent zeugmatische Konstruktion; *eine* Note ist 1 und 3 zugleich in eins. Und dieser subkutane Reichtum bei dem seiner Achttakter wegen verschrienen Schumann. In der traditionellen Musik herrschen also vielfach Pseudosymmetrien, das eigentliche Pulsieren der Musik weicht davon ab, und gerade das gilt es zu realisieren.

*

120 Pech gehabt: Schumann phrasiert das Thema anders, in ganzen Dreivierteltakten, *nicht* subkutan. Ist das nun (wie oft bei ihm) Mittel eines *Kräftespiels?* Oder hab ich recht *gegen* ihn?

*

Alle Erwägungen über die Gebundenheit der Interpretation haben ihre Grenze an der folgenden: daß die musikalische Niederschrift ja Ausdruck einer musikalischen *Idee* ist, die sie gleichsam standardisiert, verdinglicht, verändert, und die es durch »Interlinearversion« zu erwecken, wiederherzustellen gilt. In gewissem Sinn macht die wahre Interpretation die Notation *rückgängig.* Nimmt man also den Anfang des Schumannkonzertes: so ist die *Idee* das Einhalten des Motivs 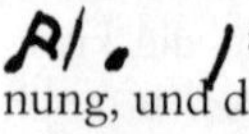 auf einer Verlängerung, als Herstellung von Spannung, und dann der Absturz, der die Spannung löst, gewissermaßen der Schwerkraft nachgibt. Das ist zu erkennen und zu realisieren. Ob dabei die geschriebenen Notenwerte diese Idee adäquat übersetzen oder nur andeuten – ob also etwa, der erkannten Idee zuliebe, die Halte zu verlängern und dann die Zeit durch ein accelerando des Absturzes einzubringen ist, das ist eine zweite, die eigentlich interpretative Frage. – Das Problem kompliziert sich aber dadurch, daß die Verdinglichung durch die Notation, Zentralmoment musikalischer Rationalisierung, der Komposition nicht *nur* äußerlich ist (so wenig wie etwa die Tonalität), sondern selbst als ein Moment, gleichsam als der Reibungskoeffizient der Äußerlichkeit, der Widerstand, an dem sie sich kräftigt, in sie eingeht. Und Interpretieren heißt darum nicht nur die Idee auskristallisieren, sondern dies Kraftfeld sichtbar machen. Dabei ist aber immer offen, wieweit das wirklich geschieht und wieweit die mensurale Treue die Idee tötet – oder wieweit die Idee bloß die kontingente Projektion des interpretierenden Bewußtseins bleibt. Das ist der eigentliche Kern der Frage der Interpretation.

*

Gegen eine bestimmte Art des »Gestaltens«, z. B. von Alfred Cortot. Sie besteht darin, in einer übertriebenen, überauffälligen Weise das herauszuarbeiten, was man ohnehin hört oder
was in einem äußerlichsten Sinn die Hauptsache ist. Eine Art 121
falscher Plastik: wie wenn man eine Skulptur durch ein Stereoskop betrachtet. Interpretation heißt hier: Musik für die Dummen. Ich hörte eine Aufnahme der Symphonischen Etüden von Schumann; das klang genau wie der Witz von dem Satz, in dem Heine und Hebbel vorkomm[en]: »Du bist wie Heine-Hebbel-*u*me«! Völlige Verzerrung durch Herausarbeiten. Daran ist Schumann nicht ganz unschuldig; durch weite Griffe entstehende Arpeggien klingen an sich schon wie Hebbelume. – Natürlich gilt Cortot, ein alter Nazi[190], im Deutschland von 1957 als großer alter Mann: sacred cow. – Schlechtes Überwiegen des neumisch mimetischen Elements. »Komödiantenpapa«.

*

zentral

Gegen die Bestimmung musikalischer Texte als Spielanweisung sowohl wie als Fixierung der Vorstellung des Komponisten wird eine positive zu halten sein. Das ist aber wohl die der *Gedächtnisfixierung* und zwar der einer *kollektiven Überlieferung,* wie sie aus dem liturgischen Gebrauch folgt. Darin ist unendlich viel enthalten. So etwa: es wird nicht sowohl ein

Für andere(s) geboten, sondern das An sich, die Idee, die Musik selber festgehalten. Dann: dies An sich ist nicht das was sich der Komponist vorstellt sondern wie es bereits in der Übung sich festgestellt hat. Das objektivierende Moment der Notation ist damit zugleich das gesellschaftliche *und* hat das geschichtliche – eben als Bild einer Tradition – in sich. Die Objektivität des Werkes gegen die Imagination des Komponisten: das ist die durch die Schrift ins Werk einwandernde Kollektivität. Solange aber diese dem Subjekt als ein Unidentisches gegenübersteht, ist jeder Text zugleich *in sich* dialektisch, und diese Dialektik ist das Problem jeder Interpretation. Das heißt: die Schrift in der Musik ist immer gegen das Subjekt wahr und unwahr. Das ist der philosophische Schlüssel der gesamten Theorie.

Frankfurt, 6. April 57

*

Das Verhältnis zur mechanischen Reproduktion aufs Neue durchdenken. Die alte These vom Verschwinden des Interpreten[191] bedarf wohl gerade angesichts der jüngsten Entwicklung, welche diese These giriert, der Revision. Denn die traditionelle Musik bis Schönberg und Webern, diese eingeschlossen, ist dem eigenen Sinn nach auf Interpreten verwiesen. Dies hängt mit dem neumischen Element der Notation aufs engste zusammen. Wo Subjektivität, Sinn, das dem Entfremdeten Entgegenstehende der Sache selbst we-
122 sentlich, aber in ihr zugleich geronnen, »verschlüsselt« ist, bedarf jenes Moment seinesgleichen, des Subjekts, zu seiner Errettung – eben um des sachlichen Gehalts willen. Meine alte Ansicht war zu undifferenziert. Hier wird auch auf gewisse, freilich psychologistisch ausgedrückte Unterscheidungen von Kurth wie die zwischen Ton- und Musikpsychologie[192] einzugehen sein; die elektronische Theorie hat bislang Ton und Musik verwechselt. Ebenso Seashore[193] kritisieren; das Moment, das ihm Abweichung heißt, ist gerade das die Musik eigentlich konstituierende, keine bloße Zutat (dies

bezeichnet eine *allgemeine* Tendenz meines Denkens gegenüber der verbreiteten). Zusehen, ob nicht die reaktionäre Theorie Furtwänglers von der »Unexaktheit«[194], und die ihr entsprechende Praxis, zu *retten* sei. Freilich dialektisch: das Unexakte, also etwa daß *keine* Zählzeiten einander mechanisch gleich sein dürfen, ist selbst exakt zu nehmen d.h. streng aus dem musikalischen Zusammenhang zu entwickeln. – Andererseits ist das Musizieren vielfach hinter den fortgeschrittensten Methoden der technischen Reproduktion – denen des Films – zurückgeblieben und vor allem das Radio hat sie, aus gesellschaftlichen Gründen, sich noch nicht zugeeignet. So geht der altmodische und ganz unzulängliche Probenbetrieb (vgl. »Neue Musik/Interpretation/Publikum«) unverändert weiter, anstatt daß das Radio beliebig viele Proben machte um authentische Aufführungen zu erzielen und dann zu fixieren. Ein Filmregisseur kann eine Szene zehnmal »schießen« und dann die beste auswählen. Dasselbe müßte bei Musik im Radio möglich sein, wobei noch auszuprobieren wäre, ob und in welchem Umfang man ebenfalls die endgültige Aufführung montieren könnte (die »lebendige Ganzheit« der Aufführung ist vor allem bei großen Formen wahrscheinlich wie in vielen anderen Bereichen eine bloße Ideologie). Übrigens: die Funktion des Dirigenten im Vergleich zu der des Filmregisseurs. Sie beruht zum großen Teil auf einer archaischen *Mangelwirtschaft.* Weil es an Probenzeit gebricht, wird vom Dirigenten die angeblich spezifische Dirigierbegabung verlangt, die der unmittelbaren, suggestiven Übertragung der Intention; und wo sie fehlt, kommen unter den gegenwärtigen Bedingungen in der Tat nur matte, insuffiziente Aufführungen zustande. Aber nirgends steht geschrieben, daß *der Sache nach* die Interpretation an Gestik und Zeichengebung mit dem Ideal *minimaler* Erklärungen gebunden sei. Es kommt allein aufs *Resultat,* die wahre Interpretation an; wie sie zustande kommt ist gleichgültig; der »faszinierende« Dirigent ist ein Fetisch wie die Meistergeige und gehört zur Kulturindustrie.

123 Schon ein Quartettprimarius kann, und wird, soviel erklären und unterbrechen wie er will. Ein Filmregisseur spielt und spricht seinen Schauspielern jede Sequenz vor. Der wahre Dirigent müßte dasselbe tun, also etwa dem Oboisten seine Phrase vorsingen, vortanzen, vorphrasieren und nicht bloß abstrakt schlagen; wollte er das jedoch tun, so würde er als unfachmännisch von allen, und am meisten vom Orchester, ausgelacht. Würde eingewandt, daß die Stimme, wie die Rolle, im Ganzen ein Selbständiges sei und der Oboist wie der Schauspieler eine Auffassung habe, so mag man das getrost konzedieren, obwohl es meist nur eine Ideologie für die Schlamperei ist. Diese Dialektik wäre dann, wie in einem Streichquartett, zwischen Dirigenten und Instrumentalisten auszutragen. Da aber im Kunstwerk die Selbständigkeit der Teilmomente *uneigentlich,* der Primat des Ganzen fraglos ist, so müßte das Entscheidungsrecht doch, wie beim Filmregisseur, schließlich beim Dirigenten, und Primarius stehen (NB dieser Gedanke wäre noch in den Kontrapunktaufsatz zu integrieren!). – Schließlich ist noch zu behandeln, daß durch Schallplatte, Radio und Tonband noch eine entscheidende *Zwischeninstanz* eingeschaltet ist, der Tonmeister. Sie ist meist von einem Elektrotechniker besetzt. Daher rühren wohl die verhängnisvollsten Verzerrungen bezw. Neutralisierungen aller mechanisch reproduzierten Musik (kulinarisches Klangideal auf Kosten des musikalischen Sinnes, Undeutlichkeit usw. Näher ausführen). Es wäre von der entscheidendsten Wichtigkeit für den gesamten Standard der Reproduktion heute, daß diese Position, von der vielfach bereits mehr abhängt als vom Dirigenten, von *höchstqualifizierten* Musikern mit genauester Kenntnis der Partitur besetzt [wird].

*

Es wird genau, konkret zu bestimmen sein, wie das Ganze vom Einzelnen, das Einzelne vom Ganzen her zu dechiffrieren ist. Jenes: von den Charakteren aus, dem tempo giusto in

Rudi [Kolischs] Sinn, den »Gestalten«; und es wird zugleich darauf ankommen, diesen Begriff genau zu formulieren (er ist das, was ich mit »Namen« meine, was Reger fehlt[195]; dazu auch meine Theorie des *Einfalls* als einer Objektivität aus dem »Musikanten«[196]). Es ist also dem je gesetzten Impuls zu folgen. Idealiter müßte aus dem »Treffen« des gesetzten Charakters alles andere hervorgehen. – Umgekehrt läßt aus dem Ganzen sich auf Teile schließen. Wenn in der »Revolutionsetüde« von Chopin bei der Reprise in der Fortsetzung ein Arpeggioakkord anstelle des einfachen Griffs in der Exposition tritt, so 124
könnte man, isoliert gesehen, schwanken, ob der Akkord breit gebrochen oder kurz gerissen werden soll. Aber bei dem sehr heftigen, dramatischen Ton des *Ganzen* kann kein Zweifel sein, daß ein kurzer Pizzicatoakkord gemeint ist. – Auf etwas anderer Ebene: die Schlußgruppe der Exposition der I. Symphonie von Mahler ist als flott (ich weiß die genaue Bezeichnung nicht auswendig)[197] bezeichnet. *Wie* flott – darüber entscheidet aber die Proportion zum Vorhergehenden. Wenn, wie bei Herrn Walter, die Entwicklung nicht zu dem flotten Tempo führt (denn vorher melodisiert er ja!), sondern, um des Einzelcharakters willen, *abrupt* einsetzt, wird's falsch. Idealiter könnte man mit dem gleichen Recht sagen, aus dem Ganzen folgten alle Teilmomente. Die beiden Thesen konvergieren aber *nicht,* finden jedenfalls nicht bruchlos zur Deckung. Das hängt aber an der Objektivität der Komposition, dem perennierenden Bruch von Allgemeinem und Besonderem (wobei natürlich die Formtotalität nicht ohne weiteres dem *umfangslogisch* Allgemeinen, wie die traditionelle Harmonik, entspricht – trotzdem ist sie in einem höheren Sinn, dialektisch, allgemeiner als das bloß individuell Gesetzte, das freilich auch wieder *in sich* allgemein vermittelt ist). In gewisser Weise ist es die Aufgabe der Interpretation, das in jeder Komposition offene Spannungsverhältnis von τὸδε τι und konkreter Totalität zu bewältigen, über den Gegensatz von Realismus und Nominalismus hinauszukommen, der in jeder Komposition ungeschlichtet liegt. Faustregel dafür aber ist, das Licht an beiden

Enden anzustecken, also vom Ganzen *und* vom Einzelnen auszugehen und beides solange aneinander sich abarbeiten zu lassen, bis ein Optimales resultiert.

*

Die Zone der Mehrdeutigkeit von Interpretation ist nicht einfach zuzugestehen, sondern möglichst genau zu bestimmen. Dabei meine alte These zu Grunde legen: Je objektiver die *vorgegebene* Musiksprache, desto größer die interpretative Freiheit (gegen die Walchas!). Nominalismus = Strenge. Dies bleibt genau zu entfalten. Das traditionelle Element, als »neumisches« der Interpretation, spielt entscheidend herein

*

Mit Solti und Hirsch[198] nach dem Holländer über Karajan gesprochen, die Aufführung der VIII. von Bruckner, die ich in Wien, mit den Philharmonikern gehört hatte. Ich sprach von der vollkommenen sinnlichen Fassade bei innerer Leere – daß
125 von Bruckner nichts übrig blieb. Beide widersprachen mir. Solti, ob mir eine zwar vergeistigte aber nicht exakte und klanglich [in]adäquate Aufführung denn lieber sei. Hirsch: wenn das Sinnliche im Kunstwerk vollkommen, so wäre eben damit das Geistige auch da. Das mußte ich denn zugestehen, allein schon um nicht der deutschen Furtwänglerei das Wort zu reden. Es gibt nicht nur eine Barbarei der Vollendung sondern auch der Imperfektion und sie predigen wäre reaktionär. Nur: bei genauester Analyse wird sich halt zeigen, daß bei Karajan das Auswendige *nicht* perfekt ist, daß hier der *Schein* der Perfektion die eigentliche verdeckt. Aber dies zu konkretisieren, bleibt unendlich schwer und noch zu leisten. – Gegen Furtwängler und Walter – *und* gegen Toscanini! Und Karajan.

*

Schwierigste Probleme von großer Form und Charakteren im 2. Satz der IX. Symphonie von Mahler. Nimmt man das 1. Thema *wirklich* als Ländler, so ist es bei der Länge seiner Exposition mit Spannung kaum durchzuhalten. Um so schwieriger wird aber der Kontrast zum 2. (Walzer), denn es soll einmal nur *etwas* rascher sein, dann aber, bei seiner Wiederkunft, schneller. Die Tempodifferenz wird also recht gering; um so notwendiger *alle* anderen Kontrastmittel. Auf jeden Fall aber muß das *3.* Thema *ganz* langsam, wirklich wie ein österreichischer langsamer Ländler genommen werden. Evt. eine metronomisierte Tempoanalyse des Satzes geben.

*

Schlecht ist jede *didaktische* Interpretation, eine solche also, die darüber belehren will, wie man interpretiert. Schlecht jeder Nachdruck, der über das von der Sache selbst Geforderte hinausgeht. Die Intention auf den Sinn kann falsch werden, sobald sie diesen unterstreicht, ihn nicht realisiert sondern, als erscheinende, auf die Realisierung reflektiert. »So spielt man das.« Es gibt eine *Schwelle* der Deutlichkeit, diese ist keine absolute Kategorie. Sie wird schlecht, sobald sie gleichsam kommentierend über die Immanenz des Gebildes hinausgeht. Es gibt Menschen, wie meinen Vetter Franz Adorno[199], die mit gehobenem Zeigefinger musizieren. Dies bleibt in genaue technische Begriffe zu übersetzen. Man kann z. B. das an sich notwendige Absetzen der Charaktere so betreiben, daß sie nicht an sich, sondern als Belehrung des Hörers hervortreten; umgekehrt aber auch den »Fluß«. Dies ist wohl eines der Geheimnisse der musikpädagogischen Musik.

*

Realisierung *mehrdeutiger* Ereignisse. Z. B. der erste Takt des 126
langsamen Satzes von op. 31, 2 [von Beethoven] ist Einleitung und thematisch zugleich. Das Arpeggio ist ein Aufrauschen-

lassen; das obere b zugleich der erste – dann auch fortgesetzte – Melodieton. *Beides* muß deutlich werden, d.h. aber der oberste Ton von dem gebrochenen Akkord sich unterscheiden, ohne doch herauszustechen. Äußerst schwierig.

*

Regel: ins Extrem gehen. Die Bereicherung der Stärkeskala durch die neue Musik kommt *aller* zugute. Je größer die Skala, desto größer auch die Möglichkeit, durch Stärkegrade die Struktur zu modellieren, dynamisch zu konstruieren. Und in eins damit extreme *Charaktere* zu treffen. Das gilt nicht nur fürs ppp sondern auch fürs fff. Die Empfindlichkeit gegen das Laute ist die Musikalität der Unmusikalischen. Manches von Mahler und Schönberg, auch Strauss bedarf dem *Sinn* nach der dynamischen Überschreitung der Grenze des Erträglichen: Kriegserklärung ans kulinarische Ideal. Natürlich war die »klassische« Dynamik *anders* – aber nachdem es die andere gibt, läßt jene sich nicht restaurieren. Gilt auch für Bach.

*

Zur Interpretation schwieriger moderner Texte: Schönberg op. 16, I. An das dreitaktige Hauptthema schließt sich ein aufgelöster, ebenfalls dreitaktiger, äußerst schwer durchzuhörender Nachsatz an. Die Dynamik ist offenbar »subjektiv« bezeichnet d.h. nach den Spielweisen der Instrumente, z.B. ein begleitender Triller von 2 Flöten f, dagegen die Hauptstimme der Klarinette p; ebenso eine profilierte Horn-Mittelstimme p, eine nicht-melodische Unterstimme der Fagotte f. Der letzte Takt ist ein Solo-Rhythmus eines gedämpften Horns, f bezeichnet. R. Kubelik hält sich in der Aufnahme ganz brav an die Bezeichnung. Aber dadurch, daß die abstürzende Klarinettenfigur, die in den Hornrhythmus mündet, in ihrer ungünstigen Lage *wirklich* p klingt, entsteht, trotz gutem »Anschluß«, zwischen ihr und dem gedämpften Horn ein dynami-

sches Loch; man kann dessen Rhythmus, durch den unvermittelten Stärkeunterschied, nicht mehr als das auffassen, was er ist, die melodische Fortsetzung der Klarinette. Damit wird die ganze, ohnehin heikle Stelle ihrem Sinn nach unverständ- 127
lich – und zugleich die ganze Exposition, die vom Verhältnis von Vordersatz und Nachsatz abhängt. Helfen könnte nur eine dynamische *Retusche*, d.h. die Klarinette relativ so stark spielen lassen, daß das gedämpfte Horn wirklich anschließt. Aber genau das – gegen den notierten Wortlaut – setzt die *Analyse* voraus; die abstürzenden 32stel der Klarinette sind thematisch (aus dem Kontrapunkt zum Hauptthema). Und genau diesen Schritt hat der musikalische und treu überwachende Dirigent *nicht* vollzogen.

*

Fritz Langs Beschreibung von dem Cabaretmädchen, das »Schöner Gigolo« mimisch illustriert. Genau so singen manche Sänger, so Herr Patzak[200], natürlich unter Herrn Walter, im Lied von der Erde. »Liegen wüst / die Gärten / der Seele / welkt hin und stirbt / die Freude[«] usw. Alles tragisch – aber das Wort Freude freudig. Auf diesem Niveau das Ganze. Der »Aufschwung« am Schluß des II. Satzes wie Brünnhilde. Die Rezitative im letzten Satz so expressiv wie die Hauptthemen – dadurch die ganze Form verfehlt. Im Allegro, nur daß es flott geht, das pesante des Grundcharakters versäumt. Die plötzlichen Temporückungen im 4. Satz alle falsch in der Proportion. Und das gilt für Mahlers Erben.

*

Sils-Maria, August 57

Wenn die Reproduktion in gewissem Sinn den – objektiven – Kompositionsprozeß nachvollzieht, so stellen sich in ihr auch ähnliche Probleme wie beim Komponieren. Ich habe im Kranichsteiner Kurs Eduard [Steuermanns] Juli 57[201] beobachtet, daß die Schüler wußten wie's anfängt und aufhört, also die Ecknoten musizierten, aber unbekümmert waren um den Sinn dessen was dazwischen geschieht (2. Bild Petruschka). »Ausspielen« ist eine große Kategorie der Reproduktion, verwandt der des »[A]uskomponierens« und genau zu formulieren. Hierher gehört das höchst aktuelle Problem rascher Melodien

*

Das Verhältnis zwischen den »Parametern«, d. h. die funktionelle Abhängigkeit der Materialschichten in der Reproduktion verfolgen. Mir fiel beim Anfang des Allegros der Barbier-
128 ouvertüre auf, wie schwierig es ist, ein spitzes, rhythmisch präzises und federndes Begleit-staccato wirklich *piano* zu spielen. Übrigens allgemeine Tendenz, den »normalen« Grundklang zu stark zu denken.

*

Wie spielt man Kontrapunkte, vor allem »harmonische«, d. h. solche in homophoner Musik? Sie müssen deutlich sein aber nicht vordringlich, mit einem ganz bestimmten, sehr schwer zu fassenden Charakter des diskreten Nachdrucks. Ob die Arbeit gelingt, hängt genau davon ab, ob solche Nuancen genau, *konkret* getroffen werden. Übrigens muß die Arbeit zusammenhängende Ausführungen über *alle* Parameter enthalten, z. B. Harmonie (»kritische Töne«, Verhältnis von vertikalem Gesamtklang und seinen einzelnen Spannungsmomenten), Form (Unterschied unmittelbar wahrnehmbarer und vermittelter, rückbezogener Formproportionen), Farbe (als Mittel zur Artikulation des Zusammenhanges, besonders auch beim Gesang) usw.

*

Nachdem Firkusny[202] das – unmögliche – g-moll-Konzert
von Mendelssohn spielte, eine Beobachtung, die etwa auch
auf Pianisten wie Backhaus und Horowitz zutrifft. Es gibt eine
bestimmte Art technische Begabung, zu der sogar die physi-
sche Kraft wesentlich dazugehört, die unmittelbar, also unter
Ausschluß des geistigen Verständnisses, mit der Darstellungsfä-
higkeit zusammenhängt, so als könnten die Hände das Ohr er-
setzen, und eine Reproduktionstheorie, die daran einfach
vorbeisieht, wäre wohl blank rationalistisch. Eduard [Steuer-
mann] sprach einmal vom »Taufrischen« des Klavierspielens
des jungen Backhaus – der doch sicher nie ein bedeutender
Musiker war. Dazu meine alte Notiz über die Möglichkeit daß
Schauspieler Rollen gut verkörpern, die sie nicht verste-
hen.[203] Ein physisches, sinnliches, vorgeistigtes Verhältnis zur
Musik, das fensterlos den Geist birgt. Ist das das neumische,
mimetische Element der Reproduktion? Es ist aber dabei zu
bemerken, daß das besondere Vermögen, das ich hier meine,
gar nicht notwendig etwas mit der Musikantenbegabung etwa
des slawischen oder ostjüdischen Typus zu tun hat; Firkusny
und Backhaus[204] haben davon kaum etwas. Sondern es geht
um etwas womöglich noch unterhalb der Psychologie des
»Temperaments«: einen Spielmechanismus, der sich gewisser-
maßen verselbständigt und gerade durch seine Verdinglichung
an den musikalischen Sinn heranreicht. Das Phänomen ist 129
äußerst schwer zu fassen, scheint mir aber Schlüsselcharakter
zu haben für das Problem der Reproduktion. Vielleicht be-
rührt es sich gerade mit der *modernen* Tendenz, daß in der wah-
ren Interpretation der Interpret erlischt. Dann wäre es sogar
dem Neumischen *entgegengesetzt*. Verfolgen.

*

Im Gloria der Missa solemnis nimmt Herr Toscanini die dynamischen Kontraste von ff und pp so extrem, daß, unterm Schatten des ff, das – isoliert sicher hörbare – pp im Zusammenhang gar nicht mehr verständlich, bloß noch wie ein Loch in der Musik ist. Es gibt also in der Treue zum Text eine Art Eulenspiegelei. Man kann Vortragsbezeichnungen so wörtlich nehmen, daß purer Unsinn resultiert. – Die ganze LP der Missa ist ein Schulfall äußerster Perfektion und völligen Verfehlens, auf Hochglanz Polierens, ein Betrug über den Rätselcharakter[205] der Missa. – Im Text der Reproduktionstheorie muß sowohl »Neue Musik Interpretation Publikum« wie die noch zu schreibende Toscanini-Analyse[206] verarbeitet werden.

*

Heteronomie der Interpretation, das unvermeidlich *Vorgeistige.* Abhängigkeit des Pianisten von den Händen, des Geigers von den Fingern, des Bläsers von der Atemkraft, des Dirigenten von der mimischen Begabung usw. Halb gehört auch das Gehör hierher. Dies *nicht* der Sache nur äußerlich. Die Pranke, die es dem Pianisten erlaubt, ins Klavier dreidimensional hineinzuspielen, ist ein Stück seines Talents. Physis und Musikalität. Weiterverfolgen.

*

Beobachtung an Crafts Webernplatten[207] November 58. Zu direkt, ohne Furcht und Zittern, die Musik ohne Isolierschicht angefaßt. Es fehlt die Sensibilität der Hände, die das Vermittelte, Symbolische jeden Tons wahrnimmt und in der Reproduktion realisiert. Äußerst wichtig. Dadurch wird alles falsch. Vielleicht auch Schlüssel für Toscanini. Die Platten enthalten subtilste Beispiele für Sinnlosigkeit durchs Verfehlen der Anschlüsse usw. und sind im empirischen Teil, zur neuen Musik, eingehend zu zitieren. Schon der Anfang, wo die Trompete der Schlußton der Flötenmelodie ist, ähnlich dann das Horn. Sonst sinnlos.

*

Ich hörte, unter Henze, eine Radio-Aufführung der Lulu- 130
suite. Sie klang abscheulich, dick, klebrig – nichts von der leuchtenden Schlankheit der Musik war übrig. Das machte, sie war nur auf den Klang hin musiziert, und dieser versagte sich eben dem. Zum Klingen zu bringen ist Musik nur, wenn sie *thematisch* gespielt, in ihrer Konstruktion artikuliert, in ihrer Entwicklung verdeutlicht wird. Der Klang ohne Rücksicht darauf verschwimmt, wird klumpig, häßlich – noch der Wohllaut ist eine Funktion der Darstellung des Sinnes. Etwas davon meinte Strauss mit der Bemerkung, nur ein sinnvoll polyphon geführtes Orchester klinge so recht.[208] Denn die Instrumentation war, bis zu ihrer jüngsten Stufe, eine Art Vermittlung von Werk und [Interpretation[209]].

*

Das Grundgesetz der Darstellung neuer Musik, der Faden der durchbrochenen Melodie, läßt sich demonstrieren, wo es verletzt wird. Besonders gutes Beispiel: Weberns op. 6, 1, in Crafts Platte. Etwa auch op. 5, 1.

*

Wichtiger Grundsatz aller musikalischen Interpretation: es gibt keine Approximationswerte. Es führt kein Kontinuum vom Falschen über das Bessere zum Wahren. Was nicht ganz richtig ist, ist schon ganz falsch; und unter Umständen ist das ganz Falsche, indem es gar nicht die Sache selbst zu sein beansprucht, besser. Die Gründe dieses Sachverhalts werden zu analysieren sein. Ist es ein allgemein ästhetischer?

*

Bei neuer *Vokal*musik entscheidet nicht einfach, ob, wie man so sagt, die Noten richtig intoniert sind, sondern die Dezision und Eindeutigkeit, mit der gesungen wird. So eigentlich falsch

singen gar nicht so viele – wohl aber so, daß die Töne nicht
absolut stehen; daß man sich gewissermaßen nicht festlegt,
sondern, weil man nicht ganz sicher ist, Modifikationen sich
vorbehält; und diese Attitüde beeinflußt dann die Distinktheit
des Klangbildes. Dahinter steht wohl ein Mangel an spezifi-
scher Imagination, d. h. es werden vor allem nicht die Inter-
valle – also das Melos – wirklich eindeutig vorgestellt sondern
nur, von einem abstrakten, von der konkreten Sache unabhän-
gigen »Gehör«, die sogenannten Tonhöhen, und die Schwan-
kungen entstehen durch Unsicherheit den Relationen gegen-
über. Im übrigen gilt *aller* neuen Musik gegenüber in
131 besonderem Maß die Forderung absoluter Deutlichkeit, Ein-
deutigkeit, Plastik – nicht nur mit Bezug auf Intonation, son-
dern auf *alle* Dimensionen. Alles muß zweifelsfrei als das
erscheinen was es ist und wozu es fungiert; z. B. auch die Kon-
traste. So ist es eine kaum noch visierte Aufgabe der *Singstimme*,
durch die Klangfarbe die verschiedenen Gestalten sowohl aus-
einanderzuhalten wie durch einander zu vermitteln. Der
Grund dieser Forderung ist evident: Mangel an einem Bezugs-
system jenseits des hic et nunc Komponierten, durch das still-
schweigend Undeutliches verdeutlicht würde. Dasselbe Pro-
blem gilt in der neuen Musik für die Komposition *selber.* Wie es
denn überhaupt bei neuer Musik darauf ankommt, alle kompo-
sitorischen Leistungen in interpretative zu übersetzen. Die In-
terpretation komponiert die Komposition. Und insofern ist
neue Musik *leichter* zu interpretieren als traditionelle.

*

Aus dem Primat der Imagination über das bloße Musikmachen folgt die zentrale Schwierigkeit aller Praxis der Wiedergabe. Richtig Musizieren verlangt die unablässige Kontrolle alles real Erklingenden am Imaginierten. Damit aber einen Prozeß der Reflexion. Der ist aber vielfach kaum zu leisten: man spielt immer wieder anders als man es sich vorstellt. Denn es gibt ein geradehin Musizieren *vor* jener Reflexion, das einen großen Teil jener Energie verbraucht, die der Reflexion zugute kommen müßte; und dazu kommt die Absorption durch die mechanischen Prozesse. Das Problem ist wohl nur pädagogisch zu lösen d. h. indem man von früh auf dazu erzieht, was immer man spielt oder singt an der Vorstellung zu messen: sich zuhören. Moderne Mittel wie Bandaufnahmen können sehr dabei helfen. – Übrigens ist der Primat der Imagination nicht als Ursachverhalt zu hypostasieren. Er ist Resultat eines geschichtlichen Prozesses, so wie alles, was Vorstellung ist, einmal real war (Traum!). Aber der Prozeß ist irreversibel. Wer heute in der Musik dem Tun den Vorrang übers Vorstellen einräumt, musiziert regressiv.

*

Einige Beobachtungen an Aufnahmen des Gezeichnetenvorspiels[210], März 1959. Jede Interpretation, vor allem aber die orchestrale, setzt die genaueste metrische Analyse voraus. Sonst entstehen Leerstellen, Zweideutigkeiten, gewissermaßen Zeitlücken; das Kontinuum des Klanges ersetzt die zeitliche Artikulation, im Grunde läßt der Zusammenhang sich gar nicht mehr wahrnehmen, und es gibt Kompositionen, wie gerade Schreker, die all das auch noch befördern. – Je mehr Orchesterwerke auf Mischklang gestellt sind, desto sorgfältiger 132
muß man darauf achten, daß nicht innerhalb der Mischklänge Einzelfarben herausstechen: der kleinste Fehler darin kann den Sinn einer ganzen Partitur auf den Kopf stellen. Wenn z. B. eine Figur der gedämpften Hörner zur Verdeutlichung auf einem Akzentton durch eine offene Trompete verstärkt ist und man diese dabei so heraushört, daß die Einheit der Phrase zerrissen wird, so ist das eine Todsünde. Dazu Bergs Wort von den herausstehenden Nägeln.[211] Natürlich können in solchen Dingen selbst die erfahrensten und besten Instrumentatoren sich *irren:* dann muß die Interpretation ausgleichen. – Zum Verhältnis von Hauptstimme und Begleitung: auch es ist nicht mechanisch aufzufassen. Es gibt Stellen, wie der Anfang jenes

Vorspiels, wo *der Intention nach* die Begleitung das Wesentliche – die »Idee« – ist und die Themen gleichsam nur dazu da ut aliquid fieri videatur. Dem muß die Aufführung gerecht werden, indem sie *nicht* einfach die Hauptstimme vom Hintergrund abhebt sondern, aber ohne dynamische Vergröberungen, den Hintergrund in den Vordergrund holt. – In üppig gesetzter Musik kann es passieren, daß man ein Hauptmotiv kaum als solches erkennen kann, wie beim ersten Auftreten in den Hörnern

(Gezeichneten-Vorspiel)

In solchen entscheidenden Fällen muß die Interpretation energisch nachhelfen.

*

Bei der Darstellung neuer Musik ist doch die wichtigste Kategorie die der Deutlichkeit, des thematischen Ausspielens. Mir ist das beim Einstudieren der Lieder op. 3 von Webern aufgegangen.[212] Das rasche, zweite, basiert auf einem Sechzehntelmotiv, das sich dann in unregelmäßige Werte (Septolen, Quintolen usw.) auflöst. Bei dem (höchst musikalischen) Pianisten gab es nun 2 einfach einander entgegengesetzte Kategorien: die thematischen Sechzehntel und die Auflösungsfelder als »Figuration«, gewissermaßen nicht mehr im Vordergrund. Dadurch kam einmal ein Bruch in die Begleitung, d. h. der Zusammenhang der Komplexe ging verloren. Dann aber wurde das Auflösungsfeld unverbindlich, ein blasses hastiges Getön, wie es buchstäblich solche Dinge unverständlich macht. Erst als wir die thematische *Präsenz* jener Partien herstellten, gab das Ganze seinen Sinn.

*

Oft läßt die wahre Interpretation nur durch Experimentieren sich finden. Man weiß immer, daß etwas falsch, oft nicht, warum es falsch, wie es richtig ist, und das läßt sich dann nur durch Ausprobieren verschiedener Möglichkeiten finden. Oft finden sich Lösungen nur durch Relationen. Z. B. eine unbetonte, aber relativ lange Gesangsnote auf den Laut e klingt in einem Lied[213] forciert, unverständlich, und entzieht sich der Korrektur; wird aber besser durch Akzent und diminuendo auf der vorhergehenden Note. 133

*

Sinnvoll, überzeugend gerät nur, was bestimmt, überzeugend vorgestellt ist. Jede Unsicherheit der Imagination überträgt sich auf die Wirkung. Dies ist eine Grundregel.

*

Interpretation, die ihrer nicht mächtig ist, immer zu *stark*. Darauf besonders merken. Überhaupt eine der wichtigsten Fehlerquellen die Differenz von Vorstellung und Realisierung. So fand ich beim Abhören meiner Trakllieder mit der Henius[214], Juli 1959, daß ich oft Akkorde *brach,* nicht exakt auf den Taktteil zusammenspielte, aus dem Bedürfnis des Ausdrucks und der Verdeutlichung des Wichtigen. Spielte ganz anders als ich es dachte. – Wegen dieses Problems ist das *Tonband* ein unschätzbares Hilfsmittel. Die wahre Interpretation wird ohne seine Hilfe nicht mehr auskommen. Auch darin Tendenz zur *Liquidation* der Interpretation.

*

Im Beruf des *Dirigenten* waltet eine objektive Unwahrheit. Die Aufführung erscheint, als wäre *er* ihr Subjekt, der Interpret, während das nur in sehr beschränktem, bei allvertrauten Werken nur in verschwindendem Maß der Fall ist, nicht nur wegen des Widerstands, den die Klangmaterie ihm entgegensetzt, besonders im Chor, sondern weil er ja gar nicht spielt sondern die Orchestermusiker, die also selber Subjekte mit Eigentümlichkeiten, Vorzügen, Schwächen sind. Nicht eine Oboe gleicht der anderen – was *vermag* der Kapellmeister darüber. Und doch imaginiert er die Aufführung. In dieser Differenz nistet die Scharlatanerie, und fast alle Untugenden und Manieren der Dirigenten entfließen daraus. Es handelt sich bei diesem Interpretationsproblem schließlich um einen Widerspruch in den *Werken*. Sie sind, als solche für Orchester, auf eine Vielfalt Exekutierender angelegt, ja *wollen* diese geradezu der eigenen Intention nach: ein Flötist *soll* schön, eine Sologeige brillant klingen usw. Zugleich aber verweisen sie als integrale Kunstwerke auf eine Einheit der Idee, wie sie nur durch den Dirigenten zu vermitteln ist. Dieser Idee gegenüber, wie in vieler anderer Hinsicht, ist das Orchester »archaisch«.

*

134 Es sind zumindest *Modelle* spezifischer Interpretationsprobleme einzelner Komponisten zu erstellen. So Bruckner (nach einer Aufführung der III. unter Kubelik[215]): die Cäsuren, Brüche sind konstitutiv, gehören zum Sinn, sind aber zugleich als Störungen kaum erträglich. Beides ist falsch: sie glätten, über sie wegdirigieren, und die Stücke auseinanderfallen lassen. Aufgabe wäre, so zu musizieren, daß sie sprechen, selber zu *Mitteln* des Zusammenhangs werden, aber was heißt das *technisch*. Hier hülfe *nur* die minutiöseste Analyse. – Sehr hübsches Wort von Klemperer über die Striche bei Bruckner: dadurch werden die Symphonien nur länger.[216] Das ist genau richtig; die Struktur wird verwischt, und das Chaotische währt stets länger als das Artikulierte. – Oder Strauss, Elektra (nach der großartigen Aufführung unter Solti, Herbst 59): das Stück, wie Strauss überhaupt, will im Schwung genommen werden, nicht verweilen; die Singstimmen sollen nicht von der Bedeutsamkeit des motivischen Lebens im Orchester erdrückt

werden. Aber eben dadurch geht das Beste verloren, das *Geprägte* gerade solcher Werke im Einzelnen, und sie nähern sich schon den mitziehenden Filmmusiken, welche die späteren sind. Z.B. der Scherzocharakter der Chrysothemispartien wird verfehlt durch ein Presto, das ihre Themen nicht profiliert und sie nur begleitet. Ich sagte Solti, es käme in der Elektra, paradox, darauf an, daß die Stimmen das Orchester nicht decken, es müsse umgekehrt sein. Das ist natürlich völlig gegen den Strom, auch gegen Straussens eigenen. Heute wäre dessen Interpretation schon wieder umzukehren.

*

Geheimnis der Interpretation: ihre doppelte Bewegung. Auseinandernehmen und wieder zusammensetzen. Z.B. Phrasierung. Die »große Linie« allein ebenso falsch wie die auseinanderfallenden Teilphrasen. Erst in diese zerlegen, dann zusammenbringen. Das geschieht aber nicht durch *Verschleifen,* sondern durch *Differenzierung* der Phrasierungsgrade nach dem Maß ihrer formbildenden Funktion, d.h. der relativen *Bedeutung* der Cäsuren.

*

Richtig in neue Gestalten kommen heißt vielfach: ritardando nur soweit führen, daß etwas von dem Schwung der alten Gestalt erhalten bleibt, der in die neue übernommen wird.

*

Immer *kritische* d.h. abweichende Noten hervorheben.

*

Intonation hat *formbildende* Funktion. Wenn in einem Stück von Webern[217] ein f in einem Instrument pizzicato, dann in einem anderen am Steg kommt, so ist die *Einheit* in dieser Differenz nur herzustellen, wenn die Intonation absolut identisch ist.

*

Artikulationsmittel: bei Imitationen in sehr polyphonen Sätzen immer den *Einsatz* verdeutlichen, dann völlig zurücktre-
135 ten lassen.

*

Alle Modifikationen sind relativ, z. B. in einem ppp-Stück von Webern[218] höchstens bis p, usw. Dies hängt aber vom *Bezugssystem* ab. In einem tonal organisierten Stück kann man mit dynamischen Modifikationen innerhalb eines Feldes viel weiter gehen als in einem nicht tonalen.

*

Nächst der Herausarbeitung des melodischen Fadens beim Springen von einer Stimme zur anderen ist das *wichtigste:* das *rhythmische* Skelett, d. h. der Hauptrhythmus, die »Schläge«, die man hört. Z. B. in Webern op. 9, No VI. – Das ist dann ein Volkslied.[219]

*

Bei sehr *kurzen* Stücken sind vor allem die Charaktere der einzelnen gegeneinander herauszuarbeiten.

*

Bei langen und sehr dichten Stücken vor allem: Luft schaffen. Ein Königreich für ein piano.[220] – Weiter hilft dazu deutliches Phrasieren *innerhalb* der verwobenen Gestalten, sowie absolutes Zurücktreten aller Begleitung, auch auf Kosten der dynamischen Vorschriften. – Überhaupt geht *Deutlichkeit* als Bedingung des Sinnes allem anderen voran. Auch agogischen Modifikationen. Lieber ein accelerando opfern.

*

Die wahre Interpretation kennt keine toten Intervalle, nur Riemann[221]. Sehr oft entstehen Löcher, Sinnlosigkeiten dadurch, daß zwei Töne, die ein melodisches Intervall bilden, auseinanderfallen, nicht aufeinander bezogen werden.

*

Klang formbildend. Hˉ in einem pianissimo-Feld sul tasto[222] spielen, damit sie im Feld bleibt und doch hervortritt. – Am Steg ist eine Formkategorie.

*

Kritische Noten sind außer Abweichungen oft: *kurze* Ecknoten in ungünstiger Lage, sowie *Zwischen*intervalle. Vorsicht mit der 1.

*

Bei sehr aufgelöster Musik wie Webern op. 9 müssen kleinste Motivgestalten aus verschiedenen Instrumenten zusammenkomponiert werden. Im 2.; Anfang des 3. Stücks.

*

Hˉ ist immer da, wo das motivische Leben sich konzentriert, auch wenn es nur ein Einzelton ist.

*

6. Dezember 1959
Frankfurt a. M.

Zur Theorie der musikalischen Reproduktion[223]:

1) man muß in der *melodischen* Hauptstimme die *harmonische* Bedeutung fühlen können.
2) man kann in sehr vielen Fällen agogische Modifikationen durch die reine Dynamik ausdrücken
3) sehr oft hängt die Formproportion an Akzenten
4) Theorie des Ritardandos, (Stetigkeit)
5) alle Auftakte, kurzen Noten z. B. $\frac{1}{16}$ nach ♪. müssen ausgespielt werden. Grundregel: die *Oberflächenartikulation* durch erste Stufen, Kadenzen, gute Taktteile hört man von selbst. Sie hat, als zum abstrakten Schema gehörig, absolut zurückzutreten zugunsten der Artikulation der konkreten, vom Schema unabhängigen thematischen Arbeit. Diese Durchleuchtung und Emanzipation von den Außenmitteln der Verdeutlichung (wie sie am extremsten Toscanini handhabt) ist das eigentliche Hauptgesetz der Interpretation. Die Konstruktion freilegen heißt *nicht:* das Schema freilegen, sondern freilegen was ihm opponiert bezw. was aus dem Zusammenstoß von Schema und Intention hervorgeht. – Diese Forderung ist zugleich eine maßlose *Über*forderung. D.h. sobald hier nur ein Augenblick nicht völlig gefüllt ist, wird alles ganz sinnlos, weil ja die Stützen der Außenartikulation wegfallen. Bei Gelegenheit von Rudi [Kolischs] Konzert in New York am 13. November 1938 (op. 59,1 und 127 [von Beethoven])

Schulheft ohne Deckel, S. 79 f.

*

Fortsetzung der Notizen zur Theorie der musikalischen Reproduktion

Wahre Gefahr des Virtuosen: die Souveränität. Durch das über der Sache sein, über sie Verfügen wird in sie nicht mehr ganz hereingegangen, die immanente Forderung nicht mehr ganz ernst genommen. Schlamperei als Korrelat der Meisterschaft. Etwa das Verschleifen der Phrase bei großen Virtuosen, auch solchen des Gesangs. – Vorzug mit jungen, unfertigen, noch nicht souveränen Musikern zu arbeiten.

Meine These von der Immanenz des richtigen Tempos als Tempo giusto belegen an einer Stelle der Frühlingssonate von Beethoven, oben auf der 2. Seite, wo es »einschnappt«.[224] – Die These kann etwa so begründet werden, daß bei zu langsamem Vortrag Gestalten, die an sich bedeutungslos sind, eine ungebührliche Bedeutung gewinnen und etwa wirken wie die Erzählung eines allgemein bekannten Witzes. *Objektive* Bedeutung des musikalisch Dummen. Zeigen etwa am langsamen Satz des Violinkonzerts von Mendelssohn. Sobald die Geige ihrem Ton genügt, werden die $\frac{6}{8}$ albern.

Das Vorkünstlerische des Virtuosen: daß Mittel Zweck werden. Ein solches ist auch der »Ton«. Sobald er sich selbst genießt, geht er auf Kosten des musikalischen Zusammenhangs. – Das Für andere anstatt des An sich. – Die kulinarischen Qualitäten sind regressiv.

Schulheft ohne Deckel

*

Ad Reproduktionstheorie

Wo Busoni sich darüber mokiert, daß jemand konventionelle Kompositionen damit verteidigt, daß sie »so musikalisch« seien[225], hat er Unrecht. Es gibt, in gewisser Weise unabhängig von der musikalischen Qualität, ein die Sprache der Musik sprechen oder nicht sprechen. Schlechte Komponisten wie Tschaikowskij, Puccini, Rachmaninoff sprechen sie – Elgar, Sibelius nicht.[226] Das wäre genau zu bestimmen.

The Scribble-In-Book II, S. 64; 1945

*

Zur Reproduktionstheorie

Die Beziehung von Mimik und Musik, zentral, wird offenbar in der Sphäre der *Reproduktion.* Musizieren und schauspielen sind nächstverwandt, wie denn oft in derselben Familie Schauspieler und Musiker vorkommen. Alle musikalischen *Unmanieren* sind unmittelbar mit solchen der Schmierenkomödianten identisch. Der Cellist, der in einem Quartett sich in den Vordergrund spielt, »chargiert«. Der Geiger der hörbar die Lagen wechselt und heftig vibriert, heult: »Du weinst, Amalia«[227]. Der Wirkungsdirigent à la Toscanini ist der Massenregisseur à la Reinhardt. In all solchen Momenten reduziert sich die Musik auf *Gesten.*

The Scribble-In-Book II, S. 76f.; ca. 1945

*

Gretel[228] fragte, wie es möglich sei, daß Schauspieler, meist von fragwürdiger Intelligenz und stets ungebildet, Menschen darstellen, Sätze vortragen könnten, welche die schwierigsten Gedanken verträten, wie Hamlet und Prospero, Faust, Mephistopheles. Ich versuchte die Antwort: jedes dichterische Werk enthält wie das bedeutungsmäßig-signifikative Element das melisch-mimische, Ton, Sprachmelodie, Gestus, und es ist wesentlich das Kriterion des Gelingens, wie tief jenes in dieses versenkt ward, d. h. ob das mimetische, »magische« das bedeutungsmäßige zu beschwören, zu *erzwingen* vermag, dergestalt, daß ein Tonfall, oder eine Geste von sich aus zur Allegorie des

Gedankens wird. Das Vermögen des Schauspielers ist mimisch im eigentlichen Sinne: er ahmt eben das melisch-gestische Moment der Sprache nach. Und je vollkommener ihm das gelingt, um so vollkommener fällt der Gedanke der Darstellung zu, auch und gerade wenn er ihn *nicht* versteht. Der entgegengesetzte Weg wäre der erklärende: aber die Intention erklären heißt sie töten anstatt beschwören. Fast könnte man sagen, es sei die *Bedingung* des Schauspielers, daß er nicht »versteht« sondern blind nachmacht. Vielleicht zur Theorie der musikalischen Reproduktion.

The Scribble-In-Book II, S. 80; ca. 1945-1947

*

Ad Reproduktionstheorie.

»Röntgenaufnahme«. Es kann im Sinn der Sache liegen, das Skelett zu *verbergen*. Aber das setzt dann selbst wieder die Röntgenphotographie *voraus*.

Braunes Oktavheft II, S. 124; April 1946

*

zur Reproduktionstheorie

Die »Sprache« der Musik, das Eingeschliffensein von Erinnerung und Vorblick, die bestimmte Erwartung dessen was kommt – kurz ihre Vergegenständlichung im positiven und negativen Sinn, all das kommt wohl wesentlich durch das relativ starre und erst mühsam zur Differenzierung zu entwikkelnde System der *Notenschrift* zustande. Dazu vgl. aus den Anbruch-Motiven über Einfluß der Notenschrift auf Komposition[229]. Wahrscheinlich ist unser ganzes Bewußtsein eines musikalischen *Zusammenhanges* durch die Schrift vermittelt.

The Scribble-In-Book II, S. 83; nach dem 6. Februar 1948

*

Zur Reproduktionstheorie: melodische Beziehungen bei weiten Intervallen herstellen. Dazu gehört vor allem unbedingte Deutlichkeit, Präzision der kritischen Noten. – Bei Mahler darf eigentlich nicht ein Viertel wie's andere dirigiert werden. Äußerste Flexibilität – dabei die Grundtempi innerhalb eines Satzes deutlich auseinanderhalten.

Schwarzes Oktavheft »B«, S. 116; ca. April 1957

*

Zur *Reproduktionstheorie.* Meine These, die Aufführung sei die Röntgenphotographie des Werkes, bedarf insofern der Korrektur, als sie nicht das Skelett sondern die ganze *Fülle* des Subkutanen gibt. Ihr gegenüber ist die erscheinende Fassade gerade *abstrakt,* so arm wie das 17. Jahrhundert.

Schwarzes Oktavheft »Q«, S. 65; Oktober 1963

Reproduktionstheorie. Das Grundproblem heute: ob man die Struktur der Musik sich von selbst mitteilen lassen, nur die Erscheinung erscheinen lassen – oder die Struktur in die Erscheinung setzen soll. Meine These ist die zweite. Die Aufgabe meines Buches ist, das zu begründen.

Schwarzes Oktavheft »V«, S. 9, August 1965

*

Reproduktionstheorie

Es darf nicht unter den Tisch fallen, daß es zunächst erfordert ist, bei aller Mannigfaltigkeit das konstitutive Einheitsprinzip zu fassen. Z. B. beim Lohengrin das der aufs höchste differenzierten Klangmischung. War in der Aufführung unter Hollreiser[230] ganz verfehlt: man hörte immerzu Forteeinsätze, die *unhörbar* sein müßten.

Die Dirigentenfähigkeit des Anziehens, sobald die Zügel schleifen.

Reproduktionstheorie. Kritik am Perfektionismus setzt diesen voraus. *Über* ihm sein, nicht drunter. Sonst ists Dilettantismus.

Schwarzes Oktavheft »X«, S. 37f., Mai 1966

*

Zur *Reproduktionstheorie.* Das stärkste Argument gegen mich kam von meinem Vetter Franz[231], und Edith Picht[232] referierte es mir als das des Herrn von Karajan. Man solle nur die sinnliche Erscheinung darstellen, die Struktur teile von selbst sich mit. »Wenn ich eine Frau liebe, will ich ihren Leib, nicht ihre Röntgenphotographie.« Aber das ist, wie meist das Plausible, pure Sophistik, Apologie des vorkünstlerisch Kulinarischen. Denn das verborgen Strukturelle ist das Sinn Verleihende. Wird es nicht in der Erscheinung realisiert, so wird diese klangmateriell-sinnlos. Zu zeigen an den subtilen Fragen der Interpunktion. Sie sind Funktion der latenten Struktur, des Subkutanen. Ohne sie aber wird das Klangbild, mag es noch so spiegelglatt sein, zum Galimathias. »Das Wesen muß erscheinen.«[233]

Schwarzes Oktavheft »W«, S. 115f.; August 1966

*

Notiz

Der Ausdruck ist bereits die Rationalisierung des Gestischen, d. h. dessen Objektivierung durch Signifikation, durch »symbolische Funktion«, das Unmittelbare durch Mittelbarkeit. Und genau dies Moment fällt der Buchstabenschrift eher als dem Notenbild zu. Es ist die Frage, ob im Sinn dieses Tatbestands nicht die vorher entwickelte Lehre von Notenbild und totaler Konstruktion, daß nämlich diese das Mimetische eigentlich festhält, zu modifizieren sei. Andererseits ist mir jedoch noch nicht ausgemacht, ob das Ausdrucksmoment, das freilich durchaus ein vermitteltes ist, in der Tat an dem signifikativen Element der Schrift haftet. Dies muß genau durchdacht werden.

Ts 49561

*

Zur Reproduktionstheorie

Die folgenden Argumente sind wesentlich für die Frage der Verwandlung des musikalischen Hörens in Lesen mit exakter Vorstellung:

A. Die Notwendigkeit, ein wesentlich Geistiges durch seine sinnlichen Repräsentanten vermittelt zu sehen, und nicht diesen Repräsentanten selber in den Geist aufzunehmen, ist infantil. So wie heute nur noch zurückgebliebene Bauern laut lesen, um überhaupt lesen zu können, und so wie nur noch beim Lesen der Gebetbücher die Lippenbewegung als ein Rudiment übrig geblieben ist, so mag es sehr leicht auch einmal mit der Musik bestellt sein. Es liegt keinerlei Grund dafür vor, den sinnlichen Klang von Musik für diese für wesentlicher zu halten als den sinnlichen Klang der Worte für die Sprache.

B. Während jede Aufführung von Musik fehlbar ist, kann die wirkliche präzise Vorstellung beim Lesen das Ideal der Aufführung geben, das als solches nicht erreichbar ist. Das musikalische Werk wird gleichsam von der Zufälligkeit seiner Realisierung gereinigt.

C. Das Aufführen von Musik hat an sich etwas Aufschwätzendes, Überredendes, Propagandistisches und zeigt sich damit der heute herrschenden Kulturindustrie verschwistert. Übertrieben könnte man sagen, jede Aufführung eines musikalischen Werkes hat etwas von Reklame für dieses. Demgegenüber würde die Realisierung der Musik in der Imagination das Werk selbst rein darstellen, ohne dem Wirkungszusammenhang das leiseste Zugeständnis zu machen.

D. Die Werke wären weitgehend dem Verschleiß und der Banalisierung entzogen.

E. Die überholte Scheidung von Werk und Reproduktion wäre liquidiert.

NB Die Reproduktionstheorie muß weit *inhaltlichere,* konkretere Anweisungen enthalten.

Ts 49562

Entwurf

I.

Seit der Antike ist die Lehre von der Aufführung als Teil der Musiktheorie anerkannt. Im Schema des Aristides Quintilianus wird die Doktrin des Vortrags – »exangeltikon« – der von der Komposition gleichgestellt: beide zusammen bilden die praktische Musikdisziplin[234]. Aber die Vortragslehre ist so wenig wie die von der Instrumentation derart entwickelt worden, daß sie den Hauptstücken der Kompositionstheorie, Harmonie und Kontrapunkt, die Waage hielt. Sie hat sich auf die Beschreibung des je herrschenden Gebrauchs, die Formulierung traditioneller Erfahrungsregeln, die Kodifizierung von Geschmacksurteilen beschränkt oder auf technische Traktate über den Gesang und das instrumentale Spiel. Ihr eigentliches Anliegen, über das Verhältnis der Wiedergabe zu den Werken zu entscheiden, ward nicht eingelöst. Keineswegs aber ist dies Verhältnis der technischen Musiklehre so unproblematisch vorgegeben, daß sie der Reflexion darauf im gleichen Sinne enthoben wäre wie etwa die mathematische Arbeit der auf die Logik. Denn den ausübenden Musiker konfrontieren seine Texte unablässig mit Fragen, die weder durch den Rekurs auf die Werke noch durch den auf die Anforderungen des eigenen Spiels ohne weiteres zu schlichten sind, sondern erst durch Erkenntnis der wesentlichen Beziehung zwischen beiden. Kein musikalischer Text, auch nicht der minutiös bezeichnete moderne, ist so eindeutig lesbar, um unvermittelt seine angemessene Interpretation zu erzwingen. Keine Verfügung des Sängers, Instrumentalisten oder Dirigenten über sein Material, wäre sie auch zu einer in sich einstimmigen und alle Möglichkeiten der musikalischen Erfahrung betreffenden Sprache entfaltet, reicht aus, von sich aus der Interpretation jenen Charakter der Wahrheit zu verleihen, welcher doch als Idee jede Aufführung unabdingbar leitet. Noch die gewissenhafte musikalische Aufführung laboriert an einem Moment des Unverbindlichen, Versuchsweisen, ja der Improvisation. Die Wiedergabe jedoch, die jenes Momentes umstandslos sich zu entäußern trachtete, würde notwendig zum Verrat an dem Werke: sie würde es nicht als solches vergegenwärtigen, sondern einzig seine brüchige Schale, das Wenige daran, was im Text manifest zutageliegt und dann leicht genug der Dechiffrierung als bloßer Schein zergeht. Im Mangel einer ausgeführten Reproduktionstheorie spricht die Not des Reproduzierenden sich aus, die ihrerseits durch jenen Mangel verstärkt wird. Sie ist zugleich die Not des preisgegebenen Werkes.

Jedoch dies Dilemma treibt keineswegs den verantwortlichen Musiker zur agnostischen Konsequenz. Er läßt die Unterscheidung von richtiger und falscher Interpretation so wenig sich verkümmern wie die eines richtig oder falsch gegriffenen Akkords, eines reinen oder unreinen Tons. Jeder Schritt der Wiedergabe stellt sich ihm als objektiv bestimmt oder notwendig dar, und unbeirrt trennt er solche wie immer auch vorläufige Notwendigkeit vom zufälligen und äußerlichen – dem Werk äußerlichen – Belieben. Dies sachliche Vertrauen eignet durchaus nicht bloß der handwerklich befangenen Naivetät. Selbst Einsicht in den geschichtlichen Wechsel der Interpretationen, die den reflektierenden Musikern zumindest seit dem neunzehnten Jahrhundert sich aufdrängte, hat es nicht vermocht, die Idee der wahren Interpretation zu brechen: die geschichtliche Veränderung als solche vielmehr ist als gesetzmäßig anerkannt und damit zur Idee der wahren Interpretation in Beziehung gesetzt worden. Das liegt implizit der Auffassung Richard Wagners in der Schrift »Über das Dirigieren« zugrunde, dem bedeutendsten Beitrag, den Komponisten zur Theorie der Reproduktion geleistet haben. Newman bezeichnet als Zweck jener Abhandlung die bündige Definition der »new demands made upon a conductor's capacity by the changes in music, and the corresponding changes in the sensitive performer's attitude towards music, that had taken place during the nineteenth century«[235]. Dem zufolge hätte Wagner nicht bloß die anwachsende subjektive Differenziertheit des Interpreten während der romantischen Ära, sondern ihren Grund, die objektiven historischen Veränderungen der Musik selber zum Kanon richtiger Darstellung erhoben. So wollte Wagner in der Tat den Kernpunkt der Schrift verstanden wissen. Er zielt auf die Lösung jenes Dilemmas der Interpretation, das seiner reflektierenden Kritik bereits bewußt war. »Mir konnte zunächst nur darum zu thun sein, das Dilemma selbst aufzudecken, und dem Gefühle eines Jeden es klar zu machen, daß seit Beethoven hinsichtlich der Behandlung und des Vortrages der Musik eine ganz wesentliche Veränderung gegen früher eingetreten ist. Was früher in einzelnen abgeschlossenen Formen zu einem Fürsichleben auseinandergehalten war, wird hier, wenigstens seinem innersten Hauptmotive nach, in den entgegengesetztesten Formen, von diesen selbst umschlossen, zu einander gehalten und gegenseitig aus sich entwickelt. Natürlich soll dem nun auch im Vortrage entsprochen werden, und hierzu gehört vor allen Dingen, daß das Zeitmaaß von nicht minderer Zartlebigkeit sei, als das thematische Gewebe, welches durch jenes sich seiner Bewegung nach kundgeben soll, selbst es ist.«[236] Wagner hat die »wesentliche Veränderung« des Vortrags der Musik nicht als bloßen Sachverhalt beschrieben, sondern als normativ bestätigt. Und zwar als Funktion von Veränderungen der kompositorischen Technik. Die Charakteristik Beethovens setzt diesen in Gegensatz zur »vorklassischen« Verfahrungsweise und gilt in Wahrheit für die gesamte Wiener Schule. Das Moment, das Wagner hervorhebt, hat seinen historischen Ursprung in der Einbeziehung der Kantabilität in den instrumentalen Satz. Es vollendet sich als Einheit in der Mannigfaltigkeit; einer aus qualitativ verschiedenen thematischen Gestalten in dialektisch vermitteltem Prozeß sich bildenden Konstruktion. Das ältere deutsche Musizieren, das Wagner in der Abhandlung beschreibt und das er in den Kapellmeisterjahren seiner Jugend mit gründlichem Widerwillen erfuhr, war hinter den Strukturveränderungen zurückgeblieben, in denen der Wiener Klassizismus resultierte. Es weiß nichts vom Einspruch des instrumentalen Gesanges gegens intrumentale Spiel. Noch spiegelte straffes, unnachgiebiges Durchtaktieren erstarrt die vorherrschende Kompositionsweise des Generalbaß-Zeitalters wider, die ihre Formen aus identischem Material schichtete, nicht als Prozeß der Synthesis von unidentischem entwickelte. Der Widerspruch jenes Typus der Darstellung, gegen dessen Verdienste Wagner im übrigen nicht blind war, zu Beethoven ist aber keiner des bloßen »Stils« und musikalischen Geschmacks. Wagners Forderung, es solle der neueren Kompositionsstruktur auch im Vortrag entsprochen werden, begründet er damit, daß das »thematische Gewebe«, also die Mannigfaltigkeit in der Einheit, durchs Zeitmaß, die Grundkategorie der Interpretation, »sich seiner Bewegung nach kundgeben soll«: also deutlich werden. Die Veränderung der Interpretation ist kein Wechsel der Moden, sondern geht, Wagner zufolge, aus der Notwendigkeit hervor, die unter dem Notentext und der einfachen Tempobezeichnung liegende Beschaffenheit der Komposition als solcher hörbar zu machen. Das Werk verlangt um seiner Objektivität willen veränderte Darstellung und zwar gerade eine der traditionellen Objektivität entgegengesetzte: dies der paradoxe Sinn von Wagners Forderung. Indem er sie aber »der Beurtheilung unseres ganzen heutigen Musikmachens«[237] zugrundelegt, läßt er kaum einen Zweifel daran, daß er die elastisch-funktionelle Darstellungsweise nicht auf die Musik seit dem Wiener Klassizismus beschränkt, sondern als allgemeines Prinzip meint. Liszts pianistische Transkriptionen Bachischer Orgelwerke etwa sind Zeugnisse dieser übergreifenden Intention. Ihr dekorativer Zug hat sich mittlerweile als jener Deutlichkeit entgegengesetzt erwiesen, um derentwillen das neudeutsche Darstellungsideal konzipiert ward. Es ist selber der historischen Dynamik verfallen, in deren Erkenntnis es entsprang. Aber es hat zugleich den Gedanken der objektiven Verbindlichkeit von Interpretation auf jene Dynamik gerade bezogen. Wagners Lehre schließt die Konsequenz ein, daß die Wahrheit der Interpretation nicht in Geschichte als ein dieser Fremdes und ihr Ausgeliefertes liegt, sondern Geschichte in der Wahrheit der Interpretation, als ein nach deren immanenten Gesetzen sich Entfaltendes. Der vorkritische wie der unverbindliche Standpunkt sind, der Tendenz nach, aufgehoben.

Wenn danach die Reproduktion von Musik als theoretisches Problem zu begreifen ist, so wird sie zugleich als Form eigenen Wesens behauptet. Alle Fragen der Reproduktion setzen in technische sich um, aber ihre Beantwortung trifft die Funktion der Technik selber. Während der Rechtsanspruch der Interpretation in dem Verhältnis konkreter Werke und empirischer Interpreten sich anmeldet und begründet, ist er doch nicht aus der Betrachtung jener beiden Pole, oder gar im Kompromiß zwischen beiden zu entscheiden, sondern erst durch Erwägungen, welche die Idee der Interpretation aus dem Begriff des musikalischen Werkes als solchem und seines geschichtlichen Lebens dartun. Eine strenge Vorstellung von den spezifischen Gesetzen der Reproduktion, also Einsicht in ihre Autonomie, läßt sich einzig in der Analyse dessen gewinnen, was von Interpretation wesentlich vorausgesetzt wird, der Existenz durch Schrift und Druck fixierter und insofern gerade vom empirischen Musizieren unabhängiger Werke. Das Ende der improvisatorischen Praxis, die Verselbständigung des Werkes und seine Trennung von der Interpretation stiftet zugleich deren Selbständigkeit. Wiedergeben läßt sich das Werk erst als einmal entfremdetes. Interpretation, als autonome Form, ist notwendig auf ihren Widerspruch verwiesen, das autonome musikalische Gebilde. Darin gemahnt sie unmittelbar an die Übersetzung sprachlicher Texte. »Übersetzung ist eine Form. Sie als solche zu erfassen, gilt es zurückzugehen auf das Original. Denn in ihm liegt deren Gesetz als in dessen Übersetzbarkeit beschlossen.«[238] Von der Übersetzung aus der fremden Sprache jedoch unterscheidet die musikalische Reproduktion grundsätzlich sich darin, daß bis zum heutigen Tage Musik ihrer bedarf, nicht jedoch die Dichtung ihres Übersetzers. Dem unübersetzten Gedicht geht nichts von seiner Schönheit ab, und eher hat es, wie das Wortspiel es will, den traduttore als traditore zu fürchten denn ihn herbeizuziehen. Die Partitur jedoch, die der Möglichkeit ihrer Aufführung radikal entzogen ist, scheint sinnlos zugleich in sich selber. Der Vorwurf, eine Komposition sei Papiermusik, mag oft genug die reaktionäre Abfertigung rationalisieren. Sein normativer Kern jedoch, es müsse jede Komposition, um als stimmig sich zu erweisen, angemessen realisierbar sein und gleichsam ihre wahre Interpretation in sich tragen, ist legitim. Er läßt in technischen Kategorien sich ausdrücken. Noch die strengste Auffassung von der Objektivität des Werkes, die jeden Gedankens an Kommunikation und Wirkung sich entschlägt, wird Kriterien wie das der sachgemäßen Interpretation sich nicht aus der Hand schlagen lassen, und solche Kriterien sind zwar von jeder empirischen Aufführung zu trennen, nicht aber vom Ideal der wahren. Der Grenzwert eines von der idealen Aufführung ganz emanzipierten Werkes erschließt sich allenfalls der Analyse von Interpretation als Form: sie liegt in deren eigener Dialektik, nicht im unkritisch vorausgesetzten Ansichsein der Werke. Aller bestehenden Musik jedoch ist das Interpretiertwerden wesentlich. Daß aber noch das schwierigste sprachliche Gebilde indifferent ist gegen seine gelungene Übersetzung, wie gegen seinen glücklichen Vortrag, während der einfachste musikalische Text, gänzlich adäquat der stummen Vorstellung des verständig Noten Lesenden gegeben, doch ein dem Aufgezeichneten transzendentes Klangbild zum Inhalt hat – das läßt sich nicht vom Aufnehmenden her erklären, sondern bloß durch die Differenz der Medien. Musik so gut wie Dichtung kann gelesen werden, nur heißt Lesen hier und dort ein Anderes. Bei der Musik erheischt Lesen notwendig die sinnliche Vorstellung, während die Dichtung die ihres eigentlichen Gehalts geradezu verbietet.[239] Die philosophische Behandlung des Problems der Reproduktion kann daher die Reflexion auf das Verhältnis von Sprache und Musik nicht vermeiden, wie es in ihrer Ähnlichkeit als Konstellation von Zeichen, ihrem Gegensatz mit Hinsicht auf [das] Postulat der Realisierbarkeit liegt. Solche Reflexion muß an den Begriff des musikalischen Textes und damit der Notenschrift sich anschließen, der das Problem der musikalischen Reproduktion konstituiert und zugleich die spezifische Differenz zur Sprache. Dieser wird Musik nur als Schrift kommensurabel.

2.

Gleich der sprachlichen ist die musikalische Schrift ein Zeichensystem. [*Marginalie von Gretel Adornos Hand*: NB TWA: auseinanderhalten: Intentionslosigkeit d. musikalischen *Schrift* + d. *Musik*. Sehr wichtig] Von den beiden Elementen, als deren Verbindung Riemann sie betrachtet[240], ist das eine das Alphabet, dessen erste Buchstaben von alters her den Tönen der diatonischen Skala zugeordnet waren. Damit involviert die Notenschrift primitive Begrifflichkeit: das Zeichen α gibt die einheitliche Tonhöhe aller je damit notierten Töne an oder markiert wenigstens, wenn man absolute Tonhöhen für die frühere Antike nicht annehmen will, stets den Ausgangston der mixolydischen Skala. Nicht zufällig aber ist solche Begrifflichkeit durch Buchstaben vermittelt und nicht durch Worte. Sie hält die Identität sinnlicher Laute fest, aber nicht die von Sachen. Die Analogie der musikalischen und sprachlichen Schrift bezieht sich allein auf die Schicht des akustischen Stoffs, dessen Elemente hier wie dort mit Zeichen bedacht werden und zwar in der Musik mit aus der Sprache entlehnten. Aber in jener fügen diese Elemente sich nicht zu Komplexen zusammen, die Gegenstände bedeuteten: die musikalische Schriftsprache ist eine ohne Intention, gleichsam eine blinde Nomenklatur, und die Einheiten des Sinnes, in denen Musik selber sich bewegt, haben mit Intentionalität nichts gemein: Musik ist eine intentionslose Sprache. Man kann denn auch bei ihr von Lauten reden und andererseits mit gutem, unmetaphorischem Grunde von Perioden und Sätzen, doch niemals von Worten. Ihrer Schrift ist das begriffliche Medium bloß peripher, ja man könnte in der musikalischen Notenschrift eine bloße Pseudomorphose ans Bereich des Begriffs erblikken. Daß sie ihre Zeichen von der Sprachschrift borgen mußte, deutet auf ihre Fremdheit zum Begriff: die Buchstaben sind den Tönen nachträglich, in der Willkür der Rationalisierung aufgeprägt und verhalten sich zu ihnen eher wie Allegorien, als daß sie mit ihnen verschmolzen wären wie die Buchstaben mit den Sprachlauten. Vom Ton a ist der Name a zu trennen, ohne daß er an musikalischer Bestimmtheit das Mindeste darüber verlöre; Buchstabe und Vokal a ebenso trennen zu wollen, wäre müßiges Beginnen. Denn das Aussprechen des Namens a zitiert den Laut a, nicht aber das Nennen des Tones a diesen. Mit anderen Worten: das Zeichensystem der Sprachschrift und die Sprache gehören einem homogenen System an, die Musik und ihre Schrift zwei verschiedenen. Die sprachlichen Zeichen ragen in den musikalischen Kosmos einzig als ein ihm selber Fremdes, Gebrochenes herein. Gerade weil Musik eine intentionslose Sprache ausmacht, ist der signifikative Charakter ihrer Schrift, die Differenz von Zeichen und Bezeichnetem, zum qualitativen Bruch gesteigert.

Wenn sonach das begriffliche Wesen als ein der musikalischen Schrift Äußerliches, nur versprengt in ihr Vorkommendes muß angesprochen werden, während doch die musikalische Schrift an Artikulation und logischer Konsequenz hinter der sprachlichen kaum zurückbleibt, so muß ihr Ursprung in einem anderen Elemente vermutet werden als dem intentionalen. Das ist aber die hypokritike, die das Aristidische Schema auf der gleichen Ebene wie Instrumentenspiel und Gesang als Feld der musikalischen Vortragslehre einzeichnet. Es ist das mimetische Element. Riemann hat an der Einbeziehung der Mimik in die musikalische Vortragslehre Anstoß genommen. »Denn wenn der Sprache zweifellos noch spezifisch musikalische Elemente im musikalischen Klange innewohnen, kann das gleiche von der lediglich zum Auge sprechenden Mimik nicht ausgesagt werden. Die Berechtigung zu der Einstellung auch dieser Kunstform ergibt sich aber wieder aus der von Anfang und fortgesetzt zu konstatierenden innigen Verbindung der sämtlichen energischen Künste, d. h. der das

Kunstwerk als ein Stück wirkliches Leben vor Auge und Ohr im zeitlichen Geschehen entwickelnden Künste; nicht nur sind im Gesange Dichtung und Musik, und im Tanze Gebärdenspiel und Musik zu fester Einheit verbunden, sondern alle drei verschmelzen im Chorreigen zu einer Gesamtkunst, für welche die Griechen den Ausdruck Musik in seiner weitesten Bedeutung anwenden.«[241] Die gewundene Verteidigung des Aristides, welche die Differenz zwischen Sprache und Musik viel zu leicht nimmt und in der summarischen Anschauung von allen energischen Künsten als »wirkliches Leben« vor Augen stellenden durch den Ausdruck hypokritike allein Lügen gestraft wird, verfehlt kraft der Nivellierung von Sprache und Musik deren mimetisches Element. Sie krankt am Riemannschen Grundfehler in der Behandlung entlegener Epochen, späte geschichtliche Züge wie eben die Trennung von Mimik und Musik als natur- und vernunftgegeben zu hypostasieren und in jedem modernen »Nacherleben« verschlossene Phänomene trugvoll sich einzufühlen, indem sie nach Kategorien des späten neunzehnten Jahrhunderts umgebogen werden. Ihm ist die Arbeitsteilung der Zeitkünste so selbstverständlich, daß er sie durch Vorstellungen musikdramatischer Art nachträglich zur Synthese bringen muß, um ihre Ungeschiedenheit in der griechischen Ästhetik zu würdigen. Weit eher aber ist die Auffassung der Mimik als eines Bestandstücks der musikalischen Vortragslehre ein archaisches Rudiment. Das besagt nicht nur, daß in der kultischen Übung, in der die Zeitkünste entsprangen, Musik, Tanz und Mimik, in der Einheit ihrer Funktion, und auch nicht bloß, daß die Gebärde des Singens selber, als willkürliches Spiel der Gesichtsmuskulatur, ein Mimisches notwendig mit sich führt. Sondern der Musik als solcher wohnt das Mimische inne. Gleichviel welchen Anteil an ihrem Ursprung die Nachahmung von Naturlauten trägt, sicherlich hat sie selber von jeher zur Nachahmung durch Gesten, seis des Tanzes seis der Arbeit, angeregt: sie hat Gesten, auf der Ebene des magischen Gebrauchs »vorgemacht«, um solche von Menschen, seis hervorzubringen seis zu regeln, und in der Differenz ihrer magischen Gestik von der empirischen ist bereits jenes Moment von Unwirklichkeit als Verstellung, von Mimik im prägnanten Sinne gesetzt, an welches der Name hypokritike erinnert und das dann zu ästhetischer Autonomie sich entfaltet. [*Marginalie:* dies zugleich das Magische der Musik, das sie dann zur Ideologie macht] Musik ist das Echo des animistischen Schauers, Mimikry ans unsichtbare, gefürchtete Mienenspiel der Naturgottheit, ein Reflex der Beschwichtigung, der noch in den jüngsten Einbildungen von der therapeutischen Wirkung der Musik nachzittert, während dies magisch mimetische Wesen der Musik schon der griechischen Aufklärung des Epikureers Philodemos zur Kritik stand. [*Marginalie:* schwach, ausführen u. *viel* tiefer fassen] Ob, wie die ältesten harmonischen Spekulationen es nahelegen, die musikalische Mimik auf Astralvorgänge sich bezog, steht dahin. Kein Zweifel kann aber daran sein, daß Musik als Sprache, allein von allen Künsten, die reine Objektivation des mimetischen Impulses leistet, frei von Gegenständlichkeit wie von Bedeuten, nichts anderes als der zum Gesetz erhobene, der Körperwelt übergeordnete und zugleich sinnliche Gestus. Die Kunst des inneren Sinnes imitiert die Gebärde des Geistes. [*Marginalie:* schwach u. dunkel]

Während aber die Ausbildung der Musik als autonomer Kunst das mimische Moment – und dessen eigenem Prinzip treu, in permanenter Opposition wider die Vergegenständlichung – immer mehr an den Rand gedrängt, vielleicht tabuiert hat, wird seine Spur dort gerade festgehalten, wo Musik selber dem Gebot der Vergegenständlichung unterlag, in ihrer Notation. Die musikalischen Zeichen, welche die Musik der Vieldeutigkeit und Vergänglichkeit des Gestus entwanden, sind dafür Bilder von Gesten. Als Rationalisierung der Magie hat die Notenschrift die mimetische Praxis festgehalten, während der musikalischen Übung das Gedächtnis an jene bereits zu entschwinden begann. Aussagen über den Ursprung der Notenschrift, der griechischen sowohl wie der Neumen, setzen dem Mißtrauen sich aus, solange die Dechiffrierung selber nicht zwingend gelungen ist. Doch drängt der Zweifel an der scheinbar natürlichen und vernunftgemäßen Ansicht sich auf. Diese geht dahin, die Notenschrift sei als Gedächtnisstütze entstanden, um die lebendige Musik, Lied und Tanz, vorm Vergessenwerden zu bewahren. Das aber ist rationalistisch: späte Bedürfnisse werden, in der Illusion ihrer Allmenschlichkeit, auf die Archaik übertragen. Gedächtnisstützen werden notwendig, wenn das Gedächtnis problematisch wird. Das geschieht erst in der Phase einer universal vermittelten Erfahrung, welche Subjekt und Objekt, als geschiedene, vergegenständlichte, wieder zusammenbringt, während das nahe, in seiner Andersheit noch nicht konstituierte Objekt im Gedächtnis die kräftige Spur hinterläßt. Das Gedächtnis, Organ fürs Gewesene, wird schwach erst gegenüber der erkannten Unwiederbringlichkeit des Gewesenen, in der Belastung mit unzähligen fernen gar nicht mehr primär erfahrenen Daten, schließlich in der totalen Anpassung an das, was augenblicklich ist. Die Hinfälligkeit des Gedächtnisses gehört zu den Schlüsseln des gegenwärtigen Bewußtseins, nicht zur ältesten Zeit. Kinder brauchen keine Gedächtnisstütze: schwer fällt ihnen nicht die sprachliche Erinnerung, sondern gerade erst deren »stützende« Vergegenständlichung; in der Schule muß man schreiben lernen nicht sprechen. Mit den Primitiven kann es kaum anders gewesen sein: die Hingabe an die Gegenwart ist die Macht des Vergangenen in dieser. Das gilt auch für die Musik. Wann immer aus bloßer Tradition, ohne Bindung an die fixierte Schrift, gespielt oder gesungen wird, erweist sich das Gedächtnis als stark. Die rhythmischen Modelle, welche die Wilden behalten, sind so komplex, daß kein Zivilisierter außer dem Fachmann die gleiche Leistung zustandebrächte; etwas vom Reiz des Jazz liegt darin. Die Modifikationen aber, denen jene Modelle im primitiven oder traditionellen Musizieren unterliegen, sind Früchte des Gedächnisses, nicht das Mal von dessen Versagen. Indem das Vergangene weiterlebt, anstatt als Entfremdetes sich abzusetzen, verbürgt seine Veränderung seine Gegenwart. Identisch festgehalten, dinghaft wird es erst als virtuell Vergessenes, wie alle Verdinglichung auf ein Vergessen hinausläuft. Die Notation ist Stütze der Erinnerung und des Gedächtnisses nur als dessen Feind, als seine Wiederherstellung durch Vernichtung.

Danach kann sie kaum als harmlose Notiz, als aide mémoire, entstanden sein. Vielmehr deutet ihr Ursprung zurück auf die Störung jener naturwüchsigen Verhältnisse, die in gewissem Sinn vor der Konstitution des Gedächtnisses und vor dessen Fragwürdigkeit liegen, weil Jetzt und Früher in ihnen noch nicht starr auseinander getreten sind. Diese Störung ist aber die Ausbildung fester gesellschaftlicher Herrschaftsverhältnisse, welche wie im festen logischen Kategoriensystem so auch in der Regelung der Zeitverhältnisse sich niederschlagen; in den letzteren vielleicht als Ausdruck einer generationsweisen Ordnung des Eigentums, die zugleich das Verbot des Inzests zwischen Mutter und Sohn einschließt. Es hat den Anschein, als hätte die musikalische Notation in sich gerade der Verdinglichung der Zeit den zähesten Widerstand geleistet: fällt doch die Mensurierung erst in jene späte Periode des Mittelalters, die der jüngsten Forschung als eine Vorrenaissance erscheinen will. Was seit ihren griechischen Ursprüngen, längst ehe ihr die vollkommene Objektivation und damit die Verselbständigung des Gebildes gegenüber der Praxis gelang, von den Noten vollbracht war, ist weniger die Bewahrung eines ohnehin in Tradition Gegenwärtigen als vielmehr die Disziplinierung der traditionellen Übung, welche die Gemeinde, also die unterworfene Masse, davon abhalten soll, im Sinn des eigenen Ausdrucksbedürfnisses das Überlieferte zu modifizieren, sondern in dessen zwangshafter Wiederholung besser gehorchen zu lernen. In der Tat verleugnet keine der theoretisch musikalischen Reformen bis zur Zeit Palestrinas eine autoritäre Absicht, die ihren bündigsten Niederschlag im Platonischen Staat und in der Augustinischen Musiklehre gefunden hat. Es ist damit von Anbeginn ein anti-mimetisches, signifikatives, gleichsam rationales Element in der musikalischen Notation gegeben, das jedoch vom mimischen Wesen der Musik nicht einfach divergiert, sondern mit ihm aufs tiefste sich verschränkt. Notation enteignet das Gedächtnis, indem sie ihm hilft: sie ist der erste Schritt zu seiner Vergesellschaftung. Die kultischen Tänze und Lieder werden der unartikulierten Einheit von Erinnerung und Veränderung entrissen: sie werden zu einer übergeordneten das Ganze der jeweiligen gesellschaftlichen Einheiten umfassenden Instanz erhoben und zugleich dem unter dieser Einheit Befaßten, dem Stammesangehörigen, entrückt: kein Text, und gewiß kein musikalischer, der nicht den Anspruch der Heiligkeit usurpierte. Es liegt darin zugleich ein Akt der Formulierung: gegenüber dem konkreten gesellschaftlichen Inhalt der musikalischen Übung konstituiert sich als dessen Form ein Gleichbleibendes, aber, um seiner gesellschaftlichen Entfremdung willen, niemals ganz Identisches: das impliziert dem genetischen Sinn nach bereits alle Problematik der musikalischen Interpretation in der Ära der voll objektivierten Texte. Notation will, daß die Musik vergessen werde, um sie zu fixieren und einzuhämmern: sie soll in die identische Wiederholung, die Verdinglichung des Gestus übergehen, welche an aller Musik barbarischer Kulturen das Trommelfell des Zuhörers martert. Indem die Musik zum kultischen Anliegen des Stammes gemacht wird, soll er der eigenen Spontaneität zugleich sich entäußern: er soll ein Ritual vollziehen, dessen Sinn in der Unverständlichkeit eben besteht und dessen Abwandlung zum Frevel, zur Treulosigkeit, zur Durchbrechung des Tabus gestempelt wird. Nichts vielleicht bezeichnet die gegenwärtige Spätphase der musikalischen Kultur als Rückschlag auf die Archaik genauer als der Tabucharakter, aus dem der musikalische Text hervorging, und der heute, in der Vollendung der ästhetischen Profanität, sich wieder herstellt. Wenn das optische Bild der musikalischen Noten seit den Neumenakzenten, und gewiß seit der Mensurierung nachahmend die Trommelschläge barbarisch-kultischer Musikübung zu beschwören scheint, so mag eine Spekulation nicht allen Grundes entbehren, welche die musikalische Schrift überhaupt ursprünglich als Nachahmung disziplinärer Musiksysteme, gewissermaßen als

Mimesis des antimimetischen Elements der Musik betrachtet. Die Verräumlichung eines Zeitlichen, Prinzip aller musikalischen Notation, stellt an sich bereits jene Enteignung, Entfremdung, Erstarrung der Musik dar, wie sie aus den gleichsam räumlichen, symmetrisch-asymmetrischen Wiederholungen der primitiven Musik blickt, die in der Unregelmäßigkeit der Modelle das mimische Moment festhalten, aber durch deren unveränderte Wiederholung es aus dem eigenen Zeitkontinuum herausbrechen, stillstellen, tot und zugleich beherrschbar machen. War jedes Notenzeichen einmal Bild eines Schlages und dann von Gewalt selber? Der Verewigung der Musik durch Schrift eignet ein tödliches Moment: was sie hält, wird zugleich unwiederbringlich. (Etwas früher stellen, verräumlichen heißt da sein: die absolute Gegenwart wäre zeitlos und nur was ganz da ist, läßt sich beherrschen. Verräumlichung ist ihrem Inhalt nach Beherrschbarkeit.) Dieser Widerspruch schreibt der Reproduktion von Kunstmusik ihre Utopie vor: durch absolute Verfügung das wiederzubringen, was durchs Verfügen selber unwiederbringlich ward. Alles Musizieren ist eine recherche du temps perdu. Das ist der Schlüssel zur Dialektik der Musik bis zu ihrer Liquidation. Denn sie konnte zur Autonomie und damit zu all ihrem Ausdruck erst sich entfalten durch ihre graphische Vermittlung, die sie praktikabel, verfügbar macht und verdinglicht. Musikalische Schrift ist das Organon der musikalischen Naturbeherrschung, und in dieser erst ist Freiheit, die musikalische Subjektivität herangereift als Trennung von der bewußtlosen Gemeinschaft. (Was ist musikalische Naturbeherrschung? Hat Musik in einem sehr frühen Stadium der Beherrschung von Menschen, wahrscheinlich im Zusammenhang des Opferrituals gedient, so wandert vermöge der Notation Beherrschung in sie selber ein, das heißt, die Gesten, welche Musik seis anregt, seis selber nachmacht, werden in ihr, als Bilder, beherrschbar, nach Belieben zu machen, wieder hervorzubringen, und darin bereitet sich die Rationalisierung des Materials der Musik vor, die an einigen ihrer entscheidenden Wendepunkte, wie bei der Liniierung der Neumen und dann bei der Einführung der festen Notenwerte, als Sprung in der Entwicklung der Notation sich vollzog. Durch die Schrift ist nicht nur das Vergangene zu vergegenwärtigen, sondern in der Vergegenwärtigung, dem »Dasein« ist alles musikalische Material übersichtlich zu machen, zu ordnen, nach einheitlichen Prinzipien zu organisieren. Schönbergs Intention, zur Zwölftontechnik, als dem Extrem der musikalischen Naturbeherrschung, welche alle musikalischen Dimensionen auf den einheitlichen Nenner bringt, eine eigene Zwölftonschrift[242] hinzuzufügen, zeugt unbewußt von einem Impuls, der die gesamte abendländische Musikgeschichte beherrscht.) Wie in der realen Gesellschaft, so ist in ihrem begriffs- und bilderlosen Abbild, der Musik, das herrschaftliche Prinzip die Voraussetzung der Freiheit, die Verdinglichung die der ästhetischen Unmittelbarkeit, die Entfremdung die der Nähe und Wärme von Kunst. Zugleich aber statuiert die musikalische Schrift ein ihrem eigenen Inhalt [nach] der Musik Konträres. Rationalisierung, Bedingung aller autonomen Kunst, zehrt an dieser zugleich. Notation reguliert, bändigt, unterdrückt immer zugleich das, dem sie dient, und an dieser Doppelschlächtigkeit leidet alle musikalische Reproduktion bis zu ihrem Untergang. Im Aufschreiben von Musik ist nicht bloß der Erscheinungsweise sondern dem Sinn nach die Differenz von dieser gesetzt und wird in die Musik um so tiefer hineingetragen, je weniger diese, als entwickelte, von ihrer Notation mehr sich ablösen läßt. Die Verräumlichung des Zeitlichen ist nicht bloß empirisch, sondern wesentlich inadäquat: Autonomie und Fetischismus, der Ursprung der Subjektivität und ihre Unterjochung unter den entfremdeten Gegensatz, das Ding, sind zwei Seiten des gleichen Sachverhalts. Das läßt an der Geschichte der Reproduktion sich ablesen, treu zum Werk ist der Gehorsam, der schließlich es selber zerstört. Einzig der gesellschaftliche Gehorsam, der in jener Treue sich reflektiert, hat Musik befähigt, der existierenden Gesellschaft zu widersprechen und er treibt sie am Ende von innen her in den gesellschaftlichen Betrieb hinein, der zugleich von außen sie aufzusaugen sich anschickt. (Bei der Stelle über die Neumen als Akzentzeichen sagen, daß dies die Basis der Neumeninterpretation seit Coussemaker ist. – Zum herrschaftlichen Charakter der Musik Hinweis auf den Zusammenhang der Musik mit dem griechischen Ideal der Männlichkeit andreia und das Sokratische Wort, der beste Tänzer sei auch der beste Krieger, auch der Platonische Satz, daß das ganze Leben des Menschen der Harmonie und Eurythmie bedürfe, Protagoras 326 B, vgl. Riemann I, 1, p. 5. Ist das nicht etwas zuviel Musikgeschichte G[retel Adorno]?)

Die Konstruktion des Ursprungs der Notenschrift aus der musikalischen Disziplin entbehrt nicht aller historischen Stütze. Riemann konzediert die Möglichkeit, »daß die Neumenschrift selbst griechischen Ursprungs ist und sich aus der Cheironomie, den Handbewegungen des die Melodiebewegung und die ihr entsprechenden Bewegungen des Chors leitenden Chordirigenten des Altertums entwickelt hat«[243]). Bleibt die Ansicht vom cheironomischen Ursprung der griechischen Notation selber hypothetisch, so ist sie weit bestimmter für das frühe Mittelalter. Oskar Fleischer hat in seinen »Neumenstudien« die Ausbildung bloßer Akzentzeichen zu komplizierten Neumen »nicht als Notation, sondern in der Praxis der die Tonbewegungen durch Handbewegungen andeutenden Dirigenten der Sängerchöre« gesucht[244]). Danach wäre die Notenschrift beides, Nachahmung der sogenannten Cheironomie eines Gestischen im wörtlichen Sinn und Abbild eines Disziplinären, der Lenkung des Chors durch den prähistorischen Dirigenten. Fleischer und Riemann schließen sich den Forschungen von Dom Mocquereau an. Dessen Ansicht vom mimischen Ursprung der Notation scheint über die ihre noch hinauszugehen, indem er die Akzentzeichen selber, aus denen die Virgen der Neumen entstanden sind, also den Grundbestandteilen der okzidentalen Notation, und nicht erst deren Zusammensetzung als Abbilder von Gesten auffaßt. (Vielleicht ist der Punkt, an dem die musikalische und die sprachliche Schrift miteinander übereinkommen, das Interpunktionszeichen, und das wäre mit der Stelle zusammenzubringen, daß die Musik Buchstaben und Sätze, aber keine Worte kennt. Das hier behandelte, selbst mimetische und zugleich dem mimischen Ausdruck feindliche Wesen der Notenschrift muß schon im vorigen Abschnitt viel schärfer hervortreten.) Mocquereau »stellt bereits mit Berufung auf die Institutio oratoria des Quintilianus fest, daß die eigentlich charakteristische Form des Acutus, dem die Virga der Neumenschrift entspricht, die links unten mit Druck angesetzte nach rechts oben spitz verlaufende ist, und die des Gravis umgekehrt die links oben mit Druck angesetzte nach rechts unten verlaufende und bezeichnet die Akzente als eine Art Nachmalen der Tonbewegung (pictographie), betont auch sehr bestimmt, daß im Mittelalter sowohl in der griechischen als in der römischen Kirche Handbewegungen des Dirigenten dazu dienten, die Hebungen und Senkungen der Melodie und zugleich den Rhythmus und das Tempo anzudeuten und somit den Chor bestimmt zu leiten«[245] – eine Praxis im übrigen, die gerade bei den differenzierten modernen Dirigenten, wie Furtwängler, überlebt, welche die Funktion des Taktschlagens mit der rechten Hand erfüllen und mit der linken gewissermaßen den musikalischen Verlauf selber in die Luft zeichnen. (Dirigieren und Ursprung der Notenschrift: die Unabhängigkeit beider Hände voneinander entspricht deren Zusammensetzung aus dem mensuralen und dem mimetischen Element. Etwas Ähnliches gilt noch für die beiden Hände des Klavierspiels, das in gewisser Weise auch ein »Schreiben« der Musik, ihr Nachahmen aus den Akzenten der Tasten ist.) Fleischer nimmt an, daß die Cheironomie, also die gestisch-optische Nachahmung von Musik »ohne schriftliche Aufzeichnung sich durch lange Jahrhunderte gehalten und fortentwickelt habe, bis endlich zu Anfang des 8. Jahrhunderts der Angelsachse (Neumenstudien II, p. 8) oder Ire (das. p. 68) Ceolfrid den ersten Versuch machte, aus den Schlagzeichen der Cheironomie eine den Texten überschriebene Tonbezeichnung zu entwickeln und damit der Erfinder der Neumenschrift wurde«[246]. Die Cheironomie wäre also die Vermittlung zwischen Musik und Schrift: mit der Musik läuft sie in der Zeit ab aber als ein Optisches, das räumlich sich fixieren, »aufschreiben« läßt. Ihr Grundelement, das »Schlagzeichen«, wäre in der Tat Abbild des Schlages barbarisch-ritualer Kulturmusiken. Zur archaischen Praxis es in Beziehung zu setzen, liegt um so mehr Anlaß vor, als die Akzentsysteme sich keineswegs auf den mittelländischen Kulturkreis beschränkten, sondern offenbar autochthon bei den spät erst in den christlichen Kulturkreis einbezogenen Kelten vorkamen, denen wiederum ein großer Anteil an der frühmittelalterlichen Klosterkultur auf dem Kontinent zukam.[247]

Angesichts der unüberwindlichen Schwierigkeiten der Deutung, insbesondere der ältesten Neumenmonumente resigniert Riemann zu dem Verdikt, es sei »die Frage nach den letzten Wurzeln der Neumenschrift für uns von sekundärer Bedeutung. Nicht die Beschaffenheit und Bedeutung der Notenschriftzeichen, sondern vielmehr die Beschaffenheit der Gesänge, welche sie fixieren sollen, ist das uns in erster Linie Interessierende«[248]. Abgesehen von dem schlagenden Einwand, daß über die Beschaffenheit jener Gesänge ohne die Dechiffrierung der Schrift gar nicht sinnvoll zu reden sei, bleibt Riemanns Trost hinter seiner eigenen an einer späteren Phase gewonnenen Erkenntnis zurück, »daß die Emanzipation des musikalischen Rhythmus von der immanenten Rhythmik des Textes durch Einführung von Notenwertzeichen sogleich durchaus einen Fortschritt der Kunst bedeutete«[249], also der Komposition zugutekam. Was aber der Mensuralnotenschrift recht ist, ist den Neumen billig: die anwachsende Genauigkeit ist die Voraussetzung für die »Rationalisierung« und Ausbildung des Komponierens ebenso wie für das sich Anmessen der Reproduktion an den dergestalt sich auskristallisierenden musikalischen Text. Der Ursprung der Neumenschrift ergibt erst die Wahrheit über die Idee der musikalischen Schrift selber und damit über das Grundproblem der Interpretation. Dem ist Riemann nahegekommen, indem er der modernen Notenschrift »Anschaulichkeit« – also eben das unintentionale mimetische Element – zuerkennt als das Erbe der Neumierung. »Wir erkennen dann mit Staunen und Bewunderung, daß das unsere heutige Notenschrift so himmelhoch über alle anderen Notierungsweisen erhebende Moment der direkten Anschaulichkeit ein Erbteil der Neumenschrift ist, daß unsere Notenschrift nur eine im Lauf der Jahrhunderte konsequent ausgebaute Neumierung ist.«[250] Aber doch nicht ganz. Wenn nämlich das objektivierende, traditionsregelnde und in gewissem Sinn ausdrucksfeindliche Element der Notenschrift gerade auf Mimesis, dem optisch erstarrten Abbild der musikalischen Geste beruht, dann wird umgekehrt die eigentliche musikalische Konkretion, in der der mimetische Impuls als solcher fortlebt, der Schrift eingesenkt gerade durch ihr zweites, abstrakt-signifikatives Element, die Buchstabentonschrift. Die musikalische Bilderschrift ist gerade »abstrakt« und setzt denn auch, wie Riemann für die Neumen ohne Linien ausführt, »die Annahme einer beschränkten Anzahl durch direkte Überlieferung mittels Vorsingens und Nachsingens weiter gegebener Melodien« voraus; »nicht die Festlegung dieser Melodien in einer jeden Einzelton genau bestimmenden Notierung ist ihr Zweck, sondern vielmehr die besondere Art ihrer Anpassung auf den jedesmaligen Text«[251] – eine höchst drastische Beschreibung des disziplinären Wesens der Gestenschrift. Die musikalische Individuation jedoch, eben die Festlegung der Melodie nach Maßgabe ihrer absolut bestimmten Einzeltöne [*Formulierungsvariante:* musikalischen Elemente], wie sie gerade die Emanzipation von der Überlieferung und damit vom priesterlichen Kommando impliziert, fordert ein nicht-mimetisches, verdinglichtes, der Musik in ihrer Unmittelbarkeit ganz entrücktes Moment, eben das allegorische des Buchstabens, das sie zur Sprache in ein Verhältnis äußerster Ferne und zugleich äußerster Nähe setzt. Dies Paradoxon wohnt der Sinnesgeschichte der musikalischen Schrift als ihr eigentliches Geheimnis inne, und es definiert die Dialektik von Ausdruck und Konstruktion, in der alles Komponieren und alle Wiedergabe von Musik spielt. (In gewissem Sinn ist die Theorie der Schrift wichtiger als die Kenntnis der alten Musik.) Ob bereits die Doppelschlächtigkeit der ältesten Instrumentalnotenschrift der Griechen, welche für die tiefere Oktave Buchstaben und für die mittlere die Namen der Saiten der Kithara verwendet, im Sinn der Zweiheit des signifikativen und gestischen Moments zu verstehen ist, läßt sich kaum entscheiden: die Saitennamen, entstanden im Zusammenhang mit der Praxis der Hervorbringung, würden dann das gestische Element repräsentieren. Fraglos indessen ist die zweifache Wurzel der Notenschrift für die neuere Zeit. Denn zur Neumisierung ist in der Ära Hucbalds bereits die lateinische Buchstabennotierung für die Noten hinzugetreten: »Zweifellos steht fest, daß im 10. Jahrhundert eine Instrumentalnotierung (für Orgel, Rotta usw.) mit den ersten Buchstaben des Alphabets im allgemeinen Gebrauch war und zwar zuerst nördlich der Alpen«[252]. Man geht kaum fehl, wenn man die Erfindung oder Renaissance der Buchstabenschrift für die Noten in Zusammenhang bringt mit der zur gleichen Periode aufkommenden Mehrstimmigkeit. Denn es erhellt, daß die Neumisierung, als reine Gestenschrift zur Festlegung selbst der primitivsten Mehrstimmigkeit im Organum untauglich war: die musikalischen Simultankomplexe lassen sich prinzipiell nicht in gestischer Sukzession abbilden und verlangen die Eindeutigkeit jedes einzelnen Tons, wenn kein Chaos resultieren soll. Es ist die Eindeutigkeit des Tons im Zusammenklang, die ihn gleichzeitig »rationalisiert« und befähigt, Ausdruck zu tragen: je mehr das Melos kultisch-ritual sich vergegenständlicht, um so mehr geht der mimetische und expressive Impuls auf den Simultankomplex, also die Harmonie, über, und es ist kein Zufall, daß die Emanzipation der Subjektivität in der gesamten abendländischen Musikgeschichte sich als Ordnung der harmonischen Perspektive, der simultanen Tiefendimension vollzog, die ihrerseits gerade Rationalisierung in einem weit radikaleren

Sinn erfordert, als sie der Gestenschrift allein je erreichbar gewesen wäre. Vielleicht sind die unabsehbaren Schwierigkeiten in der Dechiffrierung der älteren Neumen selber das Resultat eines projektiven Anachronismus, der einen Typus von Rationalität für eine Notationsphase postuliert, der dieser noch ganz fremd war: weil die Neumen gar keine »Zeichen« nach der Weise der Buchstaben sind, lassen sie sich auch gar nicht wie diese entziffern, sie bieten überhaupt keine signifikative Eindeutigkeit, sondern lediglich das exemplarische Regulativ der Tradition, und wo diese untergegangen ist, sind sie unlesbar, nicht weil es an einem Schlüssel fehlt, sondern weil sie außerhalb jener Tradition gar keinen Sinn behaupten, weil der an der Sprache gewonnene Begriff des Lesens selber ihrer Beschaffenheit widerspricht. Zugleich aber war allein die Anschaulichkeit der Gestenschrift geeignet, der Notenschrift jene Unmittelbarkeit zu verleihen, in der sie fähig ist, die Musik zu begreifen, die als intentionslose von einem dem eigenen Wesen nach intentionalen Schriftsystem gar nicht hätte erfaßt werden können. Aber der Einbruch der Intentionalität in die musikalische Notation ist selber nicht zufällig. Er ist Ausdruck der Christianisierung der Musik. Die Gestenschrift, so ließe sich sagen, beschwört Musik in ihrer Unmittelbarkeit, als Natur gleichsam, ruft sie zur ephemeren Gegenwart und ist unbekümmert um ihre Dauer. Der Intention geht es um Ewigkeit: sie tötet Musik als Naturphänomen, um sie gebrochen, als Geist, zu bewahren: das Überleben von Musik in ihrer Dauer setzt die Abtötung ihres Jetzt und Hier, und in der Schrift den Bann von dessen mimischer Repräsentation voraus. Das unabdingbare Moment der Fremdheit, das musikalischer Signifikation zukommt, eben ihre Pseudomorphose an die Sprache, ist gleichbedeutend mit der »Beseelung« der Musik, die sprechend wird nur im Bruch der eigenen Homogenität. Wird die kreatürliche Musik dem christlichen Zeitalter zur Sprache der Seele, deren Leib vergeht, die wegwirft, damit sie gewinnt, so ist das allegorische Element ihrer Signifikation nichts anderes als Ausdruck des Bruchs ihres bloßen Daseins durch die transzendierende Bedeutung: so verschränkt sich in der muskalischen Schrift gerade das Moment des Ausdrucks mit dem ihm unmittelbar entgegengesetzten des Bedeutens, und das macht die Rationalisierung der Schrift zum Organ von Subjektivität. Eine reine Signifikation der Schrift aber ist undurchführbar, weil das naturwüchsig intentionslose Wesen durch Bedeutung zwar einbrechen [kann], nie aber als solches rein in Bedeutungen aufzulösen ist. Daran hat die musikalische Schrift zu arbeiten. Die Geschichte der Notenschrift ist der Versuch einer Synthesis von Eindeutigkeit und Unmittelbarkeit. Das verleiht der Bemerkung Riemanns ihren geschichtsphilosophischen Horizont, daß die durch Guido von Arezzo bewirkte Verschmelzung der Buchstabenton- mit der Neumenschrift »schließlich die moderne Notenschrift ergab«[253]. Diese Synthesis aber ist nie gelungen und könnte so wenig gelingen wie Unmittelbarkeit in einer entfremdeten Gesellschaft. Daher perenniert musikalische Reproduktion als Problem im strengsten Sinn. Noch das genaueste Notenbild bewahrt, als Bild, etwas von der neumischen Vieldeutigkeit, und noch die genaueste Bezeichnung etwas von der signifikativen Starrheit, die dem den Tod androht, das sie zu erretten sich vornimmt. (Vielleicht umdrehen: noch bildliche Treue hat etwas von Buchstabenstarrheit, noch genaueste Bezeichnung etwas von Vieldeutigkeit). Es scheint das Gericht übers Versagen des großartigen Versuchs, die die Notenschrift während der gesamten bürgerlichen Ära, seit der Guidoschen Reform, darstellt, daß am Ende, im Zerfall der bürgerlichen Musikkultur, ohne Ahnung von den historischen Ursprüngen, an ganz verschiedenen Stellen, die Elemente wiederum auseinandertreten: Bemühungen um die Objektivierung des Kunsttanzes, zugleich mit dem Absterben der Ballett-Tradition haben Rudolf von Laban zum exzentrischen Versuch einer Tanzschrift gebracht, die wie eine Auferstehung der Neumen, jetzt aber ganz auf die musiklose Mimik beschränkt, anmutet, während die Banjodiagramme, die den amerikanischen Schlagern zur Erleichterung beigegeben werden, auf die

Abbildung der musikalischen Kurve ganz verzichten und seis mit der Tabulatur die reinen Instrumentalgriffe weisen, seis darüber hinaus isoliert das signifikative buchstabenmäßige Element beschwören. Beide Schriften, in ihrer Isolierung, sind Phänomene der Regression: die Tanzschrift als widersinnige Rationalisierung der reinen Geste, die Diagrammschrift als sich überschlagende Aufklärung, die durch reine Signifikation gerade in die primitive Nachahmung, die Anweisung zum Greifen, zurückfällt. (An der Stelle, wo vom originär mimischen Wesen der Musik die Rede ist, muß der Beziehung zwischen Musik und Weinen gedacht werden. Musik ist mimisch insofern, als bestimmte Gesten, ein bestimmtes Spiel der Gesichtsmuskulatur an sich notwendig musikalischen Klang ergibt, Musik ist gewissermaßen die akustische Objektivation des Mienenspiels, die von diesem vielleicht überhaupt erst historisch sich getrennt hat. Wenn »ein Schatten über ein Gesicht zieht«, ein Auge sich aufschlägt, Lippen sich halb öffnen, so steht das dem Ursprung der Musik am nächsten und freilich auch dem ausdruckslosen Naturschönen, dem Zug von Wolken über den Himmel, dem Erscheinen des ersten Sterns, dem Durchbruch der Sonne durchs Gewölk. Musik gleichsam in der Mitte zwischen dem Schauspiel des Himmels und dem des Gesichts. Das ist der innerste Grund der Affinität der Musik zur Naturlyrik.)

3.

Auf die genetischen Implikationen der musikalischen Schrift zurückzugehen, ist geboten, weil musikalische Werke wesentlich nur vermittelt durch die Schrift vorliegen, weil der Interpretation der Klang nicht unmittelbar sondern bloß als notierter gegeben ist und weil die Notation keineswegs die selbstverständliche Anweisung für die Interpreten bietet. Der Interpretation ist kein Gesetz für die Dechiffrierung von Texten in deren Phänomenen gewährt, sondern erst in der Besinnung aufs Wesen musikalischer Texte selber als der Einheit von Werken in der Schrift. Dieser Besinnung aber erschließt sich zugleich das Auseinanderweisen von Ideal des Klangs, Notation und Wiedergabe. Während solche Divergenz ihren empirischen Grund hat in der Flüchtigkeit des Klangs, dessen ästhetische Objektivierung unabdingbar ein außermusikalisches Element erheischt, prägt in solcher Zwieschlächtigkeit zugleich der historische Doppelcharakter von Musik als Mimik und Sprache sich aus. Als mimischen Wesens ist sie nicht rein lesbar und nicht rein imitierbar als Sprache. Daher spaltet sie sich ins Ideal des Klangs und in Schrift und bedarf der Interpretation als der immer erneuten Anstrengung zur Versöhnung der divergenten Elemente. Das rechtfertigt den Anspruch von Reproduktion als spezifische Form genommen zu werden: die Not der Musik, die auf sie verweist, ist in ihrer materiellen Unausweichlichkeit Ausdruck des Wesens von Musik selber.

Mit anderen Worten, Reproduktion ist notwendig; Musik bedarf ihrer, nicht bloß daß sie nicht stumm sei, sondern um ihres immanenten Anliegens willen, gleichsam als Lösung der Frage, die Musik als solche durch ihr Dasein zu stellen scheint: wie kann die Mimik zur Sprache werden und umgekehrt, wie das Zeichen zum Bild? Diese Notwendigkeit von Interpretation trifft einen zentralen Unterschied von Musik und Dichtung. Diese gestattet Interpretation, ohne ihrer doch absolut zu bedürfen, denn als ein Bereich von Intentionen trägt sie die Auslegung ihres sinnlichen Soseins bereits in sich selber und entfaltet sich in der geschichtlichen Dynamik zwischen dem sprachlichen Phänomen und dem Gemeinten, in jener Schicht, die Benjamin »Art des Meinens«[254] genannt hat. Musik jedoch als paradoxe Zeichensprache eines Intentionslosen bedarf eines außer ihr selbst Liegenden, das die Zeichen einlöst, ohne das Intentionslose an den Trug von Bedeutungen zu verraten. So wenig von Musik als ausgebildeter Kunst die Systeme der Bezeichnung weggedacht werden können, so wenig auch die Interpretation als ein übers bloße Dasein der Musik, ihr sinnliches An sich, Hinausgehendes und sie damit ästhetisch erst Konstituierendes. Nicht bloß wäre die prinzipiell nicht interpretierte Musik nicht lebendig, sie entriete jenes Moments der Beseelung, das sie überhaupt vom bloßen Klang erst unterscheidet und das anders als in der Dechiffrierung ihrer Zeichen ihr nicht zuwächst.

Die Notwendigkeit der Interpretation wird manifest als Bedürftigkeit der musikalischen Texte. Es ist ein Gesetz, daß jeglicher eine Zone der Unbestimmtheit enthält, eine Schicht von Fragen, die nicht unmittelbar mit dem Ideal des Klangs zu beantworten sind und die der Interpretation, als eines zum Text Hinzutretenden bedarf, um dessen Objektivität überhaupt herzustellen. »Of course, great composers have superbly transformed their ideas into scores, making the best possible use of musical notation. But it is this very notation that is imperfect and may remain so forever, notwithstanding remarkable contributions to its improvement. There are certain intangibles that cannot be expressed by our method of writing music – vital musical elements incapable of being fixed by the marks and symbols of notation. Consequently, score scripts are incomplete in representing the composer's intentions. No score, as written in manuscript and published in print, can offer complete information for its interpreter.«[255] Dorians Bemerkung gilt einem Tatbestand, der weit über die triviale Unterscheidung zwischen Totem und Lebendigem in der Kunst und über den fragwürdigen Begriff der Intention des Komponisten hinausreicht. Das rührt an das objektive Verhältnis von Musik und Schrift. [*Marginalie:* hierzu wohl Dahl-Brief von 1949[256]] Es ließe sich sagen, die Interpretation, die zum Text hinzutritt, *macht diesen überhaupt erst zum Text.* Wenn jede musikalische Interpretation an ihren Text aufs strengste sich gebunden sieht, so wird dieser verbindlich, zum Text, einzig durch Interpretation. Die Zone der Unbestimmtheit ist keine bloße Unzulänglichkeit der Notation, sondern die Konsequenz eines Zeichensystems für Intentionsloses. Es genügt das Gedankenexperiment eines in jeder Note und jedem Komplex genau bezeichneten musikalischen Textes, dessen Wiedergabe sich auf die Befolgung sämtlicher Anweisungen beschränkte. Eine solche gleichsam nicht interpretierende Wiedergabe vermöchte selbst im idealen Fall Opfer der Sinnlosigkeit zu werden, des Negativs eines ästhetisch erfüllten Intentionslosen. Keine wie immer vollkommene Notation könnte die Zone der Unbestimmtheit tilgen, und indem die Wiedergabe diese stehen ließe, anstatt an ihr die interpretative Arbeit zu leisten, würde die paradoxe Sprache der Musik zu jenem Kauderwelsch, das von so vielen treulos-treuen Aufführungen radikal moderner Werke her vertraut ist. (Zu der Stelle, wo von der Erfindung der Mehrstimmigkeit im Zusammenhang mit dem Hervortreten des signifikativen Elements der Schrift die Rede ist, muß gesagt werden, daß gerade die harmonische Dimension der Musik bis in die allerjüngste Phase hinein selber einen gewissermaßen begrifflichen, in gewisser Weise den Worten ähnlichen Charakter hat, d. h. daß eine verhältnismäßig geringe Zahl von Akkorden, vergleichbar den Worten, die »an sich« immer dasselbe bedeuten, d. h. im Zusammenhang immer die gleiche Funktion erfüllen, das harmonische Material abgeben, während das unbegriffliche, echt sprachfremde Element der Musik, das dem Gestus am nächsten kommt, immer die rhythmisch-melodische Kurve ist. Die Harmonien waren bis zur Atonalität Spielmarken, das einzige überhaupt Wortähnliche der Musik, und das bestätigt das Hervortreten des intentionalen Elements in der Phase der beginnenden Mehrstimmigkeit, insofern als jeder einzelne Akkord, relativ konstant, seine Funktion »bedeutet«, dadurch daß er als derselbe immer wieder eintritt. Akkorde haben das begriffliche Moment der Identität und der Allgemeinheit, und dieses Element ist, wie noch ausgeführt werden muß, von einem Intentionalen gar nicht zu trennen, das sich aber in der Musik stets auf die Funktion innerhalb des Ganzen bezieht. Schönbergs Begriff der funktionalen Harmonik gehört hierhin: es besteht der innigste Zusammenhang zwischen der Harmonie und der Form als Totalität. Infolgedessen ist das rein der Harmonik geltende

Schriftsystem, das gegen Ende des Mittelalters aufkam, der Generalbaß, in gewissem Sinn das Rationalste, Intentionalste, Bilderloseste: es besteht rein aus Zahlen. Es hat sich aufgelöst erst, als die Rebellion gegen die harmonische Stereotypie begann und die Harmonik, und zwar gerade vermöge ihrer subjektiven Durchdringung in das mimische Bereich hineingezogen wurde. D.h. daß in ihr enthaltene Grundelement des Ausdrucks die starre Typisierung des harmonischen Vorrats durchschlug. Es ist also der Gedanke vom Ausdruckslosen der Harmonie von Anfang an viel dialektischer zu fassen: die Harmonie hat zwar der Musik die Dimension des »Innenraums«, der subjektiven Beseelung von Anfang an verliehen, aber in einer Vergeistigung, Spiritualisierung des mimetischen Impulses, der diesen gerade gebrochen hat, so daß gerade die Harmonie, nach der andern Seite, auch wiederum das ordnungsmäßig rationale und intentionale Moment extrem ausprägte. An der Harmonie kommt die Verbindung von Subjektivität und Verdinglichung als an ihrem musikalischen Urphänomen zutage. Übrigens bezeichnet das griechische Wort Harmonie gerade das ordnungsmäßige und insofern anti-mimetische Element.)

Aber die Zone der Unbestimmtheit, die dem Werk innewohnt, ist zugleich keine Absolutheit, sondern die Einheit des Werkes in seiner schriftlichen Fixierung enthält stets zugleich das Gesetz ihrer Durchdringung. Die Fragegestalt der musikalischen Schrift, Interpretation als Problem, heißt nichts anderes, als aus der Versenkung ins Notierte die Erkenntnis zu ziehen, welche die dem Text wesentliche Unbestimmtheit in ebenso wesentliche, in der Objektivität des Werkes legitimierte Bestimmtheit umzuwandeln. Jeder musikalische Text ist beides: prinzipiell unlösbares Rätsel und Prinzip zu seiner Lösung.

Dieser Widerspruch ist bloß ein anderer Aspekt des Anliegens der Interpretation. Denn unlösbar ist das Rätsel des Textes um seiner Intentionslosigkeit willen, weil er nichts »bedeutet«, woran die Auslegung der Chiffern ihre Grenze fände; als Rätsel präsentiert sie sich, weil das Intentionslose, zum Werk geronnen, in Zeichen, gleichwie ein Intentionales erscheint; und lösbar ist das Rätsel, weil der musikalische Text als Schrift einem Gesetz unterliegt, das sein Verhältnis zum Ideal des Klangs so bestimmt regelt, daß es am Ende von der Interpretation doch eingebracht wird. Dies Gesetz ist aber kein anderes als Nachahmung selber. Wenn die musikalische Schrift Musik nachahmt und solche Nachahmung vollbringt einzig durch Anlehnung an die sprachliche Intention, die Statuierung eines Zeichensystems, dann muß die Interpretation, in der musikalischen Realisierung des Textes, ihrerseits die Schrift nachahmen, um diese zu erfüllen. Da aber die musikalische Schrift nicht rein mimetisch ist, sondern, nachdem sie einmal überhaupt auf gegenständliche Abbildung sich eingelassen hat, der Zwang der Vergegenständlichung unaufhaltsam zur signifikativen Schrift treibt, die mit der gestischen sich verschmilzt und zugleich aus ihr selber hervorgeht, so vermag auch die Nachahmung der Schrift durch die Reproduktion nicht unmittelbar zu geraten, sondern nur vermöge des Lesens der Zeichen, also vermittelt durch Intentionalität. Nur daß die einzelnen Intentionen einem ganz anderen Bereich angehören als die sprachlichen. Ihre Auflösung ergibt nicht den »Sinn« der Musik, von dem überhaupt nur metaphorisch, nämlich als dem gesamten aus der Schrift zu restituierenden Gestus zu reden sein kann. Sondern die Auflösung der musikalischen Zeichen liefert die Elemente, aus denen die Nachahmung der Musik zusammenschießt, gleichsam die einzelnen Mienen und Bewegungen, in deren richtiger Abfolge der Ausdruck des Ganzen, die musikalische Form entspringt. Gegenüber allen hochtrabenden Worten, die ihren Anspruch vom geistigen Wesen der Interpretation borgen, das doch in ihr bloße Station ist, Errungenschaften bietet, die zu nichts taugen, als in der Wiederherstellung des Gestus und seines Ausdrucks unterzugehen, behält der simple Sprachgebrauch recht, dem zufolge Musik »gemacht« wird. Gemacht nicht nur im Sinn technischer Hervorbringung, denn dieser gälte für die Malerei nicht weniger als für die Musik, und doch hat der Ausdruck ein

»Bild machen« gegenüber dem »Musikmachen« etwas Reflektiertes, das den technischen Aspekt gegenüber dem ausdrucksmäßigen protestierend schon fast hervorhebt. Musik aber wird in der Tat gemacht, weil sie nachgemacht wird und die vom Idealismus unverdorbene musikalische Erfahrung weiß sehr wohl, worum es beim Singen und Spielen geht, nicht um Deutung als Selbstzweck, sondern um die Nachahmung eines wie immer im Text versteckten und wie immer schwierig zu begreifenden Urbilds. Die Idee der musikalischen Reproduktion ist die Kopie eines nicht vohandenen Originals. (Die Stelle über Malerei weg oder umschreiben. Einen Satz hereinnehmen, daß es nicht der Sinn der Interpretation ist, die Intention eines Werkes zu erschließen, sich in sie einzufühlen und sie zu verlebendigen, sondern auf Grund der Erkenntnis der Einzelintentionen der musikalischen Zeichen die Intention des Textes zu liquidieren und in der Wiederherstellung eines virtuellen Originals aufzuheben, das nachgemacht wird. Die ideale Interpretation gibt, in vollständiger Ähnlichkeit, die Musik selbst und nicht ihr Bedeuten, und je tiefer das bedeutende Zeichen verstanden wird, um so weniger muß die Interpretation Bedeutungen mehr zu ihrem Inhalt haben.)

Interpretation hat die Idee der Kopie von den beiden Polen des Textes her zu verfolgen, vom Zeichen und vom Bild. Aber beide Elemente der musikalischen Schrift sind derart verschränkt, daß die Interpretation sich des einen je nur durch das andere zu versichern vermag. In grober Übertreibung mag man zunächst sagen, die entwickelte musikalische Schrift sei Zeichensprache im einzelnen und Bildersprache im ganzen. Wer Musik im eigentlichen Sinne liest, muß jede Note und jede Vortragsbezeichnung in Vorstellung übersetzen und diese klanglich realisieren. Wer sich dem musikalischen Gestus, den »Atem der Form« (Zitat aus Kurth oder Lorenz[257]) vergegenwärtigen will, der muß dem Schriftbild als Totalität nachgehen und dessen Kurven und Zäsuren in Nachahmung umsetzen, etwa wie ein Kapellmeister, innerlich taktierend zunächst den Überblick über eine Partitur sich verschafft. Jeder, der vom

Blatt spielt, kennt die Doppelheit der Auffassung musikalischer Schrift: er sieht sich dazu verhalten, zugleich jedes Einzelne genau, in einer Art Übersetzungsarbeit aufzufassen und durch Antezipation in den Zug des Ganzen, ins »Bild« des Satzes zu integrieren. Die Notwendigkeit des Vorauslesens, auf der die Abspieltechnik beruht, bezeugt den Versuch, beide Auffassungsweisen zur Identität zu bringen. Alle Interpretation setzt sich gewissermaßen aus Buchstabieren und Dirigieren zusammen. (Hinweis auf die beiden im Filmbuch enthaltenen Typen des Komponierens.[258]) Jedoch diese beiden Auffassungsweisen fördern keineswegs unmittelbar das mimische und das sprachähnliche Element der Musik selber zutage. Wenn nämlich alles Einzelne in Musik gelesen, in einer Art von Übersetzungsarbeit hergestellt werden muß, so ist das dabei Herzustellende selber gerade der Gestus, die Unmittelbarkeit. »Ausdruck«, die Spur, welche der Gestus der Musik eingeprägt hat, haftet vorab am Einzelnen, an jenem Detail, das signifikativ und nicht abbildlich erscheint: espressivo ist ausnahmslos die Charakteristik von Stellen und nicht von Sätzen; in einem ganzen Satz, der espressivo gespielt wäre, würde eben damit der Ausdruck, der nur am Gegensatz zu fühlen ist, sich selber aufheben. Wie jede Miene und jede Geste momentan, das »Mienenspiel« schon durchs Ich vermittelt ist, so sind die musikalischen Momente der eigentliche Schauplatz des Mimischen in der Musik und ein im eminenten Sinn mimischer Komponist wie Schubert hat wohl gewußt, warum er seinen eigentümlichsten Formen gerade jenen Namen verlieh. Gerade was in Musik zu lesen, zu entziffern ist, sind ihre mimischen Innervationen. Eine pathetische oder verhaltene oder verlöschende Stelle bedeutet nicht Pathos, Verhaltenheit, Verlöschen als ein Geistiges, sondern verhält sich nach jenen Ausdruckskategorien, bildet die ihnen eigentümlichen physiologischen und somatischen Gesten in musikalischen Konfigurationen ab, und wer sie richtig interpretieren will, muß eben jene in ihnen verkapselten Gesten finden, um sie nachzuahmen. Finden durch Lesen: die dechiffrierende Arbeit des

Interpreten, das eigentlich begriffliche Element der musikalischen Interpretation allein ist der Weg ins Reich der mimischen Charaktere. Umgekehrt ist es um die Totalität bestellt. Sie wird als Bildphänomen aufgefaßt: das »Notenbild« bezieht sich stets aufs Ganze, und es ist der Blick auf die Seite, nicht der auf den Takt oder die Stimme, dem es aufleuchtet. Aber was in solcher Unmittelbarkeit erscheint, ist selber gerade nicht das Unmittelbare. Denn die musikalische Totalität, als zeitliche, geht gerade über die Unmittelbarkeit durch Erinnerung und Erwartung hinaus. Eine musikalische Form verstehen heißt vorab, jeden musikalischen Augenblick zur Synthesis bringen mit dem Inbegriff aller zeitlichen Relationen, in denen er steht. Der Bildcharakter der musikalischen Schrift, die Verräumlichung des Zeitverlaufs, ist der primären Mimesis geradezu entgegengesetzt. In der Verräumlichung des Gestus, dem Impuls der Neumenschrift ist zugleich die Negation des gestischen Elements geleistet. Die Verewigung des Gestus durchs Bild ist zugleich dessen Vergeistigung, wie sie durch seine Einordnung in eine mit sich identische, konsistente Totalität zugleich gesetzt wird. Indem durch die bildliche Fixierung jeder musikalische Gestus durch Simultaneität in Beziehung zu den anderen gesetzt wird, hört er in gewissem Sinne auf, Gestus zu sein, wird gegenständlich, geistig, Träger gerade des organisatorischen, naturbeherrschenden Prinzips, wie es in der Cheironomie die Bilderschrift determiniert. Das musikalische Zeichen verewigt das musikalisch Ephemere, die mimische Regung; das Notenbild vergegenwärtigt das musikalisch Bleibende, die das Naturmaterial sich unterwerfende gesellschaftliche Objektivität. Musik lesen heißt sie nachmachen, ihr Bild wahrnehmen heißt sie verstehen. Mit anderen Worten, das Schriftbild ist die graphische Spur der Konstruktion, als des dialektischen Widerparts zum Ausdruck. Und es ist die begriffslose Arbeit der Auffassung musikalischer Zusammenhänge, die in der Erkenntnis das wahrhaft vermittelte, begriffliche Element der Musik determiniert: der musikalischen Logik, ihrer Organisation als Zeitkontinuum.

Seit der Romantik ist die Forderung erhoben worden, musikalische Interpretation solle aufs Original zurückgehen. Schumann insbesondere hat diese Forderung erhoben und sie, im Geist der philologischen Historie des neunzehnten Jahrhunderts begründet mit der Entstellung musikalischer Texte durch den Druck, wie etwa der berühmten Verwechslung des Simile- mit dem Pausenzeichen im ersten Satz der Pastorale[259]. Wie die Romantik insgesamt von allen musikalischen Schulen am tiefsten in Fragen der musikalischen Reproduktion eingedrungen ist – ihre Verdienste darum stehen kaum hinter denen der literarischen um Übersetzung und Kritik zurück – so hat sie auch mit der Heranziehung des Originalmanuskripts an ein entscheidendes Desiderat gerührt. Freilich in einem anderen Sinn als dem der philologischen Treue. Schumann selber hat wohl gewußt, daß das Originalmanuskript, etwa in der abgekürzten Notationsweise Beethovens, gegen den Irrtum nicht gefeit ist, und es ist selbstverständlich, daß die Zone der Unbestimmtheit dem Originalmanuskript so gut innewohnt wie dem Druck. Trotzdem hat ihm Schumann die letzte Autorität in Interpretationsfragen zugesprochen und zum ständigen Vergleich der gedruckten Noten mit dem Original geraten, wie er übrigens durch die heutigen Faksimileverfahren allgemein möglich wäre. Der Rechtsgrund dessen liegt aber weder in der Fehlerfreiheit noch in der Nähe des Manuskripts zur Intention des Autors, dem sentimentalen Persönlichkeitswert, sondern darin daß das Originalmanuskript die Bildmomente der musikalischen Schrift, die Nachahmung der Musik selber, unvergleichlich viel genauer festhält als der Druck, in dem auch die eigentlich mimetischen Charaktere der Schrift, nicht nur die Zeichen, einem Prozeß der Objektivierung und Verdinglichung unterliegen, der selbst die bildmäßige Auffassung des musikalischen Gestus in weitem Maße zur Sache des Lesens eher als des Wahrnehmens macht. Die überwältigende Erfahrung, die jeder Musiker macht, dessen Auge zum ersten Mal einen Beethovenschen Satz in der Urschrift verfolgt[260], ist nicht bloß die Ehrfurcht, welche die empirische Spur dort gerade auslöst, wo sie angesichts der ästhetischen Idealität am rührend hinfälligsten sich erweist. Sondern es ist, als wären in solchen musikalischen Schriftzügen die von der Musik nachgebildeten Regungen selber nachgebildet, als erschiene in ihnen alles Lächeln und Weinen, alles Setzen und alle Negation, von welcher die musikalische Druckschrift sonst nur noch den letzten Schatten vermittelt. Danach wäre es die Aufgabe des Interpreten, Noten so zu betrachten, bis sie dem insistenten Blick in Originalmanuskripte sich verwandeln; nicht aber als Bilder der Seelenregung des Autors – sie sind auch dies, aber nur akzidentiell – sondern als die seismographischen Kurven, die der Körper der Musik selber in seinen gestischen Erschütterungen hinterlassen hat. Solche Interpretation wäre gleichwohl gefeit vor dem schlechten Irrationalismus der graphologischen Reaktion durch das andere, das signifikative Element, ohne dessen Entzifferung keine musikalische Anschauung möglich ist. Denn Musik ist die Einbildung des Geistes ins Intentionslose, die ihn versöhnt, indem sie ihn treu an den eigenen leibhaften Ursprung erinnert.

4.

Das Ungenügen der musikalischen Schrift, ihre Mehrdeutigkeit, die unvermeidliche Zone des Unbestimmten ist kein korrigibles Übel, und wäre nicht durch angemessenere Notationssysteme zu beseitigen, so wenig auch mehr das diatonische Liniensystem, welches das Chroma nur als Abweichung zuläßt, zur Darstellung von Musik taugt, deren Struktur prinzipiell keiner Skala innerhalb der 12 Halbtöne vor den restlichen einen Vorrang einräumt. [*Marginalie:* zu oft] Sondern dies Ungenügen stammt vom Verhältnis zwischen Notation und Musik als solcher her und schließlich von der Beschaffenheit aller Musik. Die musikalische Schrift fingiert nachdrücklich womit die Phrase des Bildungsphilisters von der Tonsprache sich wichtig macht: daß Musik schlechterdings eine Sprache sei. Denn der Unterschied zwischen der musikalischen und der eigentlichen Schrift ist nicht einfach der von Intentionalität und Nichtintentionalität der Zeichen. Sind doch die musikalischen Buchstaben, als vom Bedeuteten weit unabhängigere Bedeutungsträger denn die Lautzeichen der Wortschrift, in gewissem Sinn intentionaler als diese: ihre symbolische Funktion ist um soviel ausgeprägter, als sie den Unterschied des Zeichenphänomens und des durch sie Vermittelten drastischer ausprägt. Vielmehr liegt die spezifische Differenz der Zeichen in dem, worauf sie gehen, daß nämlich die Worte Bedeutungen haben nicht aber die einzelnen Töne. Nicht daß das sprachliche Zeichen den sprachlichen Laut meint, verleiht ihm seine eigentümliche Transparenz, sondern daß die Bedeutung des Wortes durchs Zeichen gewissermaßen hindurchscheint, daß es an ihr sein Festes und seine Regel hat, die den Laut erhellt, für den das Zeichen einsteht. Sprachliches Lesen heißt nicht, optische repräsentierte Laute akustisch sich vorstellen – das entwickelte Lesen dürfte von solcher Vorstellung weitgehend emanzipiert sein –, sondern in den Zeichen für Lautliches, gerade vermöge deren eigener Vergegenständlichung im Raum, wie unter einem Blickstrahl des Bedeuteten habhaft zu werden: das Schriftzeichen hat Fenster, durch welche nicht der Laut erscheint, sondern der Sinn. Der Strahl der Intentionalität, wie ihn die Phänomenologen beschrieben haben, wird im Akt des Lesens sinnlich vom Auge wiederholt, während im Laut Bedeuten an ein prinzipiell Bedeutungsfernes, mimisch expressives Medium überging. Sprache gibt es denn eigentlich nur als Schriftsprache: muß die gegenständliche Welt sich im Reflex des Lauts, der Namengebung erst verlieren, um überhaupt zur Apperzeption zu gelangen, so wird sie aus dem Abgrund der Mimesis von Schriftzeichen wieder erweckt, das gleichsam den Weg der Lautwerdung der Dinge annulliert und sie als solche des Geistes wiederherstellt: die Sphäre der Gegenständlichkeit, der Eindeutigkeit und des Begriffs ist erst die des Zeichens für den Laut, das stets diesen tendenziell überflüssig macht, indem sie ihn in seiner grundsätzlichen Ungegenständlichkeit, dem zeitlichen Vergehen, entwindet. Ihr eignet Blindheit, nicht weil sie bedeutungslos wäre, denn sie bedeutet in der Tat ja die Musik, sondern weil die Musik selber keine Intentionen kennt, die das Zeichen ins Relief höben: keine Note und kein musikalisches Schriftbild vermag je im gleichen Maße sich zu beseelen wie das Zeichen fürs sprachliche Wort (daher »Rationalität« der musikalischen Interpretation), und das begriffslos mimische Wesen der Musik selber verurteilt den Versuch seiner intentionalen Darstellung durch die Schrift gerade zu einer nahezu mechanischen Starrheit und Härte, die zum mimischen Wesen der Musik selber im äußersten Widerspruch steht. Dieser von der Sache selbst befohlene Widerspruch, Sprachzeichen eines Sprachlosen, Bedeutungsträger eines Unbegrifflichen zu sein, in Wahrheit also die Paradoxie der Vergegenständlichung des schlechthin Ungegenständlichen selber, ohne daß dieses, wie in der Sprache, Gegenständlichem selber angeähnelt wäre, diktiert die Unzulänglichkeit der musikalischen Schrift, die wie ein Wundmal von der Gewalt zeugt, die dem gleichwohl überlebenden Impuls durch seine unabdingbare Verflechtung in den zivilisatorischen Prozeß widerfuhr. Die musikalische Schrift ist ein System von festen Zeichen für das dem eigenen Wesen nach Nichtfeste, das überhaupt nur konserviert wird als Antidot gegen die Verfestigung der Welt.

Das aber bewirkt die Veränderung der musikalischen Texte in der Zeit. Das Gewalttätige, Willkürliche in der Beziehung zwischen der Musik und ihrer Schrift zwingt sie ephemer bloß zusammen; ihr Verhältnis ist stets ein Schwanken und die komplexe Schichtung von rationalem und Ausdrucksmoment in beiden macht sich zentrifugal geltend. Die musikalische Schrift tendiert um so stärker zum dunkel Hieroglyphischen, je weniger das, was sie verewigt, selber ein Ewiges, je mehr es selber gerade das Gerinnen des Allervergänglichsten ist: Musik, an sich selber gerade das Rudiment des Vieldeutigen, wird gleichsam gegen die eigene Regung verdinglicht und bewegt darum sich weiter gegen ihre Verdinglichung und gerade in dieser. Der immanente Gestus der Musik ist immer Gegenwart, um seiner Intentionslosigkeit willen, und darum gelten noch die ältesten Zeichen der Musik dem Jetzt und nicht dem Damals: das Damals, die absolute Zeitstelle, wäre selber gerade jene Objektivation, die dem Mienenspiel der Musik entgegensteht und die Objektivation der Musik will nicht sowohl ein solches Damals festhalten als die Form des Jetzt feststellen. In der Musik, der authentischen Zeitkunst, ist gerade die Zeitdimension gleichsam leer gelassen und in diesen Hohlraum schlägt Geschichte herein und verändert das musikalische Jetzt. Sind Themen Gesten, so sind diese Gesten, die es aus den Zeichen nachzumachen gilt, nachzumachen nur als gegenwärtige, und sie wechseln nicht sowohl mit dem historischen Standort als daß dieser überhaupt den gestischen Inhalt von Musik je und je erst konstituiert: in den innersten Zellen der Musik, die frei sind von der Intention, wohnt die Geschichte. Ein Thema dechiffrieren heißt nichts anderes als in ihm die allein möglichen Gesten wiedererkennen, und die Möglichkeit der Gesten selber ist historisch determiniert. Nicht anders aber als mit dem einzelnen Zeichen verhält es sich mit dem Bilde der musikalischen Totalität. Denn das Bild reicht an die Konstruktion nicht unmittelbar heran: während es auf diese hinweist, entfaltet diese doch sich erst aus ihm in einem Prozeß der rationalen Erkenntnis, der selber wieder historisch ist: denn Zug um Zug wird in der Geschichte mehr an Konstruktion durch Erkenntnis aus den Bildern offenbar, und indem dieser Prozeß vom Bilde selber inauguriert wird, ist er einer der objektiven historischen Entfaltungen des Werkes. Daß die Zeichen in Nachahmung verwandelt werden müssen und das Bild in Erkenntnis, weil beide Elemente derart sich verschränken, daß keines rein gegeben ist, daß also die musikalische Schrift so wenig reine Bilder kennt wie reine Bedeutungen, erzwingt auf Grund der je eigenen Beschaffenheit von Bild und Musik einen Prozeß des Fragens, der den musikalischen Text in einen Schauplatz historischer Dynamik verwandelt. Die Musik, als das Bezeichnete und Abgebildete, hat ihr Leben an sich selber, weil sie die wechselnde Regung ist, die von Geschichte motiviert wird: und wie der mimetische Impuls selber vor der Individuation liegt, so bleibt diese Regung stets eine kollektive, selbst wo sie als eine des subjektiven Ausdrucks auftritt, und die gestischen Bilder der Musik beziehen sich als gesellschaftliche nicht bloß auf die einzelmenschliche Erfahrung, die sie registriert, sondern auf die gesellschaftliche Totalität und damit den konstitutiven geschichtlichen Prozeß. Die Noten aber haben kaum minder ihr Eigenleben als wofür sie einstehen. Denn identisch bleiben an ihnen bloß die ersten physikalischen Elemente, die reinen einzelnen Noten, die für jenes Tonmaterial einstehen, das nach Kurths Aufweis[261] mit dem eigentlich musikalischen noch gar nichts zu tun hat (Beleg). Der Gestaltzusammenhang aber zwischen den Noten ist nicht bloß dem Wechsel unterworfen, sondern die Bilder der Noten entspringen überhaupt in der Geschichte. Undenkbar daß der Blick auf eine Beethovensonate, dem sie als Form sich zusammendrängt, im beginnenden neunzehnten Jahrhundert möglich gewesen wäre: die Synthesis, welche die disparaten und vermittelten Elemente eines solchen Satzes in Totalität setzt, ist möglich erst als eine historische Entfaltung seiner Elemente, wie sie in den Konfigurationen der Zeichen sich manifestiert. Im strengsten Sinn hat ein Beethovenscher Satz vor 100 Jahren anders ausgesehen als heute und eben darum auch anders geklungen. Denn was Bild und Zeichen ist am Text, unterliegt selber der historischen Dynamik. Was Zeichen ist und was Bild wechselt. Immer mehr Bilder werden zu Zeichen, und diese wiederum treten zu immer neuen Bildern zusammen. Wenn selbst der Notenkopf, das festeste, rationalste Element der modernen Notenschrift, vielleicht Bild des Schlages war, dann ist gewiß aus der Ligatur, dem neumischen Bild für melodische Kurven, der Notenbalken geworden, der musikalische Sukzessivgestalten, wie sie dem Gestus am nächsten liegen, gerade in die feste

Ordnung einbezieht. Und doch sind die zuckenden Zweiunddreißigstelgruppen von Schönbergs »Erwartung« gerade wieder zu Bildern für den Angstgestus dieser Musik geworden.

Der historische Charakter der Interpretation, diktiert von der Veränderung der Werke, betrifft gleichermaßen Schrift und musikalischen Inhalt und diesen in all seinen Dimensionen. Am sinnfälligsten ist sie im Bereich der Schrift und Bezeichnung. Hier läuft durch die Geschichte eine ungebrochen durchlaufende Tendenz zur Verjüngung und Verkleinerung. Die längste Note, die das moderne System überhaupt noch kennt und die auch in ihm fast ausschließlich archaisch fungiert, die doppelte ganze Note, die selber bereits als Verkleinerung des Einheitswertes wirkt, auf den die moderne Notation bezogen ist, hieß im Mensuralsystem Brevis. Diese Veränderung bezieht sich nicht auf die absolute Dauer der Töne selbst, sondern lediglich auf die Auslegung der Symbole. »The very sight of the old notes, such as the brevis 𝅜 and semibrevis 𝅝, to a reader unaccustomed to old scores, suggests protraction – a slow atmosphere. The semibrevis, as the name implies, formerly only a subdivision, today occupies the whole measure and has thus become a false clue leading to prolongation. In other words, notes that look long to the modern eye meant something quite different in their day: the brevis 𝅜, the semibrevis 𝅝, and the minim 𝅗𝅥 are laden with connotations of slowness only in the minds of certain modern interpreters.«[262] Diese Tendenz geht aber über die Verschiebungen zwischen dem Mensural- und dem modernen Notationssystem noch weit hinaus. Es ist offenbar, daß ein Händelsches Largo im $\frac{3}{4}$ Takt unmöglich so verstanden werden kann wie die Tempobezeichnung Largo bei Beethoven, etwa im Geistertrio: würde man die Viertel auch nur entfernt so langsam spielen wie bei Beethoven, so käme musikalischer Unfug heraus, da bei der Überspannung der einzelnen Noten über den einfachsten harmonischen Verhältnissen ein melodischer Fortgang überhaupt nicht mehr zu erkennen wäre. Dabei handelt es sich aber keineswegs bloß um den Wechsel einer Schriftkonvention, sondern in jener Verkürzung wird das Zusammentreten von Zeichen zum Bilde sichtbar. Es ist, als wäre den alten einfachen Riesennoten noch die Not ihrer Dechiffrierung einbeschrieben, während diese Not, und damit die echte Bildlichkeit heute nur noch bei kleinen Werten liegt, so daß die alten großen entweder banal und selbstverständlich geworden sind oder nicht unmittelbar sondern nur durch ihre Fremdheit die Musik abbilden (Vorsicht: Theorie noch in sich widerspruchsvoll!). Wie immer jedoch es mit der absoluten Dauer der Notenwerte sich verhält, ob also die Brevis bei Palestrina oder die punktierte Halbe bei Händel in der Tat kürzer gehalten wurden als heute, es spricht sich in solchen Dechiffrierungsproblemen ein Wandel der musikalischen Erfahrung aus, der in der Struktur der Werke selber sich vollzieht und darum notwendig die Wiedergabe modifiziert.

(Die Modifizierungen der Notation bieten sehr komplizierte Verhältnisse, die auseinander gehalten werden müssen. Vor allem widerspricht die Auffassung, daß die absoluten Werte früher Kürzeres bezeichneten als heute, direkt meiner Auffassung vom Schnellerwerden der Musik. Wenn das so wäre, so müßte doch z. B. eine Sechzehntelfigur zur Zeit Händels schneller gespielt worden sein, als sie heute gespielt wird, d. h. die Musik würde gerade langsamer. Es herrschen also gar keine eindeutigen Verhältnisse, sondern das Längenproblem ist nur in Relation zum Tempo zu lösen. War nicht am Ende doch die Musik wirklich absolut genommen langsamer, und ist nicht also die Auffassung Dorians gerade abwegig und zu kritisieren? Es muß auch klar werden, wie das historische Verhältnis von Bild und Zeichen in der Schrift im einzelnen sich darstellt. Treten wirklich zunächst Zeichen zu Bildern zusammen, die wieder zu Zeichen werden, oder verwandeln sich nicht vielmehr ursprünglich Bilder in Zeichen und diese wiederum in Bilder? Das letztere scheint mir die Wahrheit zu sein, und in diesem Sinne muß die Veränderung der musikalischen Schrift behandelt werden. Das Rascherwerden ist prinzipiell die Rückverwandlung des Zeichens ins Bild, daß also größere Zusammenhänge gewissermaßen gestisch wahrgenommen werden. Am Ende dieser Entwicklung steht die »gleichzeitige« Wahrnehmung einer ganzen ausgesponnenen musikalischen Form, vgl. Lorenz[263]).

Jedoch solche Veränderungen sind uneigentlicher Art. Sie beziehen sich darauf, daß das gleiche Zeichen zu verschiedener Zeit Verschiedenes bedeuten mag, ohne die Musik selber notwendig zu treffen: könnte man einigermaßen genau die Länge jener Notenwerte zur Zeit Palestrinas oder Händels rekonstruieren, so brauchte man ihnen nur die der damaligen Praxis entsprechende Dauer zu verleihen, um der notierten Musik als eines Absoluten von den Notationssitten Unberührten sich zu versichern. In Wahrheit geht die Veränderung der Werke weit darüber hinaus. Sie betrifft, durch den Charakter des Notenbildes, die Musik selber und löst den Begriff eines von den Noten gemeinten Absoluten, Zeitlosen auf. Für die Musik gilt, was Benjamin über das Verhältnis von Dichtung und Übersetzung bemerkt, wo er den Begriff des »Originals« erörtert: ». . . in seinem Fortleben, das so nicht heißen dürfte, wenn es nicht Wandlung und Erneuerung des Lebendigen wäre, ändert sich das Original«[264]. Wenn man sinnvoll von Veränderungen des Interpretationsstils spricht, so kann das nicht heißen, daß die Musik jeder Epoche anders dargestellt wird als die einer vergangenen damals, sondern bloß daß die vergangene von der Gegenwart mitbetroffen wird. Das in der Tat ist der Kern der Wagnerschen Abhandlung übers Dirigieren: daß die vielgestaltige Formstruktur der Musik seit Haydn und Mozart eine Erkenntnisdimension aller Musik, der früheren wie der späteren eröffnet, welche die Interpretation notwendig bestimmt. Von den neueren Werken fällt Licht auf die älteren: in einem Satz etwa wie dem an der Oberfläche undurchbrochen ablaufenden letzten des Bachischen Italienischen Konzerts zeichnet sich unter der dichten Hülle der Bewegung, und in einer Zartheit und Subtilität, der gegenüber dann die explizite Formkonstruktion der eigentlichen Klassik nahezu als plump erscheint, die Struktur jenes Rondos ab, das erst in Mozart ganz sich emanzipierte: das Mozartsche Rondo verändert jenes Bachische Presto, indem es gleichsam dessen latente Formgedanken zur manifesten Architektur erhebt. Es kann aber kaum ein Zweifel daran sein, daß solche Veränderung in der Geschichte der Musik längst vor der Kopernikanischen Wendung gegen Ende des achtzehnten Jahrhunderts sich zutrug. Der absolutistische Darstellungsstil etwa, wie er von der berühmten stampfenden Dirigierpraxis Lullys, dem Gestus des musikalischen Zeremonienmeisters repräsentiert wird, muß notwendig die gesamte Wiedergabe von Musik verändert haben. Eine Bemerkung Dorians erlaubt es, den Vorgang einigermaßen zu rekonstruieren: »Generations later, Jean Jacques Rousseau protested against the noisy beating of conductors in the theaters. Rationalist that this philosopher-musician was, he finally became resigned to the idea that without the noise the measure of the music could not be distinctly felt by the singers and orchestra players«[265]. Das höfische Zeremonial, das die Musik weitgehend nach der Ostentation im Tanz formt, hat damit aus den harmonischen Symmetrieverhältnissen der Dur-Moll-Tonalität rhythmische Symmetrie abgeleitet: es ist diese Epoche, in welcher die achttaktige Periode sich durchsetzt, die dem gemeinen Bewußtsein des neunzehnten und zwanzigsten Jahrhunderts als zweite Natur erschien. Es ist diese Erfahrung der rhythmisch-harmonischen Symmetrie, wie sie den ersten Opernversuchen durchaus noch abgeht, welche die gesamte Idee der Musik affiziert und den Begriff des guten Taktteils, des Akzents, des präzisen Zusammenfallens gleichzeitiger Ereignisse hervorhebt und eine Art rationaler Integration der Musik im Sinn souveräner Willensbildung bewirkt, wie sie der kollektiv hierarchischen Auffassung der mittelalterlichen Polyphonie bis ins siebzehnte Jahrhundert hinein fremd gewesen sein muß. Es müssen einem Zeitgenossen Lullys schon Akkordverhältnisse, gleichsam das Eigengewicht des einzelnen Dreiklangs bei Palestrina hervorgetreten sein, die zu dessen Zeit noch ganz in der Stimmführung vergraben lagen, nicht anders als das Gesicht der Mozartschen c-moll-Phantasie sich wandelte, als sie einmal in der Ähnlichkeit mit manchen Wendungen der Appassionata reflektiert ward. Umgekehrt hat das musikalische Rokoko zu einer Zeit, da die harmonische Dimension und die ihr entsprechende rhythmische Symmetrie einmal etabliert war, die starre Verfahrungsweise des siebzehnten Jahrhunderts gelockert. Wenn »the Rococo lightened everything up, so the stately court courante gradually developed a moderate and eventually a fast tempo«[266], so wird ein solcher Wechsel sich nicht darauf beschränkt haben, daß man schnellere Couranten komponierte, sondern daß der Typus jenes dreiteiligen Tanzes insgesamt sich zusammenzog und daß auch ältere Couranten schneller gespielt wurden. Die Sensation von Einzelharmonie und Akzent, wie sie die Ära der Barockoper erfuhr, kann kaum mehr zugänglich, muß schwülstig-altmodisch angemutet haben, wie das barocke Trauerspiel auf der Höhe der Aufklärung. Dem Auge, das ums Jahr 1750 über eine Suite ging, müssen deren Takte sich gedrängt, gleichsam in einem Blick versammelt haben, deren jeder siebzig Jahre früher hervorgehoben werden mußte, um die Form überhaupt zu konstituieren und hervorgehoben werden wollte, um seines eigenen Gestus willen. Die Gewalt des Vergessens, die der galante Stil dem älteren gegenüber übt und die eine rätselhafte Zäsur in der Entwicklung der großen Musik bewirkte, muß alles Barocke ergriffen und jenen Charakter des Archaischen bewirkt haben, der seitdem nicht wieder gewichen ist. Und je näher die Werke der Gegenwart rücken, um so deutlicher lassen sich konstitutive Veränderungen der Wiedergabe bestimmen. Die Berichte über den weithin improvisatorischen Interpretationsstil des Pianisten Beethoven lassen keinen Zweifel daran, daß er expressive Charaktere hervorhob, die damals zugleich an den Komponisten hervortraten und befremdeten, und daß das Problem einer motivisch-konstruktiven Darstellung, das heute jede in Betracht kommende Wiedergabe Beethovens beherrscht, kaum ins Blickfeld trat. Die

Gedehntheit, mit der vermutlich Bülow den Tristan darstellte, und die aus der Neuheit der harmonischen Einzelereignisse gefordert war, müßte heute nicht bloß langweilig und sentimental erscheinen, sondern geradezu sinnentstellend. Der Tristan, aus größerer Ferne wahrgenommen, verlangt geradezu nach dem Zeitraffer, um als Kontinuität wahrgenommen zu werden und nicht in Details zu zerfallen, aus denen, als solchen, die Kraft entwichen ist, die einmal es ihnen erlaubte, von sich aus allein zum Ganzen zusammenzuschießen. Welcher subtiler organisierte Dirigent oder Kammermusiker, der in einem Werk auf ein allzu bekanntes Thema stößt, wie den Seitensatz im Allegro der h-moll-Symphonie oder des d-moll-Quartetts von Schubert stünde nicht unter dem Zwang, ein solches Thema gleichsam verschwinden zu lassen, es schamhaft in den Verlauf der Gesamtform hineinzuziehen, um es nicht durch allzu große Präsenz jener Sphäre zu überantworten, der in der bildenden Kunst die Reproduktionen der Raffaelschen Madonnen im bürgerlichen Schlafzimmer angehören (olle Kamellen!), und damit gerade zu verraten. Um jene Schubertschen Melodien zu retten vor dem Ruhm, den sie doch wiederum ihrer unvergleichlichen Schönheit verdanken, müssen sie wie aus der Erinnerung gespielt, angedeutet werden: explizit dargestellt, entarteten sie zu theme songs. Musik ist so wenig indifferent gegen die Ohren der vielen, die sie schon vernommen haben, wie die Bilder gegen die Augen, die darauf ihre Spur hinterließen. Damit aber wird die Erkenntnis des Vergangenen zur Sache nicht sowohl von Einfühlung wie von gegenwärtiger Erfahrung. Diesem Sachverhalt ist Strawinsky nahegekommen, indem er in der Autobiographie für die Komponisten aussprach (stimmt nicht, er sagt es auch von der Reproduktion!), was nicht weniger für die Reproduktion gilt: »Und dies ist unsere Überzeugung: es ist unmöglich, daß ein Mensch die Kunst einer früheren Epoche völlig begreifen und in ihr Wesen eindringen kann – in ein Wesen, das sich doch unter verschollenen Formen verbirgt und in einer Sprache ausdrückt, die man nicht mehr spricht –

wenn dieser Mensch nicht ein lebendiges Gefühl und ein echtes Verständnis für die Gegenwart hat, und wenn er nicht bewußt an dem Leben teilnimmt, das ihn umgibt! Denn nur diejenigen, die wahrhaft lebendig sind, können das Leben bei denen entdecken, die ›tot‹ sind. Daher bin ich auch der Meinung, daß es aus pädagogischen Gründen weiser wäre, wenn die Erziehung eines Schülers mit der Kenntnis der Gegenwart begänne, und man dann erst schrittweise in die Vergangenheit zurückginge.

Ich bekenne offen, daß ich kein Vertrauen zu Menschen habe, die sich als feinste Kenner gebärden, die großen Kunstgötzen bewundern, die im Baedeker einen oder mehrere Sterne haben, sich für ein unkenntliches Porträt in einer illustrierten Enzyklopädie begeistern, und die zugleich nicht das geringste Unterscheidungsvermögen besitzen, sobald es sich um die Gegenwart handelt. Welches Gewicht hat denn tatsächlich die Meinung von Leuten, die vor großen Namen in Ekstase geraten, während sie zeitgenössischen Werken gegenüber eine stumpfe Indifferenz zeigen oder höchstens ihrer Vorliebe für alles Mittelmäßige und alle Gemeinplätze Ausdruck geben?«[267] Man mag dem hinzufügen, daß die bildungsmäßig an der Vergangenheit genährte Kennerschaft in Wahrheit nie des vergangenen Werkes sondern einzig dessen falscher Gegenwart, seines konventionellen Ausdrucks habhaft wird. Wer heute Schönberg nicht versteht, kann Beethoven nicht verstehen, sondern verstellt sich durch die verdinglichte Gestalt seiner Wirkung die Beziehung zum Werke. Die Musiksachverständigen, die heutzutage den maßgebenden Teil des Publikums der Opern und Konzerte ausmachen, saugen als Parasiten die Vergangenheit aus, die sie zu bewahren meinen, und in ihrer bösen Unduldsamkeit schwingt die Ahnung der Unwahrheit dessen, worauf sie schwören.

Damit aber ist behauptet, daß die Veränderungen der Werke in der Interpretation keine bloße Sache des Geschmacks, sondern objektiv-gesetzmäßiger Art sind. Mit andern Worten, daß sie von den Werken selber vorgezeichnet sind und nicht abhängig vom Belieben oder selbst der je vorherrschenden Manier der Interpreten. Die Veränderung der Werke ist keine ihrer bloßen Auffassung, nicht solche des wechselnden Geschmacks. Eine solche Auffassung setzte voraus, daß die Eindeutigkeit der vom Werk erhobenen Forderung gleichbedeutend wäre mit einem unveränderlichen Kern, der jeweils zu den verschiedenen Epochen in verschiedenen Abschattungen sich darstellt. Die wesentliche Spannung zwischen Notation und Musik macht jedoch die Annahme des statischen Gehalts der Werke als ihres Kerns illusorisch. Es gibt kein an sich seiendes Werk an sich, das zu verschiedenen Zeiten verschieden aufgefaßt werden könnte, zugleich aber jeglicher solchen Auffassung drastische Grenzen setzt. Die Geschichte ist dem Werk nichts Äußerliches, sondern daß jedes Werk im immanenten Sinn ein Problem ausmacht, macht Geschichte zu seinem wesentlichen Substrat. Die Stufen der Lösung seines Problems sind gleichbedeutend mit seiner Entfaltung in der Zeit und nur kraft solcher Entfaltung, als deren Gesetz, und nicht als zeitloses Substratum ist das Wesen des Werkes überhaupt zu bestimmen. Solche »innere Historizität« der Werke ist aber von der auswendigen Geschichte nicht zu trennen. So wenig eine invariante Geschichte der Werke subsistiert, die nach verschiedenem Geschmack erschiene, so wenig wechselte der Geschmack als ein Regelloses und dem Werk bloß Äußerliches, sondern die geschmacklichen Modifikationen geben Zeugnis vom Gehalt der Werke nicht weniger als dessen Dynamik von der Geschichte. Wenn ein Darstellungsstil wie etwa der spätromantisch-pathetische Beethovens unerträglich ward, so besagt das nicht einfach, daß ein ernüchterter Geist gegen den Rausch der selbstherrlichen Subjektivität und ihres Ausdrucks sich sträube, sondern daß das kontrollierende Ohr des Widerspruchs gewahr wird zwischen der Darstellung und dem Werke. Das Medium solcher Einsicht ist zunächst die Notation, etwa die Tatsache, daß die in Konsequenz der Wagnerschen Theorie bei den neudeutschen Dirigenten beliebten

Tempomodifikationen in den Partituren nicht verzeichnet stehen. Aber nichts wäre verkehrter, als wollte man, wie es etwa die These der Orgelrenaissance und der Rekonstruktion der präklassischen Wiedergabe ist, in dem Rückgang auf die Texte die historistische Rekonstruktion des ursprünglichen Aufführungsideals erblicken. Wagners Schrift läßt an dessen Beschaffenheit wenig Zweifel und wenn man seiner Beschreibung nur das leiseste Vertrauen schenkt, so wäre der vorwagnerische Interpretationsstil womöglich noch unerträglicher als der tondichterisch-dramatisierende. Und zwar nicht bloß um der technischen Mängel willen, die dem durch die neuromantische Orchestervirtuosität hindurchgegangenen Ohr offen zutage lägen, sondern weil diese technische Insuffizienz, bezeichnet von der schematischen Hervorhebung der Akzente im Dienste des Zusammenhalts, jenen Aspekt des Mechanischen und Sinnwidrigen annähme, wie er etwa von gewissen zurückgebliebenen Randphänomenen der europäischen Musikkultur wie den populären Konzerten von Militär- und Palmengartenorchestern her vertraut ist. Dieser mechanische Aspekt ist aber kein bloßes subjektives Unvermögen, und ihn der »Unmusikalität« der Dirigenten zuschreiben, hieße das Problem bloß verschieben. Unmusikalisch kann eine Darstellung einzig dann genannt werden, wenn sie die Sache verfehlt. Das hieße aber hier: jene Schichten des konstruktiven Zusammenhangs, die zu Beethovens Zeiten noch verborgen sein mochten, mittlerweile aber in den Werken selber und in dem vorgeschrittenen musikalischen Bewußtsein von innen derart sich angemeldet haben, daß, wer ihnen den Gehorsam verweigert, die Sache verfehlt. Mit anderen Worten, es handelt sich hier um genau jenes Moment der mimetischen Nachbildung des gesamten musikalischen Schriftzuges, ohne welche das signifikative Verständnis der Einzelnotation, also die korrekte Wiedergabe des Textes, so illusorisch bleibt, das als ausnahmslose Regel zu gelten hat, daß, wo jene wesentlich historische Innervation bei Nachbildung des Ganzen mangelt, darüber notwendig auch die Korrektheit der Wiedergabe des

Notenbildes in die Brüche geht, auf welche gerade jene Interpretation sich beruft, welche der Nachbildung des Ganzen nicht mehr mächtig ist. Wer Beethoven heute in der von Wagner gegeißelten Weise interpretiert, wäre nicht nur der Philister, als welcher er den Neudeutschen vor Augen stand, sondern er würde mit jedem Schritt die Struktur der Sache verfehlen und zwar derart, daß dies Verfehlen wiederum schließlich in manifesten Inkorrektheiten sich durchsetzte. Das oberste Beispiel dafür ist der Darstellungsstil Arturo Toscaninis. Während dieser die Reaktion auf jenes schlampige Moment darstellt, in dem die Unwahrheit an dem neuromantischen Darstellungsstil zum Greifen kam, und diesem das Urteil widerfahren läßt, das sich das Dirigiervirtuosentum als Verfallsform des Espressivo-Musizierens redlich verdiente, hat er, auf der höheren Ebene der vom Dirigiervirtuosentum selber herangezüchteten äußersten Präzision in gewisser Weise das vorwagnerische mechanische Taktschlagen wiederhergestellt, das in der Tradition der italienischen Opernkapellmeister so wenig je ganz mag getilgt worden sein, wie der neapolitanische Operntypus bis zu Puccini. Das Toscaninische Musizieren ist nicht sowohl die Aufhebung der subjektiven Willkür im Bewußtsein von der Sache, als die Regression auf einen traditionalen Stand, in dem die Sache noch nicht als Problem erschien, sondern vermeintlich mit der sinnlichen Fassade und der signifikativen Seite der Notation zusammenfiel, während doch weder diese Tradition mehr gegenwärtig ist, noch gar die Werke, auf welche der Orchestertechniker sie projiziert, ihr angehörten und aus ihr verstanden werden könnten. Infolgedessen tritt denn auch als ein bloß äußerliches Akzidenz zu der von der Struktur abgelösten signifikativen Treue das Brio, der Schwung, die Dynamik des Theatralikers hinzu, und es resultiert ein Agglomerat von Pedanterie und Effekt, der nur in einem dem Leben der Sache entfremdeten und selber regressiven Bewußtsein als zwingende Authentizität wahrgenommen zu werden vermag. Anstatt daß das mimetische und das signifikative Element des Musizierens wechselseitig sich durchdrängen, sind sie in dem mittlerweile zu einer Art von Radiokultur ausgebreiteten Interpretationsstil nur als voneinander abgespaltene gegenwärtig: hundert trockene Richtigkeiten werden durch die Veranstaltungen eines technologischen Temperaments zu Steigerungen und Explosionen aneinander gereiht. Darüber aber büßen sie selbst die Richtigkeit ein: das Allegretto der VII. Symphonie fällt ins Andante zurück, und in der IX. Symphonie stimmt kein Satz mit der Beethovenschen Metronomisierung zusammen. Aus all dem erhellt einerseits das geschichtliche Wesen des Kerns der Werke, andererseits die Gebundenheit der interpretativen Veränderung in der historisch sich entfaltenden Objektivität des Werkes selber. Dabei ist die Treue zur Notation nur ein, freilich unabdingbares Element, die Schranke gegen das Herausfallen der Interpretation aus der historischen Gesetzlichkeit des Werkes, aber diese Treue allein genügt nicht. Weder liefert sie allein die Erkenntnis in den Stand des Werkes und damit seiner Wahrheit, noch vermag sie isoliert festgehalten sich selbst zu genügen: die bloße Treue des Lesens, auf Kosten der Nachahmung von Auge und Ohr, bewirkt eine Totenstarre, in der schließlich der Blickstrahl des Lesens selber verlischt.

(Weitere Einzelheiten zur Kritik des Toscaninischen Darstellungsstils Aufzeichnungen 3/4. Es muß das dialektische Verhältnis dabei noch schärfer hervortreten. Gegenüber dem üblichen romantisierenden Darstellungsstil besonders in Deutschland hat die Toscaninische Methode des stream lining eine außerordenlich progressive Seite gehabt und geholfen etwas von dem ornamentalen Schutt zu beseitigen, mit dem die Werke während der romantischen Periode sich überzogen hatten. Die Wirkung der ersten Toscaniniaufführungen in Deutschland hatte etwas Befreiendes, und es ist ohne Zweifel, daß ein neues Niveau an Präzision, an Funktionieren geschaffen wurde, das dem gegenwärtigen Stand der Orchestertechnik selber angemessen ist. Aber im Zusammenhang einer Bewegung des Geistes, in der an den Kunstwerken jegliches Moment des Sinnes auf Kosten der Fetischisierung der Mittel, des Funktionierens als solchem, abstirbt, hat das Toscaninische Musizierideal einen ganz anderen Aspekt angenommen. Es bedeutet im Amerika der Rekorde, des Tschaikowskykults und der Jazzmaschine etwas ganz anderes als in Europa. Was dort Entzauberung im Dienst der Sache war, wird hier zum Feind der Sache und zur Verzauberung der Apparatur und das drückt sich in der Insuffizienz der Sache aus. Theoretisch gesprochen kann das gleiche Darstellungsideal völlig verschiedene Funktionen in verschiedenen gesellschaftlichen Zusammenhängen und Bewußtseinslagen annehmen. Aber diese Funktionen sind keine bloßen subjektiven Reaktionsformen auf die Werke, sondern betreffen jeweils deren innere Zusammensetzung.)

Daß die Werke in der Zeit sich verändern und daß ihre Veränderung einen im Werke selber gelegenen Kanon der Interpretation abgibt, heißt, daß diese Veränderung nicht zu verstehen ist als ein sich Anschmiegen an die Kontingenz des geschichtlichen Verlaufs – denn dieser erscheint, als ein außerhalb des Kunstwerks gelegener von diesem aus notwendig als sachfremd und zufällig, als »Mode« – sondern daß diese Veränderung gesetzmäßig erfolgt. Diese Gesetzmäßigkeit muß aufgesucht werden im Verhältnis der Medien, in denen das Werk erscheint: des Signifikativen der Notenschrift, des Mimetischen (in der ganzen Arbeit dafür ein besseres Wort suchen) des Notenbildes und des Tonsprachlichen. Diese Gesetzmäßigkeit steht offenbar in engem Verhältnis zu einem Prozeß anwachsender Rationalisierung, zur Erhellung der Werke. Deren Entfaltung in der Zeit kommt in einem gewissen Sinn dem Fortschritt ihrer Durchsichtigkeit gleich: er führt von der Erscheinung aufs Wesen. Aber mit der Bezeichnung dieser allgemeinen Tendenz, dem Übergang von einem naiven zu einem bewußten Verhältnis zu den Werken, ist nicht allzu viel gewonnen. Insoweit der Musik selber jenes mimetische Moment eigentümlich ist, das im neumenhaften Moment der Notation seinen Niederschlag findet, kann die Entfaltung des Werkes nicht einfach als die Auflösung jenes Momentes verstanden werden – sie ließe vom Werk einzig das caput mortuum zurück – sondern was sich verändert ist viel mehr als die Konstellation, in der jenes Moment erscheint, und seine eigene Zusammensetzung. Es erhellt, daß die bloß reflektierende, jeglicher Spontaneität sich entäußernde Interpretation so wenig die wahre und fortgeschrittene ist, wie umgekehrt das verstockte und regressive Festhalten der Interpretation an der eigenen Naivetät, für das unweigerlich mit Unangemessenheit an die Sache zu zahlen ist. Näher erscheint der spezifischen Gesetzmäßigkeit der Veränderung ein Schema zu kommen, das in gewissem Sinn das Gegenteil der primitiven Annahme interpretativer Aufklärung impliziert, um freilich auf deren Idee zurückzuführen. Was nämlich an den Werken zunächst zur Auffassung gelangt, ist einerseits das signifikative Element, also die korrekte Übersetzung der musikalischen Zeichen, andererseits das Tonsprachliche. Das letztere bezeichnet genau jene Schicht von Naivetät, welche durch Geschichte kritisiert wird. Der musikalische Text der neueren Zeit, spätestens seit dem stile rappresentativo und wahrscheinlich bereits seit dem strengen italienischen Satz des sechzehnten Jahrhunderts tritt nicht isoliert, in einem Vakuum auf, sondern im Zusammenhang eines bestimmten seis traditional vermittelten, seis durch allgemeine Verbreitung garantierten Zusammenhangs, der über den je einzelnen Text hinausgeht und nach Analogie mit herrschenden Spiel- und Vortragsweisen unproblematisch darüber wacht, wie dies und jenes aufgefaßt werden soll, was in den Zeichen des Werkes an sich nicht eindeutig enthalten ist. Dieser Bezug auf unproblematisch vorgegebene, aber dem Werk selbst nicht immanente Modelle macht die Naivetät der Interpretation im üblichen Sinn aus, gleichgültig ob es sich um die Ausführung des Generalbasses und der Manieren, die Vortragsweisen des Wiener Klassizismus, die vielberufene Chopinsche Einheit von Strenge und Rubato oder jüngstens etwa um den Jazz handelt, bei dem der Schein der improvisatorischen Ungebundenheit und selbst »Unnotierbarkeit« von der Omnipräsenz jenes tonsprachlichen Mediums bewirkt wird. In der Jugend der Werke tritt demgegenüber das vom Notenbild vermittelte mimetische Element der Musik, das ihres strukturellen spezifisch zeitlichen Zusammenhangs zurück und insoweit dieses Element ein archaisches Erbe behauptet, fällt eben dies archaische Erbe je und je der Geschichte erst zu, wie denn allgemein für die Musik das Paradoxon gilt, daß ja ihr mimetisches Moment einzig durch die Konstruktion hindurch sich verwirklicht, während ihr signifikatives einzig durch die Nachahmung des Bildes, also gleichsam durch eine mimetische Funktion aufleuchtet. Was das signifikative und das tonsprachliche Element des Textes anlangt, so ist selbstverständlich jenes einigermaßen konstant. Gewiß wechselt die absolute Tonhöhe und der absolute Zeitwert der Noten, aber solcher Wechsel läßt die Relation des musikalischen Zeichensystems in sich zunächst unberührt. Es wird dynamisch bloß im Verhältnis zu den beiden anderen Momenten und zwar in einem negativen Sinn, nämlich insofern als an der Beziehung zu diesem sich erweist, daß ihm die absolute Eindeutigkeit abgeht und daß gleichsam die Hohlräume der Signifikation von der Variabilität der anderen Elemente ausgefüllt werden. Betrachtet man die gesetzmäßige Entfaltung der Werke als einen dialektischen Prozeß, so behauptet das signifikative Element, die musikalische Buchstabenschrift, in diesem die Identität der Nichtidentität (vielleicht kann man durchweg für das signifikative das Tabulatur- oder noch besser das Mensuralmoment und für das mimetische das neumische setzen. Für das tonsprachliche fehlt noch der angemessene Terminus). Demgegenüber ist das tonsprachliche Element das schlechterdings ephemere und zwar aus einem pragmatischen Grunde: es ist das, welches in den Text als solchen nicht eingeht, nicht fixiert ist, dem Text äußerlich ist und dennoch bei dessen Hervortreten das einzige Medium von dessen sinngemäßer Darstellung. Verändert sich Musikübung und Gesellschaft, so geht dies Moment unwiederbringlich verloren, weil es der Kodifizierung sich entzieht: es ließe sich sagen, daß in einem strengsten Sinn das Medium der Tradition an Musik nicht tradierbar sei. Damit aber wird der Text, verlassen von dem Sinn, der von außen ihm zuwächst, problematisch, und das neumische Element, die Frage von dem Sinn von Musik als dem Inbegriff ihres Gestus stellt sich im Zusammenhang des reinen, seiner transzendenten Vermittlungen weitgehend entäußerten Textes. Das neumische Moment tritt hervor aus dem Untergang des musiksprachlichen, die Darstellung des musikalischen Gestus aus dem Absterben der Gesten, in denen sie erscheint. Die Entfaltung des Werkes ist die Rekonstruktion des musiksprachlichen Elements aus der Immanenz des Textes, und diese Rekonstruktion ist gleichbedeutend mit der Realisierung des im neumischen Bilde begrabenen mimischen Impulses. Der Weg dazu aber ist einzig die Analysis.

(Der Mahlersche Satz: Tradition ist Schlamperei hält genau den Augenblick fest, in dem das musiksprachliche Moment sich als problematisch erweist und durch das analytisch-konstruktive ersetzt werden muß. Und zwar impliziert der Mahlersche Satz den genauen Grund dieses Übergangs, daß nämlich das musiksprachliche Element, insofern es zwar den ursprünglich erscheinenden Text wie ein Keimblatt enthüllt, aber nicht in ihm selber enthalten ist, vermöge seis seiner Eigenbewegung seis seiner Erstarrung in wachsenden Gegensatz zum mensuralen Element, zur wörtlichen Treue tritt. Diese wird gleichsam zum Vehikel, das die Erkenntnis des musikalischen Sinnes anstelle von dessen musiksprachlichem Surrogat setzt. Was die Dialektik der musikalischen Interpretation in Bewegung bringt, ist nicht einfach und sicherlich nicht stets das Absterben des musiksprachlichen Elements als dessen Verselbständigung gegenüber dem mensuralen, die es entweder so versteinert, wie es in der bekannten Anekdote des viel zu schnellen Tempos des Adagios der Freischützouvertüre berichtet wird, das Wagner vorfand, oder das musiksprachliche Element, als ein dem Text Äußerliches, wird gleichsam wild und reduziert den Text zu einem bloßen Anlaß, wie es besonders musikalischen Texten von virtuoser Beschaffenheit zu widerfahren pflegt, die in gewisser Weise auf die spielerische Freiheit des Interpreten verwiesen sind und dadurch von Anbeginn die Auflösung des mensuralen Moments und damit der eigenen Identität in sich enthalten. Diese Notiz ist die eigentliche Entfaltung des Gedankens von der Gesetzmäßigkeit der Veränderung.)

Ist das musiksprachliche Element seis abgestorben, seis in Gegensatz zum mensuralen getreten (und das musiksprachliche Element ist eigentlich das, durch welches die gesellschaftliche Verdinglichung, Konventionalisierung der Werke sich bemächtigt, ebenso wie es einmal das war, das die Werke gesellschaftlich trug, wird es zu dem, kraft dessen die Gesellschaft gegen das Werk sich kehrt), so liegt das letzte kalt, sinnverlassen, bedeutungslos da. Die in solchen Augenblicken stets wieder erhobene Forderung, man solle einfach nach dem sich richten, was da steht, ist einerseits eine Trivialität – denn die Grenzen der signifikativen Notation sind unabdingbar einzuhalten – andererseits unsinnig, denn eine Interpretation, die in der Tat streng auf das sich beschränkte, was da steht, wäre nicht bloß des Zaubers und der Aura beraubt, worüber sich reden ließe, sondern sie wäre unsinnig in dem genauen Sinn, daß ein musikalischer Zusammenhang schlechterdings nicht mehr sich wahrnehmen ließe, eben weil einer solchen Interpretation das im musiksprachlichen Element in unreiner Form enthaltene Mimische verloren ginge.

(Dies ist ein äußerst wichtiges Motiv. In der bisherigen Darstellung ist das musiksprachliche und das mimische Moment unterschieden, ohne daß andererseits ihre Affinität hervorgehoben wäre. In der Musiksprache wächst dem Werk das mimische Moment gleichsam von außen zu. In dem musiksprachlichen Element sind Teile des neumischen versprengt und unartikuliert enthalten, und zwar insofern als kein Werk jenen absoluten Mikrokosmos darstellt, als welcher es doch notwendig auftreten muß, sondern teilhat an übergreifenden, seiner Spezifikation entrückten Formen und tonsprachlichen Elementen. Die Formmomente des musikalischen Zusammenhangs sind nun weitgehend die mimischen, und diese lassen von der sozialen Allgemeinheit, die noch in Produktionen des äußersten Subjektivismus sich nicht verkennen lassen, nicht absolut sich trennen. Daß das tonsprachliche Element zum Teil bewirkt, was in Strenge Sache des neumischen ist, ist kein Zufall, sondern hängt mit jener Konvergenz zusammen: »Form« ist sowohl der Inbegriff des mikrokosmischen Gestus des Werks, seiner Mimik also, wie der das einzelne Werk übergreifenden, gesellschaftlich vorgeordneten Typen. Daher ist denn auch notwendig die interpretative Konstruktion der Werke keineswegs »rein« gegenüber dem musiksprachlichen Element, sondern enthält allemal etwas von diesem in sich: es ist gleichsam der Vorrat, von dem sie zehrt, und in einer gewissen Weise ist der zweite Pol der wahren Interpretation, gegenüber der buchstäblichen Treue die kritische Arbeit an dem musiksprachlichen Element im Bewußtsein der Konstruktion. Das musiksprachliche Element wird aufgehoben im Hegelschen Sinn.)

Die Arbeit der wahren Interpretation ist also doppelten Charakters. Sie hat einerseits die Kenntnis des Textes, das mensurale Element, ein Ergänzen durch die Analyse des Zusammenhangs und andererseits das musiksprachliche Kontinuum, mit dem sie in wie immer problematischer Weise konfrontiert ist, daraufhin abzuhören, in wieweit es mit jenen analytischen Befunden zusammentrifft. Denn beides ist ihr problematisch, sobald es einmal auseinandergetreten ist: der reine Text als sinnleerer, die bloße Musiksprache als ein dem Text Inkompatibles. Die Zone der Ungenauigkeit des Textes ist die, in welcher die Interpretation spielt: zugleich aber bietet der Notentext selber die Anweisung, jenes Vakuum zu füllen, insofern als mittelbar in der Notation alle jene Momente enthalten sind, welche die Analysis herausbringt, um sie dann durch die Interpretation zu analysieren. Die Unwahrheit des Satzes, man solle einfach spielen, was da steht, besteht in der Auffassung, das mensurale Element gebe unmittelbar den Kanon der Interpretation ab: es ist wahr insofern, als mittelbar im

Text alle jene Momente enthalten sind, welche die wahre Interpretation herauszustellen hat. Mit anderen Worten, die neumische Auslegung des mensuralen Textes ist nicht willkürlich, sondern ihre Frage: wie kann der Text sinnvoll werden, ist geleitet von dem Text selber. Die Auskristallisierung des mittelbaren Sinnes ist keine bloße Zutat, sondern die Erkenntnis des Zusammenhanges der sämtlichen mensural bezeichneten, atomistischen Momente. Der wahren Interpretation zergeht der Schein eines natürlichen, »organischen« Aspektes der Musik, der von der gesellschaftlichen Konvention bewirkt wird, und nichts anderes ist als die unreflektierte Übernahme des tonsprachlichen Elements.

(Sondernotiz: die in der Philosophie der neuen Musik berührte Dialektik zwischen dem je einzelnen Werk und dem Formentypus betrifft zentral die Theorie der Reproduktion und zwar in dem Verhältnis von neumischen und musiksprachlichen Elementen.)

Die wahre Reproduktion ist die Nachahmung eines nicht vorhandenen Originals, und dieses Nichtvorhandensein, die Nichtexistenz des Werkes an sich definiert zugleich die Objektivität, die in der subjektiven Spontaneität des Interpreten gelegen ist. Diese Nachahmung des nicht vorhandenen Originals ist aber zugleich nichts anderes als die Röntgenphotographie des Textes. Ihre Aufgabe ist es, alle Relationen, Übergänge, Kontraste, Charaktere, Spannungs- und Auflösungsfelder und was immer sonst es sei, aus welchen die Konstruktion besteht, sichtbar zu machen, während diese sonst sowohl unter der mensuralen Notation wie der sinnlichen Oberfläche des Klangs verborgen liegen. Das ist der Grund der notwendigen Entsinnlichung der musikalischen Interpretation von dem Augenblick an, in dem das musiksprachliche Element beginnt, problematisch zu werden. Man könnte das letztere geradezu definieren als das ungeschiedene und unkritische Ineinander von sinnlicher Erscheinung und musikalischem Sinn. Was in der wahren Interpretation geschieht, ist durch die bis ins verborgenste Detail reichende Artikulation der sinnlichen Erscheinung, in dieser die Totalität der Konstruktion, den Gestus des Werkes, seinen mimischen Vollzug offenbar zu machen und das setzt die analytische Auslegung des Textes wesentlich, nicht als bloßen Zusatz außermusikalischer Reflexion voraus. Während das sinnliche Moment der Musik dabei erhalten bleibt und in gewisser Weise, wie sie zumal von Wagner hervorgerufen wird, sogar verstärkt wird, wird zugleich dadurch das sinnliche Moment gebrochen. Es begibt sich des falschen Scheins, unmittelbar mit dem Sinn eins zu sein, je rücksichtsloser es in den Dienst von dessen Erscheinung tritt: den musikalischen Zusammenhang durchs sinnliche Phänomen ganz auszudrücken, heißt immer zugleich dem sinnlichen Phänomen sein an sich Sein entziehen, es zum Bilde eines anderen zu machen, es zu brechen. Je vollkommener der musikalische Sinn in der Erscheinung gegenwärtig ist, um so weniger ist die Erscheinung bloße Gegenwart – drastisch gesprochen, um so vollkommener polarisiert sie sich nach ihrem Zeithorizont, nach Protentionalität und Retentionalität, und um so weniger erschöpft sie sich im Augenblick ihres bloßen Daseins. Die vollkommene Versinnlichung der Musik kommt ihrer Entsinnlichung gleich. Wenn die Interpretation dazu gelangt, analytisch aufgefundene Beziehungen nicht hervorzuheben sondern zu verbergen, so nur, wenn darüber selber wieder erkannte strukturelle Notwendigkeit waltet: zwei Themen etwa mögen den gleichen Motivkern haben, aber ob die Interpretation diesen Motivkern zu exponieren oder zu verhüllen hat, hängt davon ab, ob die beiden Themen gemeinsamen Tonreihen lediglich die Funktion erfüllen, zwischen zwei sonst weit auseinanderliegenden melodischen Gebilden die Beziehung herzustellen – dann muß der identische Kern spürbar werden – oder ob in einem späteren Augenblick des Satzes, etwa durch unmittelbare Aufeinanderfolge der beiden latent verwandten Komplexe ihre Beziehung als Resultat der Entwicklung des Stückes in der Komposition selber manifest gemacht wird, wie es zuweilen bei Beethoven der Fall ist[268]. Dann darf die Ähnlichkeit nicht hervorgehoben werden, sondern ihre Verborgenheit selber ist ein Moment der Artikulation. Der Begriff der Deutlichkeit gibt das Maß der analytischen Interpretation ab: es muß alles deutlich werden, was an Beziehungen im mensuralen Text enthalten ist, aber dieser Begriff selber ist nicht primitiv zu fassen, als Deutlichkeit jeder überhaupt aufgespürten Einzelrelation, sondern als eine Hierarchie von Deutlichem und Undeutlichem im Sinn der Deutlichkeit der Gesamtstruktur, des mimischen Gestus. Die Deutlichkeit der wahren Interpretation unterscheidet eben darin sich von der schulmeisterlichen und pedantischen, daß diese zwar alles jeweils in den Chiffern Beschlossene herauszubringen sucht, aber ohne zugleich dessen Funktion in der Organisation des Ganzen innezuwerden und dadurch das hervorzuheben, was zwar an sich in den betreffenden Elementen enthalten sein mag, aber dann wiederum gegenüber der Deutlichkeit der Totalität zurückzutreten hat. Deutlichkeit selber ist kein Statisches, sondern ein Prozeß, und die wahre Interpretation vermag sehr wohl Undeutliches zu fordern, aber dann muß die Undeutlichkeit als solche realisiert werden, eine deutliche Undeutlichkeit.

(Der hier eingeführte Begriff der Funktion gegenüber dem Einzelereignis ist weiter zu verfolgen. Er soll nicht eine prinzipiell andere Kategorie bezeichnen, aber jenes Moment an der Interpretation des Textes, das zwar aus der Konfrontation der in der Betrachtung der mensuralen Momente erschlossenen Befunde hervortritt, zugleich aber eben diese mensuralen Momente überschreitet – mit anderen Worten, es handelt sich um genau das Phänomen, in dem die mensurale Interpretation aus sich selbst heraus dialektisch in die neumische umschlägt. Dies ist das eigentliche Zentrum aller musikalischen Interpretation.)

Es ist nicht zu verkennen, daß, je komplexer die Musik bis hinauf zu Schönberg ward, der Begriff der Deutlichkeit freilich einen immer handfesteren, buchstäblicheren Sinn annimmt, daß man nämlich alles einzelne, was überhaupt geschieht, verstehen soll, und die Wagnersche und Mahlersche

Auffassung von der Reproduktion bewegt sich trotz ihres romantischen Pathos und gleichsam als dessen Komplement durchaus im Sinn eines solchen Positivismus, während strukturell einfachere Musik wie die von Beethoven dem Postulat der Deutlichkeit und der Forderung nach Artikulation weit komplexere Verhältnisse bietet und darum in einem tieferen Sinn weit schwieriger zu interpretieren ist als die moderne Musik, ganz abgesehen davon, daß bei Beethoven etwa das tonsprachliche Element keinerlei Stütze mehr, sondern bloß noch ein Hindernis bedeutet. Die Forderung der Artikulation, gegenüber dem Idealtypus Beethoven und dem Wiener Klassizismus überhaupt, dem gegenüber in erster Linie das Ideal einer Interpretation aus Erkenntnis gilt, bezieht sich insbesondere auf die kleinsten Einheiten, in deren Beziehung die musikalische »Arbeit« jener Epoche sich erfüllt, Themen und Motive. Es ist offenbar, daß die meisten Interpreten die Artikulation der Form im Groben, die Absetzung der großen Teile der Disposition, Steigerungen, Rückleitungen, Auflösungen zustandebringen, während die offizielle, von der Massenkultur erfaßte Interpretation dem Teilganzen gegenüber versagt. Wie etwa in großen Formen die Einzelthemen nach Vordersatz und Nachsatz, Frage und Antwort sich gliedern, ist dem bloß musiksprachlich die Kurve verfolgenden Interpreten verborgen und daher erfolgt die Präsentation solcher Themen durchaus nach dem Maß ihrer Wirkung und nicht dem ihres immanent musikalischen Sinnes, eine Gewohnheit, die dann wieder in der absurden Phrasierung moderner Musik zutagekommt, die in weitestem Maße am Schein der Unverständlichkeit Schuld trägt. »A classical melody, if interpreted with inadequate phrasing, may lose something of its beauty, whereas Schönberg's would be downright incomprehensible.«[269] Oder: ein Thema, das wiedererscheint als Fortsetzung oder Nachsatz eines anderen hat einen völlig verschiedenen Sinn von dem beim ersten Auftreten und muß demgemäß ganz verschieden interpretiert werden als Konsequenz nämlich und nicht als primär Seiendes. Das einfachste Beispiel für solche Forderung ist das Auseinanderhalten von Haupt- und Nebenstimme in der Kammermusik. In früheren Phasen Beethovens, in denen das musiksprachliche Element wesentlich im Vordergrund stand und sein Schwergewicht an der Realisierung der Harmonie hatte, war die Dosierung der Stimmen, sofern nur überhaupt einigermaßen »der Faden« zu entnehmen war, primitiv. Heute, da die harmonische Dimension ohnehin durchsichtig ist und das konventionelle mit der Sprache der Musik Sich-Treiben-Lassen unmöglich ward, wird die Darstellung des Stimmengefüges gerade in Gegensatz zum harmonischen Gefälle zur Aufgabe und zwar nicht nur bei eigentlich polyphonen Stellen, sondern es wird durchweg zur Aufgabe, auch in scheinbar harmonischen Komplexen die latente Polyphonie freizulegen und damit das Werk von der bloßen harmonischen Allgmeinheit zu emanzipieren und in seiner Spezifikation zu treffen. Von der Genauigkeit und Schärfe, mit welcher solche mikrologische Arbeit geleistet wird und zwar in beiden Richtungen, erst in der Analysis des Notenbildes und dann in dessen Rückübersetzung in den Klang, hängt der Sinn musikalischer Formen, deren Verwandlung in »Inhalt«, damit die Wahrheit der Interpretation selber, ab. Die stets wieder sich stellende Aufgabe wahrer Interpretation ist der verbindliche Ausdruck der Dialektik von Ganzem und Teilen, wobei die Erkenntnis der Teile in die des Ganzen übergeht und umgekehrt das Bewußtsein vom Ganzen dem Ansatz der Teile sein spezifisches Gewicht zuteilt. Die wahre Interpretation integral komponierter Musik – und von dieser bloß ist zunächst die Rede – verliert weder das Ganze ans Detail, noch setzt sie das Detail durchs Ganze zur Ohnmacht und Nichtigkeit herab. In der Tradition der abendländischen Musik steht dafür die wie sehr auch flexible Einheit des Grundtempos im Satz ein. Wann immer Tempomodifikationen, und wären es solche subliminaler Art, die Einheit des Satzes gefährden, muß die Artikulation durch andere Mittel, Phrasierung, Agogik, Dynamik, Klangfarbe geleistet werden.

Die wahre Interpretation beruht auf Erkenntis. Damit sind

nicht rationalistische Betrachtungen über das Werk, seinen Stil, seinen historischen Standort und was immer sonst gemeint; nichts was der Erfahrung vom Werke selber als ein Fremdes, Äußerliches gegenüberstünde und der Beziehung auf den Gegenstand selber entzogen wäre. Das informatorische Wissen, das Hineintragen von Bildung in die musikalische Interpretation, gegen das bereits Wagner sich gewehrt hat, ist selber Zeichen des Verlustes der spontanen Beziehung zur Sache, wie denn der informierte Hörer, der jede Nummer des Köchelverzeichnisses und das Entstehungsjahr des gleichgültigsten Bläserstückes von Beethoven auswendig weiß, regelmäßig der ist, der die Musik selber am wenigsten versteht und den neutralisierten Abdruck des Kulturgutes anstelle des spontanen Hörens setzt. (Vgl. dazu Wagner, Über das Dirigieren, S. 312 bis etwa S. 316, zitieren und evt. bis ins einzelne besprechen.) Vielmehr ist die Erkenntnis nichts anderes als die kritische Versenkung in den Text selber, die an diesen einzig die Forderung des sinnvollen Zusammenhangs heranbringt. Das Thema der Interpretation, das analytisch herzustellen und dann durch Klang darzustellen, ist der musikalische Sinn (?). Dessen Kategorie ist prinzipiell von der des Ausdrucks zu unterscheiden, mit welcher sie in der romantischen Phase gleichgesetzt wurde und welche freilich unter den Momenten, die zum musikalischen Sinn zusammentreten, nicht das letzte ist. Der musikalische Sinn, als jeder Interpretation, »Aufgegebenes«, entzieht sich der statischen Definition. Er ist vorweg einzig negativ zu bestimmen als die Bedürftigkeit des Phänomens, das worauf das Phänomen hinweist und wessen es bedarf, um nicht bloßer Klang zu sein sondern Musik, und was gleichwohl im Phänomen nicht aufgeht. Aber er ist doch nirgends anders zu suchen als im Phänomen selber, immanent zugleich und transzendent. Mit anderen Worten, in ihrem Zusammenhang und zwar keineswegs in dem zeitlichen, der Sukzession der Komplexe, obwohl diese ein entscheidendes Moment des musikalischen Sinnes ausmacht, sondern in allen Relationen, welche das klanglich Erscheinende überhaupt bildet. Die Einheit der sinnvollen Interpretation von Musik erheischt die Realisierung der Totalität jener Momente des Zusammenhangs, und ihr primärer Gegenbegriff ist der des sinnlosen Musizierens als einem, in dem das Leben des Werkes sein Ende hat und einzig ein Totes, Verdinglichtes sich manifestiert – die Erfahrung, welche als antithesis zur Forderung der Treue jedem reproduzierenden Musiker als der Arbeit unmittelbar vertraut ist, und reguliert, wonach er seine Entscheidung innerhalb der mensuralen Schicht trifft. Dieses Moment des sinnvollen Zusammenhangs ist das, als welches das neumische des Textes in die konkrete Interpretation sich umsetzt, und seine Tendenz sich zu verabsolutieren ist es, welche das ungezügelte Musikantentum, den Virtuosen, den willkürlichen Gestus bewirkt, also genau jenes, in welchem der mimetische Impuls der Musik regressiv, ungebrochen gleichsam durchbricht und die Darstellung der Schauspielerei überantwortet. Musikalische Schauspielerei ist das Lebendige auf Kosten seiner eigenen Objektivität, und beide Momente, die Objektivität und die Lebendigkeit der Sache zusammenzuzwingen definiert das Ideal von Interpretation. Der Begriff des musikalischen Sinnes als der Totalität des Zusammenhangs der Phänomene entfaltet das telos kodifizierter Musik als eines intentionslosen Textes, denn der Sinn ist nicht oder nur fragmentarisch ein hinter dem mensural Bezeichneten Stehendes und gleichwohl verweist er insofern auf den Begriff des Textes als eines zu Verstehenden, als keines der mensural bezeichneten Momente rein als solches bereits mit dem Sinn koinzidiert: dieser Paradoxismus ist geradezu die theoretische Formulierung dessen, was stets und stets als das Geheimnisvolle an Musik erfahren ward, ihr Wesen, nur sie selber und doch mehr als sie selber zu sein. (Die wirklich verbindliche Formulierung dieser Gedanken setzt die strengste Klärung des Begriffs des intentionslosen Textes in den Anfangskapiteln voraus.) Und es ist zugleich die Bestimmung der Röntgenphotographie insofern, als diese ein über die phänomenale Schicht Hinausgehendes nicht durch deren Auslegung als Symbol, sondern durch die Einsicht in die Struktur des Phänomens selber ergibt. Der Gegenbegriff zur Intention aber, der die Vorstellung vom intentionslosen Text allein möglich macht, ist der des mimischen Wesens der Musik, also dessen worin sie sich erfüllt, ohne es zu bedeuten, und der musikalische Sinn als Zusammenhang ist nichts anderes als die Totalität ihres Gestus. Das impliziert aber die unabdingbare Verpflichtung der musikalischen Erkenntnis auf das sinnlich Erscheinende als ihr strenges Objekt. Man könnte sagen, das konsequente, zum Bewußtsein seiner selbst gesteigerte Aushören der Musik. (Vor diesem Satz kam eine große Einfügung, daher der Sprung.) Dies konsequente Aushören freilich erfolgt nicht in einem Vakuum, sondern bezieht sich jeweils auf den fortgeschrittensten Stand der kompositionstechnischen Einsicht und damit der Kompositionstechnik selbst. Denn es ist diese, die Entfaltung der Mittel des musikalischen Zusammenhangs, von der aus das Licht auf die Texte fällt, in dem stets erneute Zusammenhänge sich abheben. So verhielt es sich bereits mit Wagners Interpretationtheorie. Er hat, unter dem Zwang der Objektivität der Sache, das Postulat der in Erkenntnis fundierten Interpretation erhoben, damit weit über die Stimmung des Espressivomusizierens hinausdringend, die zunächst über seinen beiden bedeutendsten interpretationstheoretischen Schriften liegt. Selbst die Sprache der Heldenverehrung vermag die Forderung musikalischer Erkenntnis des Zusammenhangs als Grund sinnvoller Interpretation nicht zuzudecken. »Wenn wir gehörig erwägen, von welcher einzigen Wichtigkeit es bei jeder musikalischen Mittheilung ist, daß die Melodie, werde sie uns durch die Kunst des Tondichters auch oft nur in ihren kleinsten Bruchtheilen vorgeführt, unablässig uns gefesselt halte, und daß die Korrektheit dieser melodischen Sprache in gar keiner Hinsicht der logischen Korrektheit des in der Wortsprache sich gebenden begrifflichen Gedankens nachstehen darf, ohne uns durch Undeutlichkeit ebenso zu verwirren, wie ein unverständlicher Sprachsatz dieß thut, so müssen wir erkennen, daß nichts der sorgfältigsten Mühe so werth ist, als die versuchte Aufhebung der Unklarheit einer Stelle, eines Taktes, ja einer Note in der musikalischen Mittheilung eines Genius', wie des Beethoven's, an uns; denn jede noch so überraschend neue Gestaltung eines solchen urwahrhaftigen Wesens entspringt einzig dem göttlich verzehrenden Drange, uns armen Sterblichen die tiefsten Geheimnisse seiner Weltschau unwiderleglich klar zu erschließen. Wie man also einer dunkel erscheinenden Stelle eines großen Philosophen nie vorübergehen soll, ehe sie nicht deutlich verstanden worden ist, und wie man, wenn dieß nicht geschieht, beim Weiterlesen durch zunehmende Unachtsamkeit in das Misverständniß des Lehrers gerathen muß, so soll man über keinen Takt einer Tondichtung, wie der Beethoven's, ohne deutliches Bewußtsein davon hinweggleiten.«[270] Daß es sich dabei aber in Wahrheit nicht um die Reflexion auf den Genius, sondern die auf den Text handelt, zeigt sich am Inhalt der Forderungen Wagners für die Wiedergabe der IX. Symphonie. Diese Forderungen gehen aus vom Begriff der »Deutlichkeit« des Vortrags[271], und das kommt im Verlauf der Argumentation auf nichts anderes heraus als auf die Realisierung des musikalischen Zusammenhangs durch die klangliche Erscheinung. Er sieht, daß bei Beethoven das Verhältnis von musikalischem Zusammenhang und Instrumentalklang problematisch geworden ist – durch einen entbundenen Widerspruch, würde man heute sagen, zwischen musikalischer Produktivkraft und Produktionsverhältnissen, zwischen der Struktur des Werkes und den instrumentalen Mitteln seiner Realisierung. Wie er keineswegs auf Beethoven sich beschränkt, sondern die gesamte Geschichte der bürgerlichen Musik durchzieht und heute noch in der Zufälligkeit der Relation zwischen der üblichen Orchesterzusammensetzung und der fortgeschrittensten musikalischen Imagination fortexistiert. »Wir haben nun darüber zu erstaunen, wie es der Meister in das Werk setzte, mit ganz dem gleichen Orchester Konzeptionen von einer wechselvollen Mannigfaltigkeit, welche Mozart und Haydn noch ganz fern lag, zur möglichst deutlichen Ausführung zu bringen. In diesem

Bezug bleibt seine ›Sinfonia eroica‹ nicht nur ein Wunder der Konzeption, sondern nicht minder auch ein Wunder der Orchestration. Nur muthete er bereits hier dem Orchester eine Vortragsweise zu, welche es sich bis auf den heutigen Tag noch nicht aneignen konnte: der Vortrag mußte nämlich von Seiten des Orchesters ebenso genial sein, wie die orchestrale Konzeption des Meisters selbst es war. Von hier, von der ersten Aufführung der ›Eroica‹ an, beginnen daher die Schwierigkeiten des Urtheils über diese Symphonien, ja selbst die Behinderungen des Gefallens an ihnen, welches den Musikern der älteren Epoche nie wirklich hat ankommen wollen. Es fehlte diesen Werken an der Deutlichkeit der Ausführung, weil die Hervorbringung dieser Deutlichkeit nicht mehr, wie bei Haydn und Mozart, in dem verwendeten Organismus des Orchesters gewährleistet war, sondern einzig durch die, bis in das Virtuosenhafte gehende, musikalisch geniale Leistung der einzelnen Instrumentisten und ihres Dirigenten ermöglicht werden konnte.«[272] Der Begriff der Deutlichkeit, um den es dabei geht, hat offensichtlich sein Maß nicht an dem unanfechtbaren, aber banalen Gedanken, daß jedes sinnlich Erklingende an sich deutlich, plastisch, präzis sein müsse, sondern daran, daß eben der Zusammenhang der klanglichen Erscheinung die »wechselvolle Mannigfaltigkeit« erscheinen lasse, in welcher das Strukturgesetz der Beethovenschen Symphonik besteht. Es ist aber fraglos, daß die klangliche Verdeutlichung jenes Strukturmoments, und wahrscheinlich, daß seine Erkenntnis erst vom Standpunkt einer vorgeschrittenen Orchestertechnik möglich war, die sich an sich bereits tendenziell zur »Röntgenphotographie des Werkes« macht und daher erlaubt, rückblickend im älteren Werk Schichten des Strukturzusammenhangs zu erkennen, welche in dessen eigener sinnlichen Erscheinungsweise zwar enthalten, aber zugleich verborgen waren. Das verleiht der Wagnerschen Betrachtung ihr grundsätzliches Gewicht. »Jetzt, wo der Reichthum seiner Konzeptionen ein bei weitem mannigfaltigeres Material und eine viel zartere Gliederung desselben verlangte, sah Beethoven sich nämlich genöthigt, die jähesten Wechsel in Stärke und Ausdruck des Vortrages von einen und denselben Instrumentisten in der Weise ausführen zu lassen, wie sie der große Virtuos als besondere Kunst sich aneignet. Daher z.B. die Beethoven so eigenthümlich gewordene Forderung eines Crescendo, welches auf dem äußersten Punkte sich nicht in das Forte entlädt, sondern plötzlich in das Piano umschlägt: diese eine, so häufig vorkommende Nüance ist unseren Orchesterspielern meistens noch so fremd, daß vorsichtige Dirigenten, welche sich wenigstens des rechtzeitigen Eintritts des Piano versichern wollten, ihren Musikern eine kluge Umkehr des Crescendo und Einlenkung in ein behutsames Diminuendo zur Pflicht machten. Der wahre Sinn dieser so schwierigen Nüance liegt gewiß darin, daß hier dieselben Instrumente etwas ausführen sollen, was erst dann ganz deutlich wird, wenn es verschiedenen, mit einander abwechselnden Instrumenten übergeben ist. Dieß wissen neuere Komponisten, welchen das bereicherte heutige Orchester und seine üblich gewordene Verwendung zur Verfügung steht. Diesen würde es möglich gewesen sein, gewisse von Beethoven beabsichtigte Wirkungen ohne alle exzentrische Anforderung an die virtuose Leistung des Orchesters, bloß durch die ihnen erleichterte Vertheilung an unterschiedene Instrumentalkomplexe, mit großer Deutlichkeit sicher zu stellen.«[273] Nicht umsonst exemplifiziert Wagner auf neuere Komponisten, nämlich sich selbst, zumal das seit dem Lohengrin immer konsequenter gehandhabte und im Tristan allein herrschende Prinzip der instrumentalen Melodieteilung, das allein es gestattet, die durch den Ausdruck vermittelten Strukturmomente der Melodie, den Inbegriff des Sukzessionszusammenhangs, ganz und gar zu »verdeutlichen«, nämlich in Farbe und Dynamik des Orchesterklangs zureichend zu übersetzen; und die Aufgabe dieser Übersetzung ist es dann zugleich auch, die jedem älteren Werke gegenüber sich stellt und die Wagner unbedenklich zur Forderung der Retouche geführt hat, die dann über Mahler bis zu den Schönbergischen Bearbeitungen führte, welche gleichsam das Problem der Reproduktion unmittelbar vom Standpunkt der sich entfaltenden Kompositionstechnik aus stellen. Wenn Wagner das Postulat der Deutlichkeit dem des »drastischen Heraustretens der Melodie«[274] gleichsetzt, so ist darunter selbstverständlich nicht grob die Oberstimmenmelodie, sondern der »rote Faden« zu verstehen, die von Stimme zu Stimme, von Gruppe zu Gruppe springende, von Harmonie und Kontrapunkt begleitete Hauptstimme, deren Verlauf durch das gesamte Zeitalter von Bach bis Schönberg das wesentlichste Moment des gestisch-musikalischen Zusammenhangs ausmacht, und die es denn auch ist, welche der Dirigent »nachzeichnet«. Es ist freilich dies Moment zugleich, das, als Anwachsen des Bewußtseins der Interpretation, die Zerstörung des Werkes inauguriert insofern, als dieser der Widerspruch von Zusammenhang und Phänomen nicht äußerlich ist, sondern [ihr] Lebenselement bildet und, wenn er einmal nicht mehr existiert, wenn also einmal das ältere Werk sinnlich ganz und gar angemessen erscheint, ihm eben dadurch abermals ein Blankes, Totes, Verdinglichtes zuerteilt, in dem auf höherer Ebene die Verdinglichung der sturen Realisierung dessen »was da steht« sich reproduziert. Aber es wäre vergebenes Beginnen, aus Angst vor dem, was der Fortschritt in der Realisierung des Zusammenhangs durchs Phänomen dem Werk antut, ihn sistieren zu wollen, weil ja eben das Werk selber seine Substanz an solcher Bewegung hat und gar nicht ein Substrat besitzt, das seiner immanenten Bewegung entgegengehalten werden könnte. Es ist das innerste Wesen der wahren Interpretation, zum Tode seines Gegenstandes beizutragen.

(In diesem Abschnitt sind an den entsprechenden Stellen folgende Belege einzufügen: Wagners Definition des Erkenntnisideals der Interpretation als eines vom Zusammenhang, das heißt, der »Melodie«: »Hier fiel es mir denn wie Schuppen von den Augen, was auf den Vortrag ankäme, und sogleich verstand ich, was hier das Geheimniß der glücklichen Lösung der Aufgabe ausmachte. Das Orchester hatte eben gelernt, in jedem Takte die Beethoven'sche Melodie zu erkennen, welche offenbar unseren braven Leipziger Musikern damals gänzlich entgangen war; und diese Melodie sang das Orchester«[275]. Zur Definition der Darstellung des Zusammenhangs als des an Schönberg orientierten Konstruktionsideals zitieren Dorian: »The romantic interpreter who gets his result by mere temperament, by a display of fire, saddness, or agitation, is, as Rudolf Kolisch remarks, at a loss with Schönberg. The romantic method necessarily consists of a heightening of the surface luster, rather than what Schönberg demands – balance and symmetry of presentation, where true insight into the construction governs the outline as well as all the details of the interpretation.«[276])

5.

Die Forderung einer Erkenntnis des Werkes kraft dessen innerer Veränderung setzt vorab dem Verdacht des Relativismus sich aus. Wenn es das Werk an sich nicht gibt, so lautet das Argument, so ist in einem strengsten Sinn dessen Erkenntnis auch nicht möglich, sondern der Wechsel in der Auffassung ist einzig subjektive Projektion und ein dem Werke ganz äußerliches Stilgebahren. Demgegenüber ist prinzipiell vorweg an die Hegelsche Kritik des ästhetischen Relativismus als der Berufung auf den »Geschmack« zu erinnern. Der Relativismus ist ein Schein, der entsteht, sobald die Sache nach einem ihr fremden, transzendenten Maßstab gehandhabt wird. Das ist nicht mißzuverstehen im Sinn der Allerweltsweisheit des Experten, der jeglicher methodischen Besinnung gegenüber sich aufs Privileg der Sachkunde zurückzieht und dogmatisch behauptet, für den, welcher sich auskenne, verstehe das Wahre sich immer von selbst. Davon kann keine Rede sein, und jede im Material gewonnene Einsicht ist empirisch dem Irrtum offen. Technische Kenntnis als solche ist keine Garantin der Objektivität des Erkannten, allein darum schon nicht, weil sie meist von allgemeinen Disziplinen hergenommen ist, deren Gesetze keineswegs mit der Spezifikation des bestimmten Werkes identisch sind, dann aber auch, weil der Begriff der technischen Konsistenz weniger die eindeutige Entscheidbarkeit einer jeglichen ästhetischen Frage enthält als eine Anweisung darauf, wie der Horizont jeglichen ästhetischen Problems zu erschließen sei, die aber zugleich auch in ihrer Bewegung das isolierte Urteil über Richtig und Falsch eines Werkmomentes kassiert. Die ästhetische Konsistenz hat ihre Dialektik in sich, und nicht einmal der bündigste Befund eines technisch Unstimmigen reicht von sich aus hin, dem Werk das Urteil zu sprechen, sondern vermag sich in einem weiteren Horizont oder auf einer höheren Stufe der Einsicht in die Sinnstruktur des Gebildes als Element der Wahrheit, als stimmig herzustellen. Es verdient vermerkt zu werden, daß gerade Schönberg, der den Begriff der totalen Organisation in der Musik auskristallisiert hat, immer wieder den »Fehler«, das Abirren, den unretouchierbaren Fleck verteidigt hat. In Wahrheit sind die besten Kunstwerke keineswegs die vollkommensten, sondern jene, in deren Unvollkommheit die tragenden Widersprüche am tiefsten sich niederschlugen. Daher nehmen gerade sie, deren Gelingen das Mißlingen der Welt zum Maß hat, vor dem Blick der zeitgenössischen Kulturverwaltung etwas Hilfloses, Hinfälliges, Desorganisiertes an. Aber wehe dem Kunstwerk, das darum bei seiner eigenen Unvollkommenheit sich beschiede. Aber es macht allen Unterschied, ob der notwendige und doch falsche Anspruch des Absoluten, der von jedem ästhetischen Einzelurteil erhoben wird, in der Bewegung seiner eigenen Konsequenz und der der Sache zergeht, oder ob die abstrakte These subjektiver Relativität am Anfang steht, zum bestimmten Urteilen und zur Bewegung des Begriff es gar nicht kommen läßt und schließlich auf die Sabotage des ästhetischen Wahrheitsgehaltes und die Installation des Konsumentenstandpunkts herausläuft, der da verkündet, erlaubt sei, was gefällt, und nicht einmal einsieht, daß gerade das subjektive Belieben, auf das er sich zurückzieht, der bloße Reflex dessen ist, was eine genormte Produktionsmaschinerie ihm einhämmert. Die Aufhebung des ästhetischen Einzelurteils im Fortgang der Disziplin der Sache und der Überlegung ist nicht gleichbedeutend mit seiner Nichtigkeit, sondern läßt ihm allemal an seiner Stelle das Recht, das sie ihm entzieht, sobald sie über jene Stellen hinausgeht, und zugleich steht die ästhetische Wahrheit und Objektivität gerade im Ganzen jener Bewegung, der das isolierte Urteil zum Opfer fällt. So wenig die Quinten im Variationsthema der Appassionata dem Stümper zugutekommen, der das Quintenverbot nicht verstanden hat und sich darauf hinausredet, seine falschen Quinten gefielen ihm so gut; und so wenig der Unterschied zwischen seiner und Beethovens Harmonik bloß graduell und subjektiv ist, sondern auf ein Richtig oder Falsch der Sache hinweist, obwohl abstrakt gesehen, bei Beethoven das Gleiche sich zuträgt wie bei dem Stümper, aber nun als Richtiges, so wenig vermag die Dynamik und Unabgeschlossenheit der musikalischen Interpretation etwas an der bestimmten Unterscheidung des richtig oder falsch Interpretierten zu ändern, durch welche hindurch allein die geschichtliche Entfaltung der Werke sich vollzieht. Gesetzt den Fall, die fortgeschrittenste Erkenntnis etwa gewisser Instrumentalwerke von Schubert führte dazu, daß seine Werke, als prinzipiell der Struktur nach nicht integral organisierte, auch keine integrale, sondern eine fragmentarische Interpretation verlangten, also eine gegenüber dem Ideal einheitlichen Verlaufs brüchige und zerrissene. Dann würde doch eine solche Einsicht nicht etwa der Interpretation recht geben, die ohne Rücksicht auf das Strukturganze etwa in den einzelnen thematischen Augenblicken schwelgte und alles andere als Zwischenwerk erledigte, sondern die Forderung bestünde darin, die Struktur des Ganzen selber als eine fragmentarische, die Totalität als nicht totale wiederzugeben, und es würde bei jedem Detail sich genau darüber entscheiden lassen, ob die hier geforderte Auflösung des Zusammenhangs objektiv aus dessen eigener Erkenntnis sich ausweist oder kontingent und rhapsodisch bleibt.

Das Kriterium wäre, ob die von der Interpretation herzustellenden Brüche selber als sinnvoll, als wie sehr auch negative Bedeutungsträger sich erweisen, oder ob sie gegenüber den hervorgekehrten Einzelheiten zufällig und Füllsel bleiben. Noch die Zerstörung des Zusammenhangs durch die Interpretation, die wohl gefordert sein kann, steht unterm Primat des Zusammenhangs. Der ästhetische Relativismus ist das bloße Komplement zum Absolutismus: nur wo die vorkritische Vorstellung vom Werk an sich zugrundeliegt, und eben dies An-sich-sein in der Geschichte als fragwürdig sich enthüllt, verzerrt sich sein historisches Wesen zur bloßen Abschattung in verschiedenen Epochen und Subjekten und wird der Relativität überantwortet, während, ward einmal die Veränderung als Wesensgesetz bestimmt, dies Wesensgesetz zugleich das Gesetz von Wahr und Falsch von Werk und Interpretation konstituiert. Jegliche musikalische Arbeit, jede Entfaltung von Musik als Kunst, die über das bloße kulinarische Klingen hinausgeht, setzt zwar nicht die dogmatische Vorgegebenheit, wohl aber die kategoriale Möglichkeit der Unterscheidung von Richtig und Falsch voraus, beim Komponisten wie beim Interpreten. Die Apperzeption des musikalischen Sinnes, also der Vollzug des Zusammenhangs besteht gerade in dieser Unterscheidung und mit Hinblick auf diese verhält sich die musikalische Erfahrung nicht anders gegenüber elementaren Tatbeständen wie richtigen und falschen Tönen – die ja bereits nicht in der Physik sich erschöpft, sondern virtuell schon die ganze kategoriale Apparatur der Musik in sich trägt – und dem Urteil über die angemessene oder unangemessene Wiedergabe eines ganzen komplexen Stückes. Jeder Schritt der fortschreitenden Erfahrung des Subjekts von der Sache führt tiefer in diese und damit in die Notwendigkeit der Darstellung, ja das Wesen des Werkes manifestiert sich einzig durch den Stufengang solcher Notwendigkeiten hindurch. Die relativistische These von der Zufälligkeit der Interpretation ist gerade die starre, verdinglichte. Sie setzt eine Trennung des fürsichseienden Objekts und des betrachtenden Subjekts voraus, das dieses je nach Belieben verschieden auffassen [kann]. Das gilt aber nur, wo beide einander hoffnungslos entfremdet sind: erst die abgestorbenen Werke, als absolut vergegenständlichte, fielen der Relativität der Betrachtung zur Beute, wie es denn nicht zufällig ist, daß gerade an abgebrauchten, vernutzten und von der Totenstarre der Konvention überzogenen Werken die Willkür sogenannter interpretativer Auffassungen am rohesten sich betätigt. Die wahre Interpretation besteht nicht in der perspektivischen Betrachtung eines ein für allemal gegebenen Werkes, sondern das Werk selbst schließt die Dialektik seiner Betrachtung ein und erteilt dieser damit die Objektivität kraft des Wechsels. Wer da sich einbildet, vom Werk seine eigene Auffassung zu haben, ist dem Werke entfremdet und wird darum nur dessen Gipsabdruck wahrnehmen; wer es spontan versteht, der erkennt es. Der Untergang der betrachtenden Subjektivität im Werke und der Anteil des Subjekts an der Konstitution seiner Objektivität sind ein und dasselbe. Mehr nicht trifft zu am Relativismus, als daß der Zugang, den der Interpret in die Objektivität des Werkes findet, zufällig ist. Die Organisation des Ganzen als eines Sinnzusammenhangs macht es beliebig, von welchem Aspekt, von welcher Dimension die interpretative Arbeit ihren Ausgang nimmt. Die Konsequenz der hörenden Logik einmal vorausgesetzt, führt jeglicher ins Zentrum und von dort aus zu jedem anderen. Wer je mit Musikern ein Werk ausgearbeitet hat, weiß, wie wichtig es ist, überhaupt etwas zu sagen, überhaupt an einer Stelle einzusetzen, und wie gleichgültig an welcher, ja wie [gleichgültig] selbst die Richtigkeit oder Falschheit der isolierten Ausstellung, denn nach Kolischs Wort: »Irgendetwas ist immer falsch«, und darum steht noch die falsche Kritik oder der vage Vorschlag, wofern sie nur überhaupt an der Disziplin des Zusammenhangs sich messen, im Dienst der wahren Interpretation.

(Zu der Stelle, wo von der Relativität als bloßem Schein die Rede ist, der in der bestimmten Arbeit zergeht, den Satz: würde man etwa dem Leiter eines Streichquartetts bei der Arbeit die Relativität seiner Forderungen entgegenhalten und die Möglichkeit kontradiktorischer vertreten, so würde er den Einwand um so weniger verstehen, je subjektiver er im Werk eingesetzt ist, damit aber auch um so weniger um dessen Objektivität [wissen]. Je bornierter er scheinbar auf eine bloß technische Kasuistik sich wirft, um so mehr an philosophischer Wahrheit wäre auf seiner Seite. – Wo gesagt wird, daß auch der dialektische Fortgang der Interpretation in gewisser Weise relativiert, also das isolierte ästhetische Urteil aufhört, muß ausgeführt werden, worin diese Relativierung konkret vom ästhetischen Relativismus sich unterscheidet. Motiv: ein Taktierer stellt ein Werk in sinnwidriger, mechanischer Symmetrie mit Akzenten auf 1 und 3 dar. Das musikalische Bewußtsein erkennt den Widerspruch der Darstellungsweise zum Zusammenhang, nämlich zur Struktur der Komposition als einer vom Schemata der Takteinteilung verschiedene. Es ergibt sich daraus eine Forderung der Darstellung des Sinnes, und diese mag ihrerseits nun sehr leicht in Konflikt geraten seis mit der Treue zum Text, seis sogar mit der Organisation des Ganzen, indem sie etwa dem Sinn zuliebe das Ausdrucksmoment einseitig auf Kosten des Konstruktiven zusammenhält, durch Einheit des Tempos usw. hervorhebt. Kurz, der Vorgang trägt die Spuren von Relativität, aber in bestimmter Negation: mit allen Fehlern, mit Undeutlichkeit, Unpräzision und Willkür vertritt doch Furtwängler gegenüber der norddeutschen Taktschlägerei die Wahrheit. Indem er selber dabei in die Unwahrheit übergeht, wird diese darum nicht etwa wahrer. Der kritische Vorgang, auf den jene Bewegung der Interpretation herausläuft, ist die objektive Entfaltung der im Werk verschlossenen Dialektik: musikalische Interpretation ist von Kritik unabtrennbar. Solche dialektische Relativität ist nicht Gleichberechtigung der Auffassungen, sondern das Organ von deren Abschaffung. Die wahre Interpretation ist eine streng vorgezeichnete, aber noch um des antinomischen Wesens des musikalischen Kunstwerks selber nicht zu verwirklichende Idee. – Anstelle das musiksprachliche, das idiomatische Element.)

Überarbeiteter Anfang des Entwurfs

I.

Seit der Antike ist die Lehre von der Aufführung als Teil der Musiktheorie anerkannt. Im Schema des Aristides Quintilianus wird die Doktrin des Vortrags – »exangeltikon« – der von der Komposition gleichgestellt: beide zusammen bilden die praktische Musikdisziplin.[277] Aber die Vortragslehre ist so wenig wie die von der Instrumentation derart entwickelt worden, daß sie den Hauptstücken der Kompositionstheorie, Harmonie und Kontrapunkt, die Waage hielte. Sie hat sich auf die Beschreibung des je herrschenden Gebrauchs, die Formulierung traditioneller Erfahrungsregeln, die Kodifizierung von Geschmacksurteilen beschränkt, oder auf technische Traktate über den Gesang und das instrumentale Spiel. Ihr eigentliches Anliegen, über das Verhältnis der Wiedergabe zu den Werken zu entscheiden, ward nicht eingelöst. Keineswegs aber ist dies Verhältnis der technischen Musiklehre so unproblematisch vorgegeben, daß sie der Reflexion darauf im gleichen Sinne enthoben wäre, wie etwa die mathematische Arbeit der auf die Logik. Denn den ausübenden Musiker konfrontieren unablässig seine Texte mit Fragen, die weder durch den Rekurs auf die Werke noch durch den auf die Anforderungen des eigenen Spiels ohne weiteres zu schlichten sind, sondern erst durch Erkenntnis der wesentlichen Beziehung zwischen beiden. Kein musikalischer Text, auch nicht der minutiös bezeichnete moderne, ist so eindeutig lesbar, um unvermittelt seine angemessene Interpretation zu erzwingen. Keine Verfügung des Sängers, Instrumentalisten oder Dirigenten über sein Material, wäre sie auch zu einer in sich einstimmigen und alle Möglichkeiten der musikalischen Erfahrung betreffenden Sprache entfaltet, reicht aus, von sich aus der Interpretation jenen Charakter der Wahrheit zu verleihen, welcher doch als Idee jede Aufführung unabdingbar leitet. Noch die gewissenhafteste musikalische Aufführung laboriert an einem Moment des

Unverbindlichen, Versuchsweisen, ja der Improvisation. Die Wiedergabe jedoch, die jenes Momentes umstandslos sich zu entäußern trachtete, würde notwendig zum Verrat an dem Werke: sie würde es nicht als solches vergegenwärtigen, sondern einzig seine brüchige Schale, das Wenige daran, was im Text manifest zutage liegt und dann leicht genug der Dechiffrierung als bloßer Schein zergeht. Im Mangel einer ausgeführten Reproduktionstheorie spricht die Not des Reproduzierenden sich aus, die ihrerseits durch jenen Mangel verstärkt wird. Sie ist zugleich die Not des preisgegebenen Werkes.

Jedoch dies Dilemma treibt keineswegs den verantwortlichen Musiker zur agnostischen Konsequenz. Er läßt die Unterscheidung von richtiger und falscher Interpretation so wenig sich verkümmern wie die eines richtig oder falsch gegriffenen Akkords, eines reinen oder unreinen Tons. Jeder Schritt der Wiedergabe stellt sich ihm als objektiv bestimmt und notwendig dar, und unbeirrt trennt er solche wie immer auch vorläufige Notwendigkeit vom zufälligen und äußerlichen – dem Werk äußerlichen – Belieben. Dies sachliche Vertrauen eignet durchaus nicht bloß der handwerklich befangenen Naivetät. Selbst die Einsicht in den geschichtlichen Wechsel der Interpretationen, die den reflektierenden Musikern zumindest seit dem neunzehnten Jahrhundert sich aufdrängte, hat es nicht vermocht, die Idee der wahren Interpretation zu brechen: die geschichtliche Veränderung als solche vielmehr ist als gesetzmäßig erkannt und damit zur Idee der wahren Interpretation in Beziehung gesetzt worden. Das liegt implizit der Auffassung Richard Wagners in der Schrift »Über das Dirigieren« zugrunde, dem bedeutendsten Beitrag, den Komponisten zur Theorie der Reproduktion geleistet haben. Newman bezeichnet als Zweck jener Abhandlung die bündige Definition der »new demands made upon a conductor's capacity by the changes in music, and the corresponding changes in the sensitive performer's attitude towards music, that had taken place during the nineteenth century«[278]. Dem zufolge hätte Wagner nicht bloß die anwachsende subjektive Differenziertheit des Interpreten während der romantischen Ära, sondern ihren Grund, die objektiven historischen Veränderungen der Musik selber zum Kanon richtiger Darstellung erhoben. So wollte Wagner in der Tat den Kernpunkt der Schrift verstanden wissen. Er zielt auf die Lösung jenes Dilemmas der Interpretation, das seiner reflektierenden Kritik bereits bewußt war. »Mir konnte zunächst nur darum zu thun sein, das Dilemma selbst aufzudecken, und dem Gefühle eines Jeden es klar zu machen, daß seit Beethoven hinsichtlich der Behandlung und des Vortrages der Musik eine ganz wesentliche Veränderung gegen früher eingetreten ist. Was früher in einzelnen abgeschlossenen Formen zu einem Fürsichleben auseinandergehalten war, wird hier, wenigstens seinem innersten Hauptmotive nach, in den entgegengesetztesten Formen, von diesen selbst umschlossen, zu einander gehalten und gegenseitig aus sich entwickelt. Natürlich soll dem nun auch im Vortrage entsprochen werden, und hierzu gehört vor allen Dingen, daß das Zeitmaaß von nicht minderer Zartlebigkeit sei, als das thematische Gewebe, welches durch jenes sich seiner Bewegung nach kundgeben soll, selbst es ist.«[279] Wagner hat die »wesentliche Veränderung« des Vortrags der Musik nicht als bloßen Sachverhalt beschrieben, sondern als normativ bestätigt. Und zwar als Funktion von Veränderungen der kompositorischen Technik. Die Charakteristik Beethovens setzt diesen in Gegensatz zur »vorklassischen« Verfahrungsweise und gilt in Wahrheit für die gesamte Wiener Schule. Das Moment, das Wagner hervorhebt, hat seinen historischen Ursprung in der Einbeziehung der Kantabilität in den instrumentalen Satz. Es vollendet sich als Einheit in der Mannigfaltigkeit; einer aus qualitativ verschiedenen thematischen Gestalten in dialektisch vermitteltem Prozeß sich bildenden Konstruktion. Das ältere deutsche Musizieren, das Wagner in der Abhandlung beschreibt und das er in den Kapellmeisterjahren seiner Jugend mit gründlichem Widerwillen erfuhr, war hinter den Strukturveränderungen zurückgeblieben, in denen der Wiener

Klassizismus resultierte. Es weiß nichts vom Einspruch des instrumentalen Gesanges gegens instrumentale Spiel. Noch spiegelte straffes, unnachgiebiges Durchtaktieren erstarrt die vorherrschende Kompositionsweise des Generalbaß-Zeitalters wider, die ihre Formen aus identischem Material schichtete, nicht als Prozeß der Synthesis von unidentischem entwickelte. Der Widerspruch jenes Typus der Darstellung, gegen dessen Verdienste Wagner im übrigen nicht blind war, zu Beethoven ist aber keiner des bloßen »Stils« und musikalischen Geschmacks. Wagners Forderung, es solle der neueren Kompositionsstruktur auch im Vortrag entsprochen werden, begründet er damit, daß das »thematische Gewebe«, also die Mannigfaltigkeit in der Einheit, durchs Zeitmaß, die Grundkategorie der Interpretation, »sich seiner Bewegung nach kundgeben soll«: also deutlich werden. Die Veränderung der Interpretation ist kein Wechsel der Moden, sondern geht, Wagner zufolge, aus der Notwendigkeit hervor, die unter dem Notentext und der einfachen Tempobezeichnung liegende Beschaffenheit der Komposition als solcher hörbar zu machen. Das Werk verlangt um seiner Objektivität willen veränderte Darstellung und zwar gerade eine der traditionellen Objektivität entgegengesetzte: dies der paradoxe Sinn von Wagners Forderung. Indem er sie aber »der Beurtheilung unseres ganzen heutigen Musikmachens«[280] zugrundelegt, läßt er kaum einen Zweifel daran, daß er die elastisch-funktionelle Darstellungsweise nicht auf die Musik seit dem Wiener Klassizismus beschränkt, sondern als allgemeines Prinzip meint. Liszts pianistische Transkriptionen Bachischer Orgelwerke etwa sind Zeugnisse dieser übergreifenden Intention. Ihr dekorativer Zug hat sich mittlerweile als jener Deutlichkeit entgegengesetzt erwiesen, um deretwillen das neudeutsche Darstellungsideal konzipiert ward. Es ist selber der historischen Dynamik verfallen, in deren Erkenntnis es entsprang. Aber es hat zugleich den Gedanken der objektiven Verbindlichkeit von Interpretation auf jene Dynamik gerade bezogen. Wagners Lehre schließt die Konsequenz ein, daß die Wahrheit der Interpretation nicht in Geschichte als ein dieser Fremdes und ihr Ausgeliefertes liegt, sondern Geschichte in der Wahrheit der Interpretation als ein nach deren immanenten Gesetzen sich Entfaltendes. Der vorkritische wie der unverbindliche Standpunkt sind, der Tendenz nach, aufgehoben.

Wenn danach die Reproduktion von Musik als theoretisches Problem zu begreifen ist, so wird sie zugleich als Form eigenen Wesens behauptet. Alle Fragen der Reproduktion setzen in technische sich um, aber ihre Beantwortung trifft die Funktion der Technik selber. Während der Rechtsanspruch der Interpretation in dem Verhältnis konkreter Werke und empirischer Interpreten sich anmeldet und begründet, ist er doch nicht aus der Betrachtung jener beiden Pole, oder gar im Kompromiß zwischen beiden zu entscheiden, sondern erst durch Erwägungen, welche die Idee der Interpretation aus dem Begriff des musikalischen Werkes als solchem und seines geschichtlichen Lebens dartun. Eine strenge Vorstellung von den spezifischen Gesetzen der Reproduktion, also Einsicht in ihre Autonomie, läßt sich einzig in der Analyse dessen gewinnen, was von Interpretation wesentlich vorausgesetzt wird, der Existenz durch Schrift und Druck fixierter und insofern gerade vom empirischen Musizieren unabhängiger Werke. Das Ende der improvisatorischen Praxis, die Verselbständigung des Werkes und seine Trennung von der Interpretation stiftet zugleich deren Selbständigkeit. Wiedergeben läßt sich das Werk erst als einmal entfremdetes. Interpretation, als autonome Form, ist notwendig auf ihren Widerspruch verwiesen, das autonome musikalische Gebilde. Darin gemahnt sie unmittelbar an die Übersetzung sprachlicher Texte. »Übersetzung ist eine Form. Sie als solche zu erfassen, gilt es zurückzugehen auf das Original. Denn in ihm liegt deren Gesetz als in dessen Übersetzbarkeit beschlossen.«[281] Von der Übersetzung aus der fremden Sprache jedoch unterscheidet die musikalische Reproduktion grundsätzlich sich darin, daß bis zum heutigen Tage Musik ihrer bedarf, nicht jedoch die Dichtung ihres Übersetzers. Dem unübersetzten Gedicht geht nichts von seiner Schönheit ab, und eher hat es, wie das Wortspiel es will, den traduttore als traditore zu fürchten denn ihn herbeizuziehen. Die Partitur jedoch, die der Möglichkeit ihrer Aufführung radikal entzogen ist, scheint sinnlos zugleich in sich selber. Der Vorwurf, eine Komposition sei Papiermusik, mag oft genug die reaktionäre Abfertigung rationalisieren. Sein normativer Kern jedoch, es müsse jede Komposition, um als stimmig sich zu erweisen, angemessen realisierbar sein und gleichsam ihre wahre Interpretation in sich tragen, ist legitim. Er läßt in technischen Kategorien sich ausdrücken. Noch die strengste Auffassung von der Objektivität des Werkes, die jeden Gedankens an Kommunikation und Wirkung sich entschlägt, wird Kriterien wie das der sachgemäßen Instrumentation sich nicht aus der Hand schlagen lassen, und solche Kriterien sind zwar von jeder empirischen Aufführung zu trennen, nicht aber vom Ideal der wahren. Der Grenzwert eines von der idealen Aufführung ganz emanzipierten Werkes erschließt sich allenfalls der Analyse von Interpretation als Form: sie liegt in deren eigener Dialektik, nicht im unkritisch vorausgesetzten Ansichsein der Werke. Aller bestehenden Musik jedoch ist das Interpretiertwerden wesentlich. Daß aber noch das schwierigste sprachliche Gebilde indifferent ist gegen seine gelungene Übersetzung wie gegen seinen glücklichen Vortrag, während der einfachste musikalische Text gänzlich adäquat der stummen Vorstellung des verständig Noten Lesenden gegeben, doch ein dem Aufgezeichneten transzendentes Klangbild zum Inhalt hat – das läßt sich nicht vom Aufnehmenden her erklären, sondern bloß durch die Differenz der Medien. Musik so gut wie Dichtung kann gelesen werden, nur heißt Lesen hier und dort ein Anderes. Bei der Musik erheischt Lesen notwendig die sinnliche Vorstellung, während Dichtung die ihres wesentlichen Gehalts geradezu verbietet[282]. Die philosophische Behandlung des Problems der Reproduktion kann daher die Reflexion auf das Verhältnis von Sprache und Musik nicht vermeiden, wie es in ihrer Ähnlichkeit als Konstellation von Zeichen, ihrem Gegensatz mit Hinsicht aufs Postulat der Realisierbarkeit liegt. Solche Reflexion muß an den Begriff des musikalischen Textes und damit der Notenschrift sich anschließen, der das Problem der musikalischen Reproduktion konstituiert und zugleich die spezifische Differenz zur Sprache. Dieser wird Musik nur als Schrift kommensurabel.

2.

Gleich der sprachlichen ist die musikalische Schrift ein Zeichensystem. [*Marginalie:* NB auseinanderhalten: Intentionslosigkeit der musikalischen *Schrift,* und der *Musik.* Sehr wichtig.] Von den beiden Elementen, als deren Verbindung Riemann sie betrachtet[283], ist das eine das Alphabet, dessen erste Buchstaben von alters her den Tönen der diatonischen Skala zugeordnet waren. Damit involviert die Notenschrift primitive Begrifflichkeit: das Zeichen α gibt die einheitliche Tonhöhe aller je damit notierten Töne an, oder markiert wenigstens, wenn man absolute Tonhöhen für die frühere Antike nicht annehmen will, stets den Ausgangston der mixolydischen Skala. Nicht zufällig aber ist solche Begrifflichkeit durch Buchstaben vermittelt und nicht durch Worte. Sie hält die Identität sinnlicher Laute fest, aber nicht die von Sachen. Die Analogie der musikalischen und sprachlichen Schrift bezieht sich allein auf die Schicht des akustischen Stoffs, dessen Elemente hier wie dort mit Zeichen bedacht werden und zwar in der Musik mit aus der Sprache entlehnten. Aber in jener fügen diese Elemente sich nicht zu Komplexen zusammen, die Gegenstände bedeuteten: die musikalische Schriftsprache ist eine ohne Intentionen, gleichsam eine blinde Nomenklatur, und die Einheiten des Sinnes, in denen Musik selber sich bewegt, haben mit Intentionalität nichts gemein: Musik ist eine intentionslose Sprache. Man kann denn auch bei ihr von Lauten reden und andererseits mit gutem, unmetaphorischem Grunde von Perioden und Sätzen, doch niemals von Worten. Ihrer Schrift ist das begriffliche Medium bloß peripher, ja man könnte in der musikalischen Notenschrift eine bloße Pseudomorphose ans Bereich des Begriff erblicken. Daß sie ihre Zeichen von der Sprachschrift borgen mußte, deutet auf ihre Fremdheit zum Begriff: die Buchstaben sind den Tönen nachträglich, in der Willkür der Rationalisierung aufgeprägt und verhalten sich zu ihnen eher wie Allegorien, als daß sie mit ihnen verschmolzen wären wie die Buchstaben mit den Sprachlauten. Vom Ton a ist der Name a zu trennen, ohne daß er an musikalischer Bestimmtheit das Mindeste darüber verlöre; Buchstabe und Vokal a ebenso trennen zu wollen, wäre müßiges Beginnen. Denn das Aussprechen des Namens a zitiert den Laut a, nicht aber das Nennen des Tones a diesen. Mit anderen Worten: das Zeichensystem der Sprachschrift und die Sprache gehören einem homogenen System an, die Musik und ihre Schrift zwei verschiedenen. Die sprachlichen Zeichen ragen in den musikalischen Kosmos einzig als ein ihm selber Fremdes, Gebrochenes herein. Gerade weil Musik eine intentionslose Sprache ausmacht, ist der signifikative Charakter ihrer Schrift, die Differenz von Zeichen und Bezeichnetem, zum qualitativen Bruch gesteigert.

Wenn sonach das begriffliche Wesen als ein der musikalischen Schrift äußerliches, nur versprengt in ihr vorkommendes muß angesprochen werden, während doch die musikalische Schrift an Artikulation und logischer Konsequenz hinter der sprachlichen kaum zurückbleibt, so muß ihr Ursprung in einem anderen Elemente vermutet werden als dem intentionalen. Das aber ist die hypokritike, die das Aristidische Schema auf der gleichen Ebene wie Instrumentenspiel und Gesang als Feld der musikalischen Vortragslehre einzeichnet. Es ist das mimetische Element. Riemann hat an der Einbeziehung der Mimik in die musikalische Vortragslehre Anstoß genommen. »Denn wenn der Sprache zweifellos noch spezifisch musikalische Elemente im musikalischen Klange innewohnen, kann das gleiche von der lediglich zum Auge sprechenden Mimik nicht ausgesagt werden. Die Berechtigung zu der Einstellung auch dieser Kunstform ergibt sich aber wieder aus der von Anfang und fortgesetzt zu konstatierenden innigen Verbindung der sämtlichen energischen Künste, d.h. der das Kunstwerk als ein Stück wirkliches Leben vor Auge und Ohr im zeitlichen Geschehen entwickelnden Künste; nicht nur sind im Gesange Dichtung und Musik, und im Tanze Gebärdenspiel und Musik zu fester Einheit verbunden, sondern alle drei verschmelzen im Chorreigen zu einer Gesamtkunst, für welche die Griechen den Ausdruck Musik in seiner weitesten Bedeutung anwenden.«[284] Die gewundene Verteidigung des Aristides, welche die Differenz zwischen Sprache und Musik viel zu leicht nimmt und in der summarischen Anschauung von allen energischen Künsten als »wirkliches Leben« vor Augen stellenden durch den Ausdruck hypokritike allein Lügen gestraft wird, verfehlt kraft der Nivellierung von Sprache und Musik deren mimetisches Element. Sie krankt am Riemannschen Grundfehler in der Behandlung entlegener Epochen, späte geschichtliche Züge wie eben die Trennung von Mimik und der Musik als natur- und vernunftgegeben zu hypostasieren und in jedem modernen »Nacherleben« verschlossene Phänomene trugvoll sich einzufühlen, indem sie nach Kategorien des späten neunzehnten Jahrhunderts umgebogen werden. Ihm ist die Arbeitsteilung der Zeitkünste so selbstverständlich, daß er sie durch Vorstellungen musikdramatischer Art nachträglich zur Synthese bringen muß, um ihre Ungeschiedenheit in der griechischen Ästhetik zu würdigen.

2.

Zeichensystem, Begrifflichkeit
Buchstaben
Absenz der Intention und Pseudomorphose an den Begriff.
Rekurs auf das mimische Moment
Meine Theorie Aufzeichnungen 20 ff
historische Stützen

Folgerungen	1) Notwendigkeit der Interpretation 2) die Zone der Unbestimmtheit und das Begriffliche s. Dorian
Interpretation geht nicht auf »Intentionen«	Paradoxie des Zeichens für den Gestus Interpretation als Wiederherstellung des Gestus. Nachahmung. (Originalmanuskript) Veränderung des Ausdrucks der Schrift als deren Maß. Diese Veränderung nicht unmittelbar sondern Ausdruck nur durch Begriff zu erretten, d. h. Konfrontation der Schrift mit dem Ideal des Klanges.

NB der Zusammenhang der Musik, ihr Sinn, ist also selber nicht intentional sondern gestisch

Der Ausdruck von Musik ist ihre Anweisung auf den Gestus, den sie »vormacht«.

NB die Notwendigkeit des Hereinragens der Sprache in Musik *trotz* ihrer Äußerlichkeit muß hervortreten

4.

a) Das Auseinandertreten von Musik in Text und Interpretation selber ist nicht zufällig sondern Ausdruck ihres Doppelcharakters als Mimik und Sprache. Nicht rein lesbar als mimisch, nicht rein imitierbar als sprachlich. Daher Reproduktion Form.
b) Reproduktion notwendig.
c) die Zone der Unbestimmtheit strukturell bestimmt, kein bloßer Mangel, aber keine absolute sondern fragende Unbestimmtheit.
d) Interpretation als Wiederherstellung des Gestus durch die Intention.
e) es ist nicht die Aufgabe der Interpretation Intentionen zu realisieren sondern sie durch Erfüllung zu liquidieren.
f) dies möglich von den beiden Polen
   α) die Interpretation des Zeichens durch das neumische Bild des Ganzen, den mimischen Zusammenhang.
   β) die Imitation des Schriftbildes durch die Treue gegen das Zeichen.
g) das Originalmanuskript.

5.

Veränderung aus Schrifttheorie ableiten.
historischer Charakter der Interpretation.
Kategorien und Beispiele der Veränderung.
Nachweis der Objektivität der Veränderung
Gesetzmäßigkeit der Veränderung als Entfaltung der immanenten Charaktere, das »Leben« der Werke.

Materialien zur Reproduktionstheorie[285]

Ordnung [illegible]. Und doch [illegible] Klanggruppen von Schönbergs ›Erwartung‹ gerade wieder zu Bildern für den Ausdruck dieser Musik geworden.

Der historische Charakter der Interpretation [illegible] von der Veränderung der Werke [illegible] Schrift und Bezeichnung [illegible] durch die Geschichte eine [illegible] durchlaufende Tendenz zur Verringerung und Verkleinerung. Die längste Note, die das moderne System überhaupt noch kennt [illegible], die doppelte ganze Note, ist seiner Herkunft [illegible] Verkleinerung des Einheitswertes [illegible] Notation [illegible] im Mensuralsystem: Brevis. Die Verkleinerung bezieht sich nicht auf die absolute Dauer der Töne selbst, sondern lediglich auf die [illegible] Symbole: »The very sight of the old notes such as the brevis ▭ and semibreve ◇, [illegible] slow [illegible] merely a subdivision [illegible] the whole measure and has thus become a false clue [illegible] In other words, notes that look to the modern eye [illegible] meant something quite different in their day; the brevis ▭, the semibrevis ◇ and the minima [illegible] connotations of slowness only in the minds of certain modern interpreters.« Diese Tendenz geht aber über die Verschiebung zwischen dem Mittelalter und dem modernen Notationssystem [illegible] [illegible] ist nur möglich so verstanden werden kann [illegible] Gegenwart würde man die Viertel [illegible] spielen [illegible] musikalisch [illegible] bei der [illegible] der einzelnen Noten über den [illegible] metrischen Verhältnissen [illegible] Steigerung [illegible]

LA.

Reproduktion als Form 21. Juni 1946

Weder eindeutig durchs Werk vorgeschrieben noch vom Interpreten aus entscheidbar. (Pult + Taktstock 2. Jhg. Heft 4 S. 51 ff.[286])

Bedürftigkeit des Werkes wie der Interpretation nach einander

Dazu: Interpretation als historisches Problem. Dorian 23[287], evt. Über das Dirigieren[288] 290 *[Von Dorian aus Pfeil nach unten:]* stets wieder als solches NB ergänzen: Interpretation nur durch Schrift gegeben

Reproduktion als Form Aufzeichnungen 20[289].

Problem: Text und Freiheit. Zum Problem der Reproduktion 51 bis 52[290]. (Ausgangsfrage)

Übersetzung als Form Benjamin VII[291].

Titel vielleicht: TWA

Reproduktionstheorie

Ein musikphilosophischer Versuch

Der musikalische Text + die musikalische Schrift

Was ist ein musikalischer Text Aufzeichnungen 2. Ibd. Notenschrift + Schrift *[Marginalie:]* NB Riemann, »Studien zur Geschichte der Notenschrift« 1878

Intentionslosigkeit des Textes Aufzeichnungen 4 (vielleicht an spätere Stelle)

Zone der Unbestimmtheit Dorian 27. Ungenügen der Schrift Dorian 28

Schrift und Druck Dorian 61

historische Relativität der Schrift Dorian 181

Originalmanuskript u. Kritik Dorian 224-225. NB pro Originalmanuskript: sein Bildcharakter

Wagners These vom Primat des Sinnes über die Notation Über das Dirigieren 275. *[Marginalie:]* leitet zu Sinn

erster großer Entwurf Aufzeichnungen 20-22

Auswendigspielen Aufzeichnungen 23. Schumann I 147-148

cf. ad Sinnakzente Wagner Oper und Drama, 2. Abschnitt, 3. Teil, S. 148-160. Ad Riemann I, 2, 94[292]

NB es muß hervortreten warum Musik Interpretation verlangt, nicht die Dichtung (weil diese als Intention sich selbst interpretiert und an ihr sich entfaltet, die intentionslose Musik ihr Leben an einem außerhalb ihrer selbst Seienden hat). Der Zwang der Aufführbarkeit liegt im mimetischen Moment. Schrift der Musik will nachgeahmt werden
NB die Veränderung der Texte aus ihrem mimetischen Wesen ableiten.

Verdinglichung + Subjektivität (Hauptthese: nicht Gegensatz sondern polar anwachsend)
Mangel an Bezeichnung, Arbeitsteilung und Dorian 29
Hauptbeleg Dorian 57
Funktionsteilung usw. Dorian 62 f.
Verdinglichung des Komponierens Dorian 70
[Auf der Rückseite des Blattes:] Das Ende der improvisatorischen Praxis, die Verselbständigung des Werkes, und seine Trennung von der Interpretation, stiftet zugleich deren eigene Selbständigkeit.

Reproduktion als Funktion der Verdinglichung
Reproduktion ist ein Problem auf Grund der Entfremdung von Hervorbringung und Produkt, der vergebliche Versuch der Versöhnung.
Aufzeichnungen 7. Askese und Verdinglichung Dorian 44
NB jede gute Interpretation setzt die Verfremdung des Werkes gegenüber dem vertrauten Erinnerungsbild voraus, gleichsam die Wiederholung dessen, was alle Niederschrift aller Musik einmal antat. (Cf. Kapitel 1, S. 5 unten[293])

Konstruktion + Ausdruck
[Marginalie:] nahe [?] Mimesis
»espressivo« Aufzeichnungen 9 Rubato als Ausdruck Dorian 190
Dialektik Aufzeichnungen 10 oben.
espressivo als ritardando Dorian 207[294]

seelenvoll belebt Über das Dirigieren 269 und Notiz
Ton als Umschlagsmoment Über das Dirigieren 282 und Aufzeichnungen 12
expressiver Sinn als thematische Absicht Über das Dirigieren 283
Adagiocharakter Über das Dirigieren 285
Ausdruck, Form, Beethoven + Neue Tempi Neue Tempi 5-6[295]
Diskussion von Strawinskys These[296] (im Anschluß an den Terminus espressivo)

Interpretation + Mimesis
[Marginalie:] mit Spiel wohl zusammen
»Spielen« Aufzeichnungen 2.
Entweichen der mimetischen Charaktere [Aufzeichnungen] 5
Subjektivismus und Identifikation (NB in gewissem Sinn befördert die Verdinglichung die Mimesis) Dorian 49
Affektenlehre Dorian 139-144 (NB Mimesis tritt, in der Rationalisierung, in den Dienst des Wirkungszusammenhanges)
Interpretation als Nachahmung Dorian 144
Klassizismus als verdrängte Mimesis Über das Dirigieren 316f.
Riemanns Leugnung Riemann I, 1, 9[297].

Die Idee der wahren Interpretation
Anfang der »Aufzeichnungen«
NB Auswendigspielen.
Nachahmung des nichtvorhandenen Originals (dessen Begriff hier ins Zentrum)

Die Idee der Veränderung der Werke These: die Veränderung *gesetzmäßig* im Sinne der Entfaltung der immanenten Charaktere des Werkes
Veränderung durch Gehörtwerden Aufzeichnungen 5.
Nicht nur Entweichen, auch Bilden *neuer* Charaktere Aufzeichnungen 5 (NB das neue Moment der Dialektik der Aufklärung. Dazu Wagner über die Wildheit des Scherzos der IX.

Wagner Zum Vortrag der IX. Symphonie Beethovens 240 (Aufzeichnungen 16)
[Marginalie am linken Rand:] Damit das Kapitel beginnen Dorian *28*
Insuffizienz berühmter älterer Platten Aufzeichnungen 5-6 (NB dazu Liszt[s] Bearbeitungen als Index)
Der absolutistische Darstellungsstil Dorian 69
Schnellerwerden im Rokoko Dorian 117.
Historischer Charakter der Interpretation Über das Dirigieren 290 (vielleicht an den Anfang dieses Absatzes)
Historischer Charakter der Interpretation jüngste Phase Aufzeichnungen 14
These der *objektiven* Veränderung der Werke Nachtmusik 2-3[298]. *(Begründen!)*
Gesetzmäßigkeit der Veränderung Neue Tempi 1-2[299].
Text gebrochen Neue Tempi 3. Ausgeführt 4-5[300].
Erste zus[ammenhängende] Darstellung »Zur gesellschaftlichen Lage der Musik«, II, 356 ff[301]
Veränderung des Originals Benjamin X[302]
[Marginalie am linken Rand:] evt. eigener Absatz über historischen Charakter der Interpretation *vor* »Veränderung der Werke«. Motive Aufzeichnungen 25
Hierzu noch gegen die leichtere Verständlichkeit älterer im Vergleich zu zeitgenössischer Musik. Cf. Strawinsky Autobiographie[303] *[Marginalie am linken Rand:]* NB Beispiel: der Seitensatz der h-moll-Symphonie [von Schubert]
NB Zone der Unbestimmtheit nicht Unzulänglichkeit der Notation = *historisch.* Daher Veränderung Dorian *181*

Das Subjekt-Objekt-Problem der Interpretation
Objektivität durch Tiefe der subjektiven Auffassung Aufzeichnungen 7
Kritik der starren Teilung Subjekt und Objekt ad Dorian 31. (NB aber beide Momente müssen *festgehalten* werden)
Differenzierung der »subjektiven« Seite Aufzeichnungen 7 unten

Undialektische Auffassung von Subjekt und Objekt Dorian 157-159 (suchen)
Phantasie und Treue Dorian 220.
subjektives Element objektiver Interpretation gegen Dorian 284-286
Das Nichtaufgehen des Subjekts und das Idiom Aufzeichnungen 24-25

Das Problem der Virtuosität + die Verselbständigung der Reproduktion
Übergewicht Aufzeichnungen 6-7
NB Kritik des Musikanten[304]
Rückfall der Musik ins Glücksspiel. Regression. Allmacht.

Interpretation als Rettung + Kritik
Rettung anschließen Über das Dirigieren 299 ff., Aufzeichnungen 13. *[Marginalie am linken Rand:]* mit dem folgenden zusammennehmen.

Dialektik der Retusche evt. »Rettung und Kritik«
[Marginalie am linken Rand:] vgl. »Erkenntnis«
Schumann III, p. 66 ff.[305]
Wagner Zum Vortrag der IX. Symphonie Beethoven's und Aufzeichnungen 15-16.
Wagner Zum Vortrag der IX. Symphonie Beethoven's
231 Deutlichkeit. Plastik.
232 Einwand der Undeutlichkeit
234 Deutlichkeit als Drastik (Doppelcharakter des Deutlichen: an sich und für [die Zuhörer])
235 f strukturelle Notwendigkeit der Retouche
237 Gewinn und Verlust
[Marginalie am linken Rand:] NB Tristanpartitur Vorwort[306] gilt auch für die alten Instrumente
239 wie Wagners Theorie weitertreibt.

241 Gesetz der Retouche und Vorstellungstheorie (Grund der Insuffizienz)

245 Kritik der VIII. [Symphonie von Beethoven] (und meine Notiz über IX. Durchführung-Anfang[307])
246 das retardierende Moment der Vorsicht.
255 ff (Aufzeichnungen 16-17) ausgeführte Dialektik der Retouche

[Marginalie am linken Rand:] NB bei Beethoven natürlich *nicht* die Taubheit verantwortlich

Zum Beschluß dieses Komplexes: Zus[ammenhang] mit Idee des integralen Werkes Aufzeichnungen 19 f.

Interpretation als Erkenntnis

Analyse Aufzeichnungen 2.

Schönbergs Erkenntnisideal Dorian 333

Melodie Erkennen Über das Dirigieren 271.

Deutlichkeit und Sinn Aufzeichnungen 15, Wagner Zum Vortrag der IX. Symphonie Beethoven's 231, 232, 234, 238

Wagners Formel über Erkenntnis Wagner Zum Vortrag der IX. Symphonie Beethoven's 252[308], Aufzeichnungen 16

Wagner Zum Vortrag der IX. Symphonie Beethoven's 233. Instrumentation als Konstruktion.

ad Sinn *Interpretation, Einheit der Elemente, integrales Werk + dessen Problematik*

Substituierbarkeit der Elemente Aufzeichnungen 1-2.

Dynamik und Phrasierung (zentral) Dorian 163.

Thema und Dynamik Dorian 168

Gesetz der gegenseitigem Beziehungen zueinander Über das Dirigieren 287

Hauptstelle zum Zus[ammenhang] der Elemente Wagner Zum Vortrag der IX. Symphonie Beethoven's *251* (Aufzeichnungen *16)*

Dynamisches Proportionsproblem und instrumentale Farbe

(Zus[ammenhang] der Elemente). Wagner Zum Vortrag der IX. Symphonie Beethoven's 253

Konstruktive Konsequenz neuer Tempi Neue Tempi 5-6[309]

ad Uninterpretierbarwerden *Integration + der Zerfall der Werke*

Relativismus
Aufzeichnungen 23-24

Idee des Uninterpretierbar Werdens + das Verstummen
Ideal des stummen Musizierens Aufzeichnungen 2
Lesen von Musik Aufzeichnungen 4.
Wachsende Eindeutigkeit der Texte heute Dorian 29
Erleichterung der Notation und Regression des Interpreten Dorian 42 (vom Generalbaß bis Jazz)
objektive Interpretation gerade subjektiver Musik Dorian 247
Eliminierung des Interpreten als Vermittler usw. Dorian *342 bis 344*
Ausgangstheorie Nachtmusik 1[310].
Ende der Interpretierbarkeit = Transparenz, reine Erkenntnis Nachtmusik 3[311]
Zerfall als Zerfall der Inwendigkeit Nachtmusik 4[312]
Beschwörung des Uninterpretierbaren: Furtwängleraufsatz[313]
Schein der objektivistischen Darstellung (und der objektivistischen Musik) behandeln

Tempo, Metronomisierung usw. NB hier beginnt die Behandlung der kritischen Zonen der Interpretation.

Pulsschlag Dorian 115 (mit Kritik)
Dorians Regel Dorian 180
Schnellerwerden durch Wiederholung Dorian 186
Metronom Dorian 198, 300. cf. Aufzeichnungen 10.
Wagners Modifikationslehre Dorian zwischen 227 und 239, Über das Dirigieren 281-283
Tempo als Zentralproblem Dorian 280. (begründen: Zusammenstoß von Allgemeinem und Besonderem, das Nominalismusproblem) *[Marginalie:]* versetzen
Tempo Funktion des »Melos« Über das Dirigieren 274. (Aufzeichnungen 11 f)

These des Rascherwerdens Neue Tempi 2[314]
»Leben« als Geschichte, nicht vitalistisch Metronomisierung 130f.[315] Gegen Metronomisierung alter Werke Metronomisierung 130
Starrheit und Genauigkeit Metronomisierung 132 / Tempobeziehung Metronomisierung 133
Crescendo, Dynamik
Dorian 149, 151. (NB Problem der eingelegten Dynamik bei Beethoven)
Stärke und Dissonanz Dorian 168 (cf. Wagnerarbeit IV[316])
Langsamkeit des Organum und Einzelereignis (cf. Neue Tempi[317]). Riemann I, 2, 137.[318]

Der musikalische Sinn
Aufzeichnungen 3
Dorians These von der Interpretation des Sinnes aus Schrift. Dorian 28
Phrasierung als kritisches Problem des Sinnes Dorian 159. (NB. ad intentionslose Sprache)
Sulzers Warnung vorm guten Taktteil Dorian 162
[Marginalie zu diesen Notizen am linken Rand:] zu »Einheit der Elemente« usw.
Sinn und Phrasierung Dorian *164*
Charakter durch musikalischen Inhalt: Rückschluß Dorian *227*
Rückschließende Interpretation Über das Dirigieren 268f., cf. Über das Dirigieren 285
Melodie = roter Faden = Zusammenhang Über das Dirigieren 271 und 286
Sinn und Technik Über das Dirigieren 273 (Aufzeichnungen *11)*. Ad intentionslose Sprache.
Modifikation im Dienst der Verständlichkeit Über das Dirigieren 327.
[Marginalie am linken Rand:] s. Subjektivismus Zusammenhang mit Veränderung der Werke

Dirigent (These: Koordinator der arbeitsteilig entfremdeten Funktionen)
Autorität Über das Dirigieren 264

Kritik der Theorie von der Vorstellung des Komponisten
Aufzeichnungen 2-3. Dorian 31.
hierher Kritik alles musikalischen Psychologismus d.h. die mimetischen Impulse nicht die des Subjekts
und das »Geistige« ist die gesellschaftliche Instanz.

Kritik der Lehre vom Text als Spielanweisung
Positivismus
Aufzeichnungen 2-3
Strawinskys Positivismus Dorian 329

Kritik des Historismus
Ausnutzung späterer Resourcen Dorian 81
gegen falsche Objektivität Dorian 163
»musikologisches Tempo« Dorian 180
gegen die Antithese theatralisch-historisch Dorian 293
Historische Korrektheit usw. Dorian 311, und Aufzeichnungen 10
Keine Prästabilierte Harmonie Dorian 312. Schönbergs Bach Dorian 313. *318* diskutieren
Wagner: relatives Recht der falschen Interpretation Über das Dirigieren 282.
Hauptstelle bei Wagner Über das Dirigieren 310
Argumentation Aufzeichnungen 14f
Argumentation: das Präsubjektive als Reiz Aufzeichnungen 18f.
[Marginalie am linken Rand:] natürlich auch gegen *Willkür* – aus der inneren Geschichte ableiten.

ad Sinn *»Buchstabe« + »Geist«*

Wechselwirkung von Sinn + Schrift

Für »Buchstabe« Aufzeichnungen 2

Kritik des romantischen und des positivistischen Darstellungsstils

Toscanini Aufzeichnungen 3-4

Dirigentenaufsatz Anbruch[319]. / Strawinsky Dorian 30

gegen Aufgehen in Gegenwart Aufzeichnungen 11, ad Über das Dirigieren 268

Kritik der Romantik im Zusammenhang mit Veränderung der Werke Über das Dirigieren 285-86, 294, 298

Wagner und die Manie des Übergangs Über das Dirigieren 292-93, Aufzeichnungen 12. *[Marginalie am linken Rand:] Romantik*

Das Moment der »Vernunft« bei Wagner Über das Dirigieren 299.

Diskussion der Einwände gegen Wagner. Setz[ung] und Nominalismus Über das Dirigieren 308 ff.

Objektivismus und Ressentiment Über das Dirigieren 319 f.

»mathematisches« und »idealisches Hören« Über das Dirigieren 334.

[Marginalie am linken Rand:] NB Theorie des Auswendigspielens.

Kritik des Stilbegriffs überhaupt

Anschließen an Dorian 31.

Der Stil als ein von außen an die Komposition Herangebrachtes, nur *im* Werk, nicht als Rahmen. Dazu Wagners »Gebildetheit« Wagners Theorie Über das Dirigieren 312-316.

Schrift + Instrument

Problem Aufzeichnungen 6.

Gesang Aufzeichnungen 6. Geige und Gesang Dorian 66

»Spiel«

Spiel und Risiko Aufzeichnungen 6 (vergl. Zirkus. Verschrän-

kung des mimetischen und naturbeherrschenden Elements)
Virtuos und Zirkus Dorian 299
Spiel zum Schein geworden. Zum Problem der Reproduktion 53[320]

Fetischismus: Mittel anstatt Zweck
Massenkultur und Interpretation – Problem Dorian 55.
Standardisierung des Tanzes Dorian 107
NB der Fetischismus ist nichts der Reproduktion Fremdes, sondern in der Fixierung mitgesetzt
[Marginalie am linken Rand:] NB Fetischarbeit[321]

Musik als Sprache
Dorian 44-46
Beim Interpreten Aufzeichnungen 24-25
NB paradox: das sprachliche Moment der Musik, das Mimetische, ist zugleich das Refugium des objektiv traditionalen.

Problem des Ornaments
an Dorian 89 anschließen
Schlüsselcharakter der Manieren und Generalbaß ad Dorian 92

Wagners Theorie
Bemerkung über Wagners Sprachstil Aufzeichnungen 13

Dialektisches Bild
Erste Entwürfe Aufzeichnungen 17 und 18
aufs Mimetische rückbeziehen.

Nachleben der Werke; leichte Musik als Interpretation
Ausgangstheorie Nachtmusik 1-2.[322]
Die absolute Negativität Nachtmusik 4-5[323]

Mechanische Musik
Debussys Antimechanismus Dorian 300 (dazu meine Notiz aus blauem Buch[324])

Satie Dada Jazz Dorian 305 (Mechanisierung nicht nur von außen)
Mechanisierung notwendig und nichtauthentisch Aufzeichnungen 20
Mechanisierung als Zerfall der Werke. Radio Voice.[325] Dazu aber: Mechanisierung als immanente Konsequenz des Schrumpfens der interpretativen Freiheit.

Kritik des kulinarischen Ideals (Verfall des Idiomatischen)
Aufzeichnungen 4-5
Vgl. Radio Symphony[326], Damrosch-Studie[327], Fetischarbeit.

Rubato, Zeit »stehlen«, interpretative Freiheit [Marginalie am linken Rand:] Rubato und Ornament sind die Rudimente der Improvisation im Text
Aufzeichnungen 6. Interpretation stets »Rubato« ibd.
Vorschrift der Freiheit Dorian 54-55
Ende des Generalbasses als Ende der Freiheit Dorian 157
Mozarts Rubato Dorian 189 (kritisieren). Rubato als Ausdruck Dorian 190
funktionelles Rubato Dorian 239
Freiheit Zum Problem der Reproduktion 51[328] *[Marginalie am linken Rand:]* evt. abspalten und Freiheit allein ziemlich im Anfang behandeln
Formen – Freiheit, Nominalismus – Strenge Zum Problem der Reproduktion 52f[329]
sehr gute Stelle über Verfall der Freiheit bei Beethoven Zur gesellschaftlichen Lage der Musik II, 359 unten – 360[330]
Im Vordergrund stehen der Interpretation in alter Zeit Riemann I, S. VIII

in die Nähe von Stil. *Konvention, Tradition* usw.
Dorian 72, 77.
Zum Problem der Reproduktion 52f[331]
Busoni ad Bach + Schönberg Zum Problem der Reproduktion 54[332]

Zwei Schemata

Theorie der musikalischen Reproduktion.
Erstes Schema.

I. Reproduktion, Werk, Geschichte.
II. Die Wahrheitsgehalte der Werke und ihr Zerfall.
III. Die Dialektik zwischen der Geschichte der Werke und der der Reproduktion. Reproduktion als Form.
IV. Die Geschichtsphilosophische Struktur der Veränderung der Werke, das Subjekt-Objektproblem und die Reproduktion. Das Problem der Freiheit der Reproduktion.
V. Das Problem der Tradition, die immanente Geschichtsphilosophie der Reproduktion und ihre strukturelle Bezogenheit auf die der Werke. Das Nichtaufgehen.
VI. Beethoven-Analyse.
VII. Die aktuelle Problematik der Reproduktion. Mechanisierung.
VIII. Die Konvergenz zur Erkenntnis und die Idee des Verstummens.

29. Dezember 1927.

Ts 49564

Zweites Schema

Reproduktion als Form
Der musikalische Text und die musikalische Schrift, Schrift und Instrument
Die Idee der Veränderung der Werke
Veränderung objektiv
Die Idee der wahren Interpretation und Interpretation als Erkenntnis
Relativismus
Kritik der Theorie von der Vorstellung des Komponisten
Kritik der Lehre vom Text als Spielanweisung, Positivismus
Kritik des romantischen und des positivistischen Darstellungsstils

Kritik des Historismus
Kritik des Stilbegriffs überhaupt dazu: Zu Sprache und Stil
Das Subjekt-Objekt-Problem der Interpretation
»Buchstabe« und »Geist«
Verdinglichung und Subjektivität
Reproduktion als Funktion der Verdinglichung
Konvention, Tradition, usw.
Musik als Sprache
Konstruktion und Ausdruck
Interpretation und Mimesis
Der musikalische Sinn
Interpretation, Einheit der Elemente, integrales Werk, dessen Problematik
Tempo, Metronomisierung, Crescendo usw.
Problem des Ornaments
Rubato, Zeit »stehlen«, interpretative Freiheit
Interpretation als Rettung und Kritik
Dialektik der Retusche (Wagners Theorie)
Interpretation und Zerfall der Werke; Idee des Uninterpretierbarwerdens und des Verstummens
Das Problem der Virtuosität und der Verselbständigung der Reproduktion; »Spiel«?
Fetischismus: Mittel anstatt Zweck
Kritik des kulinarischen Ideals
Mechanische Musik
Nachleben der Werke: leichte Musik als Interpretation [-] die Werke im Zeitalter ihres Zerfalles
Dialektisches Bild

NB musikalische Sprache: Brief an Dahl[333]
Aufz[eichnungen?] in grünem Buch[334]

LA
21. Juni 1946

Ts 49560

Anhang
Stichworte zum Darmstädter Seminar
1954

Musikalische Reproduktion keine Frage des Stils sondern des musikalischen Sinns. Herstellung des musikalischen Zusammenhangs. Elemente der thematischen Arbeit müssen verdeutlicht werden.
Klang tritt an die Stelle der Konstruktion. Aufräumen mit dem Begriff des gut Klingens.
Es ist falsch, die Erwartung des Publikums einzulösen
Farbe als Mittel der Formbildung.
Frage der Extreme: Plastik der Musik, Haupt- und Nebenstimmen.
Was heißt thematisch spielen? Verschiedenes Gewicht der Themen. Phrasierung.
Anfangen mit Tempo, 1. Satz von f-moll-Quartett [op. 95 von Beethoven]
Gegen den Strich musizieren. Sie lassen sich vom Musikstrom treiben anstatt die Gestalt zu realisieren, lassen sich von den Fingern treiben. Der Musikstrom muß gestaut oder durchbrochen werden.
Rudi [Kolisch]: Lob der Papiermusik.
Bei Beethoven muß die Spannung zwischen dem Subkutanen und der Oberfläche realisiert werden. Bei Schönberg hat das Subkutane die Haut verzehrt.
Kritik des Musikanten. Einseitiges Hervorheben des Idiomatischen.
Rudi [Kolisch]: allgemeine Kritik des Standes der heutigen Streichmusik[335]. Streichinstrumente veraltet müssen in chromatische umgewandelt werden.
1. Stunde allgemeine Einleitung
2. Stunde: Tempo, Dynamik, Klang, Überwiegen der Koloristik über die Konstruktion.
3./4. Stunde thematische Arbeit, op. 59 No. 2 [von Beethoven].
Über[be]tonung des guten Taktteils
Dissonanzen spielen. Frage des kritischen Tons. Harm[on]ien richtig spielen.

Frage der Deutlichkeit, Pseudo- und wirkliche Deutlichkeit
Rhythmus. In thematischer Musik gibt es nicht zwei einander gleiche Takteinheiten. Gegen den herkömmlichen Begriff des rhythmischen Spielens.
Das Metrische und das Rhythmische darf nicht verwechselt werden
Was heißt eigentlich eine Melodie spielen?
Es gibt keine Spezialprobleme für moderne Musik, der Unterschied liegt darin, daß die Moderne ganz anders vorgstellt wird und ganz anders verstanden als die traditionelle.
Tonfall, Deklamation, Mozart, Adagio aus dem g-moll-Quintett [KV 516]

Ts 49563

*

Kranichstein 1954. 13. August.

Einleitender Vortrag.[336]

Gegen hermetische Absonderung neuer Musik, keine spezialistische Sekte.
Dadurch alte museal
Versuch dies zu durchbrechen, alte aktualisieren.
Nicht modernistisch aufputzen, sondern fragen: was können wir über die traditionelle Musik an der neuen lernen.
Dies Thema des Kurses.

Ist das nun nicht »Willkür«, »Hineininterpretieren«[?]
Kritik der Unveränderlichkeit
Wille des Autors unbekannt.
Tradition als Schlamperei (soziologisch: Kulturindustrie).
Interpret vor Problemen, stets.
Aber: Gewißheit des »Richtigen«, Möglichkeit der konkreten Entscheidung.
Idee des musikalischen Sinnes. Sinnloses Musizieren
Qualität dessen vollständige Realisierung.

»Röntgenphotographie«.
Einwand dagegen
Antwort: Geschichte der Musik: Doppelstruktur, das Hervortreten des Subkutanen.
Dieser Tendenz ist Rechnung zu tragen.

Reflexion auf die musikalische *Schrift.*
Der Text enthält 3 Elemente
1) das materiale (signifikative, der Inbegriff alles durch Zeichen eindeutig Gegebenen).
2) das idiomatische (»musiksprachliche«, das aus der je vorgegebenen und das Werk einschließende[n Musiksprache zu erschließende][337]; »tempo giusto«, »wienerisch« usw.)
3) das neumische (= mimisch-gestische), die alte Unmittelbarkeit der Interpretation.

Das Problem der Interpretation wird vorgezeichnet vom Verhältnis dieser Elemente.

(2) stirbt ab. Größere Freiheit bei *älteren* Texten, Anwachsen der Strenge.
(1) ist relativ konstant aber insuffizient. Versuchung der Beschränkung darauf als das Schema. Musikalischer Positivismus + Historismus. Orgel. Sinnlosigkeit. Exkurs über Subjektivismus + Objektivismus. Jener hat Grenze an der geschichtlich-objektiven Veränderung der Werke. Dieser als Residualtheorie. Wahr ist nicht was durchs Eliminieren des Subjekts übrig bleibt: es bedarf aller subjektiven Innervation um in der Sache zu erlöschen.
Begriff des Musikalischen.
(2) Das Problem. Nicht mehr unmittelbar sondern durch (1) vermittelt, ein zu erschließendes. Analyse als Bedingung der musikalischen Interpretation.

Entfalten. Kein Rationalismus.
(a) das idiomatische Element notwendig, aber muß aufgezehrt werden. »Gegen den Strich musizieren«.

(b) Aufgabe der Analyse ist die Rekonstruktion des Neumischen aus dem Zusammenhang. Er tritt, als realisierter, anstelle von »Stil«. Reproduktion ist *mehr* als Realisierung der Analyse.

All dies nur am konkreten Werk, nicht in abstracto zu leisten, weil der Sinn sich nur in Werken konstituiert. Die *Idee* der *Interpretation* ist die der objektiven Wahrheit, ihre *Realisierung* stets unzulänglich. Es gibt keine gute Interpretation. Das Ende der Interpretation.

Einige Probleme:

1) nicht mit dem Musikstrom d. h. dem Gefälle der Tonalität sondern (bei thematischer Musik) thematisch musizieren. Verfremdung. NB. Bruckner. Vorstellung realisieren.
2) nicht von der instrumentalen Spielweise her (einschränken. NB Tonalität *zugleich* Konvention und Konstruktion.)
3) Gegen kulinarisches Musizieren, Schönheit als Selbstzweck. Atomistisches Musizieren. Glätten. Farbe, Ton als Darstellungsmittel.
4) Primat der Deutlichkeit (Mahler)
5) Beispiel wie *eine* falsch interpretierte Note Musik sinnlos machen kann Berg op. 3
das unter den Tisch gefallene [Zweiunddreißigstel] Takt 91 und die Identität mit dem Codathema Takt 51-52.
6) ad gegen den Strich: schlechte Taktteile, Dissonanzen usw. Aber auch dies nicht mechanisch.

Schließen: »Selbstverständlichkeit«. Aber es wird sich in concreto das gar nicht Selbstverständliche zeigen.

[Ad 6)] es kommt darauf an, nicht *nur* das Subkutane sondern den *Prozeß* zwischen ihm und der Oberfläche [zu] realisieren. Interpretieren heißt: Musik als Kraftfeld aufschließen.

*

NB nicht isoliert, eins kann fürs andere eintreten

3. Vorl. 15. Aug. Elemente der Darstellung.

54

1) Tempo

a) Das anti-atomistische. Ganze Formen heißt *rascher* spielen

Idee der Zeit als Augenblick.

Einheit des Ganzen.

Unterschied von Stimmung und Darstellung im Tempo.

Langsame Sätze aus [op.] 59, 2 und a-moll-Quartett [op. 132 von Beethoven].

b) Einheit eines Mannigfaltigen.

»Das« Tempo als Idee.

Rudi [Kolischs] These

Differenzierung im Satz, Schnabel. Problem der Einheit.

Antagonismus der darzustellenden Gestalt und der Totalität

c) Wie kommt man zum richtigen Tempo.

Regel: untere Schwelle die Einheit des Durchzufühlenden

" [des] Grundmetrums, etwa die Deutlichkeit der Gestalten. (Beispiel Bergsonate[338])

Extrapolation des Tempos Beispiel Beethoven op. 10,1.

Im allgemeinen ausgehen von der Vorstellung der Totalität als einem Charakter

Provisorische Regel: Einheit finden. Oft sehr schwer. Beispiel Beethoven c-moll-Konzert ₵ Allegro con brio, das A. c. b. heißt *nicht* 𝅗𝅥 = 138, sondern: so rasche ♩ daß man Halbe zählt, also etwa 𝅗𝅥 = 80.

[Marginalien am linken Rand:]

Nicht nachlassen Eroica S. 12 nach Generalpause[339]

einen Satz *im Fluß halten:* op. 59, 2, S. 3, Takt 5-6

Eroica S. 16

Tempo ist Anwalt des Ganzen gegen das Detail

Konsequenz der raschen Tempi: Klang in *stärkstem* Maß als Mittel der Differenzierung.

Tempogestaltung abhängig vom *Inhalt* der Musik, also bei

thematischer Musik flexibler als bei rhythmischer
Musik muß verweilen können, aber nicht sich selbst zuhören.

[Marginalie am linken Rand:]
Tempo + Ausdruck. Mimetisches

2) Dynamik
nicht aus der Spielweise: Neue Musik und dynamische Extreme
Gegen mittlere Dynamik. Falsch: die Stärke *durch* Modifikation aus mittlerem mf entwickeln. Richtig: von den Charakteren *und* ihrer Proportion aus.
Größerer dynamischer Umfang.
Größere dynamische Differenzierung z. B. mf + mp, F und FF usw.
Dynamisch *Luft* für die Musik schaffen (Akzente und weg)
ein Akzent kann für eine F-Fläche stehen.
Dynamik und Präsenz, Dynamik als *qualitativer* Begriff Unterschied von H⁻ und N⁻ in der Klassik.
Problem einer richtig zu spielenden Nebenstimme op. 59, 1, S. 34 Takt 9 1. Geige [= Takt 9. des 2. Satzes] op. 59, 2, 1. Satz, Takt 13
Unterschied durchbrochen kontrapunktischer und eigentlich polyphoner Darstellung, Forderung des sofortigen *Zurücktretens*

Dynamik kann für *Tempo* – als das subtilere Mittel – eintreten z. B. Eroica S. 7 [= Takt 55 f.]. Hier schon in der Komposition; oft erst durch Interpretation.

*

ad Dynamik (Fortsetzung)

Ausgangsklang nicht mf
Musik nicht als Normalzustand, darum –

3) Phrasierung.
Darstellung von Gestalten
Emanzipation vom Taktstrich.
Einheit der Zählzeit, nicht 1 betonen
gegen Binnenbetonung gebundener Noten.
Interpunktion d. h. verschiedene Grade der Phrasierung
Überkreuzung von Phrasierungen
Phrasierung und Formverlauf: Beispiel Verminderung der Phrasenunterschiede.
Betonung kritischer Noten
richtige Phrasierung d. h. sinnvoller Vortrag von Themen leistet das, was bei primitivem Musizieren das Rubato *von außen her* vergeblich unternimmt.
Regel: Vermeidung toter Noten, des Mechanischen. / Gegen Riemann tote Intervalle.
Die *strengere* moderne Darstellung ist zugleich die flexiblere.

*

ad op. 59, No. 2.

S. 1
Takt 1 *melodisch* spielen
Takt 13. Rhyth[mus] (Akzent auf e)
Auflösungsfeld spielen d. h. keine Akzente, vgl. Takt 155
Takt 21 NB das vorschlagende F [recte: E] als Konsequenz aus [Takt] 13
S. 2 Akzente im 1. System [Takt 26 f.]
Takt 35 vorher Luftpause – C nicht fallen lassen
S. 3 Takt 48 Sextensprung thematisch spielen wegen [Takt] 18
[Takt] 49 nicht als Ende des crescendo sondern subito wegen der neuen Gestalt (aber Vorsicht wegen der 2. Stelle) vgl. Eroica 1. Satz
[Takt] 51 Bratsche, quasi Variation von [Takt] 48
[Takt] 55 das »Auffangen« wie im Finale Les Adieux und Eroica 1. [Satz]

S. 4 [Takt] 78 Mittelstimme thematisch spielen
S. 5 oben [= Takt 82 f.] Phrasierung *sehr wichtig*
S. 6 [Takt] 107 Cello + Bratsche thematisch.

II. Satz nicht feierliche Stimmung sondern Thema
2. Strophe Oberstimme spielen

Anmerkungen des Herausgebers

1. Adorno hat die Kritik Toscaninis, der in den »Aufzeichnungen« eine prominente Rolle spielt, in seinem Aufsatz »Die Meisterschaft des Maestro« entfaltet, der im Oktoberheft 1958 des »Merkur« zuerst veröffentlicht wurde; vgl. jetzt Theodor W. Adorno, Gesammelte Schriften, hrsg. von Rolf Tiedemann unter Mitwirkung von Gretel Adorno, Susan Buck-Morss und Klaus Schultz, Band 16: Musikalische Schriften I-III, Frankfurt am Main 1978, S. 52-67. Die »Gesammelten Schriften« Adornos werden im folgenden mit der Sigle GS und der Bandzahl abgekürzt.

2. Vgl. Lessings Schriften gegen den Hamburger Hauptpastor Johann Melchior Goeze, besonders den dritten Abschnitt aus den »Axiomata, wenn es deren in dergleichen Dingen gibt«, der den Titel trägt: »Der Buchstabe ist nicht der Geist, und die Bibel ist nicht die Religion«.

3. Zum Schauspieler vgl. vor allem die unten S. 206 f. stehende Aufzeichnung.

4. Die Mehrzahl der im folgenden notierten Motive kehrt in Adornos Toscanini-Aufsatz »Die Meisterschaft des Maestro« wieder.

5. In dem Toscanini-Aufsatz erscheint der Name Sibelius nicht, wohl aber der Toscaninis in der 1938 geschriebenen »Glosse über Sibelius« (vgl. GS 17, S. 247-252): »Kommt man nach England oder gar nach Amerika, so beginnt der Name [scil. Sibelius'] ins Ungemessene zu wachsen. Er wird so häufig genannt wie der einer Automarke. Radio und Konzert hallen von den Tönen aus Finnland wider. Toscaninis Programme sind Sibelius offen.« (Ebd., S. 247) – Adorno hatte offenbar daran gedacht, in der »Analyse des Darstellungsstils von Toscanini« an die zum Schluß seiner Sibeliusglosse diagnostizierte Tendenz anzuknüpfen: »Seine Musik ist in gewissem Sinn die einzig ›zersetzende‹ aus diesen Tagen. Aber nicht im Sinn der Destruktion des schlechten Bestehenden, sondern dem der Calibanischen Zerstörung aller musikalischen Resultate der Naturbeherrschung, die sich die Menschheit teuer genug im Umgang mit der temperierten Skala erworben hat. Wenn Sibelius gut ist, dann sind die Maßstäbe der musikalischen Qualität als des Beziehungsreichtums, der Artikulation, der Einheit in der Mannigfaltigkeit, der Vielfalt im Einen hinfällig, die von Bach bis Schönberg perennieren. All das wird von Sibelius an eine Natur ver-

raten, die keine ist, sondern die schäbige Photographie der elterlichen Wohnung. Zu seinem Teile trägt er in der Kunstmusik zum großen Verschleiß bei, in dem ihn doch die industrialisierte leichte spielend überbietet. Aber solche Destruktion maskiert sich in seinen Symphonien als Schöpfung. Ihre Wirkung ist gefährlich.« (Ebd., S. 251 f.)

6. Adornos Aufsatz »Drei Dirigenten. Rettung: Wilhelm Furtwängler – Darstellung: Hermann Scherchen – Beschwörung: Anton Webern« war im September-Heft 1926 der »Musikblätter des Anbruch« erschienen (S. 315-319); vgl. jetzt GS 19, S. 453-459.

7. Rudolf Kolisch (1896-1978), mit dem Adorno seit seinen Wiener Studien 1925 befreundet war, studierte Violine bei Otakar Ševčic in Wien und Komposition zunächst bei Franz Schreker, von 1919 bis 1922 dann bei Arnold Schönberg. Er war der Primarius mehrerer Streichquartette; das erste, das »Wiener Streichquartett«, spielte Ende 1926 Adornos »Zwei Stücke für Streichquartett« zum ersten Mal öffentlich. 1935 planten Kolisch und Adorno, die »Theorie der musikalischen Reproduktion« gemeinsam zu schreiben, wie aus Adornos Brief an Ernst Krenek vom 23.3.1935 hervorgeht (vgl. Theodor W. Adorno und Ernst Krenek, Briefwechsel, hrsg. von Wolfgang Rogge, Frankfurt a. M. 1974, S. 72). Nach dem Kriegsausbruch 1939 kehrte Kolisch, der 1937 in die USA emigriert war, mit seinem Quartett von einer Tournee in den Vereinigten Staaten nicht nach Europa zurück. 1944 wurde Kolisch Primarius des Pro-Arte-Quartetts, das als »Quartet in residence« an der University of Wisconsin in Madison arbeitete. 1953 nahm Kolisch, der zum erstenmal nach Kriegsende in Europa konzertierte, an den Darmstädter Ferienkursen für Neue Musik teil, wo er Kurse und Konzerte gab sowie Seminare zu Interpretationsfragen hielt. Vgl. auch Adornos Aufsatz von 1956 »Kolisch und die neue Interpretation« (GS 19, S. 460-462).

8. Adorno bezieht sich, wie aus der Angabe unten S. 74 hervorgeht, auf Schumanns Aphorismus »Das öffentliche Auswendigspielen«: »Nennt es nun ein Wagstück, oder Charlatanerie, so wird das doch immer von großer Kraft des musikalischen Geistes zeugen. Wozu auch diesen Souffleurkasten? warum den Fußblock an die Sohle, wenn Flügel am Haupt sind? Wißt ihr nicht, daß ein noch so frei angeschlagener Accord, von Noten gespielt, noch nicht halbmal so frei

klingt, wie einer aus der Phantasie? O, ich will aus eurer Seele antworten: allerdings kleb' ich am Hergebrachten, denn ich bin ein Deutscher, – erstaunen würde ich freilich in etwas, brächte plötzlich die Tänzerin ihre Touren, der Schauspieler oder Deklamator seine Rollen aus der Tasche, um sicherer zu tanzen, spielen, deklamieren; aber ich bin wirklich wie jener Philister, der, als einem Virtuosen die Noten vom Pult fielen und dieser trotzdem ruhig weiter spielte, siegend ausrief: ›Seht, seht! das ist eine große Kunst! der kann's auswendig!‹« (Robert Schumann, Gesammelte Schriften über Musik und Musiker, hrsg. von Heinrich Simon, Leipzig o. J., Bd. I, S. 147f.)

9. Gemeint ist vermutlich Stefan Auber, der dem Kolisch-Quartett von 1939 bis 1942 angehörte, wie aus einer Stelle von Adornos »Reflexionen über Musikkritik« von 1967 hervorzugehen scheint: »Ich erinnere mich, daß ich einmal meinem Freund Rudolf Kolisch über einen neuen Cellisten seines Quartetts sagte, er hätte doch einen so abscheulichen Ton, und Kolisch antwortete: ›Aber das ist doch das Beste an ihm‹.« (GS 19, S. 583)

10. In Adornos Rundfunkvortrag über Franz Schreker von 1959, 1963 in die Sammlung von Aufsätzen »Quasi una fantasia« aufgenommen (vgl. jetzt GS 16, S. 368-381), heißt es dazu: »Die Fermente seines Klanges sind allesamt, vollständig von der Unterhaltungsmusik absorbiert worden, sei es, daß deren Matadore an Schreker lernten, sei es, daß seine Art, Klänge gleichsam abzuschmecken, an sich bereits zur Sphäre U tendierte und daß diese von selbst hervorbrachte, was bei ihm alles andere sein möchte als Amusement. [. . .] Dabei wollte Schreker mit seinen Mixturen hoch hinaus. Der Rausch, den sie bereiten, meinte die Schimäre eines spülend Lauen, Chaotischen wie aus dem hetärischen Zeitalter, einer Musik ohne irgendein fest Umrissenes, gleichviel in welcher Dimension. Sie sträubt sich dagegen wie gegen Verdinglichung; Kunst, die noch die eigenen, rein-musikalischen Stoffe verübelt, als wären sie außermusikalisch, kunstfremd.« (Ebd., S. 374)

11. Die »Vorlesungen über Musik mit Berücksichtigung der Dilettanten« des Schweizers Hans Georg Nägeli (1773-1836) waren 1826 bei Cotta erschienen; darin heißt es: »Aber ein anderer gieng, bald nach ihm [scil. Haydn] aufgetreten, ihm zur Seite, der in jenem theo-

retischen Sinne ein ›unreiner‹ Instrumental-Componist genannt werden muß, der die Cantabilität mit dem freyen, instrumentalischen Ideenspiel auf tausendfach bunte Art vermengte und vermischte, vermöge seiner Erfindungsgabe, seines Ideenreichthums eine ungeheure Fermentation in das ganze Kunstgebiet hineinbrachte, dadurch vielleicht mehr mißbildend als bildend, aber mächtig aufregend wirkte, und das war Mozart. Gefühlsheld und Phantasieheld in gleichem Maaße, voll Drang und Kraft, erscheint er in vielen seiner Compositionen augenblicklich – um mich bildlich auszudrücken – als Schäfer und Krieger, als Schmeichler und Stürmer; weiche Melodien wechseln häufig mit scharfem, schneidendem Tonspiel, Anmuth der Bewegung mit Ungestüm. Groß war sein Genie, aber eben so groß sein Genie*fehler,* durch Contraste zu wirken. Fehlerhaft war dieß hier um so mehr, als er das Nichtinstrumentalische mit dem Instrumentalischen, die Cantabilität mit dem freyen Tonspiel in steten Contrast setzte. Unkünstlerisch war es, wie es in allen Künsten ist, wenn etwas *nur durch sein Gegentheil* Wirkung gewinnen muß. Mißbildend war es, zunächst für ihn selbst, weil man, so wie das ewige Contrastiren zum Hauptwirkungsmittel erhoben wird, die *schöne Proportion der Theile* eines Kunstwerks außer Acht läßt.« (Hans Georg Nägeli, Vorlesungen über Musik mit besonderer Berücksichtigung der Dilettanten. Mit einem Vorwort zum Neudruck von Martin Staehelin, Darmstadt 1983 [Reprographischer Nachdruck der Ausgabe Stuttgart und Tübingen, Cotta 1826], S. 157)

12. Vgl. E. T. A. Hoffmanns »Beethovens Instrumental-Musik«, das vierte Stück der »Kreisleriana« aus den »Fantasiestücken in Callots Manier«.

13. Der Violinist und Dirigent Joseph Joachim (1831-1907), der mit Franz Liszt, Hans von Bülow und Johannes Brahms befreundet war, gründete 1869 das Joachim-Quartett, mit dem er in ganz Europa Beethoven-Abende gab.

14. Der spanische Violinist und Komponist Pablo de Sarasate (eigentlich: Pablo Martín Sarasate y Navascuez, 1844-1908) unternahm Tourneen durch Europa und Amerika; überliefert wird, daß er über höchste technische Fähigkeiten verfügte und ein stark ausgeprägtes Vibrato hatte.

15. Der polnische Pianist und Komponist Ignacy Jan Paderewski (1860-1941) arbeitete neben seinen Konzert- und Lehrverpflichtungen seit 1936 an einer Neuedition der Werke Chopins, die erst nach dem Ende des Zweiten Weltkriegs erscheinen konnte. Er gab zahlreiche Konzerte in den USA.

16. Der amerikanische Dirigent und Cellist Alfred Wallenstein (1898-1983) arbeitete als Solo-Cellist mit Toscanini in New York, bevor er sich als Dirigent betätigte; er leitete von 1943 bis 1956 das philharmonische Orchester von Los Angeles, wo Adorno ihn gehört haben dürfte.

17. Der in Frankreich geborene Dirigent Pierre Monteux (1875 bis 1964) leitete von 1935 bis 1952 das Symphonie-Orchester von San Francisco. Er dirigierte das mit seiner Unterstützung gegründete NBC-Orchester, bevor Toscanini dessen Leitung übernahm.

18. Vladimir Samojlowitsch Horowitz (1904-1989), der 1933 Toscaninis Tochter geheiratet hatte, ging 1939 endgültig in die USA, wo er bis 1953 durch zahlreiche Konzerte und Schallplattenaufnahmen wirkte.

19. Der aus Litauen stammende amerikanische Violinist Jascha (eigentlich: Iossif Robertowitsch) Heifetz (1901-1987) gab 1917 sein amerikanisches Debüt in der New Yorker Carnegie Hall.

20. Frederick Dorian, The History of Music in Performance. The Art of Musical Interpretation from the Renaissance to Our Day, New York 1942. – Adorno hat das Buch ›mit dem Bleistift in der Hand‹ durchgearbeitet und die als Marginalien notierten Stichworte anschließend in das Heft mit den »Aufzeichnungen zu einer Theorie der musikalischen Reproduktion« übertragen. Der leichteren Lesbarkeit und Übersicht wegen werden die Zitate aus dem Buch von Dorian unmittelbar im Anschluß an Adornos Stichworte in Kursivschrift und mit Anführungszeichen wiedergegeben; da Adorno bei der Notierung der Seitenzahlen Satzanfänge auf der vorangehenden Seite nicht immer berücksichtigt hat, wurden die Seitenangaben in solchen Fällen stillschweigend korrigiert. – Frederick Dorian (1902-1991), der vor seiner amerikanischen Einbürgerung Friedrich Deutsch hieß und

aus Wien stammte – der Komponist Max Deutsch (1892-1982) war sein Bruder –, studierte Musikwissenschaft bei Guido Adler (er promovierte 1924 mit einer Arbeit über »Die Fugenarbeit in den Werken Beethovens«), Kompositionstheorie und Dirigieren bei Anton Webern, Klavier bei Eduard Steuermann und war Mitglied des Wiener Schönbergseminars. Seit 1930 arbeitete Dorian als Musikkritiker und war im Jahr 1934 der Pariser Musikkorrespondent der »Frankfurter Zeitung«. In den USA war er Professor an der Carnegie-Mellon University.

21. Adorno bezieht sich auf die Fermaten im Thema des ersten Satzes der 5. Symphonie von Beethoven. Die Marginalie in Dorians Buch auf S. 27 lautet vollständig: »aber die Fermate muß nach dem *Sinn* entschieden werden d. h. dem Zusammenhang«.

22. Die Notiz bezieht sich auf das vorangehende Zitat aus Dorian, S. 31. – Der Verweis auf die »Phänomenologie des Geistes« von Hegel zielt vermutlich auf jene berühmte Stelle gegen Ende der Einleitung, die Adorno auch in der mittleren seiner »Drei Studien zu Hegel« (vgl. GS 5, S. 247-380; dort S. 295) auszugsweise zitiert: »Diese *dialektische* Bewegung, welche das Bewußtsein an ihm selbst, sowohl an seinem Wissen, als an seinem Gegenstande ausübt, *insofern ihm der neue wahre Gegenstand* daraus *entspringt*, ist eigentlich dasjenige, was *Erfahrung* genannt wird. Es ist in dieser Beziehung an dem soeben erwähnten Verlaufe ein Moment noch näher herauszuheben, wodurch sich über die wissenschaftliche Seite der folgenden Darstellung ein neues Licht verbreiten wird. Das Bewußtsein weiß *etwas*, dieser Gegenstand ist das Wesen oder das *Ansich*; er ist aber auch für das Bewußtsein das *Ansich*; damit tritt die Zweideutigkeit dieses Wahren ein. Wir sehen, daß das Bewußtsein jetzt zwei Gegenstände hat, den einen das erste *Ansich*, den zweiten das *Für-es-Sein dieses Ansich*. Der letztere scheint zunächst nur die Reflexion des Bewußtseins in sich selbst zu sein, ein Vorstellen nicht eines Gegenstandes, sondern nur seines Wissens von jenem ersten. Allein wie vorhin gezeigt worden, ändert sich ihm dabei der erste Gegenstand; er hört auf, das Ansich zu sein, und wird ihm zu einem solchen, der nur *für es* das *Ansich* ist; somit aber ist dann dies: *das Für-es-Sein dieses Ansich*, das Wahre, das heißt aber, dies ist das *Wesen* oder sein *Gegenstand*. Dieser neue Gegenstand enthält die Nichtigkeit des ersten, er ist die über ihn gemachte Erfahrung.«

(Georg Wilhelm Friedrich Hegel, Werke. Auf der Grundlage der Werke von 1832-1845 neu edierte Ausgabe, Redaktion: Eva Moldenhauer und Karl Markus Michel, Bd. 3: Phänomenologie des Geistes, Frankfurt a.M. 1970, S. 78 f.)

23. Adornos Aufsatz »Über den Fetischcharakter in der Musik und die Regression des Hörens«, der die ersten Erfahrungen mit dem amerikanischen Musikleben und mit der Funktion Toscaninis in diesem niederlegte, ist im Sommer 1938 entstanden und in demselben Jahr in der »Zeitschrift für Sozialforschung« erschienen; vgl. jetzt GS 14, S. 14-50.

24. In einer Aufzeichnung zum Beethovenbuch notierte Adorno: »Bei der Betrachtung des Originalmanuskripts von Beethovens Geistertrio: die außerordentlich weitgehenden Abkürzungen können nicht auf Eile zurückgeführt werden. Beethoven hat relativ wenig komponiert. Auch sind – anders als bei Schubert – zahllose Änderungen im Ms [Manuskript] zu finden. Dagegen ist auffällig die *Undeutlichkeit* der Niederschrift. Sie wirkt wie eine bloße *Stütze* des Eigentlichen, nämlich des dargestellten Klanges.« (Adorno, Beethoven. Philosophie der Musik. Fragmente und Texte, hrsg. von Rolf Tiedemann, Frankfurt a. M. 1993, S. 29, fr. 20)

25. Von Adornos »Versuch über Wagner« (vgl. jetzt GS 13, S. 7-148) lagen zur Zeit der Niederschrift dieser Aufzeichnungen nur das erste, sechste, neunte und zehnte Kapitel gedruckt vor; sie waren 1939 in der »Zeitschrift für Sozialforschung« erschienen. Das vierte – »Klang« überschriebene – Kapitel (ebd., S. 59-67) des Wagnerbuches handelt von der Dissonanz, vgl. vor allem S. 62 f.

26. Die Schumannstelle, die Dorian (S. 227) in englischer Übersetzung gibt, lautet im deutschen Original: »Du weißt, wie wenig ich die Streite über Temponahme leiden mag und wie für mich das innere Maß der Bewegung allein unterscheidet. So klingt das schnellere Allegro eines Kalten immer träger, als das langsamere eines Sanguinischen. Beim Orchester kommen aber auch die Massen in Anschlag: rohere, dichtere vermögen dem Einzelnen wie dem Ganzen mehr Nachdruck und Bedeutung zu geben; bei kleineren, feineren hingegen, wie unserm Firlenzer, muß man dem Mangel der Resonanz

durch treibende Tempos zu Hilfe kommen.« (Robert Schumann, Gesammelte Schriften, a.a.O., Bd. I [Anm. 8], S. 137 [»Schwärmbriefe«])

27. Schönbergs Bearbeitungen der Choralvorspiele »Komm, Gott, Schöpfer, Heilger Geist« für großes Orchester und »Schmücke dich, o liebe Seele« für Soloviolоncello und großes Orchester sowie des Präludiums und der Fuge in Es-Dur für großes Orchester.

28. Adorno hat das Stichwort von Strawinskys Positivismus im zweiten Teil der »Philosophie der neuen Musik« ausgeführt: »Der impliziten Philosophie nach gehört er zum Machischen Positivismus: ›das Ich ist nicht zu retten‹; der Verhaltensweise nach zu einer westlichen Kunst, deren höchste Erhebung das Werk Baudelaires ausmacht, wo das Individuum kraft der Sensation die eigene Annihilierung genießt. Daher setzt die mythologisierende Tendenz des Sacre die Wagnerische fort und verneint sie zugleich. Strawinskys Positivismus hält sich an die Vorwelt wie an eine faktische Gegebenheit. Er konstruiert ein imaginär-völkerkundliches Modell des Präindividuierten, das er exakt herauspräparieren möchte.« (GS 12, S. 153)

29. Die numerierten Stichworte sind Marginalien auf der S. 343 von Dorians Buch.

30. Vgl. Richard Wagner, Gesammelte Schriften und Dichtungen, 2. Auflage, Bd. 8, Leipzig 1888, S. 261-337.

31. »Wollen wir uns erklären, was wir unter dem ›Effekte‹ zu verstehen haben, so ist es wichtig, zu beachten, dass wir uns gemeinhin des näherliegenden Wortes ›Wirkung‹ hierbei nicht bedienen. Unser natürliches Gefühl stellt sich den Begriff ›Wirkung‹ immer nur im Zusammenhange mit der vorhergehenden *Ursache* vor: wo wir nun unwillkürlich zweifelhaft werden, ob ein solcher Zusammenhang bestehe, oder wenn wir sogar darüber belehrt sind, dass ein solcher Zusammenhang gar nicht vorhanden sei, so sehen wir in der Verlegenheit uns nach einem Worte um, das den Eindruck, den wir z. B. von Meyerbeer'schen Musikstücken erhalten zu haben vermeinen, doch irgendwie bezeichne, und so wenden wir ein ausländisches, unserem natürlichen Gefühle nicht unmittelbar nahe stehendes Wort, wie

eben diesen ›Effekt‹ an. Wollen wir daher genauer Das bezeichnen, was wir unter diesem Worte verstehen, so dürfen wir ›Effekt‹ übersetzen durch ›Wirkung ohne Ursache‹.« (Zit. Wagner-Lexikon. Hauptbegriffe der Kunst- und Weltanschauung Richard Wagner's in wörtlichen Anführungen aus seinen Schriften zusammengestellt von Carl Fr. Glasenapp und Heinrich von Stein, Stuttgart 1883, S. 129f.)

32. Adorno bezieht sich vermutlich auf mündliche Äußerungen Bruno Walters oder vielleicht auch auf Berichte Thomas Manns, denn Walters Buch zu Fragen der musikalischen Interpretation ist erst 1957 erschienen; vgl. Bruno Walter, Von der Musik und vom Musizieren, Frankfurt a. M. 1957. Dort schreibt Walter: »[. . .] daß von aller Thematik am stärksten die der langsamen Sätze, vor allem des Beethovenschen Adagio, zu mir sprach. Mir war, als ob in ihm sich mir das tiefste Geheimnis der Musik offenbarte. Doch konnte es nicht fehlen, daß ich Spuren dieses ›Ewig Weiblichen‹ in der Musik, das uns hinanzieht, bis weit jenseits des Gebietes der langsamen Sätze, ja auch in zahlreichen thematischen Bildungen der schnellen Sätze empfand. Eigentlich schien mir jedes Thema oder Motiv, das auch energisch-männlichste, noch Spuren aus jener Welt des gesanglich Urmusikhaften zu enthalten, so wie wiederum fast alle Gesangsphrasen auch Elemente von Bewegtheit und rhythmischen Leben aufwiesen. [. . .] Denn es wäre falsch, unter *Gesangsthema* nur zu verstehen, was wir wirklich singen können, das heißt eine Phrase, deren Wiedergabe menschlicher Stimmumfang und vokale Technik gewachsen sind. [. . .] *Gesanglich* im eigentlichen Sinn ist also alles, was von Instrument oder Stimme in singendem Ausdruck – cantabile – vorgetragen werden kann und soll, und genau das ist es, was wir unter dem Begriff des Lyrischen zu verstehen haben.« (Ebd., S. 67f.)

33. Vgl. dazu Adornos »Versuch über Wagner«, GS 13, S. 97f.

34. Ernest Newman – The Life of Richard Wagner, Bd. 4: 1866 bis 1883, New York 1946 – schreibt an der angegebenen Stelle über Anklänge der Wagnerschen Schriften in Nietzsches Werk: »The reference to *On conducting* relates to the paragraph in which Wagner protests against the superficial ›classicity‹ of most of the time-beaters of the day, the tradition of which he traces back to Mendelssohn's ›cheerful-Grecian‹ conducting of great works. Neither of these citations has

any particular bearing on music and Greek tragedy as such.« – Newman bezieht sich auf das unveröffentlichte »Vorwort an Richard Wagner« zu »Die Geburt der Tragödie« vom Februar 1871, worin es heißt: »Von Ihnen weiß ich es, mein verehrter Freund, von Ihnen allein, daß Sie mit mir einen wahren und falschen Begriff der ›griechischen Heiterkeit‹ unterscheiden und den letzteren – den falschen – im Zustande ungefährdeten Behagens auf allen Wegen und Stegen antreffen; von Ihnen weiß ich gleichfalls, daß Sie es für unmöglich halten, von jenem falschen Heiterkeitsbegriffe aus zur Einsicht in das Wesen der Tragoedie zu kommen. Deshalb gebührt Ihnen die nachfolgende Erörterung über Ursprung und Ziel des tragischen Kunstwerks, in der der schwierige Versuch gemacht worden ist, unsere in diesem ernsten Probleme so wunderbar consonierende Empfindung in Begriffe zu übertragen.« (Friedrich Nietzsche, Nachgelassene Fragmente 1869 bis 1874. Kritische Studienausgabe, hrsg. von Giorgio Colli und Mazzino Montinari, Band 7, München 1988, S. 351)

35. Adorno denkt hier vermutlich an die Stelle aus seinem »Versuch über Wagner«, GS 13, S. 53 f.

36. Diese Notiz ist dem Hrsg. rätselhaft geblieben.

37. Der Violinist Adolf Busch (1891-1952) gründete 1913 das nach ihm benannte Streichquartett, das in den zwanziger Jahren des vergangenen Jahrhunderts berühmt wurde.

38. Das Argument kehrt in Adornos Aufsatz »Tradition« (GS 14, S. 127-142) wieder, wo es gegen Ende heißt: »Der Historismus verleumdet sein eigenes Prinzip, die Gewalt der Geschichte. Deshalb wird er der Sache nirgends gerecht. Seine Treue ist Untreue etwa in der Insistenz auf den zu Bachs Zeiten üblichen Originalbesetzungen. Daß damals, wie das Musikalische Opfer und die Kunst der Fuge kraß demonstrieren, Besetzungen und Instrumentalfarben nicht ebenso eindeutig waren wie heute, bekundet einen zentralen Unterschied: Farbe fungierte nicht im gleichen Sinne als der integrale Bestandteil der Komposition, zu dem es seit dem neunzehnten Jahrhundert bis zur Klangfarbenmelodie und der Organisation von Farbskalen als Reihen geworden war.« (Ebd., S. 141 f.) – Vgl. auch Adornos Vorlesung »Funktion der Farbe in der Musik«, die er 1966 während der

Darmstädter Ferienkurse für Neue Musik hielt; eine Transkription nach den erhaltenen Tonbandaufnahmen erschien 1999 in dem von Heinz-Klaus Metzger und Rainer Riehn herausgegebenen Sonderband »Darmstadt-Dokumente I« der »Musik-Konzepte«.

39. Vgl. Text, S. 58.

40. Wagner schreibt dort: »Durch die Einführung der Ventile ist für dieses Instrument unstreitig so viel gewonnen, daß es schwer fällt, diese Vervollständigung unbeachtet zu lassen, obgleich dadurch das Horn unleugbar an der Schönheit seines Tones, wie namentlich auch an der Fähigkeit, die Töne weich zu binden, verloren hat.«

41. In seinem Aufsatz »Bach gegen seine Liebhaber verteidigt« (vgl. jetzt GS 10·1, S. 138-151) hat Adorno diesen Gedanken entwickelt: »Der objektiv in seinem Werke verschlossenen Dynamik gebührt einzig eine Interpretation, welche sie realisiert. Denn die wahre Interpretation ist die Röntgenphotographie des Werks: ihr obliegt, im sinnlichen Phänomen die Totalität all der Charaktere und Zusammenhänge hervortreten zu lassen, welche Erkenntnis aus der Versenkung in den Notentext sich erarbeitet.« (Ebd., S. 149)

42. Vgl. Richard Wagner, Zum Vortrag der neunten Symphonie Beethoven's, in: Gesammelte Schriften und Dichtungen, 2. Aufl., Neunter Band, Leipzig 1888, S. 231-257.

43. Zu Mahlers *Instrumentationspraxis* vgl. auch den zweiten Abschnitt des Kapitels »Dimensionen der Technik« von Adornos »Mahler«, GS 13, S. 261-266.

44. In seinem Aufsatz »Zur Vorgeschichte der Reihenkomposition« (GS 16, S. 68-84) schreibt Adorno: »Daß die idée fixe der ›Phantastischen Symphonie‹, Allegorie der Traumgeliebten, im letzten Satz verzerrt und erniedrigt wird, sagt zugleich etwas Absolut-Musikalisches. Berlioz fühlt noch gleichsam, was er dem traditionellen, statischen Begriff des Themas, auch des Beethovenschen, antut, und wagt dennoch das bei Beethoven Undenkbare – die Idee von Verzerrung und Karikatur deckt, wie vielfach in der Geschichte der Musik, das Hervortreten der neuen Qualität. Bei Wagner dann ist, unter dem Na-

men der psychologischen Variation, was bei Berlioz noch schockhaft war, bereits zur unproblematischen, selbstverständlichen und durchgebildeten Kompositionstechnik: zum Stilprinzip geronnen.« (S. 71)

45. Adornos Aufzeichnungen dazu für das Beethovenbuch, vgl. Theodor W. Adorno, Beethoven. Philosophie der Musik, a. a. O. [Anm. 24], S. 167-172, besonders S. 167 f.

46. Adorno bezieht sich auf seinen 1928 in den »Musikblättern des Anbruch« innerhalb der »Motive II« veröffentlichten Aphorismus (vgl. jetzt GS 18, S. 14 f.) und seine Opernkritik von 1932 (vgl. jetzt GS 19, S. 219 f.). Vgl. auch Adornos »Zur Bilderwelt des Freischütz« (GS 17, S. 36-41) von 1961/62.

47. Die Formulierung entstammt Victor Hugos Brief vom 6. Oktober 1859 an Charles Baudelaire: »Que faites-vous quand vous écrivez ces vers saisissants: *Les Sept Vieillards* et *Les Petites Vieilles* que vous me dédiez, et dont je vous remercie? Que faites-vous? Vous marchez. Vous allez en avant. Vous dotez le ciel de l'art d'on ne sait quel rayon macabre. Vous créez un frisson nouveau.« (Zit. Baudelaire, Œuvres complètes. Texte établi, présenté et annoté par Claude Pichois, Bd. II, Paris: Bibliothèque de la Pléiade 1976, S. 1129) – Von Edgar Allan Poe ist in Hugos Brief nicht die Rede.

48. Zu einer Neuinszenierung des »Lohengrin« in Frankfurt am Main schrieb Adorno im Februar 1930: »Ein Wort noch über die Pointe der Aufführung: den fortgelassenen Schwan. In der Tat, was kann ein Regisseur viel anderes tun, als das symbolische Märchentier streichen? Naiv-leibhaftig löst es Komik aus, ornamental-stilisiert nicht minder; einen aus Lichtkegeln konstruierten Schwan lassen sich die reaktionären Opernhörer nicht gefallen. So bleibt vom Schwan der Hohlraum zurück. Nur freilich, fällt der Schwan auf der Bühne, muß ihm Text und Musik nach; es geht nicht an, daß Lohengrin die Leere, der er entsteigt, mit seinem Danklied besingt, sondern jedes Wort und jeder Ton im Lohengrin, der von der Macht der Bilder lebt, müßte mit ihm getilgt werden; und was würde dann aus dem Werk? Oder vielmehr: wie ist es heute wirklich um den ›Lohengrin‹ bestellt?« (GS 19, S. 170) – Vgl. auch Adornos Aufsatz »Bürgerliche Oper« von 1955 (jetzt GS 16, S. 24-39, besonders S. 25).

49. Der aus Schottland stammende Pianist und Komponist Eugen d'Albert (1864-1932), der bei Franz Liszt in Weimar studiert hatte, spielte vor allem Bach und Beethoven. Er lehrte seit 1907 an der Berliner Musikhochschule. Unter seinen Schülern waren Edwin Fischer und Wilhelm Backhaus. – In einer Konzertkritik sagt Adorno von d'Albert, daß er »stets noch [der] größte aller Pianisten« sei (GS 19, S. 314).

50. Vgl. Adornos Aufsatz »Die gegängelte Musik« von 1948, jetzt GS 14, S. 51-66.

51. Diesen zentralen Gedanken hat Adorno in den folgenden Jahren immer wieder in seine Arbeiten eingesenkt – so in den Schönbergaufsatz von 1952 (vgl. jetzt GS 10·1, S. 152-180, dort S. 163), in »Das Altern der neuen Musik« (vgl. jetzt GS 14, S. 143-167, dort S. 157) und in »Vers une musique informelle« (vgl. jetzt GS 16, S. 493-540, dort S. 521).

52. Vgl. Adornos Aufzeichnung zum Verhältnis »der späten Werke des mittleren Beethoven« zu Schubert in den Fragmenten zum geplanten Beethovenbuch (Adorno, Beethoven. Philosophie der Musik, a. a. O. [Anm. 24], S. 137 f.). – Im letzten Kapitel seines Mahler-Buches schreibt Adorno über eine Stelle des sechsten Satzes des »Lieds von der Erde« (Philharmonia-Partitur, S. 117, um Ziffer 37): »Häufig wird die Musik ihrer selbst müde und klafft auseinander: dann trägt der innere Fluß über das Versiegen des äußeren hinweg, das Leere wird selber Musik.« (GS 13, S. 296)

53. Vgl. den Nachweis in Anm. 6.

54. Die 1929 im »Anbruch« gekürzt veröffentlichte Arbeit nahm Adorno 1964 vollständig in die Sammlung »Moments musicaux« auf (vgl. jetzt GS 17, S. 52-59).

55. Vgl. ebd., S. 53 f.

56. Vgl. ebd., S. 52 f.

57. Vgl. ebd., S. 52 u. S. 56 f.

58. So auch schon wörtlich in Adornos Brief vom 29. Februar 1940 an Walter Benjamin (vgl. Theodor W. Adorno / Walter Benjamin, Briefwechsel 1928-1940, hrsg. von Henri Lonitz, Frankfurt a. M. ²1995, S. 417).

59. Vgl. Anm. 8.

60. Im »Getreuen Korrepetitor« heißt es in den Interpretationsanalysen von Anton Weberns op. 3 und op. 12: »Bei der Entfaltung der Interpretationsprobleme orientiere ich mich diesmal nicht systematisch an verschiedenen Kompositionsdimensionen und ihrem Verhältnis zueinander, sondern lasse mir die verschiedensten Darstellungsfragen vom Verlauf der Lieder so zutragen, wie sie in der Praxis des Probierens sich enthüllt haben. Ein gewisses Maß an Willkür ist dabei zu konzedieren. Denn in jedes Kunstwerk, und in die Interpretation eines jeglichen davon führen buchstäblich unendlich viele Zugänge; die Wahl eines jeden hat etwas Zufälliges; nur müssen alle im Kern des Werks, in seinem Gehalt konvergieren. Auch der Möglichkeiten, ein Werk zu verfehlen, sind unendlich viele, und es läßt da ebenfalls mit Beliebigem sich anheben. Aber von jedem solchen Beginn her müßten, wofern er aus der wahren Anschauung des Gebildes abgeleitet ist, seine sämtlichen Interpretationsaspekte sich eröffnen. So sagte mir Rudolf Kolisch einmal bei einer Probe, es sei relativ gleichgültig, was man beanstande; stimme irgend etwas nicht, und fange man nur an einer Stelle kritisch zu arbeiten an, so folge daraus das andere von selbst.« (GS 15, S. 252)

61. Ernst Wendel (1876-1938) leitete von 1909 bis 1935 das Philharmonische Staatsorchester der Freien Hansestadt Bremen. Adorno hörte am 8. März 1926 Wendels Aufführung der 4. Symphonie von Ernst Krenek in Frankfurt a. M.; seine Konzertkritik, vgl. GS 19, S. 70f. – Im Dezember 1924 schrieb Adorno über ein Frankfurter Museumskonzert: »Ernst Wendel holte sich seine Hauptererfolge mit Bruckners Achter und Beethovens Neunter. Wie dankbar man immer dem gründlichen Orchestererzieher und erfahrenen Dirigenten für den Aufbau seiner Montagskonzerte sein muß – hinter dem frenetischen Beifall seines Publikums birgt sich doch viel Bequemlichkeit und das Behagen, hier der Mühe um Fremdes und Problematisches in Programm und Darbietung ledig zu sein. Wendel läßt sich von der Tradition tragen, und es gibt keine tragfähige Dirigiertradition mehr

heute; wo sie etwa im Handwerk noch geblieben, fehlt ihr der menschliche Ausweis, und auch im Handwerk vermag sie freischwebend sich nicht zu bewahren. Die Aufführung der Neunten war sachlich und kontrolliert, man freute sich zu hören, wie klug Wendel etwa in der Coda des ersten Satzes der Versuchung billiger Nibelungendämonie auswich. Aber es fehlt ihm die Kraft des Beginnens, die Sicherheit, ein in jahrzehntelanger Musikübung fixiertes Werk von seiner und der eigenen Wurzel aus neu zu hören; der Mut auch, irrend über sich hinauszugreifen; kurz, all das, was an Furtwängler stets wieder zwingt mit ganzer Gewalt. Es ist nicht die Schuld der Dirigenten, daß kein anderes, geborgenes, umfangenes Dirigieren mehr gelingen mag, wohl aber bezeichnet es die Tragik der Situation, der jetzt der reproduzierende wie der produzierende Künstler sich gegenüberfindet. Bei aller ernsten Absicht bleibt Wendel letztlich verhaftet in kapellmeisterlicher Routine.« (GS 19, S. 44 f.)

62. Der in Wien geborene Violinist Fritz Kreisler (1875-1962).

63. Von dem Tenor Enrico Caruso (1873-1921) haben sich in Adornos Nachlaß mehrere Tonträgeraufnahmen erhalten.

64. Adorno verweist auf Benjamins Vorwort – »Die Aufgabe des Übersetzers« – zu den Baudelaire-Übertragungen, die 1923 in Heidelberg erschienen waren; auf der genannten Seite heißt es: »Um das echte Verhältnis zwischen Original und Übersetzung zu erfassen, ist eine Erwägung anzustellen, deren Absicht durchaus den Gedankengängen analog ist, in denen die Erkenntniskritik die Unmöglichkeit einer Abbildtheorie zu erweisen hat. Wird dort gezeigt, daß es in der Erkenntnis keine Objektivität und sogar nicht einmal den Anspruch darauf geben könnte, wenn sie in Abbildern des Wirklichen bestünde, so ist hier erweisbar, daß keine Übersetzung möglich wäre, wenn sie Ähnlichkeit mit dem Original ihrem letzten Wesen nach anstreben würde. Denn in seinem Fortleben, das so nicht heißen dürfte, wenn es nicht Wandlung und Erneuerung des Lebendigen wäre, ändert sich das Original. Es gibt eine Nachreife auch der festgelegten Worte.« (Walter Benjamin, Gesammelte Schriften. Unter Mitwirkung von Theodor W. Adorno und Gershom Scholem hrsg. von Rolf Tiedemann und Hermann Schweppenhäuser, Bd. IV·1, hrsg. von Tillman Rexroth, Frankfurt a. M. 1972, S. 12)

65. Hugo Riemann, Handbuch der Musikgeschichte, Erster Band: Altertum und Mittelalter (bis 1300), Erster Teil: Die Musik des Altertums, 3. von Alfred Einstein durchgesehene Auflage, Leipzig 1923.

66. Riemann gibt an der Stelle die »schematische Übersicht der einzelnen Felder [...], in welche das gesamte Gebiet der Musikwissenschaft sich für die Betrachtung scheidet«, wie er sie bei Aristeides Quintilianus gefunden hat – einem griechischen Musiktheoretiker, dessen Schrift περὶ μουσικῆς vermutlich aus dem 3. Jahrhundert n. Chr. stammt.

67. Riemann übersetzt den Terminus mit »Vortrag«.

68. Hugo Riemann, Handbuch der Musikgeschichte, Erster Band: Altertum und Mittelalter (bis 1300), Zweiter Teil: Die Musik des Mittelalters (bis 1450), Leipzig 1920.

69. Adorno bezieht sich auf den zweiten Teil des ersten Bandes von Riemanns »Handbuch«.

70. Der französische Musikwissenschaftler Edmond de Coussemaker (1805-1876) ist vor allem durch seine Forschungen auf dem Gebiet der mittelalterlichen Musik und Musiktheorie hervorgetreten.

71. Der Musikwissenschaftler Oskar Fleischer (1856-1933), Schüler von Philipp Spitta, lehrte von 1895 bis 1925 in Berlin; Verfasser der dreiteiligen »Neumenstudien« (1895-1904).

72. Vgl. das im Text S. 78 schon gegebene Zitat.

73. Auf die Wiedergabe der Akzentzeichen und der ihnen entsprechenden Zeichen der Neumenschrift ist hier verzichtet worden.

74. Adorno verweist auf die Erstausgabe von Benjamins Schrift aus dem Jahre 1928; vgl. jetzt Walter Benjamin, Ursprung des deutschen Trauerspiels, in: Gesammelte Schriften, Bd. I·1, hrsg. von Rolf Tiedemann und Hermann Schweppenhäuser, Frankfurt a. M. ²1978, S. 387-389.

75. Bei Riemann ist die zweite Buchstabenfolge über der ersten plaziert.

76. Das Fragezeichen ist im Manuskript durch einen Pfeil mit der Notiz »Das Bild reicht an die Konstruktion nicht unmittelbar heran« verbunden.

77. Adorno dachte dabei vermutlich vor allem an die in Anm. 74 nachgewiesenen Seiten aus Benjamins »Ursprung des deutschen Trauerspiels«.

78. Ingolf Dahl (1912-1970), aus einer schwedisch-deutschen Familie stammend, studierte zunächst an der Kölner Musikhochschule, mußte 1933 Deutschland verlassen und ging, nach einigen Jahren in der Schweiz, 1938 in die USA, wo er in Kalifornien bei Nadia Boulanger studierte; von 1945 bis 1970 lehrte er an der University of Southern California. Er war als Komponist, Dirigent und Pianist tätig; er arbeitete mit Strawinsky zusammen. – Dahl hatte am 2. Januar 1949 an Adorno geschrieben und dessen Forderung, auch Jazz müsse sich notieren lassen, kritisiert. Die ›beanstandete Formulierung‹ stand in Adornos Rezension zweier Bücher über Jazz (vgl. jetzt GS 19, S. 382-399) und war bereits 1941 erschienen, sie lautet: »Die Autorität der geschriebenen Musik bleibt hinter der Freiheit der gespielten in jedem Augenblick spürbar. Dann aber ist die Grenze der Notierbarkeit keineswegs bloß der Volksmusik, sondern ebenso der Kunstmusik gesetzt. Ein Beethovenquartett, von dem nichts gespielt würde, als was in den Noten steht, wäre sinnlos. Endlich ist in der vorgeschrittenen europäischen Kunstmusik mittlerweile die Kunst der rhythmischen Notation so weit entwickelt, daß zumindest die von Sargeant als unnotierbar betrachteten Improvisationen durchaus ins Bereich des Notierbaren fallen. Der Gedanke, daß ein Solochorus von Armstrong graphisch nicht faßbar sein soll, während ein Quartettstück von Webern sich aufschreiben läßt, ist einigermaßen riskiert – zu schweigen von der Frage, wo und wann in der tatsächlichen Jazzpraxis überhaupt noch improvisiert wird.« (Ebd., S. 383 f.) – Adornos Antwort an Dahl, von der ein Typoskriptdurchschlag sich erhalten hat, datiert vom 10. Januar 1949: »Lieber Herr Dahl, [Absatz] haben Sie schönsten Dank für Ihren Brief. Ich halte die Probleme, die Sie anrühren, für so wichtig, daß ich versuchen möchte, meinen Stand-

punkt etwas näher zu begründen. [Absatz] Zunächst die Frage der Notation. Die von Ihnen beanstandete Formulierung, daß Jazz sich müsse notieren lassen, wenn es bei Webern möglich ist, hatte den Sinn, mystische Vorstellungen über die vermeintliche Irrationalität der ›improvisatorischen‹ solo chorusses zu zerstören. Aber das soll natürlich nicht bedeuten, daß ich dafür im Ernst einen blinden Rationalismus in Notationsfragen verträte. Nun würde ich sagen, daß *alle* musikalische Notation bis zu einem gewissen Grad ungenau ist, d. h. daß jede Musik, wenn man in einem allerstrengsten Sinn nur das spielt, was da steht, sinnlos wird. Das Lesen von Musik hat zwei Dimensionen. Die eine bezieht sich auf die Notation, die andere auf etwas, was ich das tonsprachliche Element nennen möchte, also Kenntnis und Erfahrung von dem *strukturierten* Material, das jeglichem Kompositionsstil zugrundeliegt. Diese Sprache muß man aber bei jeder Beethovenschen Violinsonate genau so gut kennen wie beim Jazz: keine Notation spielt in einem Vakuum, sondern jede ist eine Art von Fixierung innerhalb eines jeweils vorgegebenen tonsprachlichen Kontinuums. Der Jazz stellt bis zu einem gewissen Grad ein solches Kontinuum sui generis dar, und was das Unnotierbare daran scheint, ist in Wahrheit nichts anderes als daß das zugrundeliegende tonsprachliche Kontinuum – vulgär gesprochen, der Inbegriff aller Konventionen des Vortrags – von dem der abendländischen Kunstmusik einigermaßen verschieden ist. Ist man aber einmal in diesem Kontinuum drin, so kann man genau so gut notieren, wie sich abendländische Kunstmusik innerhalb ihres Kontinuums notieren läßt. Die Schwierigkeiten der Jazznotation beziehen sich ja ohnehin im wesentlichen bloß auf die Differenzen in der Skandierung der Hauptstimme von den rhythmischen Eckpunkten des Begleitsystems. Diese Differenzen kann man ganz weitgehend aufschreiben – aber lebendige Musik wird natürlich daraus nur, wenn man den Sinn der Sprache als ganzer versteht. Und selbst das ist der technischen Bestimmung keineswegs so ganz entzogen. Eines der wichtigsten tonsprachlichen Elemente scheint mir die Differenzierung zwischen Gegenakzenten und Synkopen, die in der abendländischen Musik bis zur jüngsten Entwicklung im allgemeinen miteinander gleichgesetzt waren. [Absatz] Ihr zweiter Hauptpunkt, das Verhältnis von ›dirty notes› usw. zu sozialem Sadismus [vgl. jetzt GS 19, S. 386-388], läßt sich nicht isoliert, in rein musikalischen Begriffen beantworten. Die betreffenden Stellen meiner Kritik beziehen sich auf eine gesellschaftliche Theorie des Jazz, die ich 1936 in unserer Zeitschrift für Sozialforschung pseudonym veröffentlicht habe. Der betreffende Aufsatz war in Europa geschrieben und ist in vielen Details überholt, aber zur Grundkonzeption stehe ich heute noch, und da ich selber die Arbeit nur in einem Sammelband habe, können Sie sie vielleicht nachschlagen: ›Über Jazz‹, von Hektor Rottweiler, Zeitschrift für Sozialforschung, Jahrgang V, 1936, S. 235 ff. [Vgl. jetzt GS 17, S. 74-100.] Heute nur soviel: der Ursprung jener Trübungen in nicht rationalisierten Musiksystemen ist mir wohl vertraut. Aber ich glaube, das Entscheidende beim Jazz ist die Frage, was die Pseudomorphose von amerikanischer Tanzmusik mit jenen exotischen Elementen bedeutet. Und da meine ich allerdings, daß es sich nicht bloß um einen Reiz, sondern um ein Ausdrucksmoment von Versagen, Antasten, Degradieren handelt, tief verwandt der gesamten Sitte der ›adaptation‹ in der gegenwärtigen Massenkultur. Anstatt daß die konventionelle Musiksprache aufgelöst wird, wird sie starr festgehalten, zugleich aber als gewissermaßen unwahre dargestellt und einer Art hämisch-burschikoser Prozedur unterworfen, und es ist wesentlich diese *Funktion,* der das Hereinnehmen der exotischen Elemente dient. Das Phänomen, das ich meine, läßt sich etwa der Sprechweise eines ressentimenterfüllten Mädchens vergleichen, das, wenn es den Namen eines eleganten Restaurants hört, sagt: ›da bin ich noch nicht gewesen, das ist zu foin für mich‹, oder der eines Antiintellektuellen, der anstatt Psychologie immerzu Pychologie sagt. Aber wie gesagt, solche Beobachtungen gewinnen ihren Stellenwert einzig in einer prinzipiellen Jazztheorie, nicht als isolierte Interpretationen. Ich gebe Ihnen gern zu, daß der strenge hot jazz solche valeurs in den Dienst einer anderen Ausdrucksfunktion stellt, aber der Jazz als Massenphänomen der amerikanischen Gesellschaft, der in diesem Zusammenhang mich hauptsächlich interessierte, macht eben das daraus, was ich versucht habe zu bezeichnen. Übrigens ist das auch ganz auf der Linie der Schlagertexte – nicht umsonst hieß einer der berühmtesten vor zehn Jahren ›Goddy. Goody‹. [. . .] Hoffentlich auf sehr bald! [Absatz] Herzlichst Ihr«.

79. Zitat aus der letzten Strophe des Gedichts »Der sterbende Mensch« von Karl Kraus.

80. Der Ausspruch Gustav Mahlers ist von dem Künstler Alfred Roller, der seit 1902 an der Wiener Hofoper als Bühnenbildner und auch

gelegentlich als Regisseur mit Mahler zusammenarbeitete, überliefert: »Bei jeder neuen Inszenierungsarbeit erfand er gleichsam die Sprache der Bühne von neuem, war er, aus seiner ungeheuren Kraft verschwenderisch schöpfend, jung, unternehmungslustig, und kühn wie am ersten Tage. Er verspottete das bequeme Schema und verabscheute den Ariadnefaden der Routine. In solchem Zusammenhange fiel einmal das immer wieder und immer falsch zitierte Wort von der Tradition. ›Was Ihr Theaterleute Eure Tradition nennt, das ist Eure Bequemlichkeit und Schlamperei!‹« (Alfred Roller, Mahler und die Inszenierung, in: Musikblätter des Anbruch 2 [1920], S. 273)

81. Vgl. Ferruccio Busoni, Entwurf einer neuen Ästhetik der Tonkunst. Neue Ausgabe mit einem Nachwort von H. H. Stuckenschmidt, Wiesbaden 1954, S. 25 f.

82. Der Pianist und Komponist Arthur Schnabel (1882-1951) spielt als pianistischer Interpret und auch als Herausgeber der Beethovenschen Klaviersonaten in Adornos Aufzeichnungen eine ähnlich prominente Rolle wie Toscanini, Walter und Furtwängler. Im »Getreuen Korrepetitor« lobt Adorno Schnabels »volles, rundes Pianissimo, ein Klang, wie ihn Arthur Schnabel unvergleichlich meisterte« (GS 15, S. 263).

83. »Was heißt denn aber *musikalisch* sein? Du bist es nicht, wenn du, die Augen ängstlich auf die Noten gerichtet, dein Stück mühsam zu Ende spielst; du bist es nicht, wenn du (es wendet dir jemand etwa zwei Seiten auf einmal um) stecken bleibst und nicht fortkannst. Du bist es aber, wenn du bei einem neuen Stück das, was kommt, ohngefähr ahnest, bei einem dir bekannten auswendig weißt, – mit einem Worte, wenn du Musik nicht allein in den Fingern, sondern auch im Kopf und Herzen hast.« (Robert Schumann, Gesammelte Schriften über Musik und Musiker, hrsg. von Heinrich Simon, Bd. 3, Leipzig o. J., S. 171)

84. Vgl. GS 12, S. 55 und 180 f.

85. Ein amerikanisches Vokalquintett, dem die deutschen »Comedian Harmonists« nacheiferten; vgl. auch unten S. 172.

86. Es ist – wie das Notenbeispiel zeigt – die erste der »Trois Nouvel-

les Études. Composées pour la *Méthode des Méthodes* de Moscheles et Fétis«, die in f-moll geschrieben ist, also nur vier vorgezeichnete b hat.

87. Vgl. Adorno, Fragment über Musik und Sprache (jetzt in: GS 16, S. 251-256); das »Fragment« ist 1956/57 – drei Jahre nach der Abfassung – erstmals publiziert worden.

88. Der Violinist Arnold Rosé (1863-1946) gründete 1883 das Rosé-Quartett, mit dem er die beiden ersten Streichquartette von Schönberg uraufführte. Er war bis 1938, als er nach England emigrieren mußte, auch Konzertmeister an der Wiener Hofoper und durch seine Heirat mit Justine Mahler Schwager von Gustav Mahler. – Vgl. auch Adornos Wiedergabe dieser Erinnerung im »Getreuen Korrepetitor« (GS 19, S. 319).

89. Mit diesem Begriff bezeichnet Riemann die Intervalle zwischen den »Grenztönen der aufeinanderfolgenden einzeln aufgefaßten Motive« im Gegensatz zu allen »in ein Motiv hineinfallenden Melodieschritten«, die nach ihm als »geschehende Tonbewegung aufzufassen« seien (Hugo Riemann, System der musikalischen Rhythmik und Metrik, Leipzig 1903, S. 14).

90. So in Adornos Handschrift.

91. Vgl. Text, S. 213-286.

92. Der Pianist und Komponist Eduard Steuermann (1892-1964), der bei Ferruccio Busoni und Arnold Schönberg studiert hatte und zu den bedeutendsten Interpreten der zweiten Wiener Schule gehörte, war 1925 Adornos pianistischer Lehrer in Wien und bis zu seinem Tode ein enger Freund; vgl. Adornos Nachruf »Nach Steuermanns Tod« (jetzt GS 17, S. 311-317) und »Die Komponisten Eduard Steuermann und Theodor W. Adorno. Aus ihrem Briefwechsel«, in: Adorno-Noten, hrsg. von Rolf Tiedemann, Berlin 1984, S. 40-72.

93. Adornos Aufsatz »Arnold Schönberg. 1874-1951« war 1953 in der »Neuen Rundschau« erschienen; vgl. jetzt GS 10·1, S. 152-180; zum »Subkutanen« vgl. besonders S. 157 und S. 166.

94. Unter diesem Titel war 1932 in der »Frankfurter Zeitung« ein Aufsatz Adornos erschienen, der sich kritisch mit Paul Hindemith befaßte und den Adorno später in seine Dokumentation »Ad vocem Hindemith« (vgl. GS 17, S. 222-229) aufnahm. Vgl. auch Adornos gleichnamigen Aufsatz, der auf Erfahrungen mit der musikalischen Jugendbewegung zurückgeht und die Kritik von 1932 fortführt, GS 14, S. 67-111.

95. Beethovens Trio B-Dur für Klavier, Violine und Violoncello op. 97 ist 1811 entstanden und 1816 gedruckt erschienen.

96. Der Liederkreis »An die ferne Geliebte«, op. 98, 1816 komponiert.

97. Die Ouvertüre zum »Märchen von der schönen Melusine«, op. 32 von Felix Mendelssohn-Bartholdy.

98. Vgl. etwa das Kapitel »Vom Tempo« in Walters Buch »Von der Musik und vom Musizieren« (a. a. O. [Anm. 32], S. 33-52), wo es an einer Stelle heißt: »Stellen wir also fest, daß der Begriff vom richtigen Tempo für ein Tonstück relativ ist, ungefähr wie der von einer richtigen Kleidung für eine Reise, während der er mit dem Wetter und anderen Umständen wechseln muß. Trotzdem heißt unser Problem nicht *Tempi,* sondern bleibt das *Tempo.* [...] Der richtige Vortrag, den uns das richtige Tempo ermöglichen soll, bedarf einer unstarren Kontinuität der Tempoführung – nennen wir sie ›anscheinende Kontinuität‹.« (Ebd., S. 35)

99. Schuberts 1819 komponierte Klaviersonate A-Dur (D 664).

100. Der Urheber dieses Satzes ist nicht ermittelt; Adorno zitiert ihn auch in seiner »Einleitung in die Musiksoziologie« (GS 14, S. 304).

101. Vermutlich ist die Notiz auf S. 91 gemeint.

102. Über den 1901 in Frankfurt am Main geborenen Pianisten und Begleiter Heinz Hirschland konnte nichts ermittelt werden. In einem Brief an Alban Berg vom 27. Dezember 1925 nennt Adorno ihn einen Freund des Komponisten Karol Rathaus.

103. Vgl. Anm. 83.

104. Vgl. die Takte 40 bis 50 des ersten Satzes der VII. Symphonie von Anton Bruckner.

105. Die von Adorno mehrfach in seinem Werk zitierte Wendung ist von dem Schönbergschüler Karl Linke (1884-1939) überliefert worden; vgl. Arnold Schönberg. Mit Beiträgen von Alban Berg, Paris von Gütersloh, K. Horwitz, Heinrich Jalowetz, W. Kandinsky, Paul Königer, Karl Linke, Robert Neumann, Erwin Stein, Ant. v. Webern, Egon Wellesz, München 1912, S. 78.

106. Der Komponist Erich Wolfgang Korngold (1897-1957) war eines der berühmtesten Wunderkinder dieses Jahrhunderts (Verdrängte Musik. Berliner Komponisten im Exil, hrsg. von Habakuk Traber und Elmar Weingarten, Berlin 1987, S. 285); er studierte 1907 bis 1911 bei Alexander von Zemlinsky und komponierte Opern. Für Max Reinhardt arrangierte er 1929 »Die Fledermaus« und 1931 »Die schöne Helena« von Jacques Offenbach. Zwischen 1938 und 1945 schrieb er vor allem Filmmusiken für Hollywood, sein 1945 entstandenes Violinkonzert basiert auf Filmmusikthemen (ebd.).

107. Agathe Calvelli-Adorno (1868-1935), die Schwester von Adornos Mutter, war Pianistin und lebte im Hause Wiesengrund.

108. Von Oktober 1952 bis August 1953 arbeitete Adorno an der Hacker-Foundation in Beverly Hills. Die Untersuchungen, die Adorno dort wissenschaftlich dirigierte, waren der Astrologiekolumne der »Los Angeles Times« gewidmet (vgl. The Stars down to Earth, in GS 9·2, S. 7-120) und dem Fernsehen (vgl. dazu die beiden 1953 veröffentlichten Aufsätze »Prolog zum Fernsehen« und »Fernsehen als Ideologie« in GS 10·2, S. 507-533).

109. Der Aphorismus von Karl Kraus, den Adorno zitiert und der bei der Titeltaufe eines Adornoschen aus den »Minima Moralia« Pate stand (vgl. GS 4, S. 33 f.), ist dem Kapitel »Eros« der Sammlung »Nachts« entnommen: »Vieles, was bei Tisch geschmacklos ist, ist im Bett eine Würze. Die meisten Verbindungen sind darum so unglücklich, weil diese Trennung von Tisch und Bett nicht vorgenommen

wird.« (Karl Kraus, Schriften, hrsg. von Christian Wagenknecht, Bd. 8: Sprüche und Widersprüche. Pro domo et mundo. Nachts, Frankfurt a.M 1986, S. 315)

110. Vgl. dazu Adornos Interpretationsanalyse von Schönbergs Phantasie für Geige mit Klavierbegleitung op. 47 aus dem »Getreuen Korrepetitor«, jetzt in: GS 15, S. 313-337.

111. Vgl. den Nachweis in Anm. 41.

112. Vgl. dazu etwa das Argument aus Adornos »Metakritik der Erkenntnistheorie«: »Ihre Subjektivität wenden sie daran, von der Wahrheit das Subjekt zu substrahieren und Objektivität stellen sie sich als Rest vor. Alle prima philosophia bis zu Heideggers Anspruch der ›Destruktion‹ war wesentlich Residualtheorie; Wahrheit soll sein, was übrig bleibt, die Neige, das Allerschalste.« (GS 5, S. 23)

113. Die ausführliche Wiedergabe der Anekdote findet sich in Adornos »Einleitung in die Musiksoziologie«: »[Der Dirigent] hat [dem Publikum] gegenüber [. . .] a priori etwas Propagandistisch-Demagogisches. Daran erinnert der alte Witz von der Besucherin des Gewandhauskonzerts, die ihre sachverständige Nachbarin bittet, sie doch darauf aufmerksam zu machen, wenn Nikisch zu faszinieren beginne.« (GS 14, S. 293)

114. Über Adornos Erfahrung in Reutenen bei Ravensburg mit dem von Thomas Mann sehr geschätzten Tenor Karl Erb (1877-1958) konnte nichts ermittelt werden.

115. Der 1914 in Budapest geborene Pianist Julian von Károlyi, der seit 1972 in Würzburg lehrte, bevorzugte in seinen Konzerten das romantische Repertoire.

116. Adorno hielt den Vortrag (vgl. jetzt GS 14, S. 143-167) im April 1954 im Süddeutschen Rundfunk.

117. Im Schönbergteil der »Philosophie der neuen Musik« sagt Adorno: »Alle Formen der Musik, nicht erst die des Expressionismus, sind niedergeschlagene Inhalte. In ihnen überlebt was sonst vergessen

ist und unmittelbar nicht mehr zu reden vermag. Was einmal Zuflucht suchte bei der Form, besteht namenlos in deren Dauer. Die Formen der Kunst verzeichnen die Geschichte der Menschheit gerechter als die Dokumente.« (GS 12, S. 47)

118. Adorno, Kolisch und Steuermann leiteten während der »Internationalen Ferienkurse für Neue Musik« ein Seminar über »Neue Musik und Interpretation«; vgl. die unten im Anhang wiedergegebenen Stichworte Adornos zu seinem einleitenden Vortrag am 13. August 1954 und zu den Seminaren.

119. Vgl. Adornos »Einführung in die zweite Kammersymphonie von Schönberg« in GS 18, S. 627-629.

120. Vgl. vor allem Adornos Aufsatz »Funktionalismus heute«, GS 10·1, S. 375-395.

121. Der wiedergegebene Rhythmus tritt im ersten Satz, Takt 49 zum erstenmal auf, die »Quint« ist die thematische e-h der 1. Violine in Takt 1.

122. Adornos Aufsatz von 1953, vgl. jetzt GS 18, S. 149-176.

123. Im »Getreuen Korrepetitor« wird Schönbergs vermutlich mündlich überlieferte Verteidigung des Textes gegen den Interpreten wiederholt: »Dieser [scil. der Text] hat, durchweg in der Wiener Schule, vor dem, was der Interpret als Sinn sich zurecht gelegt hat, im Konfliktfall den Vorrang; Schönberg selbst hat beim Probieren zuweilen das einmal Geschriebene gegen den eigenen Impuls verfochten.« (GS 15, S. 300)

124. Vgl. das erste Kapitel des mit Max Horkheimer gemeinsam geschriebenen Buchs: »Begriff der Aufklärung« (jetzt GS 3, S. 19-60, bes. S. 27, 33 f. und S. 40).

125. Die Orgelbewegung, die nach 1900 einsetzte, suchte den sogenannten alten – also ›vororchestralen‹, aus dem Orgelbau des 19. Jahrhunderts herrührenden – Klang der Orgel wiederherzustellen, weil er der polyphonen Darstellung mehr entspräche. Die Orgelbewegung

ist die erste Gestalt des Historismus in der Musikdarstellung. Adornos Kritik ist entfaltet in seinen Aufsätzen »Bach gegen seine Liebhaber verteidigt« (GS 10·1, S. 138-151) und »Tradition« (GS 14, S. 127-142).

126. Der Organist Helmut Walcha (1907-1991), weltweit bekannt für seine Bachkonzerte, spielte seit 1946 an der Orgel der Dreikönigskirche in Frankfurt a. M.

127. In der »Philosophie der neuen Musik« heißt es: »Beethoven hat den Sinn von Tonalität aus subjektiver Freiheit reproduziert.« (GS 12, S. 70) Vgl. auch Adornos Fragmente über Beethoven, a. a. O. [Anm. 24], S. 82-96.

128. Gemeint sind die Variationen für Klavier op. 27. Über Steuermanns Deutung ist nichts ermittelt.

129. Sie steht in dem Aphorismus »Fächer« aus der »Einbahnstraße«: »Das Vermögen der Phantasie ist die Gabe, im unendlich Kleinen zu interpolieren [. . .]«. (Benjamin, Gesammelte Schriften, a. a. O. [Anm. 74], Band IV·1, S. 117)

130. Der Violinist und Bratschist Michael Mann (1919-1977) war bis 1957 als Orchestermusiker in den USA beschäftigt; er studierte anschließend Germanistik und lehrte von 1962 bis zu seinem Tod in Berkeley. Näheres über seine Teilnahme an dem Kranichsteiner Seminar ist nicht ermittelt.

131. Vgl. den VIII. und IX. Abschnitt von »Brahms the Progressive« aus Schönbergs »Style and Idea«.

132. Vgl. das »Fragment über Musik und Sprache« (GS 16, S. 251 bis 256).

133. Nach der Überlieferung soll das Wort anläßlich der Aufführung des Streichquartetts op. 130 (mit der Großen Fuge) an den Primarius Ignaz Schuppanzigh gerichtet worden sein: »Glaubt Er, daß ich an seine elende Geige denke, wenn der Geist zu mir spricht?«

134. Vgl. den dritten Text von »Ad vocem Hindemith«, GS 17, S. 222-229, besonders S. 227 f.

135. Das Adjektiv »crack« als Slangausdruck sagt soviel wie »first-class«, »excellent«.

136. Möglicherweise kommt dem nicht mitgeteilten »Ausspruch« Kolischs eine Stelle aus dessen Aufsatz »Über die Krise der Streicher« nahe: »Die Priester dieser Religion haben nur ein einziges Ideal auf ihren Altar gestellt, das des *schönen Tons.* Dieser ist insofern eine außermusikalische Kategorie, als kein Werk der Kunstmusik je für ›schönen Ton‹ geschrieben wurde. Seine ausschließliche Pflege substituiert ein subjektiv-sensualistisches, musikalisch-indifferentes Moment für alle dynamisch-expressiven der Musiksprache. Unter seiner Ägide vollzieht sich musikalische Reproduktion jenseits ihrer eigentlichen Aufgabe, der Enthüllung von Konstruktion, lediglich als Kult des Schönen.« (Rudolf Kolisch, Über die Krise der Streicher, Darmstädter Beiträge zur Neuen Musik I, hrsg. von Wolfgang Steinecke, Darmstadt 1958, S. 86)

137. Artur Schnabels Ausgabe der 32 Klaviersonaten und der Diabelli-Variationen von Beethoven in Einzelheften erschien in den zwanziger Jahren im Ullstein-Verlag, eine amerikanische Ausgabe in zwei Bänden in den dreißiger Jahren bei Simon & Schuster.

138. Vgl. die oben S. 43-46 wiedergegebenen Zitate aus Wagners Schrift »Über das Dirigieren« (S. 287, 290, 294 und 298).

139. Vgl. dazu die Stelle aus der »Philosophie der neuen Musik«: »Die Sonate erfüllt prinzipiell bei durchgehaltener Identität wenn nicht der wörtlichen Zählzeit, so doch des Tempos die Form mit einer solchen Mannigfaltigkeit rhythmisch-melodischer Gestalten und Profile, daß die ›mathematische‹ und in ihrer Objektivität anerkannte, quasi-räumliche Zeit tendenziell mit der subjektiven Erfahrungszeit zusammenfällt im glücklichen Einstand des Augenblicks.« (GS 12, S. 180)

140. Vgl. Rudolf Kolisch, Tempo and Character in Beethoven's Music, in: Musical Quarterly 29 (1943), S. 169-187 (Part I) und S. 291-312 (Part II). Eine deutsche – von Regina Busch besorgte – Ausgabe erschien als Doppelheft 1976/77 in den von Heinz-Klaus Metzger und Rainer Riehn herausgegebenen Musik-Konzepten.

141. »Lieber Junge, die überraschenden Wirkungen, welche viele nur dem Naturgenie der Komponisten zuschreiben, erzielt man oft genug ganz leicht durch richtige Anwendung und Auflösung der verminderten Septimenakkorde.« (Zit. Paul Bekker, Beethoven, Stuttgart/Berlin 1922, S. 189)

142. Vgl. auch Adornos Analyse der Klaviersonate op. 1 von Alban Berg in seiner Bergmonographie von 1968 (GS 13, S. 374-382).

143. So in Adornos Handschrift.

144. Vgl. Takt 95.

145. Gemeint sind offenbar die Takte 132 ff.

146. Vermutlich denkt Adorno an folgende Stelle aus Schönbergs Aufsatz »Faschismus ist kein Exportartikel«: »Homophone Musik konzentriert die ganze Entwicklung auf eine Hauptstimme und weist den anderen Elementen eine untergeordnete Bedeutung zu, indem sie nur die Entwicklung und Verständlichkeit der Hauptstimme fördert. Daher kann diese Hauptstimme sich aus sich selbst heraus recht schnell entwickeln und sehr verschiedene Charaktere, Stimmungen, Gestalten, Bilder und Klänge produzieren, ohne den Zusammenhang zu verlieren, ohne unverständlich zu werden. Dagegen verlangt die kontrapunktische Methode die volle Aufmerksamkeit des Hörers nicht nur für eine Hauptstimme, sondern gleichzeitig für zwei, drei oder mehr Stimmen, von denen keine die Hauptstimme ist, denn sie sind alle Hauptstimmen.« (Arnold Schönberg, Stil und Gedanke. Aufsätze zur Musik, hrsg. von Ivan Vojtěch, Frankfurt a. M. 1976, S. 318)

147. Vgl. Takt 65 ff. in der 1. Violine.

148. Vgl. etwa Eroica, 1. Satz, Takt 93 f. – In seinen Aufzeichnungen zu Beethoven hat Adorno dazu notiert: »Weiter die Sitte ein crescendo auf 1, und dem Höhepunkt, mit einem piano abzuschließen (oft bemerkt). Wahrscheinlich Mittel der in der stufenarmen und begrenzten Harmonik stets sehr schwierigen *Verknüpfung.* Anstatt daß es schließt und dann (brüchig) ein Neues beginnt, wird durchs *p* der

Schluß verweigert – man könnte von dynamischem Trugschluß reden – zugleich Widerstand gegen das Gefälle der Kadenz. – Vielleicht hat sich der Spätstil durch das Hervortreten solcher Eigenheiten gebildet – nach dem klassizistischen Maß wäre er Manierismus. – Die Violinsonaten sind besonders reich an solchen Eigenheiten.« (Adorno, Beethoven. Philosophie der Musik, a. a. O. [Anm. 24], S. 87 f.)

149. In der von Adorno benutzten Eulenburg-Ausgabe der siebzehn Streichquartette.

150. Adorno denkt offenbar an das ff der Takte 55 f.

151. In Adornos Aufsatz von 1953 heißt es: »Die Kunst wird entkunstet: sie tritt selber als ein Stück jener Anpassung auf, der ihr eigenes Prinzip widerspricht.« (GS 10·1, S. 135)

152. Diese häufig von Adorno verwendete und als von Schönberg herrührend bezeichnete Formel ist wörtlich nicht zu finden. Möglicherweise hat Adorno sie aus zwei von ihm angestrichenen Stellen aus Schönbergs »Style and Idea« zusammenkomponiert; in »Brahms the Progressive» heißt es: »The most important capacity of a composer is to cast a glance into the most remote future of his themes or motives.« (Style and Idea, a. a. O., S. 80) Und in »The Blessing of the Dressing«: »I used to say that the composer must be able to look very far ahead in the future of his music. It seems to me this is the masculine way of thinking: thinking at once of the whole future, of the whole destiny of the idea, and preparing beforehand for every possible detail.« (Ebd., S. 216 f.)

153. Steuermann spielte am 22. August 1954 das gesamte Klavierwerk von Schönberg in der Reihenfolge op. 11, 25, 19, 33 und 23. (Vgl. Volker Rülke, Zu Eduard Steuermann, in: Von Kranichstein zur Gegenwart. 50 Jahre Darmstädter Ferienkurse, hrsg. von Rudolf Stephan, Lothar Knessl, Otto Tomek, Klaus Trapp, Christopher Fox, Darmstadt 1996, S. 114)

154. Der Pianistin und Malerin Maria Proelss (1892-1962), mit der Adorno seit seiner Jugend bekannt war, schrieb er einen Nachruf, in

dem es heißt: »Höchst unkonventionell spielte sie Klavier: ohne Rücksicht, einzig aus dem Bedürfnis heraus, den Sinn der Musik zu realisieren. Ihm ordnete sie die technische Erscheinung gänzlich unter: erkannte Technik unabhängig vom je Darzustellenden kaum an, in schroffem Gegensatz zu den positivistischen Stromlinienmusikern, die in den letzten vierzig Jahren obenauf kamen. Was ihr vorschwebte, nannte sie mit Vorliebe fluidieren.« (GS 19, S. 465)

155. Vgl. Chopin, op. 10, Nr. 12, Takt 27.

156. Vgl. dazu das Kapitel »Dirigent und Orchester« aus Adornos »Einleitung in die Musiksoziologie« (jetzt in GS 14, S. 292-307).

157. Maria Wiesengrund (1865-1952) war ausgebildete Sängerin; sie hatte in der Saison 1885/86 ein Engagement in Wien.

158. Vgl. Adorno / Hanns Eisler, Komposition für den Film, jetzt in GS 15, S. 7-155; zur Reproduktion vgl. S. 52-55.

159. Vgl. vor allem den vierten Abschnitt – »Erscheinungsformen des Bewegungsverlaufs« – der »Musikpsychologie« des Musikwissenschaftlers Ernst Kurth (1886-1946), der in Wien bei Guido Adler studiert hatte und sich 1912 in Bern habilitierte. Adorno hat das 1931 erschienene Buch 1933 besprochen (vgl. GS 19, S. 350-358).

160. Das Zitat beginnt schon auf S. 65 des dritten Bandes der siebenbändigen deutschen Übersetzung von Eva Rechel-Mertens.

161. Vgl. GS 14, S. 279-282, bes. S. 281.

162. Georg Solti (1912-1997) war von 1952 bis 1961 Generalmusikdirektor an der Frankfurter Oper.

163. Adornos Vortrag und die Aufführung des Kammerkonzerts aus dem Jahre 1954, vgl. jetzt GS 18, S. 630-640.

164. Vgl. ebd., S. 635.

165. Zum Arrangement vgl. GS 14, S. 28-30; Adornos Kritik des Hi-

storismus findet sich im fünften Abschnitt des Bachaufsatzes (vgl. GS 10·1, S. 147-151).

166. Der Dirigent Ludwig Rottenberg (1864-1932) war von 1893 bis 1924 Generalmusikdirektor an den Städtischen Bühnen Frankfurt am Main. – Adorno gibt Rottenbergs resignierenden Ausspruch auch in dem Vortrag »Konzeption eines Wiener Operntheaters« aus dem Jahre 1969 wieder (vgl. GS 19, S. 498).

167. Der Komponist und Dirigent Winfried Zillig (1905-1963), Schüler Schönbergs, war offenbar der Dirigent der oben S. 157 von Adorno kritisierten Aufnahme des Bergschen Kammerkonzerts. Er scheint der namentlich nicht genannte Dirigent zu sein, von dem es in Adornos Aufsatz »Neue Musik, Interpretation, Publikum« heißt: »Ich habe es erlebt, daß ein im übrigen ausgezeichneter und in der verantwortlichen Tradition der neuen Musik aufgewachsener Dirigent nach der Aufführung eines freilich besonders schwierigen Werkes auf meinen zweifelnden Blick, sich selbst beschwichtigend, sagte: noch eine Probe, und es wäre gegangen wie eine Haydnsymphonie. Beim nachträglichen Abhören vermochte ich an einer der wichtigsten, imitatorischen Stellen des Werkes das Entscheidende, die Kombination des Themas mit seiner Vergrößerung und Verkleinerung nicht mehr wahrzunehmen.« (GS 16, S. 40) – Vgl. zu dem Komponisten Zillig auch Adornos Nachruf »Winfried Zillig. Möglichkeit und Wirklichkeit«, in: GS 17, S. 318-326.

168. Nicht ermittelt.

169. Der tschechoslowakische Violinist Otakar Ševčik (1852-1934), Kolischs Lehrer, war ein bedeutender Pädagoge. Zur »Halbtonmethode«, in welcher die Finger auf allen Saiten gleich gesetzt werden und ihre Lage in bezug auf ganze und halbe Töne sich nach und nach in systematisch-progressiven Absätzen verändert (vgl. den Artikel Ševčik in: Die Musik in Geschichte und Gegenwart, Kassel/London/New York 1965), vgl. Ševčiks Violinschule für Anfänger, op. 6.

170. Im Sommer 1956 hielt Adorno in Kranichstein eine vierstündige Vorlesung über »Schönbergs Kontrapunkt«, aus deren Bearbeitung ein Jahr später der Aufsatz »Die Funktion des Kontrapunkts in der neuen Musik« hervorging (vgl. jetzt GS 16, S. 145-169).

171. So auch Adornos Erinnerung in den »Epilegomena zum Kammerkonzert« aus der Bergmonographie (vgl. GS 13, S. 442).

172. So in Adornos Handschrift; zu konjizieren ist »neumisch«.

173. Clara Haskil (1895-1960) spielte den Solopart in Mozarts Klavierkonzert KV 595.

174. Vgl. GS 13, S. 504-508.

175. Vgl. Bertolt Brecht, Übungsstücke für Schauspieler, in: Versuche, Heft 11 (Versuche 25/26/35), Berlin 1951, S. 107-128.

176. Adornos Aufsatz von 1957, vgl. jetzt GS 16, S. 40-51.

177. Gemeint ist wahrscheinlich der Aphorismus Nr. 202 des ersten Teils von »Menschliches, Allzumenschliches« mit dem Titel »Nah und zu fern«: »Der Leser und der Autor verstehen sich häufig deshalb nicht, weil der Autor sein Thema zu gut kennt und es beinahe langweilig findet, so dass er sich die Beispiele erlässt, die er zu hunderten weiss; der Leser aber ist der Sache fremd und findet sie leicht schlecht begründet, wenn ihm die Beispiele vorenthalten werden.«

178. Adornos Mutter und Tante; vgl. die Anm. 157 und 107.

179. Der Satz Schönbergs, den Adorno in seiner Bergmonographie als »spaßhaftes Gebot« (vgl. GS 13, S. 443) bezeichnet, konnte nicht ermittelt werden. Vermutlich handelt es sich um eine mündliche Überlieferung.

180. Es sind wohl die Takte vor dem ff in Takt 51 gemeint.

181. Vgl. die Takte 40ff.

182. Vgl. Adorno / Hanns Eisler, Komposition für den Film, jetzt in: GS 15, S. 7-155; zur ›sinnwidrigen Interpretation‹ vgl. bes. S. 27f. (»Standardisierung der musikalischen Interpretation«).

183. Vgl. Hugo Riemann, Vademecum der Phrasierung, Leipzig

1900. – In Riemanns Buch sind S. 7 ff. Auszüge aus Johann Abraham Peter Schulz' (1747-1800) Artikel über den musikalischen »Vortrag« abgedruckt, der zuerst 1772 in Johann Georg Sulzers (1720-1779) Buch »Allgemeine Theorie der Schönen Künste« (1771-1774) erschienen war.

184. Vielleicht denkt Adorno an das »Lehrbuch der Fugenkomposition« von Iwan Knorr (Leipzig 1911), das in der Reihe der »Lehrgänge an Dr. Hochs Konservatorium in Frankfurt a. M.« erschienen und in Adornos Bibliothek erhalten ist; dort heißt es auf S. 2: »[Das Thema] soll nicht aus Vorder- und Nachsatz (Periodenform) bestehen, da der zu erwartenden ›Antwort‹ gewissermaßen die Rolle des Nachsatzes zufallen wird.«

185. Vgl. Anm. 105.

186. Vgl. GS 13, S. 65 f.

187. Vgl. Adorno, Die Funktion des Kontrapunkts in der neuen Musik, in: GS 16, S. 145-169.

188. Die Stelle »a tempo, animato«.

189. Vgl. die Takte 8 bis 11 von Schumanns op. 41, Nr. 3.

190. Der französische Pianist Alfred Cortot (1877-1962) gehörte als Funktionär der Vichy-Regierung an und spielte während der Judenverfolgungen eine mehr als unrühmliche Rolle.

191. Vgl. vor allem Adornos Aufsatz von 1925 »Zum Problem der Reproduktion« (jetzt in GS 19, S. 440-444) und den zweiten Teil der Arbeit »Zur gesellschaftlichen Lage der Musik« von 1932 (jetzt in GS 18, S. 752-777).

192. Vgl. Ernst Kurth, Musikpsychologie, Berlin 1931. – Zur Unterscheidung von Ton- und Musikpsychologie, vgl. Adornos Rezension, GS 19, S. 351 f.

193. Vgl. Carl E. Seashore, Psychology of Music, New York und

London 1938. – Adornos Rezension von 1940 ist erst posthum veröffentlicht worden in GS 19, S. 375-381.

194. Ein Zitat, in dem Furtwängler sich zum Anwalt der »Unexaktheit« machte, ist nicht ermittelt worden. In den »Gesprächen über Musik«, die Furtwängler mit Walter Abendroth führte, heißt es: »Ein bekannter Dirigent soll gesagt haben: Man muß so lange probieren, bis der Dirigent nicht mehr nötig erscheint. Dies ist ein grundsätzlicher Irrtum, der nicht nur in einer falschen Vorstellung von Detailfragen des Weniger- oder Mehrprobierens, sondern von dem, was Musizieren überhaupt ist und soll, seinen Ursprung hat. Der Drang, alle Einzelheiten bis ins kleinste festzulegen, entstammt nämlich im letzten Grunde einer Angst der Interpreten, sich der Inspiration des Moments allzusehr überlassen zu müssen. Sie versuchen, diese Inspiration durch minutiöse Vorbereitung möglichst in den Hintergrund zu drängen, und schließlich *zu ersetzen* und *überflüssig zu machen*. Sie wollen die einzelnen Wirkungen bis ins letzte festlegen, gleichsam am Schreibtisch ausrechnen, ›in Spiritus setzen‹. Dies ist deshalb falsch, weil man *lebendigen Werken damit nicht gerecht wird*. Die großen musikalischen Meisterwerke stehen in weit höherem Maße, als gewöhnlich angenommen wird, unter dem *Gesetz der Improvisation*.« (Wilhelm Furtwängler, Gespräche über Musik, Zürich 1948, S. 66) – Zu Furtwängler vgl. auch den ersten Teil von Adornos Aufsatz »Drei Dirigenten« (jetzt in GS 19, S. 453-455) und »Wilhelm Furtwängler« von 1968 (jetzt in GS 19, S. 468 f.).

195. In seinem Aufsatz »Über das gegenwärtige Verhältnis von Philosophie und Musik« von 1953 schreibt Adorno: »Als Sprache geht Musik auf den reinen Namen, die absolute Einheit von Sache und Zeichen, die in ihrer Unmittelbarkeit allem menschlichen Wissen verloren ist. In den utopischen und zugleich hoffnungslosen Anstrengungen um den Namen liegt die Beziehung der Musik zur Philosophie, der sie eben darum in ihrer Idee unvergleichlich viel näher steht als jede andere Kunst. Aber der Name erscheint in der Musik einzig als reiner Laut, losgelöst von seinem Träger, und damit das Gegenteil eines jeglichen Bedeutens, einer jeglichen Intention auf den Sinn. Da aber Musik den Namen – das Absolute als Laut – nicht unmittelbar weiß, sondern, wenn man es so wenden darf, um dessen beschwörende Konstruktion durch ein Ganzes, einen Prozeß sich bemüht, so

ist sie zugleich selbst verflochten in den Prozeß, in dem Kategorien wie Rationalität, Sinn, Bedeutung, Sprache gelten. Es ist das Paradoxon aller Musik, daß sie, als Anstrengung um jenes Intentionslose, für welches das unzulängliche Wort Namen gewählt ward, sich entfaltet gerade vermöge ihrer Teilhabe an Rationalität im weitesten Sinne.« (GS 18, S. 154) – Ad Reger heißt es in dem »Versuch über Wagner«: »Die Wagnersche Typenfeindschaft endet absurd beim Namenlosen, Unspezifischen, Abstrakten derart, daß man etwa bei Max Reger schließlich jedes Thema und jeden Takt aus jedem Werk in jedes andere transponieren könnte, während die innere Brüchigkeit des Motivmaterials bei seinen neudeutschen Nachfolgern Strauss und Pfitzner an den Extremen auftrumpfender Banalität und hilfloser Undeutlichkeit offenbar wird.« (GS 13, S. 51)

196. Vgl. GS 14, S. 98-100.

197. Takt 135: »Hier ist nach allmählicher Steigerung ein frisches, belebtes Zeitmaß eingetreten.«

198. Der Kunsthistoriker Rudolf Hirsch (1905-1996) hatte Deutschland 1933 verlassen müssen und bis 1950 in den Niederlanden, während der deutschen Besatzung im Untergrund, gelebt. Er war 1950 nach Deutschland zurückgekehrt. Herausgeber der »Neuen Rundschau«, Nachlaßverwalter Hofmannsthals und Hauptherausgeber der historisch-kritischen Hofmannsthal-Ausgabe.

199. Der Jurist Franz Calvelli-Adorno (1897-1984) war selbst ein ausgezeichneter Pianist und Geiger. 1933 mußte er seinen Posten als Landgerichtsrat in Frankfurt am Main aufgeben, weil seine Mutter Jüdin war. Er legte das Privatmusiklehrerexamen in Dortmund ab und unterrichtete bis 1945 Klavier und Geige in Privathäusern. Von 1934 bis 1938 spielte er im Orchester des Jüdischen Kulturbunds unter der Leitung des ehemaligen Generalmusikdirektors der Frankfurter Oper Wilhelm Steinberg. Nach 1945 wurde er von den Amerikanern als Präsident des Senats für Wiedergutmachung eingesetzt und arbeitete bis zu seiner Pensionierung als leitender Richter. Er war im Vorstand der Frankfurter Museumsgesellschaft. Neben Aufsätzen zur Musik publizierte er ein Buch »Über die religiöse Sprache. Kritische Erfahrungen«. (Für diese Angaben dankt der Hrsg. Frau Elisabeth Reinhuber-Adorno.)

200. Der österreichische Tenor Julius Patzak (1898-1974) wollte zunächst Dirigent werden und studierte in Wien bei Franz Schmidt und Guido Adler, bevor er sich autodidaktisch zum Sänger ausbildete. Er war Mitglied des Wiener und des Münchener Opernhauses, galt aber auch als bedeutender Liedsänger.

201. Es war der erste Klavierkurs, den Steuermann nach 1954 in Kranichstein gab. – Adorno hielt in dem Sommer dort eine vierstündige Vorlesung mit dem Titel »Kriterien der neuen Musik«.

202. Der Pianist und Komponist Rudolf Firkušný (1912-1994), der nach seiner Ausbildung in Prag sich 1938 bei Artur Schnabel weiterbildete, lebte seit 1940 in den USA.

203. Vgl. Text, S. 206 f.

204. Für den Pianisten Wilhelm Backhaus (1884-1969), der als Junge von zehn oder elf Jahren noch Johannes Brahms kennengelernt hatte, waren für die musikalische Darstellung Partiturstudium und theoretische Beschäftigung mit der Musik ebenso wichtig wie die Spieltechnik.

205. Vgl. Adorno, Verfremdetes Hauptwerk. Zur Missa Solemnis (jetzt in GS 17, S. 145-161); der Vortrag wurde am 16. Dezember 1957 im Norddeutschen Rundfunk gesendet. Adorno hat die Schallplattenaufnahme offenbar während der Arbeit an dem Aufsatz gehört.

206. »Die Meisterschaft des Maestro« entstand bald darauf.

207. Der amerikanische Dirigent Robert Craft (geb. 1923) leitete die erste Einspielung des Gesamtwerks von Anton Webern.

208. »Und nur wahrhaft sinnvolle Polyphonie erschließt die höchsten Klangwunder des Orchesters. Ein Orchestersatz, in dem ungeschickt oder, sagen wir nur, gleichgültig geführte Mittel- und Unterstimmen sich befinden, wird selten einer gewissen Härte entbehren und niemals die Klangfülle ergeben, in der eine Partitur erstrahlt, bei deren Ausführung auch die zweiten Bläser, zweiten Violinen, Bratschen, Violoncelli, Bässe sich in der Belebung schön geschwungener

melodischer Linien seelisch beteiligen.« (Instrumentationslehre von Hector Berlioz, ergänzt und revidiert von Richard Strauss, Teil I, Leipzig o. J., S. III)

209. Adorno hat irrtümlich »Instrumentation« wiederholt. – Vgl. dazu die Stelle aus »Neue Musik, Interpretation, Publikum« (jetzt in: GS 16, S. 44 f.) und Adornos Kranichsteiner Vorlesung »Funktion der Farbe in der Musik« von 1966, in: Musik-Konzepte, hrsg. von Heinz-Klaus Metzger und Rainer Riehn, Sonderband: Darmstadt-Dokumente I, München 1999, S. 263-312, bes. S. 305.

210. Vgl. dazu auch die längere Passage in Adornos Aufsatz über Schreker GS 16, S. 377 f.

211. »Nach einer Äußerung von Alban Berg [hat] der Instrumentator zu verfahren wie ein Schreiner, der kontrolliert, daß an seinem Tisch nicht die Nägel herausstehen und nicht der Geruch des Leims bemerkbar bleibt [. . .].« (GS 13, S. 76)

212. Adorno hat den Liedern, die er mit jungen Musikern der Frankfurter Musikhochschule einstudierte, eine der »Interpretationsanalysen« gewidmet, die er in den »Getreuen Korrepetitor« aufnahm; vgl. jetzt GS 15, S. 251-265.

213. Das Lied ist nicht sicher zu ermitteln. – Bei der Durchsicht der Lieder, die Adorno in den späten fünfziger Jahren mit der Sängerin Carla Henius studierte, fällt immerhin der fünfte Takt von Alexander von Zemlinskys op. 13, Nr. 4 auf, wo auf die unbetonte zweite Silbe von »hörte« ein e – nach einem fis auf der ersten Silbe – mit dem Wert einer Dreiachtelnote in einem Dreivierteltakt entfällt. Adornos Vorschlag paßte sehr gut zur Lösung des Problems.

214. Neben seinem op. 5 – »Klage. Sechs Gedichte von Georg Trakl für Singstimme und Klavier« (vgl. Adorno, Kompositionen, hrsg. von Heinz-Klaus Metzger und Rainer Riehn, Bd. 1: Lieder für Singstimme und Klavier, München 1980, S. 48-65) – hat Adorno auch seine George-Lieder op. 7 (vgl. ebd., S. 76-85) mit Carla Henius studiert und letztere auch aufgeführt. – Carla Henius hat über ihre Zusammenarbeit mit Adorno in mehreren Aufsätzen berichtet, die in

ihrem Buch »Schnebel, Nono, Schönberg oder Die wirkliche und die erdachte Musik« (Hamburg 1993, S. 79-116) nachzulesen sind.

215. Der Dirigent Rafael Kubelik (1914-1996) war von 1955 bis 1958 Musikdirektor am Covent Garden und leitete von 1961 bis 1968 das Symphonie-Orchester des Bayerischen Rundfunks.

216. Die Quelle für Klemperers Wort ist nicht ermittelt.

217. Vgl. die Takte 3 (1. Geige) und 4 (Cello) der fünften Bagatelle für Streichquartett aus op. 9 von Webern. – Vgl. hierzu und im folgenden Adornos Interpretationsanalyse von Weberns op. 9 im »Getreuen Korrepetitor« (GS 15, S. 277-300).

218. Nicht sicher zu ermitteln, da es in Weberns op. 7 und op. 9, die Adorno zu der Zeit studierte, mehr als ein Stück gibt, das der Beschreibung entspricht, doch spricht seine Interpretationsanalyse des dritten Stücks aus Weberns op. 7 dafür, daß Adorno hier an dieses »Adagio« dachte.

219. Vgl. die ausgeführte Interpretationsanalyse von Weberns Stück im »Getreuen Korrepetitor«, GS 15, S. 295-300.

220. Anspielung auf Shakespeare, König Richard III., V, 4.

221. Vgl. den Nachweis in Anm. 89.

222. So in Adornos Handschrift; gemeint ist wahrscheinlich »sulla tastiera«, das dem »Am Steg« entspricht.

223. Die beiden folgenden Aufzeichnungen sind die ältesten überlieferten; Adorno hat sie in das von ihm so genannte »blaue Buch« eingetragen, das der Hrsg. der Beethoven-Aufzeichnungen als »Schulheft ohne Deckel« (vgl. Adorno, Beethoven. Philosophie der Musik, a. a. O. [Anm. 24], S. 361) bezeichnet und das bis zur Drucklegung der »Aufzeichnungen zu einer Theorie der musikalischen Reproduktion« nicht einsehbar war. Die Wiedergabe der Notizen folgt einer Abschrift, die Elfriede Olbrich angefertigt hat.

224. Wahrscheinlich denkt Adorno an die Takte 29ff. der Violinsonate op. 24.

225. Vgl. Anm. 81.

226. Vgl. die Aufzeichnung S. 90.

227. Friedrich Schiller, Die Räuber, IV, 4: »*Du weinst, Amalia?* – und das sprach er mit einer Stimme! mit einer Stimme – mir war's, als ob die Zeit sich verjüngete – die genossenen Lenze der Liebe dämmerten auf mit der Stimme! Die Nachtigall schlug wie damals – die Blumen hauchten wie damals – und ich lag wonneberauscht an seinem Hals [...].«

228. Die promovierte Chemikerin Gretel Adorno (1902-1993), geb. Karplus, war seit 1937 mit Adorno verheiratet.

229. Adornos Aphorismus aus dem Jahre 1929, vgl. jetzt GS 18, S. 19.

230. Der Dirigent Heinrich Hollreiser (geb. 1913) arbeitete seit 1964 hauptsächlich als Gastdirigent.

231. Vgl. Anm. 199.

232. Die Pianistin und Cembalistin Edith Picht-Axenfeld (1914 bis 2001) lehrte seit 1947 an der Freiburger Musikhochschule; sie war mit dem Philosophen Georg Picht verheiratet.

233. Mit diesem Satz beginnt der zweite Abschnitt - »Die Erscheinung« – des zweiten Bandes von Hegels »Wissenschaft der Logik«.

234. Hugo Riemann, Handbuch der Musikgeschichte, 1. Band, 1. Teil, 3. Aufl. Leipzig 1923, p. 8. [Anm. Adorno]

235. Ernest Newman, The Life of Richard Wagner, New York 1946, Vol. IV, p. 261 f. [Anm. Adorno]

236. Richard Wagner, Gesammelte Schriften, 2. Aufl. Leipzig 1888, 8. Band, p. 290 f. [Anm. Adorno]

237. L. c. p. 290f. [Anm. Adorno]

238. Walter Benjamin, Vorwort über die Aufgabe des Übersetzers zur deutschen Übertragung der Tableaux Parisiens von Charles Baudelaire, Heidelberg 1923, p. VII. [Anm. Adorno]

239. Cf. Theodor A. Meyer, Das Stilgesetz der Poesie, [Leipzig 1901,] p. 55ff. [Anm. Adorno]

240. Cf. Riemann, l. c., I, 1, p. 61 und »Studien zur Geschichte der Notenschrift« (1878) [Anm. Adorno]

241. Riemann, l. c. I, 1, p. 9. [Anm. Adorno]

242. Vgl. Arnold Schönberg, Eine neue Zwölfton-Schrift, in: Stil und Gedanke. Aufsätze zur Musik, a. a. O. [Anm. 146], S. 198-205.

243. Riemann, l. c., I, 1, p. 31. [Anm. Adorno]

244. Riemann, l. c., I, 2, p. 84. [Anm. Adorno]

245. Riemann, l. c., I, 2, p. 84. [Anm. Adorno]

246. Riemann, l. c., I, 2, p. 84f. [Anm. Adorno]

247. Cf. Riemann, l. c., I, 2, p. 85. [Anm. Adorno]

248. Riemann, l. c., I, 2, p. 89. [Anm. Adorno]

249. Riemann, l. c., I, 2, p. 199. [Anm. Adorno]

250. Riemann, l. c., I, 2, p. 95. [Anm. Adorno]

251. Riemann, l. c., I, 2, ibd. [Anm. Adorno]

252. Riemann, l. c., I, 2, p. 106. [Anm. Adorno]

253. Riemann, l. c., I, 2, p. 107. [Anm. Adorno]

254. Benjamin, l. c., [p.] XI. [Anm. Adorno]

255. Frederick Dorian, The History of Music in Performance, New York 1942, p. 28. [Anm. Adorno]

256. Vgl. Anm. 78.

257. Die schon im »Versuch über Wagner« zitierte Stelle aus Alfred Lorenz' »Das Geheimnis der Form bei Richard Wagner«, vgl. GS 13, S. 30.

258. »Es lassen sich grob übertreibend zwei Typen des Komponierens unterscheiden, mit Rücksicht auf die Logik der Sache ebenso wie auf ihre Genesis. Der erste Typus ist der, welcher von der Anschauung des Details, einer Art musikalischen Keimzelle, blind, nur dem Zwang der Triebrichtung jener Details folgend, zum Ganzen gelangt. Schubert, Schumann gehören diesem Typus an; der ursprünglichen Anlage nach auch Schönberg, der einmal sagte, bei der Komposition eines Liedes lasse er sich von den Anfangsworten treiben, ohne sich auch nur über das Gedicht als ganzes Rechenschaft zu geben. Der entgegengesetzte Typus ist der, bei dem der Primat des Ganzen herrscht und alle Details als Funktion des Ganzen konstituiert. Beethoven gehört wohl dem zweiten Typus an. Das Vollbringen eines Komponisten besteht wesentlich in der Tiefe, in der beide Typen in der Logik seines Werkes sich durchdringen: Bach, Mozart, Beethoven, Schönberg sind darin exemplarisch. Bleibt der erste Typus undialektisch bei sich stehen, wie etwa Dvořák, so kommt ein Potpourri von ›Einfällen‹ mit willkürlichen oder schematischen Vermittlungen zustande; umgekehrt ist die Gefahr eines zweiten Typus – Händel wäre ein gutes Beispiel – die leere und unverbindliche Anschauung des Ganzen, bei skizzierten, unausgeführten, oft flachen Details.« (Adorno und Hanns Eisler, Komposition für den Film, in: GS 15, S. 7 bis 146; die Stelle S. 91)

259. Cf. ibd., p. 224 f.; cf. Wagner, l. c., p. . . . [Anm. Adorno] – Den beabsichtigten Nachweis aus Wagners Schrift glaubt der Hrsg. durch den Nachweis der Schrift Schumanns, aus der Dorian an der Stelle zitiert, ersetzen zu sollen: »Über einige mutmaßlich korrumpierte Stellen in Bachschen, Mozartschen und Beethovenschen Werken«, in:

Robert Schumann, Gesammelte Schriften über Musik und Musiker, a. a. O. [Anm. 8], Bd. 3, S. 66-72; die Stelle über die Pastorale findet sich S. 70-72.

260. Vgl. Anm. 24.

261. Vgl. Ernst Kurth, Musikpsychologie, a. a. O. [Anm. 192], S. 1-3.

262. Ibd. [Anm. 255], p. 181. [Anm. Adorno]

263. »Wenn man ein großes Werk mit allen seinen Einzelheiten vollständig auswendig beherrscht, so kommen manchmal Augenblicke vor, wo das Zeitbewußtsein plötzlich weg ist und das ganze Werk, ich möchte sagen ›räumlich‹ alles in höchster Genauigkeit zusammen, im Bewußtsein gleichzeitig vorhanden ist.« (Alfred Lorenz, a. a. O. [Anm. 257], S. 292; zit. GS 13, S. 30f.)

264. Benjamin, l. c., p. X. [Anm. Adorno]

265. Dorian, l. c., p. 69. [Anm. Adorno] – Dorian bezieht sich auf den Artikel »Battre la mesure« in Rousseaus »Dictionnaire de Musique«.

266. Dorian, l. c., p. 117. [Anm. Adorno]

267. Igor Strawinsky, Erinnerungen, Zürich-Berlin 1937, p. 98 ff. [Anm. Adorno]

268. Beethoven, Sonate für Violine und Klavier [G-Dur, op. 96], Finale, nach der Generalpause, 8 Takte vor Buchstaben L und 8 Takte nach L. [Anm. Adorno]

269. Eduard Steuermann, zitiert bei Dorian, l. c., S. 332. [Anm. Adorno] – Dorian zitiert ohne Seitenangabe Steuermanns Aufsatz »The Piano Music of Schönberg«, in: M. Armitage, Schönberg, New York 1937.

270. Richard Wagner, Gesammelte Schriften und Dichtungen, Leipzig 1888, IX, S. 251 f. [Anm. Adorno]

271. L. c., S. 232. [Anm. Adorno]

272. Ibd. [Anm. Adorno]

273. L. c., S. 232 f. [Anm. Adorno]

274. L. c., S. 234. [Anm. Adorno]

275. L. c., VIII, S. 271. [Anm. Adorno]

276. Dorian, l. c., p. 333. [Anm. Adorno]

277. Vgl. Anm. 234.

278. Vgl. Anm. 235.

279. Vgl. Anm. 236.

280. Vgl. Anm. 237.

281. Vgl. Anm. 238.

282. Cf. Theodor M. Meyer, Das Stilgesetz der Poesie, p. 55 ff. [Anm. Adorno]

283. Vgl. Anm. 240.

284. Vgl. Anm. 241.

285. Adorno versammelte hier – jeweils unter den in kleinerem Schriftgrad wiedergegebenen Stichworten, die Gretel Adorno für ihn aus den »Aufzeichnungen« ausgezogen hatte – dasjenige, was er zur Niederschrift heranzuziehen gedachte. – Das Datum bezieht sich auf den Beginn der Arbeit an den »Materialien«. Vgl. auch im Text S. 316 das Datum der Stichworte des »Zweiten Schemas«. – Die Verweise auf Dorian, Wagners Schriften, beziehen sich zumeist auf die Stellen, die am Anfang der »Aufzeichnungen« wiedergegeben sind, wo nicht, werden sie in Anm. wiedergegeben.

286. Vgl. Adorno, Das Problem der Reproduktion, jetzt in: GS 19, S. 440-444.

287. »Music lives through interpretation. Between a musical work and the world stands the interpreter who brings the score to life by his performance. The relationship between the performing and the creative artist, however, has changed profoundly in the history of music and continues to do so.«

288. Gemeint ist Wagners Schrift »Über das Dirigieren«, vgl. Anm. 30.

289. Die Seitenzahlen beziehen sich auf die Zählung in Adornos »Heft«, die im Druck am Rand wiedergegeben sind.

290. »Die eigentümliche Problematik der Reproduktion hebt an vielmehr erst mit der Frage nach der *Freiheit* des Interpreten, die, will sie nicht offene Willkür diskutieren, in jenen Grenzen nur statthat. Und auch diese Frage, wird behauptet, findet ihre Antwort nicht allein beim Interpreten, sondern wesentlich und konstitutiv in der Struktur des Werkes. Auf welche Weise man vom Werke ablese, welche Freiheit es dem Interpreten läßt, der es als Werk interpretiert – das zu erforschen scheint die zentrale Aufgabe einer Theorie der Reproduktion, die freilich, als Theorie, nicht durchdringen könnte, was unlöslich verquickt das Gebilde in seiner Fülle, den Nachbildner als ganzen Menschen umschlossen hält.« (GS 19, S. 440)

291. Vgl. Anm. 238.

292. Die Stelle in Riemanns »Handbuch der Musikgeschichte« lautet: »Weiter ergibt die Vergleichung, daß diejenigen Silben, welche bei natürlicher Deklamation die *Hauptträger von Sinnakzenten* sind, bei allen Textunterlagen dieselben Hauptausbiegungen der Melodie erhalten, so daß man schließen muß, daß auch ein *idealer Rhythmus* durch schnelleren Vortrag sich einschaltender Silbenhäufungen oder umgekehrt durch breiteren Vortrag silbenärmerer Teile gewahrt wird. Die Bedeutung eines solchen idealen Rhythmus ist von keinem geringeren als *Richard Wagner* in einer jeden Widerspruch ausschließenden Fassung in seiner Schrift ›Oper und Drama‹ im zweiten Abschnitt des dritten Teiles dargelegt worden (Ges.-Ausg. IV S. 148).«

293. Adorno bezieht sich auf seinen »Entwurf«, vgl. oben S. 219, vor dem Benjamin-Zitat.

294. »We can find nowhere in Beethoven a specifically prescribed rubato. [. . .] Yet there are evidently passages where the aggregate of Beethoven's markings amounts to what the rubato instruction represents in later periods: a variation of time with gradual modification. For example, in the opening movement of Opus 111, the original instruction, *allegro con brio ed appassionato,* dissolves completely upon the very first appearance of the second theme. Here, *meno allegro* appears in the second half of the measure, followed by two measures marked *ritardando.* [. . .] Similar situations are to be found in many other of Beethoven's last works – at the end of Opus 90, and in Opera 101, 109, and 110. It is only in such places of agitated emotion, of intense expression, that we are obliged to perform with an appropriate amount of *tempo rubato.* Such slight and controlled rubato would coincide with the style of Beethoven's own rendition, as described by those who were privileged to hear him.«

295. Adornos Aufsatz »Neue Tempi« ist zuerst in Heft 1 des siebenten Jahrgangs (1930) von »Pult & Taktstock« erschienen; vgl. jetzt GS 17, S. 66-73, die von Adorno hier bezeichnete Stelle S. 71 f.

296. Nicht sicher zu ermitteln; vermutlich ist die Stelle aus Dorian, S. 30 (vgl. oben S. 18) gemeint.

297. Vgl. Anm. 241.

298. Vgl. jetzt GS 17, S. 54-56.

299. Vgl. ebd., S. 66 f.

300. Vgl. ebd., S. 68-70.

301. Der zweite – von der »Reproduktion« und dem »Konsum« handelnde – Teil des Aufsatzes war 1932 im dritten Heft der »Zeitschrift für Sozialforschung« erschienen; vgl. jetzt GS 18, S. 752-777.

302. Vgl. oben S. 254 und die Anm. dort.

303. Vgl. Text, S. 257f.

304. Vgl. den Nachweis in Anm. 94.

305. Der schon oben (Anm. 259) nachgewiesene Aufsatz »Über einige mutmaßlich korrumpierte Stellen in Bachschen, Mozartschen und Beethovenschen Werken«.

306. Vgl. Anm. 40.

307. Vgl. Anm. 45.

308. Vgl. Text, S. 276f.

309. Vgl. jetzt GS 17, S. 71-73.

310. Vgl. jetzt GS 17, S. 52f.

311. Vgl. ebd., S. 56f.

312. Vgl. ebd., S. 57f.

313. Vgl. den Nachweis in Anm. 6.

314. Vgl. GS 17, S. 67f.

315. Der Aufsatz ist 1926 in Heft 7/8 (S. 130-134) von »Pult & Taktstock« zuerst erschienen; vgl. jetzt GS 17, S. 307-310.

316. Vgl. Anm. 25.

317. Vgl. jetzt GS 17, S. 66-73.

318. »Das Schreckgespenst dieser dem modernen Musiker direkt kunstwidrig dünkenden fortgesetzten falschen Parallelfortschreitungen verlor nur wenig von seiner Fürchterlichkeit durch die Bestimmung, daß das Organum mit einer gewissen Bedächtigkeit (modesta morositate) vorzutragen sei, wobei ja weniger die schneidenden Folgen der Quinten und Oktaven als vielmehr der Wohlklang der einzel-

nen Akkorde zur Geltung kommen konnte. Rätselhaft blieb für das heutige Musikgefühl trotz aller Hinweise auf die Mixturregister der Orgel und das Phänomen der Obertöne, daß jemals längere Zeit und allgemein als schön sollte empfunden worden sein, was nun seit einem halben Jahrtausend als fehlerhaft und ohrenbeleidigend gilt.« (Riemann, Handbuch der Musikgeschichte, a.a.O. [Anm. 65], I, 2, S. 137) – Adornos Marginalie dazu: »Riemann hypostasiert durchwegs das entwickelte tonale System als ›natürlich‹«.

319. Vgl. Anm. 6.

320. Vgl. GS 19, S. 440-444, bes. S. 441 f.

321. Vgl. den Nachweis in Anm. 23.

322. Vgl. GS 17, S. 52-54.

323. Vgl. ebd., S. 56-59.

324. Vgl. die Aufzeichnungen S. 205. – Das von Adorno so genannte »blaue Buch« ist identisch mit dem »Schulheft ohne Deckel«.

325. Das ist der zweite Teil des in Zusammenhang mit seiner Arbeit am »Princeton Radio Research Project« von Adorno geplanten Buches »Current of Music«, das Fragment geblieben ist. Es wird als dritter Band von Adornos »Fragment gebliebenen Schriften« veröffentlicht werden.

326. Vgl. Adorno, The Radio Symphony. An Experiment in Theory, in: Radio Research 1941, hrsg. von Paul F. Lazarsfeld und Frank N. Stanton, New York 1941, S. 110-139. – Adornos Aufsatz »Über die musikalische Verwendung des Radios« aus dem »Getreuen Korrepetitor« (vgl. jetzt GS 15, S. 369-401) geht auf diese Studie, die ihrerseits eine gekürzte Version der »Radio Voice« ist, zurück.

327. Ebenso wie die »Radio Symphony« ist die «NBC Music Appreciation Hour« – eine Sendereihe, geleitet von dem Dirigenten Walter Johannes Damrosch (1862-1950) – aus Adornos Arbeit am »Princeton

Radio Research Project« hervorgegangen; vgl. die deutsche Fassung »Die gewürdigte Musik« (GS 15, S. 163-187).

328. Vgl. GS 19, S. 440.

329. Vgl. ebd., S. 440-442.

330. Vgl. jetzt GS 18, S. 756: »Die Forderung sachlich adäquater Wiedergabe der Werke hat sich dabei von dem – ohnehin schwer kontrollierbaren – Willen der Autoren ganz emanzipiert und gerade in solcher Emanzipation kommt der geschichtliche Charakter von Reproduktion bündig zutage. Wollte man etwa eine frühere Beethovensche Klaviersonate so ›frei‹, mit so willkürlich-improvisatorischen Veränderungen zumal der Grundzeitmaße der einzelnen Sätze spielen, wie es, nach zeitgenössischen Berichten, der Pianist Beethoven tat – vor der heute erst, durch die spätere Produktion, ganz erkennbaren konstruktiven Einheit solcher Sätze müßte die scheinbar authentische Interpretationsweise schlechterdings als sinnwidrig sich darstellen.«

331. Vgl. Anm. 329.

332. Vgl. GS 19, S. 442 f.

333. Vgl. Anm. 78.

334. Aufgrund der Abkürzung ist es nicht sicher, ob Adorno an eine oder mehrere Aufzeichnungen in dem »grünen Buch«, dem ersten in der Chronologie seiner Notizbücher, denkt. Die eine Aufzeichnung, die hier gemeint zu sein scheint und nach dem 1. Februar 1942 entstanden ist, lautet: »Das Paradoxon der Musik: daß sie die äußerste unsinnliche Bestimmtheit jeglichen Moments mit der völligen Absenz des Begriffs vereint. Am Gegensatz zur Lyrik der Sprache erkennbar, die allemal begrifflich aber unbestimmt ist.« (S. 53)

335. Vgl. Rudolf Kolisch, Über die Krise der Streicher, in: Darmstädter Beiträge zur neuen Musik I, Mainz 1958, S. 84-90.

336. Die Stichworte, die Adorno zu seinem Einleitungsvortrag no-

tierte und die erkennbar in engstem Zusammenhang mit seinen »Aufzeichnungen zu einer Theorie der musikalischen Reproduktion« stehen, sind auszugsweise bereits veröffentlicht worden; vgl. Rolf Tiedemann, Nur ein Gast in der Tafelrunde. Theodor W. Adorno: kritisch und kritisiert, in: Von Kranichstein zur Gegenwart. 50 Jahre Darmstädter Ferienkurse, hrsg. von Rudolf Stephan u. a., Darmstadt 1996, S. 150.

337. Vgl. Text, S. 88.

338. Vgl. Anm. 142.

339. Vgl. Anm. 144.

Editorische Nachbemerkung

Für das Buch, zu dem Adorno Aufzeichnungen in ein von ihm »Schwarzes Buch« genanntes Notizheft eintrug, notierte er zwei provisorische Titel: »Die wahre Aufführung« und »Reproduktionstheorie. Ein musikphilosophischer Versuch«. Beide Titel sind gleichsam an den Extremen einer Theorie der Interpretation angesiedelt: dem der sinnlichen Darstellung der Musik und dem, was in der notierten Komposition auf Interpretation, Darstellung hin angelegt und auf sie verwiesen ist. Sie terminieren in der Erkenntnis des objektiven Gehalts des Komponierten, und diese ist der richtigen Darstellung vorausgesetzt. Das hat Adorno schon früh dazu bewogen, die musikalische Reproduktion als eigene Form anzusehen, deren »Maß [nicht durchaus] in die Hände des Reproduzierenden gegeben ist«, wie es einleitend in dem Aufsatz »Zum Problem der Reproduktion« von 1925 heißt. Ist aber die Reproduktion eine »autonome« Form, dann folgt sie auch nicht unmittelbar aus der Komposition, ist sie nicht die einfache Ausführung eines verbindlich Notierten und objektiv Geltenden, sondern Schauplatz der in der schriftlichen Fixierung von Musik nur scheinbar zur Ruhe gekommenen Auseinandersetzung derjenigen Kräfte, die die musikalische Form begründen. – Wenn weder der Interpret noch die Komposition das Maß der Darstellung ist, so ist diese doch nicht unabhängig vom Komponierten. Die musikalische Interpretation muß zur Erkenntnis werden, um die Erkenntnis, die nach Adorno den musikalischen Werken immanent ist, erscheinen zu lassen. Dies ist zugleich die Bedingung der Möglichkeit dafür, daß zwischen richtiger und falscher Interpretation mit Gründen unterschieden werden kann, daß die wahre musikalische Darstellung sich im eminenten Sinne von einer bloßen Wiedergabe des Notentextes unterscheidet. Daß die Reproduktion zum Problem der Moderne wurde, hat Adorno gleichermaßen gegen den historistischen Objektivismus wie gegen den Irrationalismus der subjektiven Einfühlung damit begründet, daß sich die Werke in der Geschichte nicht als identische erhalten, sondern sich objektiv in ihr verändern, ja, daß sie in ihr zerfallen. Von dieser These, die den Ausgangspunkt seiner Überlegungen in den zwanziger Jahren bildete, sagt Adorno in einer Aufzeichnung, daß sie »nicht herzubeten sondern zu begründen« sei. Das eben sollte die ausgeführte Theorie der musikalischen Reproduktion leisten.

Die Arbeit an dem Buch, das Adorno und Rudolf Kolisch noch 1935 gemeinsam zu schreiben planten – erste Gespräche darüber dürften bereits in den zwanziger Jahren, als Adorno Beiträge für die Wiener Zeitschriften »Musikblätter des Anbruch« und »Pult & Taktstock« schrieb, geführt worden sein –, hat Adorno im Frühjahr 1946 in Los Angeles begonnen, als die in enger Zusammenarbeit mit Max Horkheimer entstandene »Dialektik der Aufklärung«, der Schönbergteil der »Philosophie der neuen Musik«, das mit Hanns Eisler geschriebene Buch »Komposition für den Film« und der größere Teil des Aphorismenbuchs »Minima Moralia« beendet, wenn auch noch nicht gedruckt waren. Diese großen Arbeiten aus den Jahren 1940 bis 1945 waren den zahlreichen und aufreibenden Verpflichtungen, die die Arbeit an den Forschungsprojekten des Instituts für Sozialforschung mit sich brachte, abgerungen. In den Jahren 1945 und 1946 trat die Belastung etwas zurück, Adorno konnte sich wieder eigenen Dingen zuwenden und erneut mit systematischem Klavierüben und Musizieren beginnen, so daß die am 21. Juni 1946 begonnene Schematisierung des Buches über die musikalische Reproduktion die begründete Hoffnung dokumentiert, diese Arbeit sehr weit treiben, wenn nicht gar beenden zu können. Während er die ersten »Aufzeichnungen« notierte, die zentrale Motive seiner Theorie der musikalischen Interpretation versammeln, studierte Adorno die »History of Music in Performance» des Schönbergschülers Frederick Dorian und Richard Wagners Schriften »Über das Dirigiren» und »Zum Vortrag der IX. Symphonie Beethoven's« – auch dies ein Zeichen dafür, daß die »Theorie der musikalischen Reproduktion« das nächste Buch werden sollte. In der zweiten Hälfte des Jahres 1946 mußte jedoch die Arbeit daran hinter der an der »Authoritarian Personality« und damit zusammenhängenden Research-Arbeiten zurücktreten. Erst im Sommer 1949 konnte Adorno die Arbeit an der Reproduktionstheorie fortsetzen, wie die Datierungen auf den Seiten 30 und 33 seines »Schwarzen Buches« belegen. Ob das Studium von Teilen des Riemannschen »Handbuchs der Musikgeschichte« noch 1946 erfolgte oder erst 1949, ist aufgrund der Datierungen im Notizbuch nicht sicher zu sagen. In das Jahr 1949 scheint auch der Gretel Adorno diktierte große Entwurf zu fallen; der letzte Versuch, das Buch zu schreiben, bevor Adorno nach Deutschland zurückkehrte. Erst 1953 wurden die »Aufzeichnungen« während eines Aufenthalts in Los Angeles fortgesetzt. Im Sommer 1954 hielten Adorno, Rudolf Kolisch und Eduard Steuermann in Kranichstein einen Kurs über »Neue Musik und Interpretation«, zu dessen Intention Adorno am 4. Juni 1954 an Kolisch schrieb: »Den Kurs selber habe ich mir eigentlich so gedacht, daß wir drei ihn wirklich gemeinsam halten, und daß jeder dann etwas sagt, wenn er es für richtig hält – so wie Horkheimer und ich seit Jahren und mit sehr gutem Erfolg unsere Seminare zusammen abhalten –. Natürlich ist die Tempofrage nur ein Teilproblem, und nicht einmal das wichtigste. Am meisten kommt es doch wohl darauf an, den Schülern klar zu machen, was strukturell-sinnvolles Interpretieren eigentlich heißt. Ich habe mir vorgestellt, aus meinen ungemein zahlreichen Aufzeichnungen zur Theorie der musikalischen Reproduktion eine Art von Einleitungsreferat zu machen, an das wir dann praktisch anschließen können; wenn Du und Eduard das selber für ungünstig halten, so ist es mir ebenso recht, wenn wir unmittelbar in die Praxis eintreten. In dem Einleitungsreferat könnte man vor allem auch die Zonen der Interpretationsprobleme abstecken und Einseitigkeiten wie die der Tempofrage von vornherein vermeiden.« Äußerungen Kolischs und Diskussionen im Verlauf dieses Kurses hat Adorno in den »Aufzeichnungen« festgehalten. Am 6. Dezember 1959 notierte er den letzten Eintrag auf der letzten Seite des »Schwarzen Buchs«, das bis auf die »Nachweise zum Kierkegaardbuch«, die die ersten Seiten füllen, ganz den »Aufzeichnungen zur Theorie der musikalischen Reproduktion« vorbehalten war.

Adorno hat in den »Materialien zur Reproduktionstheorie« und in dem »zweiten Schema« von 1946 versucht, eine Ordnung herzustellen, die die Argumentation des Buches organisieren helfen sollte. Diesen Versuchen liegen seine »Aufzeichnungen«, seine Aufsätze aus den zwanziger und frühen dreißiger Jahren und die stichwortartig kommentierten Stellen aus den Arbeiten von Dorian, Wagner und Riemann zugrunde. Bei den Verweisen bezieht sich Adorno natürlich auf die Seitenzahlen seiner Aufzeichnungen, so wie er es auch bei Rückbezügen innerhalb derselben gehalten hat. Diese Orientierungshilfen beizubehalten hat den Herausgeber bewogen, in die Abfolge der Aufzeichnungen nicht einzugreifen und auf eine eigene – nach Themen und Motiven zusammengestellte – Anordnung der Fragmente zu verzichten; aber das allein war nicht der ausschlaggebende Grund. Mag immer die Kritik einer chronologischen Wiedergabe von Fragmenten einer gewissen Plausibilität nicht entbehren, so ist doch festzuhalten, daß Adornos Aufzeichnungen zur Reproduktionstheorie *einen* Gegenstand haben, dem sie zu verschiedenen Zeiten mit unterschiedlichen Gewichtungen zu folgen sich bemühen. Eine nicht-chronologische Anordnung der Fragmente erkaufte mit dem Anschein größerer Nähe zum vollendeten Werk, daß das Moment des Einblicks in den Arbeitsprozeß verdeckt und damit auch das biographisch Zufällige der Nichtvollendung der Arbeit unkenntlich gemacht würde. – Wenn sich die Veröffentlichung von Fragmenten überhaupt rechtfertigen läßt, dann durch die Hoffnung, daß mit ihnen etwas in die Welt kommt, was dem Bedürfnis denkender Menschen Abhilfe schafft: Gedanken lesen zu können, deren Nervenpunkte das schmerzhafte Bewußtsein des Verlustes der Tradition sind; von der bürgerlichen Kultur hat sich einzig ihr Rätselbild erhalten. Unter den problematischen Bedingungen der Selbsterhaltung dieser Kultur in der Kulturindustrie ist alle Tradition eine Sammlung von Fragmenten, die der Leser harrt.

Unter dem Titel »Aufzeichnungen I« sind die Notate aus dem »Schwarzen Buch« in der Reihenfolge ihrer Niederschrift wiedergegeben. Die Notenbeispiele sind nach dem Faksimile von Adornos Handschriften gedruckt worden. Aufzeichnungen, die vor 1946 und nach dem 6. Dezember 1959 entstanden, hat Adorno in andere Notizbücher geschrieben; wenn er das »Schwarze Buch« nicht zur Hand hatte, notierte er Aufzeichnungen zur Reproduktionstheorie gelegentlich auch in das je aktuell geführte Notizbuch. Diese Notizen sind unter dem Titel »Aufzeichnungen II« versammelt; der Fundort ist in kleinerem Schriftgrad jeweils unter der betreffenden Aufzeichnung angegeben. Die zwei als Typoskripte überlieferten Notizen sind mit der Sigle Ts und der Blattzahl der Archivierung versehen.

Zur editorischen Verfahrensweise sei gesagt, daß, bis auf die gebräuchlichen, alle Abkürzungen in dem handschriftlichen Text Adornos aufgelöst wurden, um die Lektüre nicht unnötig zu behindern. Beibehalten wurden lediglich die geläufigen Bezeichnungen p für piano, pp für pianissimo, f für forte, ff für fortissimo, mf für mezzoforte und sf für sforzato. Da Geschlossenheit und Einheitlichkeit kein Charakteristikum für Notate ist, wurde in die Adornosche Orthographie sowenig wie in die Interpunktion regulierend eingegriffen, allenfalls Verschreibungen wurden stillschweigend berichtigt. Hervorhebungen von Adorno sind *kursiv* gesetzt. Ebenfalls *kursiv* und in ekkigen Klammern wiedergegeben sind Bemerkungen des Herausgebers, Ergänzungen oder Korrekturen dagegen in eckigen Klammern und geradem Schriftgrad. – Zur Erleichterung der Lektüre glaubte der Herausgeber die Stellen, die Adorno aus dem Buch von Dorian, den Aufsätzen Wagners und dem Handbuch von Riemann mit Seitenangabe und kurzen Stichworten in den »Aufzeichnungen« regestenartig verzeichnete, nach der Seitenangabe und den Stichworten bzw. vor dem Stichwort, wenn dies wie bei Wagner wegen des Kommentarcharakters geboten schien, *kursiv* und mit Anführungszeichen in den Haupttext aufnehmen zu sollen. Die Randpaginierung gibt die Seitenzählung der «Aufzeichnungen« in dem »Schwarzen Buch« wieder, um dem Leser das Auffinden der Stellen, auf die Adorno verweist, ohne den Umweg einer Anmerkung zu ermöglichen. Alle in den Anmerkungen gegebenen Seitenzahlen beziehen sich dagegen auf die des gedruckten Buches. Die Anmerkungen dienen der Erläuterung der erwähnten Namen, dem Nachweis von Zitaten und der Identifizierung von Kompositionen, wenn diese sich nicht aus Adornos Angaben zweifelsfrei ergeben, und Taktangaben, sofern sie nicht in eckigen Klammern im Text selbst ergänzt wurden. Im Register sind unter dem Namen der Komponisten die erwähnten Kompositionen aufgeführt. – Jedem kundigen Leser werden zahlreiche Überschneidungen mit Stellen aus den veröffentlichten »Musikalischen Schriften« Adornos, nicht nur die, die Adorno selbst nennt, geläufig sein; sie alle zu verzeichnen, nähme sowohl den Fragmenten wie den publizierten Aufsätzen ihr je eigenes Recht.

Das in der Übersicht wiedergegebene Verzeichnis der »Aufzeichnungen« folgt dem von Gretel Adorno angelegten, das als Typoskript im Theodor W. Adorno-Archiv sich erhalten hat.

Danken möchte der Herausgeber Elfriede Olbrich, der langjährigen Sekretärin Adornos, die eine Entzifferung der »Aufzeichnungen« hergestellt hat, die bei unsicheren Lesungen zu Rate gezogen wurde.

Juli 2001

Personenregister

Das Register erschließt allein den Text Adornos, während alle Zitate aus Dorian, Riemann und Wagner sowie die Anmerkungen des Hrsg. unberücksichtigt bleiben; die Verweise beziehen sich auf die Buchseiten.

Übersicht